WHERE TO STAY IN GERMANY
& Austria
1994

Produced by AA Publishing

Directory taken from the accommodation database of the ANWB (Royal Dutch Touring Club), and generated by the AA's Establishment Database, Information Research and Control, Hotel and Touring Services Department

Maps prepared by the ANWB (Royal Dutch Touring Club)
© ANWB

Editor: Virginia Langer

Cover designed by the Paul Hampson Parnership, Southampton
Cover illustration by Diana Ledbetter

Hotel descriptions translated by Bernadette Hickman,
Anke van Lenteren and Nigel Stevenson

Advertisements
Head of advertisement sales: Christopher Heard,
telephone 0256 20123 ext 21544
Advertisement production: Karen Weeks,
telephone 0256 20123 ext 21545

Typeset by Gardata BV, Leersum, Netherlands
Printed by BPCC Hazell Books, Member of BPCC Ltd, Aylesbury

The contents of this publication are believed correct at the time of printing. Nevertheless the Publisher cannot be held responsible for any errors or omissions or for changes in the details given in this guide or for the consequences of any reliance on the information provided in the same. Although every effort has been made to ensure accuracy we always welcome any information from readers to assist in such efforts and to keep the book up to date.

Assessments of hotels and restaurants are based on the experience(s) of the ANWB's professional hotel inspectors on the occasion(s) of their visit(s) and therefore the descriptions given in this guide may contain an element of subjective opinion which may not dictate a reader's experience on another occasion.

© The Automobile Association and ANWB (Royal Dutch Touring Club) January 1994

All rights reserved. No part of this publication may be reproduced, stored in a retrieval system, or transmitted in any form by any means – electronic, mechanical, photocopying, recording or otherwise – unless the written permission of the Publisher has been given beforehand. This book may not be lent, resold, hired out or otherwise disposed of by way of trade in any form of binding or cover other than that in which it is published, without the prior written consent of the Publisher.

A CIP catalogue record for this book is available from the British Library.

Published by AA Publishing which is a trading name of Automobile Association Developments Limited whose registered office is Norfolk House, Basingstoke, Hampshire RG24 9NY, registered number 1878835

ISBN 0 7495 0812 4

Contents

V	**FOREWORD**
VI	**HOW TO USE THIS GUIDE**
IX	**TRAVELLERS' DIRECTORY**
IX	Before you go
IX	General and touring information
XV	Personal health and safety
XVII	Preparing your car
XX	On the road
XXIV	Road accidents and breakdowns
2	**MAPS**
2	Germany
26	Austria
34	**GERMANY**
34	Preface
37	Munich city plan
39	Berlin city plan
40	Frankfurt city plan
41	Hotels directory
203	**AUSTRIA**
203	Preface
206	Vienna city plan
207	Salzburg city plan
208	Hotels directory
259	**INDEX**

AA

WHERE TO STAY

A series of European hotel guides from two of Europe's leading motoring organisations: the Automobile Association of Britain (AA) and the Royal Dutch Touring Club (ANWB).

Your complete guides to accommodation in Europe; the whole series lists over 5000 hotels, with around 1500 that have been specially recommended by the AA and ANWB.

Updated annually, there are comprehensive details of facilities, prices and opening times of establishments. The books also contain a Travellers' directory – a comprehensive section of invaluable information to help you plan and make the most of your holiday. A section of location maps and town plans will help you find your hotel.

Where to Stay in Spain, Portugal and Andorra

Where to Stay in Italy and Switzerland

Where to Stay in Germany and Austria

Where to Stay in France, Belgium and Luxembourg

MORE GREAT GUIDES FROM THE AA

Foreword

This is the second year that the Automobile Association of Great Britain and the Royal Dutch Touring Club (ANWB) of the Netherlands have joined forces to produce this series of guides to accommodation throughout Europe. The two motoring organisations are highly respected for their wide-ranging resources and expertise, and this is reflected in the *Where to Stay* guides.

All of the accommodation listed in these pages is regularly visited by ANWB inspectors to ensure that acceptable standards are maintained. Establishments that the inspectors have especially recommended have the AA/ANWB symbols in the top corner of their entry; they are briefly described and are often illustrated as well. These especially recommended establishments are entitled to display the 1994 sticker illustrated.

Although we list a wide range of accommodation – from luxury hotels to simple guesthouses – we have aimed for a bigger choice of budget accommodation, and have concentrated on known popular tourist destinations.

We are always pleased to receive your comments on hotels you have visited; fill in and send the report form on the card at the back of the book. The *Where to Stay* guides are updated annually, so make sure that you are using an up-to-date book.

Finally, when you stay at hotels listed in this book please mention this guide – owners kindly supply us with information for their entry every year, and appreciate knowing when guests have found it useful.

How to Use This Guide

TRAVELLERS' DIRECTORY ➢

The *Travellers' directory* is a section of information for the Continental traveller, whether in a car or travelling by air or rail. Information in the sections on *Health and safety* and *General and touring information* will be useful to all travellers; especially for independent motorists are sections on *Preparing your car, On the road,* and *Road accidents and breakdowns*. When planning your holiday, refer to this section of essential information first.

MAPS ➢

The maps begin on page 2. There is a separate map section for the countries in this guide. The first page for each country is the key map; this is divided into boxes, and numbers in the top corners indicate map numbers of detailed sections which follow. The maps indicate main roads and rivers.
The following symbols are used for towns:
■.......... a large town with one or more hotels
☐.......... a large town included for location purposes
●.......... a small town with one or more hotels
○.......... a small town included for location purposes

> To find a hotel in a certain area, refer first to the *Maps*, where towns with hotels are indicated by solid squares and circles.
> To find a hotel in a specific town, refer first to the relevant *Hotels directory* (see below), where towns are arranged alphabetically in each country.

COUNTRY SECTIONS ➢

Preface   A short introduction to each country has a description of the hotel classification system, plus general information on motoring, accident procedures, currency, telephones, etc.

City plans   Following the *Preface* are plans of major cities in the country. The location of listed hotels in these cities is indicated by a city plan grid reference in the hotel entry (for example, 'City Plan C3').

Hotels directory   The directory listing of inspected accommodation and recommended hotels is arranged alphabetically according to towns and cities within the country.

AA/ANWB selected hotels: If a hotel name appears in red, it has been specially recommended by the AA and ANWB. These hotels are entitled to display a sticker with the AA and ANWB symbols, indicating that it reaches approved standards of quality.
All hotels in this guide receive a sticker with the year 1994 printed on it. This is

HOW TO USE THIS GUIDE

different from the joint recommendation badge described above which, in addition, displays the symbols of the AA and the ANWB.

Hotel classification: Many countries in Europe have hotel classification schemes. These schemes are sometimes operated by national authorities, as in France, and sometimes by national motoring organisations, as in Britain. The classification system used for each country is explained in the country introduction. In each hotel entry, the classification precedes the establishment name.

Hotel charges: Charges (quoted in the local currency) are indications of the lowest room price to the highest room price. Prices may vary according to season; some establishments may have special group rates.

These prices are guides only. Although every effort is made to publish current charges, these may change without notification. Prices in this book are based mainly on 1993 charges; where the prices reflect increases for 1994, they are preceded by an asterisk (see *Abbreviations and symbols*).

If there is a dash in front of the symbol for single room, this indicates that there are no special single rooms in the hotel, and the price given is for single occupancy of a double room. If no prices are given, the hotel did not supply price information.

Continental breakfast is usually included in the room price. In some hotels half-board is obligatory, and if the extra meal service is ignored, the price may be increased.

Abbreviations and symbols: Abbreviations indicating the type of establishment appear in brackets following each establishment name; these are explained on the next page. Symbols indicating the facilities and services offered by hotels are also listed and explained on the next page. Facilities listed as being in the room (shower, toilet, television, etc) are available in some rooms, and not necessarily *every* room.

Some hotels do not allow pets for hygiene reasons. Although the information about pets has been checked for this guide, the policy of individual hotels can change without notification. Therefore the AA and ANWB cannot take responsibility for information about pets. It is best to confirm the policy of each hotel in writing when booking, or on arrival.

To avoid misunderstanding it is always best to check prices when booking, or on arrival at the hotel.

HOW TO USE THIS GUIDE

READING A DIRECTORY ENTRY

Abbreviations and symbols

HCR	hotel-café-restaurant. Built and furnished for accommodation, with licence for a café and restaurant		American Express Diners Club Eurocard Visa		indoor terrace outdoor swimming pool indoor swimming pool lift
HR	hotel-restaurant. As HCR above, but with restaurant only		in quiet surroundings		rooms on ground floor
HP	hotel-pension. A hotel catering mainly for longer-staying guests		in wooded surroundings		rooms with bath
HG	hotel-garni. Provides bed and breakfast accommodation only		beside a river beside a lake		rooms with shower rooms with toilet
HA	hotel-apartment. Lets flats for certain periods, also provides meals		within 500 metres of the seafront		rooms with television special diets on request
MT	motel. An HR or HCR close to a motorway, adapted to the requirements of motorists		in the town centre outside the town on a main road car park on hotel premises hotel garage terrace		half-board only permission required to bring pets no pets
*	1994 price				
	single room				
	double room				

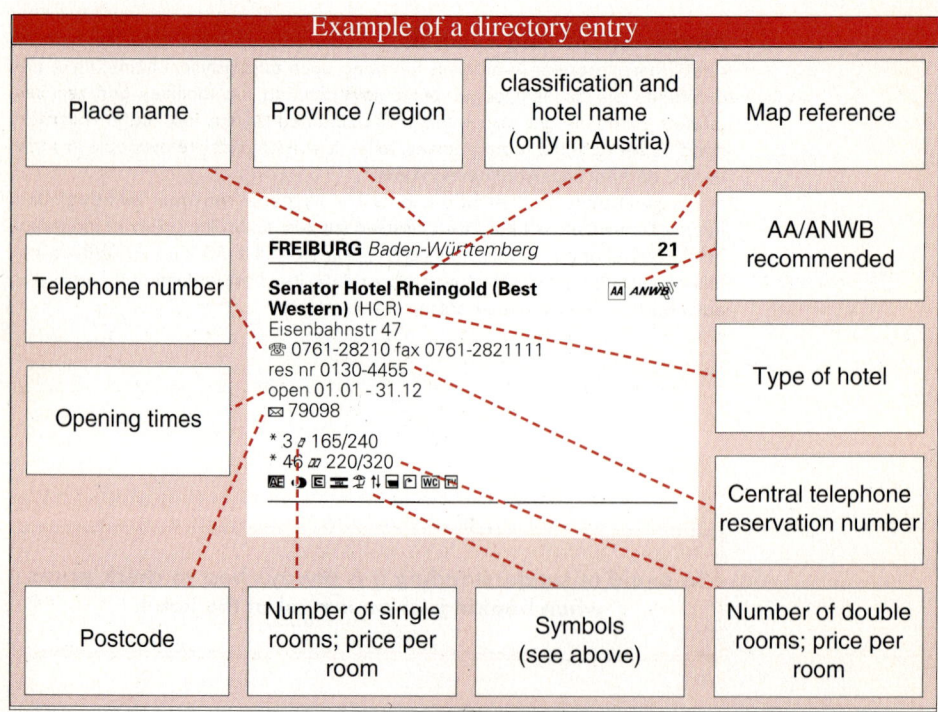

Example of a directory entry

- Place name
- Province / region
- classification and hotel name (only in Austria)
- Map reference
- Telephone number
- AA/ANWB recommended
- Opening times
- Type of hotel
- Central telephone reservation number
- Postcode
- Number of single rooms; price per room
- Symbols (see above)
- Number of double rooms; price per room

Travellers' DIRECTORY

BEFORE YOU GO ➤

*M*any people travelling around the continent of Europe will choose to fly or to go by train or coach, and for them only the *General and touring information, Health and safety* and the individual country prefaces will be relevant. Motorists, however, have to cope with many different regulations.

The motoring regulations specific to a particular country are in the country prefaces, and the sections below, *Preparing your car* and *On the road*, list a few generally applicable regulations and things to watch out for. If you are in trouble on the road, refer to the section on *Road accidents and breakdowns*.

Motoring in Europe should not and usually does not cause any more worries than motoring at home, nevertheless you should bear the following points in mind; it is inconvenient enough to have your vehicle break down in your own country, but it is much more of a nuisance if you are abroad, when you may have a language difficulty, delays in getting spare parts, a restricted holiday period and many unbudgeted expenses to meet. Making the effort to have your car thoroughly checked and serviced, and equipping yourself with a few essential spares could save you a lot of irritation.

GENERAL AND TOURING INFORMATION ➤

Buses and trams See *Public transport*, below.

Boats Generally speaking, there is free movement of boats within EC member countries, but you should carry the boat's registration and insurance documents, and in some European countries a Helmsman's Overseas Certificate of Competence is required. For more information contact your local motoring organisation, or the tourist offices of the countries you plan to visit. See also *Identification plate* under *Preparing your car*.

Channel Tunnel Scheduled to open in 1994, the Channel Tunnel links Britain and France by rail; the British terminal is near Folkestone, and the French terminal is just outside Calais. Trains operate daily, every 15 minutes at peak periods, and the crossing takes 35 minutes. There are no reservations; motorists drive on to the next available train. Travellers pass through customs and passport control for both Britain and France before departure, so there are no further formalities after the crossing.

Children If you are travelling with very young children, remember that supplies of your usual baby food, drinks, disposable nappies, health remedies, etc, may not be available at your destination, and it may be best to bring sufficient supplies from home. Make sure the hotels you will be staying at will accept children, and that they have things such as cots and high chairs that you may need. Remember that people traditionally go to the *Kurparks* of Germany and Austria for peace and quiet, and the enthusiasm and noise of small children may not be welcome.

≪≪≪ TRAVELLERS' DIRECTORY – General and touring information ≫≫≫

If you will be visiting hot areas, remember that young children can have a lower tolerance to high temperatures. All children are very susceptible to fierce summer sun on Mediterranean beaches, so take sun hats and plenty of high-protection sun cream. See also *Children* under *Preparing your car*.

Credit/charge cards Major credit cards are widely used in Europe, and payment by card can be a more convenient and safer way of paying for larger items like accommodation and fuel. Generally speaking, credit cards are less widely accepted in Germany. In some countries garages do not generally accept cards for fuel, and sometimes payment by card incurs a small additional charge (refer to the country prefaces – *Fuel*). For the conditions of using your credit card abroad contact the issuing company.

Currency There are generous allowances on the amount of currency you can take from country to country in Europe, but if you plan to carry large amounts of currency across borders consult your bank before you travel. Carrying large amounts of currency leaves you vulnerable to theft; credit cards and travellers' cheques are safer alternatives.

Customs regulations Tourists travelling across borders within the EC will not necessarily need to pass through customs nor make any customs declarations. However, you may still be stopped for selective checks by customs officers for illegal items: drugs, weapons, indecent material, and items which may pose threats to health or the environment.

> **EC COUNTRIES:**
> Belgium,
> Denmark,
> France,
> Germany,
> Greece,
> Ireland,
> Italy,
> Luxembourg,
> Netherlands,
> Portugal,
> Spain (not the Canary Islands),
> UK (not the Channel Islands)

Goods which you buy in the EC for your own use (or gifts) are not subject to import tax when you cross EC borders. However, very large quantities may arouse suspicions that you are buying for the purposes of commercial re-sale. If you will be carrying more than is reasonable for your personal use, check in advance whether this will be acceptable with the customs or tourist office of the country.

If you travel between an EC and non-EC country, you will normally be required to pass through customs, and tax-free allowances tend to be lower; these lower limits also apply for purchases from a duty-free shop within the EC. Again, check with the authorities if you will be carrying goods of quantity or value in excess of reasonable personal needs. No one under 17 is entitled to tobacco or alcohol allowances.

If you are a non-EC national, remember to check what duty-free allowances you will be entitled to on your return home.

If you are carrying items of obvious high value (computers, video recorders, etc), you may find it useful to carry the sales receipt as proof that any duty has been paid.

Disabled travellers Facilities and accommodation for disabled travellers vary widely throughout Europe. Plan well in advance: contact your local motoring club and disability organisations before leaving home, and the tourist offices of the countries you will visit may prove helpful. As far as possible, make prior arrangements with airlines, railways, hotels, etc, specifying exactly what your special requirements will be, and give them time to prepare and confirm arrangements. If you will be travelling with a guide dog, you will need to check veterinary requirements for the countries you plan to visit.

◄◄◄ TRAVELLERS' DIRECTORY – General and touring information ►►►

Drugs Avoid narcotic drugs altogether, and also beware of anyone who asks you to take a parcel or drive a car over a border. If you need to carry any drugs for legitimate health reasons, you may find passage through customs easier if you have a letter from your doctor explaining the treatment.

Electrical Electricity in Europe is predominantly AC 220v, but can occasionally be as low as 110v. Circular two-pin plugs and screw-type light bulbs are usual. British and Irish travellers can buy plug adapters from electrical shops; visitors from North America will need voltage transformers as well as plug adapters for their appliances.

Embassies and consulates Generally embassies and consulates are ready to help their nationals overseas, within certain limits. They generally cannot help with expenses, nor do they serve as information bureaux. Any loss or theft of property should be reported to the local police, not the embassy or consulate.

Contact embassies or consulates on such matters as obtaining an emergency passport, guidance on how to transfer money, or if you are in difficulties with police or other local officials. Status of consulates varies, and services and working hours of smaller consulates may be restricted in some cases.

Emergencies It is worth being aware of emergency procedures and emergency service telephone numbers in the country you are visiting. See the boxed information in the country prefaces for specific information. Always cooperate fully with the police and emergency services.

Messages to relatives in an emergency can usually be arranged through the local police or hospital authorities, or you can try the local tourist office or motoring organisation for advice and help.

Eurocheques This scheme, operated by a network of European banks, is a system of money transfer, enabling you to write cheques in the currency of the country you are visiting. You will need a special chequebook, and you should contact your bankers well in advance of your departure for futher information. Most European banks will cash Eurocheques and retail acceptance is fairly widespread, but do confirm acceptance before committing yourself to goods or services.

Ferry crossings If your holiday involves a sea crossing, check schedules and prices in advance, and remember that in the summer season ferries may often be full. Book ahead if possible. If you are taking your car on the boat, find out if there are any special requirements or restrictions. Also see *Fuel* under *On the road*.

Lost property Report any property losses to the local police – you will usually need to advise them in order to make an insurance claim. Always keep the numbers of travellers' cheques and credit cards separately, and if you lose them notify the issuing company immediately, as well as local police.

Also contact your consulate if you lose passports or visas. Railway stations usually have lost property offices for items left on trains, and if you note the number (if any) of any taxis you use, it could help in case you leave anything behind.

◁◁◁ TRAVELLERS' DIRECTORY – General and touring information ▷▷▷

Maps For maps while planning your trip, contact the tourist offices of the countries you will visit, otherwise your local motoring organisation may have European maps for sale or facilities for ordering them. Motoring organisations in Europe which produce their own series of maps are the Automobile Association of Britain, the Touring Club Italiano and the ÖAMTC of Austria. Official cartographers for France produce Cartes IGN, the Swiss firms Hallwag, and Kümmerly and Frey produce maps covering the whole of western Europe, as does the Austrian Freytag and Berndt (F&B Autokarten). The well known French Michelin maps are available in large and small scales, and also cover all of western Europe.

A good source of free maps as you travel are the large hotel/motel chains (Novotel, Mercure, etc). Contact local tourist offices for local maps and town plans.

Money One of the safest ways to carry money is travellers' cheques, which can be changed at banks, exchange bureaux, larger hotels and sometimes at post offices, larger shops or businesses. Exchange rates are usually best at banks and worst at hotels. For information on individual countries, see the country prefaces. See also *Currency*, and *Credit/charge cards*.

Motoring organisations Local offices of national motoring organisations are often a good source of information and help. You may need to be a member of a motoring organisation in your own country to be eligible for reciprocal services in another. For addresses and information about individual countries, see the country prefaces.

Newspapers English-language newspapers are widely available in Europe. Particularly in large towns and cities and major resorts you will find a varying choice of British newspapers (from the *Times* to the *Sun*); the *International Herald Tribute* and *USA Today*, and news magazines *Time* and *Newsweek* come from the USA. Depending upon where you are, they will be anything from one to three or four days late.

Opening times Business hours vary; see the country prefaces for specific information. Remember that in southern European countries shops, offices, churches and many tourist attractions may close for up to three hours for lunch. Also, especially in France, many shops and businesses close for the entire month of August for annual holidays.

Passports and visas Always carry your passport and visas, and keep a separate note of the passport number, and the date and place where it was issued. Make sure that you have all the necessary documents for the countries you plan to visit, and that they will not expire while you are away. See also *Valuables*, below.

Photography Photography is usually allowed without restriction, although flash photography is sometimes prohibited in churches, art galleries and museums; if in doubt always ask first. If there is a charge for photography inside buildings there will be signs saying so. If photography is prohibited, usually near military or other official establishments, there will be prominent signs – usually a diagonal line across a camera.

◀◀◀ TRAVELLERS' DIRECTORY – General and touring information ▶▶▶

Public transport Long-distance train travel in Europe between countries and large population centres is usually efficient and fast; as services become more localised they can deteriorate somewhat, and in some instances (Spain and Portugal in particular), quite dramatically. It is worthwhile getting a seat reservation for any long journey, as services can sometimes be unpredictably busy. If you plan to travel extensively by train enquire about special tourist tickets giving unlimited travel for a specified period of time; they can be excellent value for money depending upon how much you use them. However, these tickets are usually available only to non-resident tourists, and are often only available for purchase outside the country.

For travelling about in large cities, ask at tourist offices about tourist tickets which will enable you to travel about at much reduced rates, as well as saving you the trouble of buying single tickets. Sometimes you will need a passport photograph for these special tickets – it is worthwhile taking one just in case. Alternatively, transport tickets are often available in batches (called *carnets*, *Mehrfahrtenkarten*, *Tageskarte*, *blocco*, etc) which work out cheaper than buying the equivalent number of single tickets, and are available (according to the country) in stations, travel offices, and sometimes at newsagents, tobacconists or banks. Very often, especially in large cities, you must insert your ticket in a time-stamping machine, either as you enter the station or when you board a bus, train or tram, before it is valid. In cities where there is more than one form of transport, tickets are often interchangeable on everything – buses, trains, trolleys, funiculars, and sometimes boats and ferries.

Radio The BBC World Service offers a full range of English-language programmes throughout Europe on various medium-wave (try 648 KHz) and long-wave frequencies for certain periods of the day and night. The BBC World Service and Voice of America also operate short-wave services, with best reception during the evening and night. Many European state radio services have English-language segments, broadcasting on various bands. Frequencies and times vary; it is probably best to scan your dial for the broadcast and reception that suits you. If your car radio is a good one, you should be able to receive the domestic long-wave BBC Radio 4 (198 KHz) well into northern and central areas of France and Germany, with continuous broadcasting from early morning until past midnight.

Radio telephones, CB radios Many countries control the temporary importation and use of telephones and radio transmitters. If you will be travelling with this equipment, contact your local motoring organisation or the tourist board of the countries you will visit.

Registration for tourists Residents of EC countries are not required to carry out any national registration formalities in EC countries. However, EC visitors to non-EC countries, and non-EC visitors to EC countries are required to register with the police. In practice, formalities are straightforward for short holidays, and the registration requirement is normally satisfied by completion of a card or certificate when booking into a hotel or other accommodation. If you will be staying with friends or relatives, it is usually the responsibility of the host to seek advice from the police. If you will be staying in a country for longer than three months, different rules apply and you should seek advice from the authorities before you leave home.

⋘ TRAVELLERS' DIRECTORY – General and touring information ⋙

Stamps Obtain postage stamps from post offices, but also, according to the country, from tobacconists, newsagents, hotel receptions, tourist offices and travel stations.

Telephones See the country prefaces for information on calling from public call boxes, but it may be best to try to get help if you encounter language problems. In many countries you can buy phonecards, usually available from post offices, shops and tobacconists. You will need to know the country code (IDD code; see box) for the country you want to call: Calls you make from your hotel bedroom usually incur a surcharge. For specific information about individual countries see the country prefaces.

Australia =	61
Britain =	44
Canada and USA =	1
Ireland =	353
New Zealand =	64
South Africa =	27

Television Most larger hotels in Europe will have cable or satellite services which may include the English-language channels Sky, Super and CNN. Otherwise, take your pick from the local stations – even if you cannot understand the language you should be able to get the essentials of the weather forecast to plan your activities.

Time zones The following are comparisons with (Britain's) Greenwich Mean Time. No allowances have been made below for summer time/daylight saving time.

Australia:
Canberra area, New South Wales, Queensland, Tasmania, Victoria – 10 hours ahead
Broken Hill area NSW, Northern Territory, South Australia – 9.5 hours ahead
Western Australia – 8 hours ahead

Canada:
Alberta – 7 hours behind
British Columbia – 8 hours behind
Manitoba – 6 hours behind
Ontario – 5 to 6 hours behind
Quebec – 4 to 5 hours behind
Saskatchewan – 6 hours behind

Europe (continental western):
1 hour ahead

New Zealand:
12 hours ahead

South Africa:
2 hours ahead

United States:
Eastern time – 5 hours behind
Central time – 6 hours behind
Mountain time – 7 hours behind
Pacific time – 8 hours behind
Alaska – 9 to 10 hours behind
Hawaii – 11 hours behind

Tourist information National tourist offices are well equipped to deal with local enquiries, and are especially helpful for information on current events, tourist sights, car and equipment hire and sports facilities. Their offices abroad are helpful, but local offices will have detailed local information. Ask for the address of the local tourist office at your hotel.

Travellers' cheques Take any substantial amounts of money in the form of travellers' cheques. You can often use them like cash, or change them for currency anywhere in Europe, but remember that you will usually need to show your passport when you cash them. Always keep a separate note of the cheque numbers and the information on procedures in case of loss.

‹‹‹ TRAVELLERS' DIRECTORY – Personal health and safety ›››

Valuables — Pay particular attention to the security of your money and valuables. Whenever possible leave excess cash and travellers' cheques with your hotel safe-deposit against a receipt. Always remove valuables from a parked car, even if it is in a supervised car park or locked garage.

VAT refunds — Value Added Tax is a form of EC sales tax levied on goods and services. It is included in the marked price, but visitors from non-EC countries can request a partial refund of VAT at some large stores for goods above a certain price. Ask for an invoice for VAT refund when you make your purchase, and when you leave the EC, present your invoice and purchase to a customs officer. When you return home, claim your refund by post. Since VAT is charged at varying amounts up to around 25 per cent, the refund, although only a proportion of the tax paid, is worth claiming for substantial purchases. You will be responsible for declaring these purchases to customs in the normal way.

Weather information — If the weather is important to your journey, contact the nearest branch of the local motoring club for information. To check informally on conditions ahead as you go along, ask your hotel, garages and tourist offices.

Swimming — Although European coastlines and beaches have improved in recent years, sea pollution around coasts may still pose serious health risks. Some countries publish detailed information on the quality of their beaches, including maps, which are available from national authorities. In many (though not all) resorts where the water may be dangerous there are signs (generally small) which forbid swimming.

Watch for these signs:
French: *Défense de se baigner* (no swimming); *Il est défendu de se baigner* (swimming prohibited).
Italian: *Vietato bágnarse* (no swimming); *É vietato bégnarsi* (swimming prohibited).
Spanish: *Prohibido bañarse* (no swimming); *Se prohibe bañarse* (swimming prohibited).

Toilets — Toilet facilities on the continent of Europe are very variable, ranging from ultra-modern, spotless pay-cubicles on the street corners of large cities, to primitive unsanitary basements or out-houses with doubtful or non-existent plumbing and no paper in less frequented rural areas. Finding a toilet can sometimes be a challenge: train stations and museums usually have facilities, after that try cafés or restaurants, or if you are dressed appropriately reception areas of large hotels usually have facilities signed.

PERSONAL HEALTH AND SAFETY ›

Health — Usually no immunisations are required for travelling in Europe unless you have recently come from an infected area. Tourist boards will have up-to-date information.

Take sensible precautions. If you are visiting a hot region, make sure you use protective sun cream, cover your head against the sun, drink plenty of non-alcoholic liquids, and avoid going out in the middle of the day. Also, remember that you will be more vulnerable to the sun in high altitudes.

TRAVELLERS' DIRECTORY – Personal health and safety

Water from the tap is usually safe to drink throughout Europe, but ask before you drink if you are in any doubt. Bottled water – usually more pleasant to drink – is sometimes a sensible precaution anyway.

Sexually transmitted diseases, including AIDS, exist in most countries, especially in the more popular holiday destinations; condoms are available from pharmacies.

Rabies is endemic in continental Europe, so do not touch any tame or wild animal. If you are scratched or bitten go to a doctor and report the incident to the police immediately.

Before you leave home pack a personal first-aid kit with your usual remedies from home: pain, indigestion, travel-sickness and diarrhoea tablets, plus treatment for hay-fever or allergies that may be set off by unfamiliar vegetation.

Insurance Be sure to take out personal insurance before you travel to cover unforseen circumstances such as holiday cancellation, delayed flights, theft, damage, loss and medical expenses.

Medical care If you are a resident of an EC country, you will be entitled to reciprocal medical care in other member countries, but it is always advisable to take out adequate insurance to cover expenses connected with illness – including a longer hotel stay or air-ambulance transport home if necessary. Usually you will need to pay for any professional medical treatment you receive; keep receipts for all treatment and medicines and claim from your insurance company after you return home.

Medicines and prescriptions In some countries, medicines normally regarded as prescriptive are available over the counter at pharmacists, and it is worthwhile visiting a pharmacy for advice in the first instance for minor conditions (also see *Pharmacies* below).

Personal safety Petty theft is a problem in virtually every tourist honey-pot and big city in Europe. Avoid well known dubious areas, especially at night; also avoid dark lonely streets and empty train and metro carriages. Make sure your bag has a strong strap and secure clasp, carry it under your arm with shoulder strap across your body. A money belt or neck purse under your clothing is a good idea for extra security. Be aware that anything in an exposed outside pocket is easy prey for pickpockets; in some larger cities gangs of children snatch and thieve. If you are personally threatened, make as much noise and fuss as possible to attract help.

Lone women should take extra care. Learn the emergency telephone numbers, and keep enough money and change for telephone calls and bus or taxi rides. Ignore any unwelcome attention as any reply, however discouraging, could be misconstrued. At the same time be aware of what is going on around you. Be confident and look as though you know where you are going; if you are lost ask women or couples the way. Remember that the way you dress can possibly attract unwanted attention and send unintentional non-verbal messages.

Have a look around your hotel when you arrive; check the emergency exits and procedures and the location of fire extinguishers. A small torch is reassuring if the lights fail for any reason.

‹‹‹ TRAVELLERS' DIRECTORY – Preparing your car ›››

Pharmacies Pharmacies are a good first stop for any health problems, and in some countries can dispense medicines normally available only on prescription. Pharmacists can usually put you in touch with a doctor for more serious ailments. If you are likely to need a prescription filled, ask your own doctor to write (legibly) the prescription using the generic name for the medicine, since brand names for drugs may vary.

PREPARING YOUR CAR ➢

For more specific rules and regulations, refer to the country prefaces.

Automatic gearboxes If you plan to travel in more remote areas with an automatic car, automatic transmission fluid may be difficult to obtain so it is a good idea to carry an emergency supply. Also, if you are towing a trailer, you may need to fit a gearbox oil cooler – check with your car manufacturer.

Brakes Before beginning a touring holiday in Europe, you should change the brake fluid, and check the thickness of the brake lining or pad material. Be aware that long drives through hilly or mountainous areas can be especially hard on brakes.

Children Most European countries either prohibit children travelling in the front seat of a car, or lay down conditions which must be complied with. Also see the country prefaces *(Children in cars)*, or check with tourist offices for more information.

Compulsory equipment Regulations on required equipment for cars vary from country to country, but generally domestic laws are not enforced on tourists. However in some cases they are: for example, where there is a safety priority.
  Warning triangles are nearly always required, and a first-aid kit and a spare set of vehicle bulbs are sometimes needed. Refer to the country prefaces for specific information.

Dimension and weight restrictions For ordinary private cars the limits of 4 metres high and 2.5 metres wide are generally imposed. All vehicles have a specified individual weight limit; for information on how this relates to private cars, see *Overloading*, below.
  If you plan to use one of the major road tunnels through a mountainous area there may be additional restrictions. If your vehicle is especially large or if you are towing a trailer, contact your local motoring organisation or the tourist office of the country in which you will travel for more information.

Direction indicators Direction indicators should work at between 60 and 120 flashes per minute. Most standard car-flasher units are overloaded by the extra lamps of a trailer, and you should fit a heavy-duty unit or relay device.

Electrical As a precaution, you should have the electrical connections in your car checked before you travel. If you have problems with the charging system, you should always get help from a qualified auto-electrician.

Fire extinguisher Although not compulsory for the countries in this guide, it is a sensible precaution to equip your car with a fire extinguisher.

TRAVELLERS' DIRECTORY – Preparing your car

First-aid kit   Of the countries in the *Where to Stay* guides, only Austria requires motorists to carry a first-aid kit. However, it is always a sensible precaution to have a first-aid kit in your car.

Insurance (Green Card)   Before you travel, ask your car insurance company to extend your cover to apply in the countries you will be visiting (usually there is a charge for this). Normally your insurer will issue you with an International Motor Insurance Certificate, known as a Green Card. It is internationally recognised proof that you have the minimum required insurance cover. Sign the Green Card when you receive it, and always carry it with you when travelling – if you have an accident the police or other authorities may need to see it. If you are towing a trailer or caravan, it will need separate insurance and mention on your Green Card. Also check with your insurers to make sure you will be covered if your vehicle is damaged on the motorail or ferries.

Identification plate   All boats and trailers taken across national borders must have a unique chassis number for identification purposes.

International distinguishing sign   If you cross national borders, the back of your car must have an approved international distinguishing sign – oval with a white background, and black letters indicating the country of the vehicle's registration. In some countries there are police checks for the signs, and fines are imposed for missing or incorrect ones. If you are towing a trailer, that must also have a sign.

Keys   If you are driving your own car, make sure you have the number of your car keys, just in case they are lost or mislaid.

Lights   If you are taking a car from Britain or Ireland to continental Europe (or vice versa), remember that for driving on the other side of the road you will need to alter your headlights so that the dipped beam does not dazzle oncoming drivers. Headlamp or beam converter kits are available from motoring shops.

Always use dipped lights in fog, snow and heavy rain. Also you must use dipped lights when passing through a tunnel, no matter how long it is, or whether it has internal lights. The police will sometimes wait at the end of the tunnel to make sure drivers are using their lights. It is sensible, and compulsory in some countries, to carry a spare set of bulbs for your lights. For specific regulations see the country prefaces. Finally, remember that more passengers or a heavy load will affect the beam of your lights; reset them if necessary.

Mirrors   Always make sure you have good all-round vision. Your car should have outside wing mirrors on both sides – important if you will be driving a right-hand-drive car in continental Europe, or a left-hand-drive car in Britain or Ireland. If you are towing a trailer, consider fitting wing-mirror extensions to improve your rear vision.

Overloading   Overloading your car is dangerous, and in some countries is an offence subject to an on-the-spot fine. If you are stopped for overloading, you would also be made to reduce your load before being allowed to continue. Every vehicle has a maximum load weight and requirements for distribution of the weight between each axle. If this information is not in your car handbook, contact the

◀◀◀ TRAVELLERS' DIRECTORY – Preparing your car ▶▶▶

manufacturer. To check your car's weight (fully laden with passengers and holiday luggage), take it to a public weighbridge. When you load your car make sure that nothing impairs your vision, and that luggage on a roof-rack is secure and stable.

Registration documents
You must carry the original vehicle registration document with you at all times. If you plan to use a borrowed car, you must also carry a letter of authority to use the car from the registered owner. For leased or rented cars, check that you receive the appropriate authority documents from the hire company.

Seat belts
Regulations in all European countries require wearing of seat belts. Failure to comply will put you at risk of a police fine. Also see *Children in cars* in the country prefaces.

Servicing, mechanical precautions
Basic checks on your car before you leave home could save a lot of inconvenience and expense: have your car serviced by a franchised dealer; check all your lights, brakes, tyres (including the spare), oil level and any leaks, windscreen wipers and washer fluid, battery connections, brake fluid; make sure there are no dashboard warning lights on, and that there are no unusual noises or handling characteristics.
If you have a hire car, notify any faults to the company as soon as possible.

Spares
Any spare parts you take will depend on your car and how long you will be away. If you have to order spare parts, identify the parts as clearly as possible, giving the manufacturer's part number if you know it, and always quote the engine and chassis number of your car.

Trailers
See *Dimensions and weight restrictions*, *Identification plate*, and *Automatic gearboxes*.

Tyres
Examine your tyres carefully; if you think they are likely to be more than three-quarters worn before you return home, replace them before you leave. If you notice uneven wear, scuffed treads or damaged tyre walls, seek advice from your repairer. The minimum requirement in most European countries is for a tread depth of 1.6mm over the central three-quarters of the tyre width around the circumference. If your car is heavily loaded, or if you plan to do much high-speed driving your tyre pressures may need to be raised – check your car handbook. Check pressures when your tyres are cold, and remember to check the spare.

Warning triangles
Use of a warning triangle is compulsory in most European countries – also see the country prefaces. You should set the warning triangle behind your car if you have stopped on the road for any reason. The triangle should be clearly visible to the traffic coming up behind – about 30m behind on an ordinary road, but up to 100m on a motorway. It should be about 60cm from the side of the road, but make sure that the triangle itself is not obstructing traffic.

Winter: snow tyres/chains
If you plan to visit continental Europe in winter, in certain areas you may find that the use of snow tyres or wheel chains is compulsory. Ask advice from your motoring organisation and from the tourist boards of countries you will visit.

TRAVELLERS' DIRECTORY – On the road

ON THE ROAD ➢

In continental Europe vehicles drive on the right. However, vehicles in Britain and Ireland drive on the left. If you come from a country which drives on the right and you will be using a British-made car for your visit to the contintent, you will find, firstly, that the steering wheel and other controls will be on the opposite side to the one you are used to, and secondly, both your rear and forward vision will be affected. This is important when trying to overtake. See *Overtaking* below, and *Mirrors* under *Preparing your car*. For more specific motoring rules and regulations, refer to the country prefaces.

Children Most European countries either prohibit children travelling in the front seat of a car, or lay down conditions which must be complied with. Also see the country prefaces *(Children in cars)*, or check with tourist offices for more information.

Courtesy on the road An extra degree of courtesy and patience may gain you a little more time and tolerance from drivers who may be characteristically impetuous and impatient. In Germany it is a legal offence to be abusive to other drivers.

Crash (safety) helmets In nearly all European countries it is a legal requirement for motorcyclists and their passengers to wear crash helmets.

Drinking and driving There is only one safe rule: If you drink, do not drive. The laws are strict and penalties severe.

Driving age For the minimum age at which tourists are allowed to drive temporarily imported cars, refer to the country prefaces. For hire cars different companies will have their own restrictions; check in advance with them.

Driving licence Always carry your national driving licence with you, and make sure that it is not due to expire while you are away. If you plan to drive a hired or borrowed car in the country you will visit, make local enquiries. In some countries you will need an International Driving Permit; refer to the country prefaces.

Fines Some countries impose on-the-spot fines for minor traffic offences. You must pay the fine in the local currency to the police or to the local post office. In France you will be liable to an immediate deposit; a subsequent court fine could be even more. Disputing a fine usually leads to court appearance, delay and more expense. In some countries, the authorities will immobilise your vehicle until the fine is paid, and may even sell it to pay the penalty. Once you have paid the fine you generally cannot recover it, but always get a receipt as proof of payment. If you disagree with the fine, the local motoring organisation may be able to help you; refer to the country prefaces.

Fuel Both leaded and unleaded fuel under familiar brand names are widely available throughout Europe. In Austria leaded petrol is not sold, although unleaded super has an additive which makes it suitable for cars which take leaded fuel. Fuel is usually graded normal and super with recognisable local terms; some countries are supplying 98 octane unleaded (super plus or premium) either in addition to or instead of 95 octane. Diesel is also widely

TRAVELLERS' DIRECTORY – On the road

available, generally called either *diesel* or *gas-oil*. Also see *Fuel* in the country prefaces. If you intend to carry a fuel reserve in a can, check the local regulations first, since there are legal restrictions on the amount you can carry, and in some countries it is forbidden. Also, if you are taking your car on a ferry or by motorail, carrying fuel in cans is prohibited.

Fuel is widely available, with 24-hour service on motorways. It is best to keep your fuel tank topped up, especially in more remote areas, and remember that a roof-rack or trailer will make an appreciable difference to your fuel consumption. In Germany it is considered negligent to run out of fuel on a motorway, and you may be fined for doing so. See also *Credit/charge cards* under *General and touring information*.

Garages and service stations

Generally European garages are open from 08.00 to 18.00 (sometimes with a break at midday, 12.00 to 15.00), Monday to Saturday. On Sunday and public holidays fuel and service are often unobtainable, and in some countries, especially France, it may be difficult to get repairs done in August, when many firms close for the annual holidays. Ask your local dealer for a list of franchised repairers in Europe before you leave.

Always ask for an estimate before you have repairs done; it can save disputes later. Always settle any dispute with a garage before you leave; subsequent negotiations by post are usually lengthy and unsatisfactory. Also see information in the country prefaces under *Fuel*.

Hazard warning lights

Hazard warning lights are almost always considered a supplement to a warning triangle, and not a substitute for it. In an accident or breakdown, a warning triangle will give plenty of advance warning to drivers coming up behind; hazard lights (if they are working) will not be seen around bends or obstructions, or over a rise in the road. Also see *Warning triangle* under *Preparing your car*.

Headlight flashing and hooting

Headlight flashing and sounding your horn are used only as a warning of approach, or as a passing signal at night. Otherwise both are commonly understood as a sign of irritation, so use with caution to avoid misunderstanding.

Holiday traffic

Remember that during peak holiday times traffic will be very heavy, and delays are likely in some places. Times to avoid travelling are at weekends, at the beginning and end of school holidays, before and after public holidays, and religious feast and festival days at religious centres. Contact local tourist boards for information on when and where roads are likely to be congested. Refer to the public holiday dates and the information on *Roads* in the country prefaces.

Journey times

When estimating how long a journey will take, remember to allow for road and weather conditions, customs clearance, volume of traffic, queues at toll booths, and any major local events and roadworks. Also allow plenty of time for stops for rest, refreshments and fuel. On motorways your average speed will probably be something like 100kph (60mph), on main and secondary rural roads about 70kph (45mph), and in towns and cities it may be 25 to 30kph (15 to 20mph) or even less. If you have a plane or ferry to catch, allow plenty of time for unforeseen delays and checking in, and it is probably

TRAVELLERS' DIRECTORY – On the road

a good idea to contact a local tourist office to see if they know of anything on the way that may hold you up.

Motorways For specific information see *Motorways* or *Roads* in the country prefaces.

Overtaking Always be particularly careful when overtaking, especially if you are driving a right-hand-drive car in continental Europe, or a left-hand-drive car in Britain or Ireland. Signal beforehand in good time, and signal again afterwards. On roads with two or more lanes in each direction, always return to the inside lane (failure to do this will incur on-the-spot fines in some countries).

Parking Parking is a problem in every major city in Europe, and police are strict with offenders. There are large fines, with offending cars impounded and heavy charges for recovering them. If you can, always park in an authorised car park or by the side of the road in the direction of traffic; as far as possible park off the main road, but not on cycle or bus lanes or tram tracks (also see country prefaces).

Priority in traffic *The following does not apply to driving in Britain and Ireland.*

The general rule in continental Europe is to give way to traffic entering a junction from the right, but this is not always the case at roundabouts (traffic circles) – see below. Learn the international signs that indicate priority and give way.

Never rely on having the right of way at intersections: in rural areas farm vehicles are liable to pull out on to a larger road regardless of oncoming traffic. You must always give way to emergency and military vehicles, and blind and disabled people, funerals and marching columns also have priority. Buses and coaches carrying many passengers will expect, and should be allowed, priority. At roundabouts, generally give way to traffic entering the roundabout unless signposted to the contrary. If possible, keep to the outside lane on a roundabout to make your exit easier.

There are specific rules for individual countries – refer to the country prefaces.

Railway crossings – guarded and unguarded Almost all level railway crossings are indicated by the international road signs; guarded crossings are usually lifting barriers, sometimes with bells or flashing lights when a train is approaching.

Road conditions Main roads in Europe are generally good, with extensive and efficient motorway systems in northern Europe and Italy. Secondary roads may occasionally degenerate into long stretches of badly worn surfaces with steep cambers and corrugated edges. Also refer to the country prefaces – *Roads* and *Motorways*.

Road signs Most road signs in Europe are the familiar international ones. Watch for road markings – do not cross a solid white or yellow line in the centre of the road.

Be aware that place names on signposts may change as you cross borders, or even within countries: the French city of Lille may be signed Rijsel in Belgium. In Belgium, French and Flemish are both official languages: 'Anvers' is the French equivalent of the Flemish 'Antwerpen'. Similarly, in Basque and Catalonian areas of Spain, local and national place names both appear on

◀◀◀ TRAVELLERS' DIRECTORY – On the road ▶▶▶

signs (San Sebastian = Donostia). Switzerland has three national languages – French, Italian and German. Also, some areas of northeastern Italy are German-speaking, with signs in German.

Seat belts Regulations in all European countries require wearing of seat belts if fitted. Failure to comply will put you at risk of a police fine. Also see *Children in cars* in the country prefaces.

Security The problem of car theft is increasing, but much more common is petty theft from vehicles. Make sure you take everything out of your car before leaving it for any length of time. Cars with foreign number plates are easy to spot and tempting prey for a petty criminal. If you plan to stay in a large town or city, it is worthwhile finding a hotel with an adequate secure car park. Make sure you are well insured.

Speed-control detection devices The use or possession of devices to detect police speed controls, either inside or outside of vehicles, is illegal in most European countries. Penalties are severe: the equipment may be confiscated, there may be an immediate deposit payable which may not cover any subsequent fine, the driver may be banned from driving, and in serious cases the vehicle may be confiscated and the driver imprisoned.

Speed limits Always obey local speed limits – see the country prefaces for detailed information. Remember that it can be illegal to obstruct traffic by travelling too slowly; offenders can be fined and their driving licences confiscated on the spot. Legal speed limits can be varied by road signs, so be aware of these and keep to the lower limit.

Tolls Tolls are charged on most motorways in France, Italy, Portugal and Spain, and for some major bridges and tunnels. For Switzerland, a motorway tax is levied, and you must display a disc to show that you have paid (available at the Swiss border). Toll charges can mount up over long distances; primary and secondary roads (with a good map), although not as quick, can be less congested and more pleasant. Always have enough local currency to pay tolls, since travellers' cheques are not accepted. Credit cards are accepted at toll booths in France and Spain.

Traffic lights Traffic lights in continental Europe follow a similar pattern. See the country prefaces for specific information. Sometimes traffic lights can be quite dim and they can easily be missed – especially those suspended over the road. Usually there is only one set of lights on the right side of the road some way before the junction; make sure that you stop before the light, otherwise you will not be able to see it. Watch for 'filter' lights that will enable you to turn right at a junction against the main lights. If you are going straight ahead, make sure that you are not in the 'filter' lane, otherwise you will obstruct cars wanting to turn.

Trams Trams are common in many European cities, and always take priority over other vehicles. Give way to passengers boarding and alighting. Never allow your car to interfere with the passage of a tram. Overtake trams on the right except in one-way streets.

≪≪≪ TRAVELLERS' DIRECTORY – Road accidents and breakdowns ≫≫≫

Warm-climate driving In hot weather and at high altitudes, heat in the engine compartment can cause carburation problems. If you are towing a trailer, consult the manufacturers of your car about any limitations of the cooling system, and about the operating temperature of the gearbox fluid if you have automatic transmission. Also see *Automatic gearboxes* under *Preparing your car*, above.

Winter driving If you plan to visit continental Europe in winter, you should be aware that driving is always more or less restricted in the mountainous regions; some passes are closed every winter, and some are closed as required during periods of bad weather. In certain areas you may find the use of snow tyres or wheel chains compulsory. Make full enquiries well in advance from your motoring organisation and from the tourist boards of countries you will visit.

ROAD ACCIDENTS AND BREAKDOWNS ➢

Accidents on the road
- ▶ If you are involved in an accident, stop and place your warning triangle on the road behind the accident to warn following traffic. Turn on your hazard warning lights as an additional warning.
- ▶ Obtain medical help for anyone injured.
- ▶ You must call the police if the accident has caused injury, if an unoccupied vehicle or property has been damaged, or if it is required by law in the country (see country prefaces).
- ▶ If you are calling the police, do not move your car unless it seriously obstructs traffic; if you must move it, first photograph the scene or mark the car's position on the road with independent confirmation if possible.
- ▶ Notify your insurance company in writing within 24 hours (or the time limit for your policy). If a third party has been injured, notify the company or bureau given on your Green Card.
- ▶ Record all essential details of the accident (again, photograph the scene if possible, including other vehicles, registration plates and background which may help later enquiries).
- ▶ Cooperate with officials seeking information.

If you stop to help at an accident park your car carefully well away from the scene.

> **Emergency telephone numbers are given in the country prefaces**

Breakdowns If your car breaks down, try to stop where you will not obstruct traffic. Place your warning triangle behind your car where following traffic will be warned of obstruction. Use your hazard warning lights as well, though remember that they will not be effective around bends or over hills. If you cannot deal with the fault yourself, see the country prefaces for specific advice on seeking help. Also see *Warning triangles* under *Preparing your car*.

Insurance and third-party claims If you intend to make a third-party insurance claim resulting from an accident in Europe, be aware that levels of settlement may be low, and there are special difficulties relating to the recovery of car-hire expenses. Negotiation of claims against foreign insurers is extremely protracted, and translation of all documents slows progress even more. Legal costs and expenses are not recoverable in many European countries, although if you have personal insurance, you may be eligible for a discretionary payment.

SPECIMEN
Letters

ENGLISH
Your address
Street
Town
County
Country

Hotel address
Street
Town
County
Country

00.00.1993

Dear Sir

Please send me by return your terms with tax and service included, and confirm availability of accommodation with:

full board/half board/bed and breakfast.

I would arrive on _____
and leave on. _____

I would need ____ rooms with single bed with/without bath/shower

____ rooms with double bed with/without bath/shower

____ rooms with twin beds with/without bath/shower

____ cots in parents' room.

We are ____ adults. Our party also includes ____ children; ____ boys aged ____ years and ____ girls aged ____ years.

I look forward to receiving your reply and thank you in advance.

Yours faithfully

Specimen letters for booking hotel rooms

Print your letter clearly, and enclose an International Reply Coupon, available from post offices.

GERMAN
Sehr geehrter Herr

Bitte senden Sie mir umgehend Angaben Ihrer Preise, einschl.

Stauer-und Bedienungskosten, und bestätigen, ob Sie Zimmer frei haben, für eine Unterbringung mit:

Vollpension/Halbpension/Zimmer mit Frühstück.

Ankunftsdatum _____
Abfahrtsdatum _____

Ich möchte ____ Einzelzimmer mit/ohne Bad/Dusche

____ Zimmer mit Doppelbett mit/ohne Bad/Dusche

____ Zimmer mit Zwei Betten mit/ohne Bad/Dusche

____ Kinderbettchen im Elternzimmer.

Wir sind ____ Erwachsene, und zusätzlich ____ Kinder; ____ Jungen ____ Jahre und ____ Mädchen ____ Jahre.

Ich sehe ihre Antwort gern entgegen und danke Ihnen im voraus für Ihre Bemühungen.

Mit freundlichen Grüssen

Germany D 1

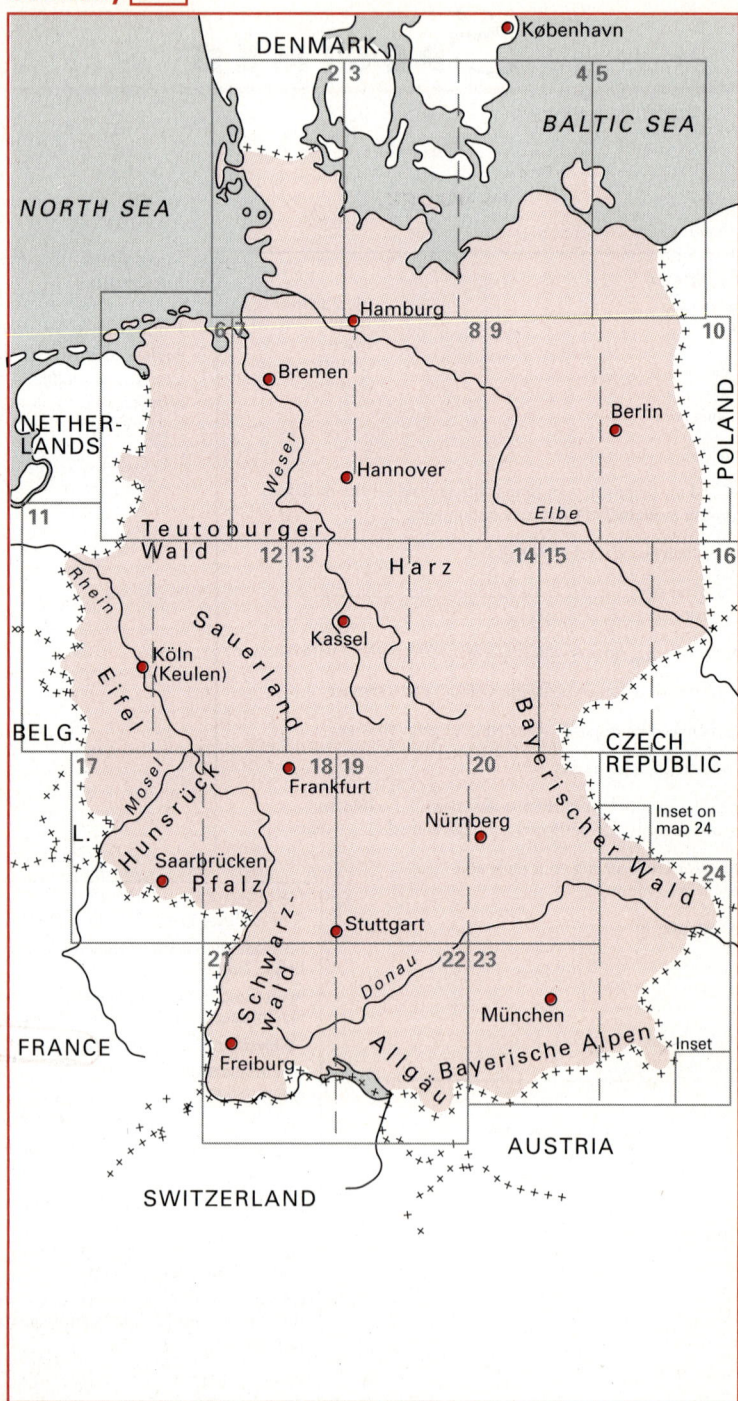

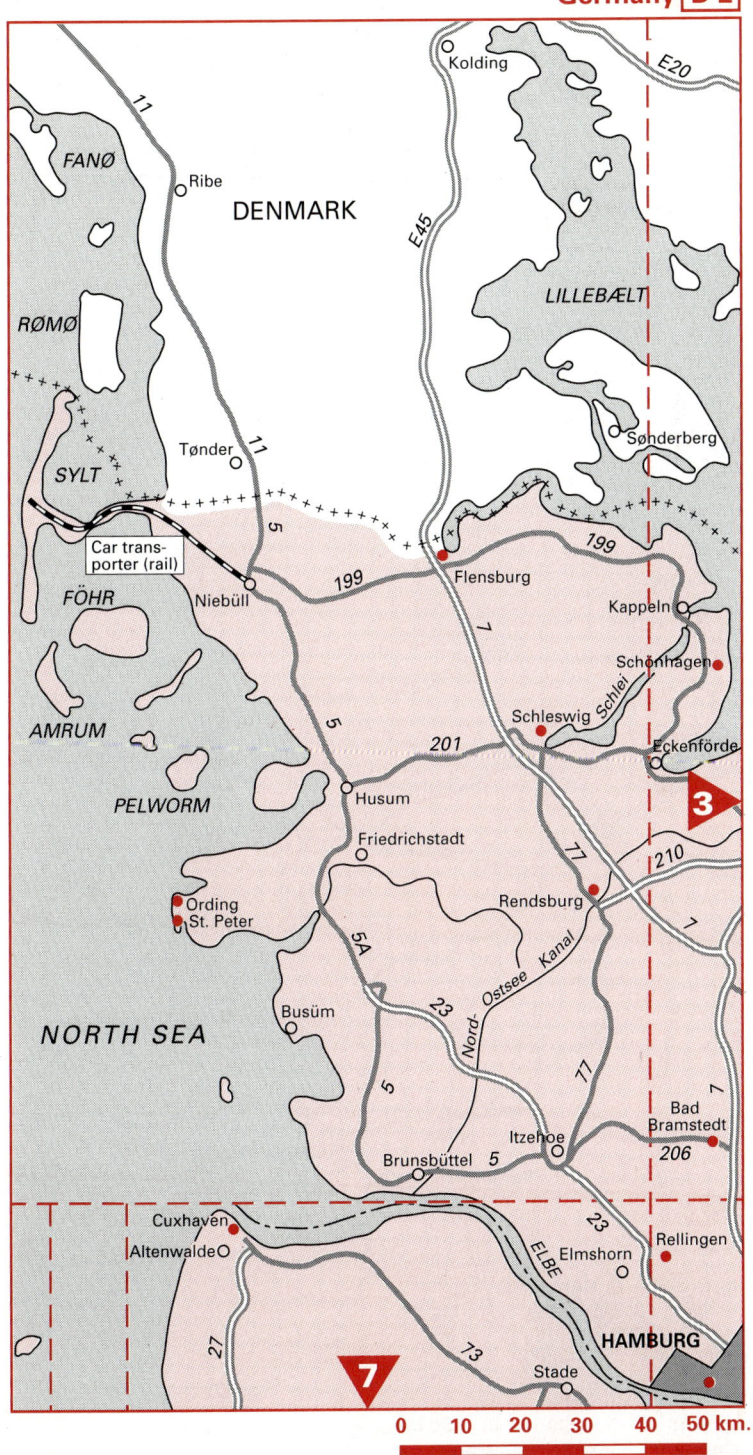

Germany D 3

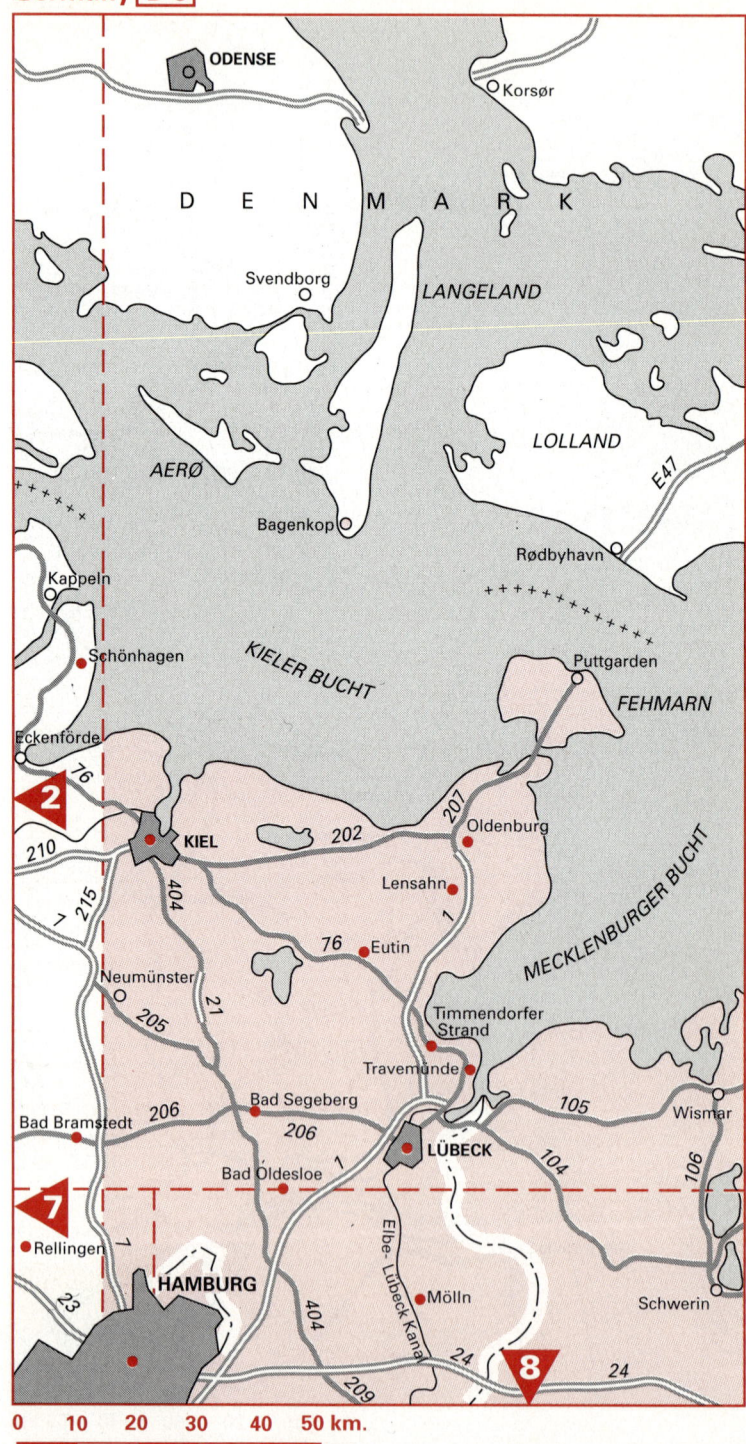

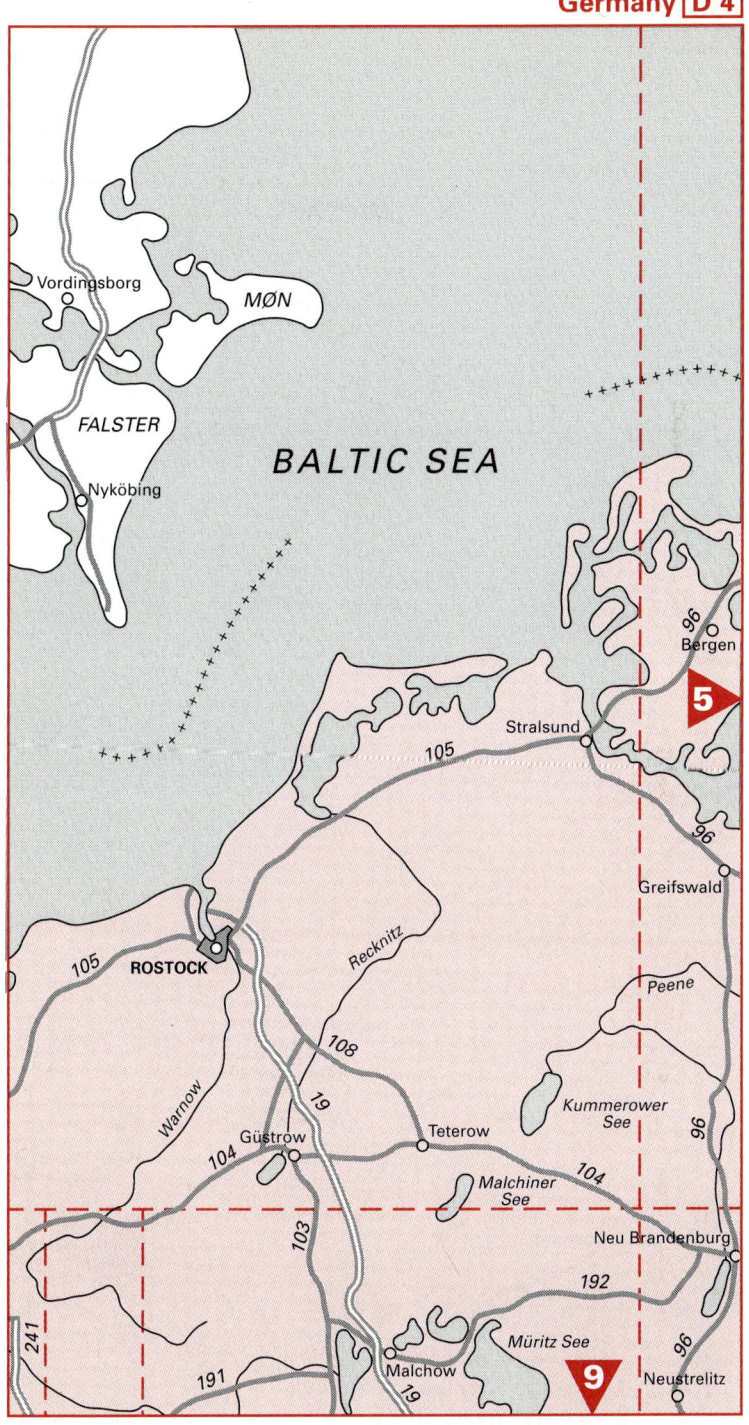

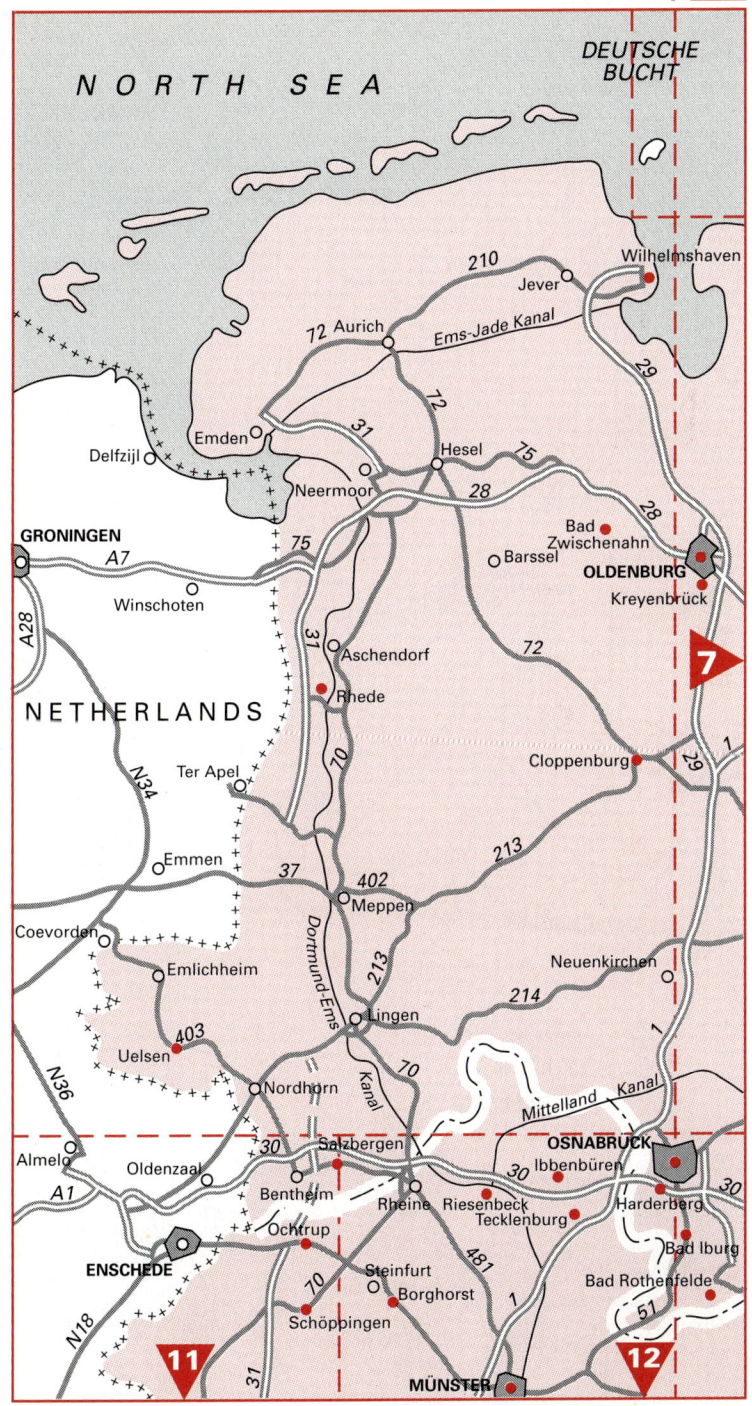

Germany D 7

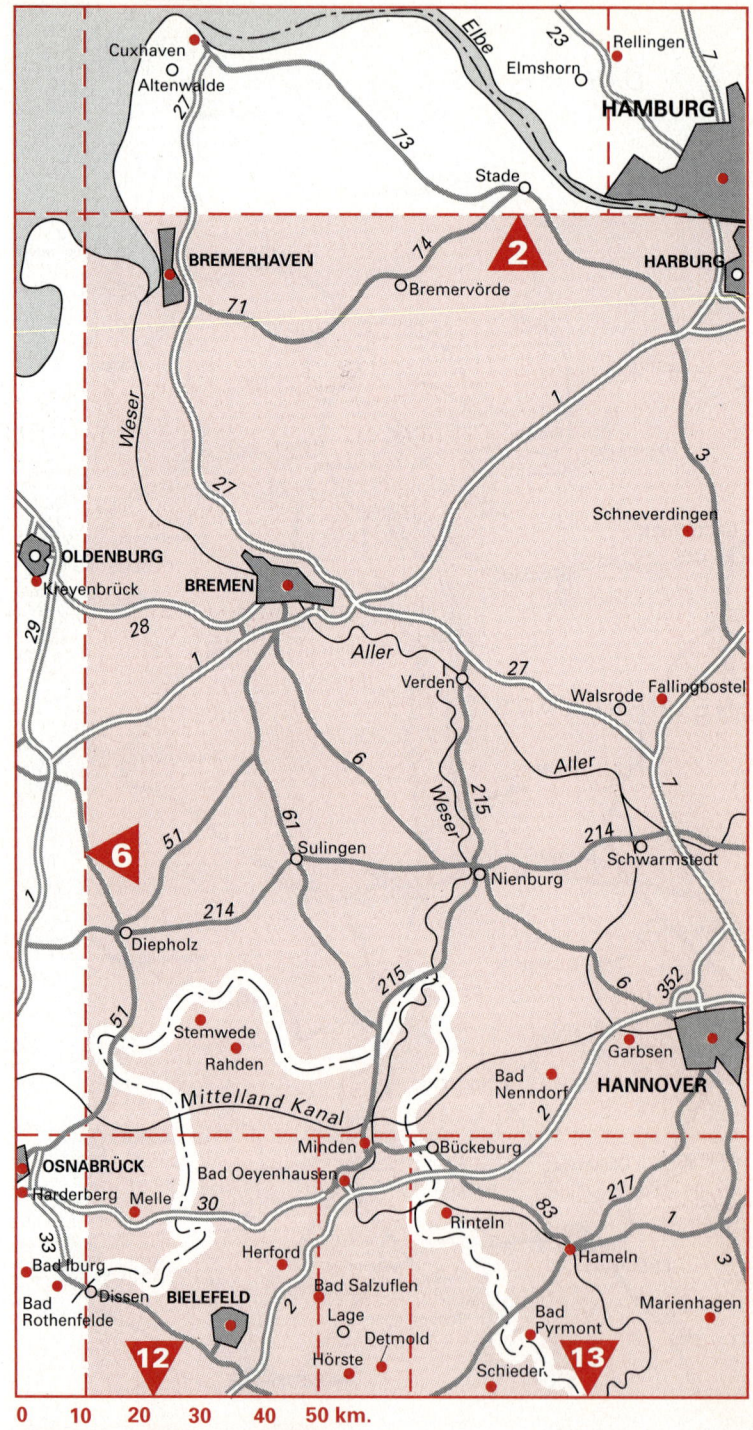

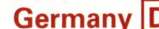

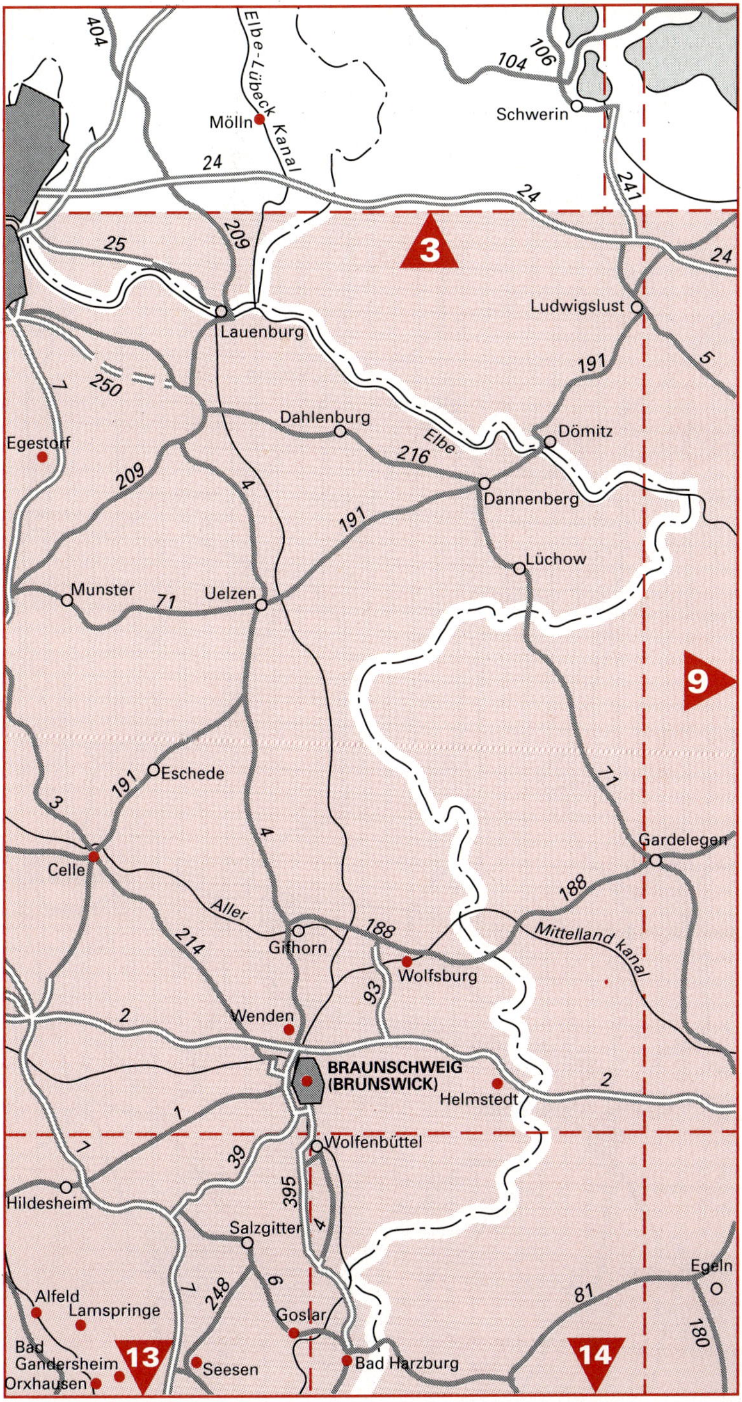
Elbe-Lübeck Kanal
Mölln
Schwerin
Lauenburg
Ludwigslust
Dahlenburg
Elbe
Dömitz
Egestorf
Dannenberg
Lüchow
Munster
Uelzen
Eschede
Gardelegen
Celle
Aller
Gifhorn
Wolfsburg
Mittelland kanal
Wenden
BRAUNSCHWEIG
(BRUNSWICK)
Helmstedt
Wolfenbüttel
Hildesheim
Salzgitter
Egeln
Alfeld
Lamspringe
Goslar
Bad
Gandersheim
Orxhausen
Seesen
Bad Harzburg
404
104
106
1
24
241
25
209
250
7
191
5
216
4
71
3
188
214
93
2
39
395
248
6
81
180
3
9
13
14

Germany D 9

Germany D 11

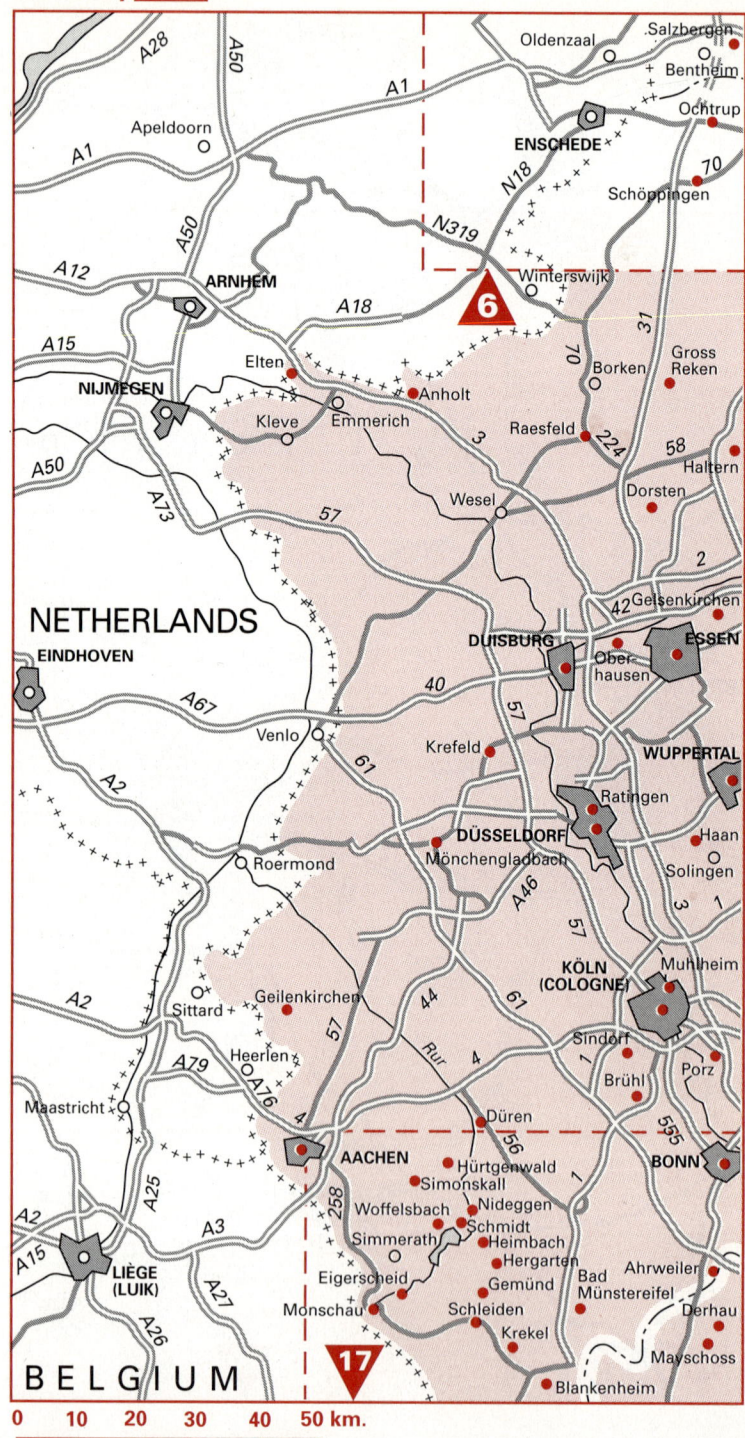

Germany D 12

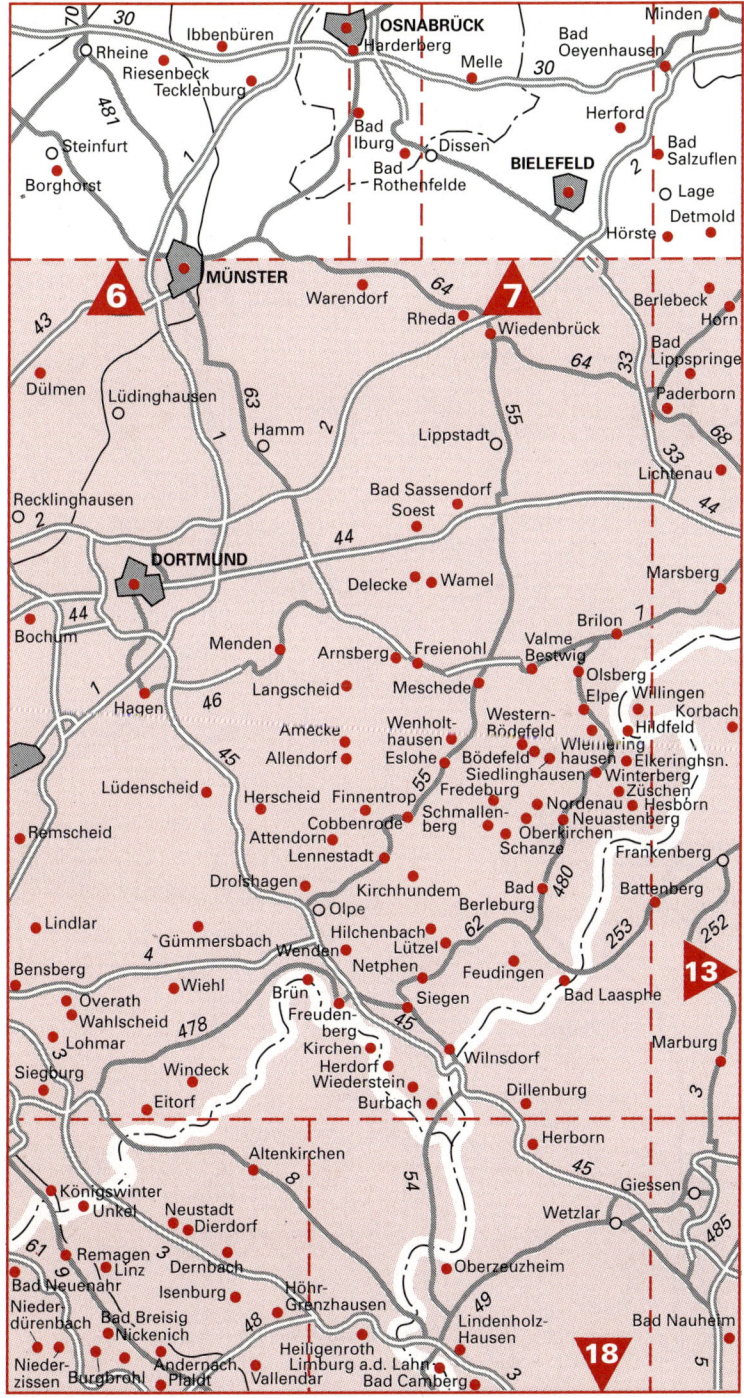

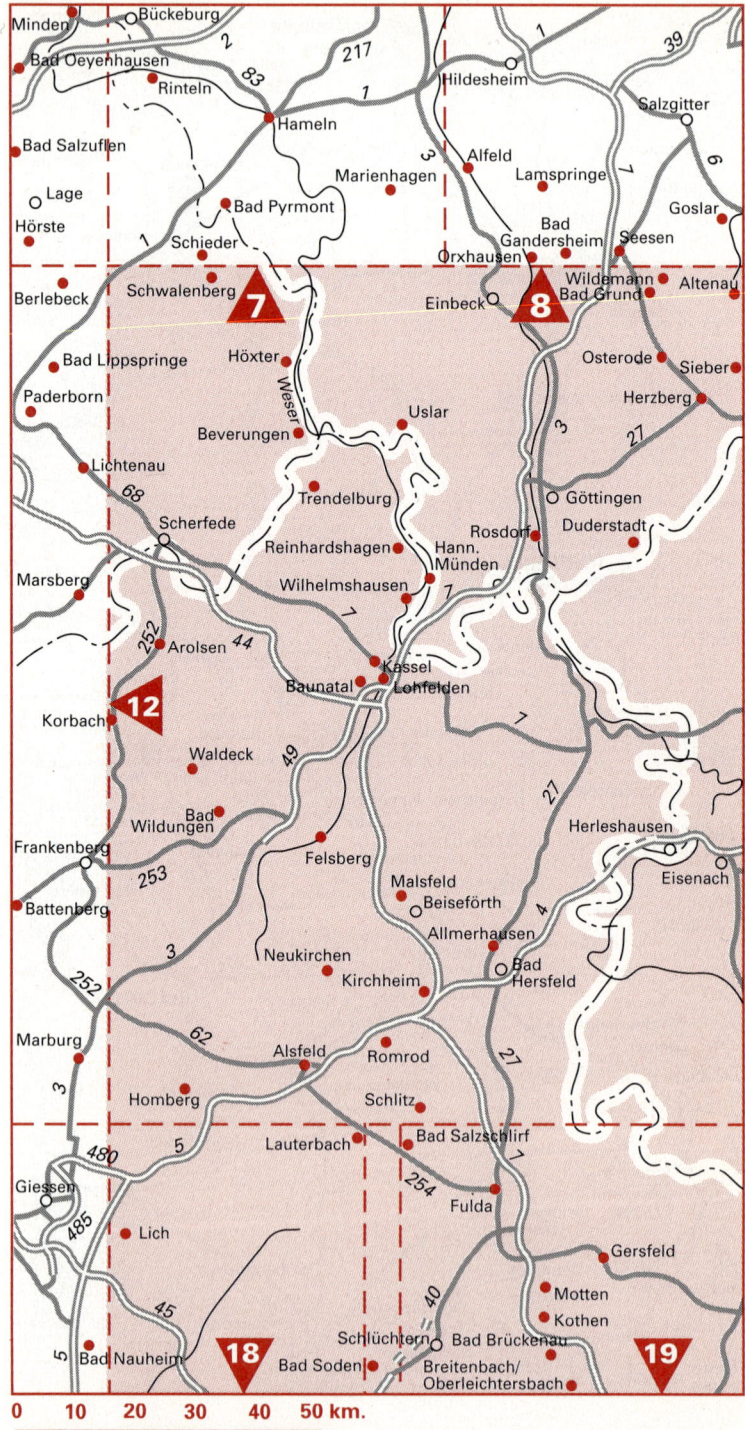

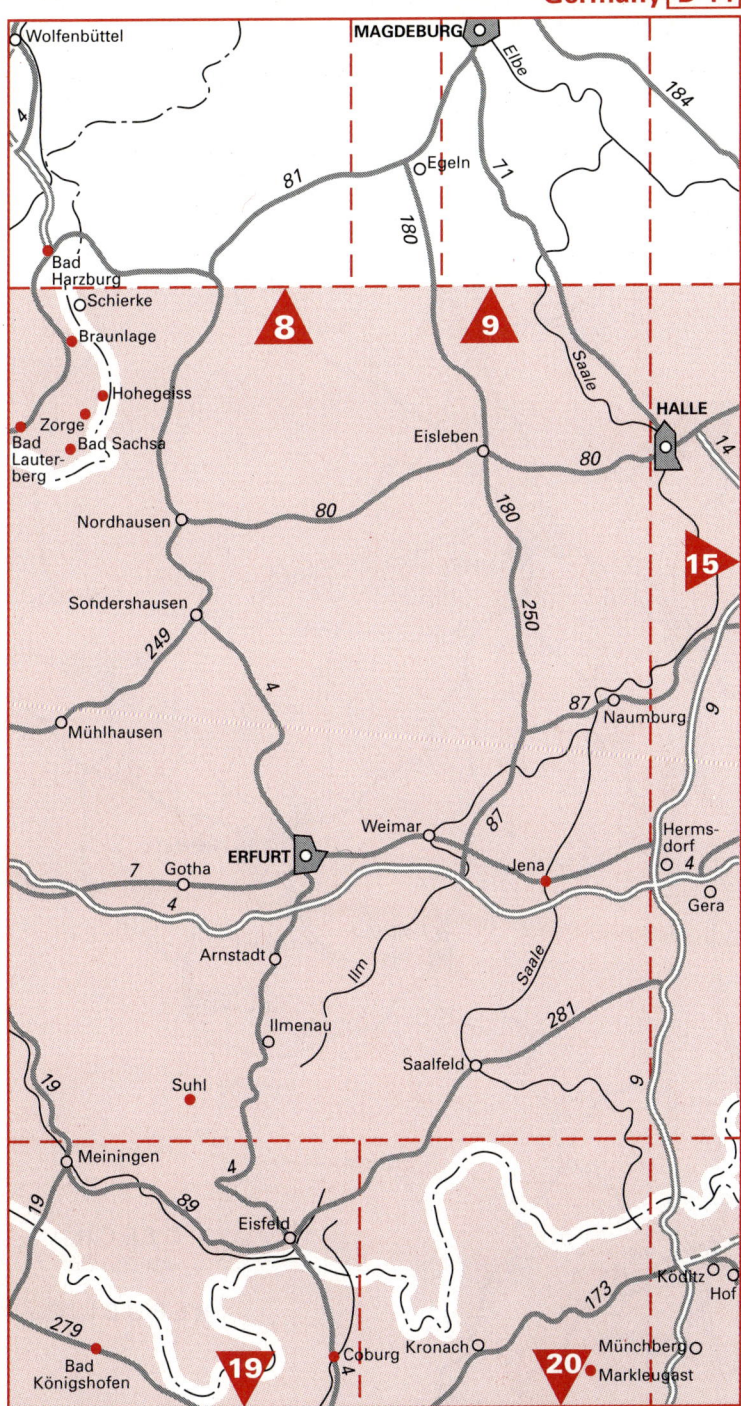

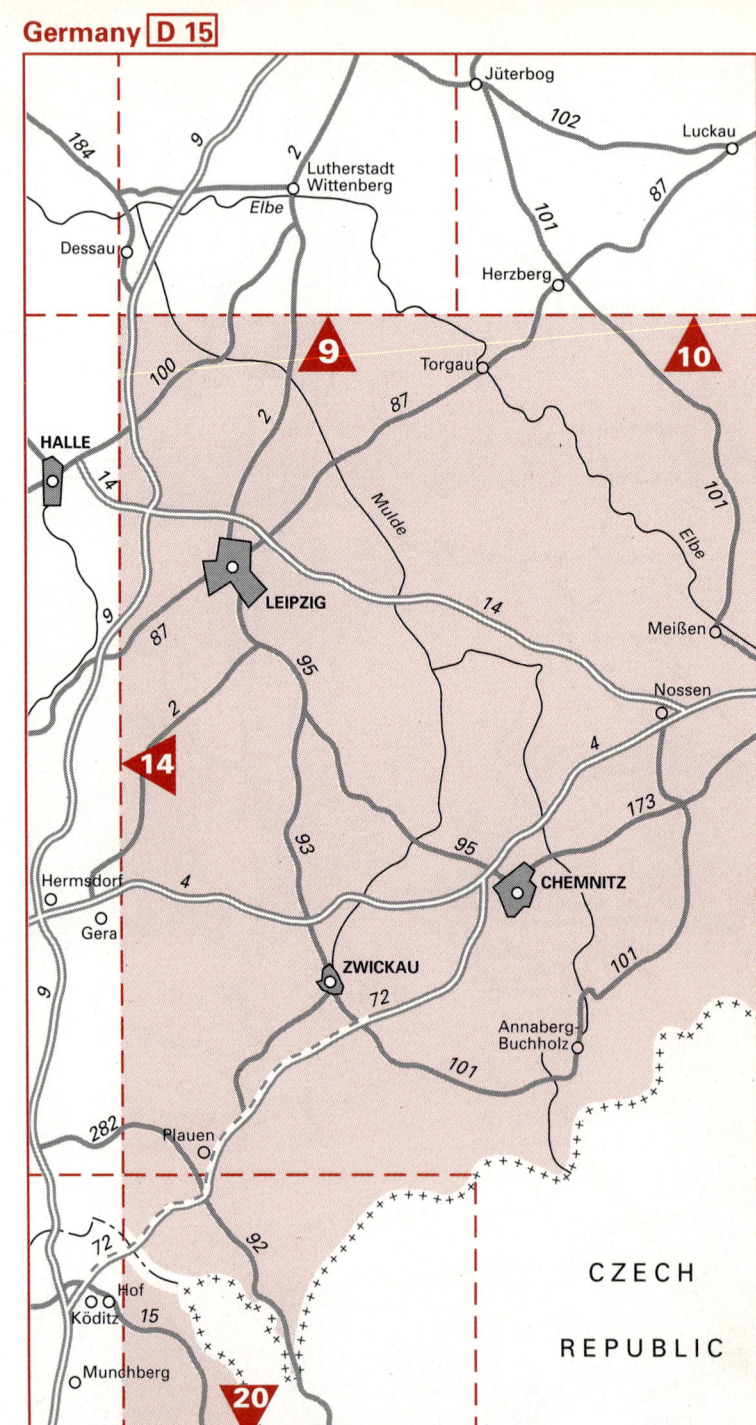

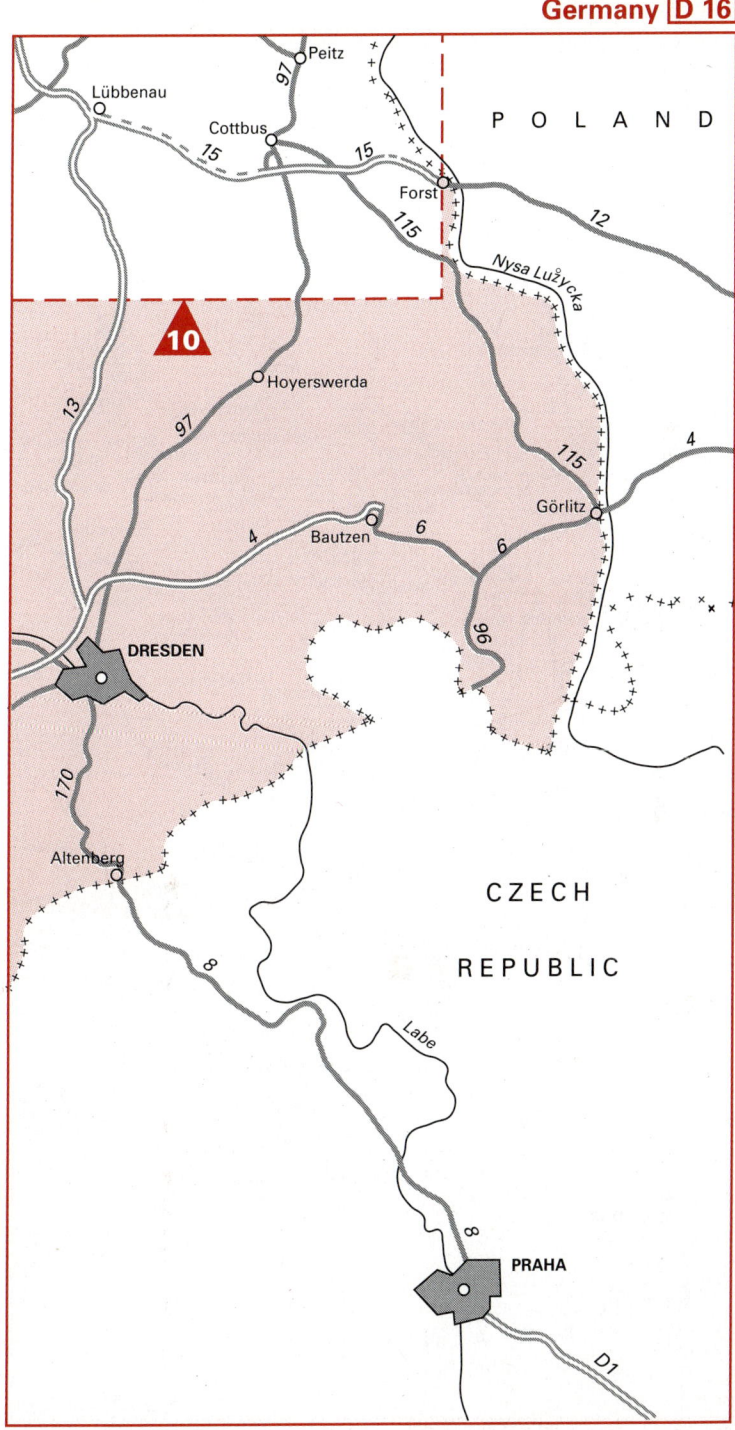

Germany D 17

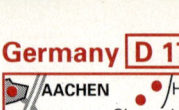

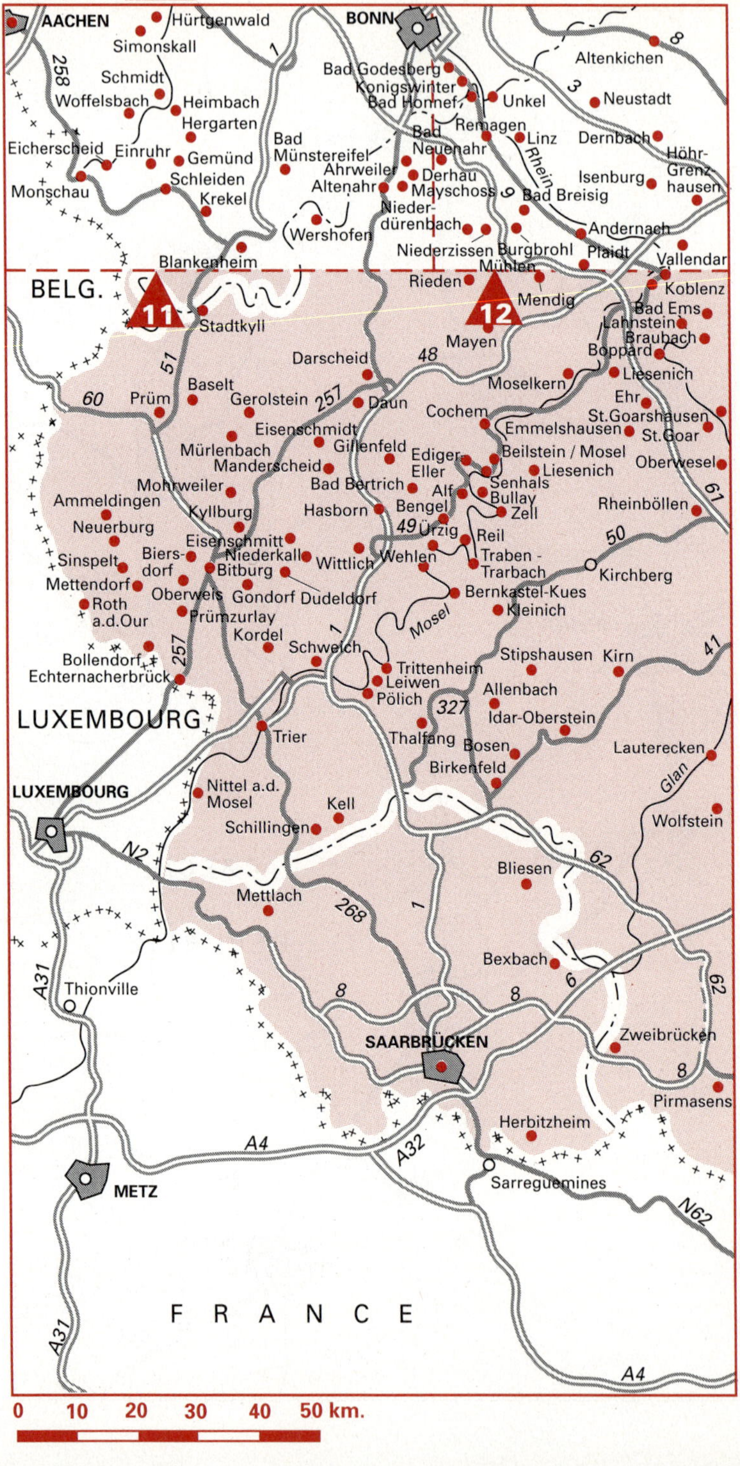
AACHEN
Hürtgenwald
Simonskall
Schmidt
Woffelsbach
Heimbach
Hergarten
Eicherscheid
Einruhr
Gemünd
Monschau
Schleiden
Krekel
Blankenheim
Bad Münstereifel
Wershofen
BONN
Bad Godesberg
Konigswinter
Bad Honnef
Unkel
Altenkichen
Neustadt
Remagen
Linz
Dernbach
Höhr-Grenzhausen
Bad Neuenahr
Ahrweiler
Altenahr
Derhau
Mayschoss
Bad Breisig
Isenburg
Nieder-dürenbach
Niederzissen
Burgbrohl
Andernach
Plaidt
Vallendar
Mühlen
Rieden
Mendig
Koblenz
Bad Ems
Lahnstein
Braubach
Boppard
Liesenich
Mayen
BELG.
11
12
Stadtkyll
Darscheid
Baselt
Prüm
Gerolstein
Daun
Moselkern
Ehr
Cochem
St.Goarshausen
Emmelshausen
St.Goar
Eisenschmidt
Mürlenbach
Gillenfeld
Ediger
Eller
Beilstein / Mosel
Liesenich
Oberwesel
Manderscheid
Bad Bertrich
Alf
Senhals
Bullay
Mohrweiler
Ammeldingen
Kyllburg
Hasborn
Bengel
Zell
Rheinböllen
Neuerburg
Ürzig
Reil
Eisenschmitt
Niederkall
Wittlich
Wehlen
Traben - Trarbach
Kirchberg
Sinspelt
Biers-dorf
Bitburg
Mettendorf
Oberweis
Gondorf
Dudeldorf
Bernkastel-Kues
Roth a.d.Our
Prümzurlay
Kleinich
Mosel
Kordel
Bollendorf
Schweich
Stipshausen
Kirn
Echternacherbrück
Trittenheim
Leiwen
Pölich
Allenbach
LUXEMBOURG
Idar-Oberstein
Trier
Thalfang
Bosen
Lauterecken
Birkenfeld
Glan
LUXEMBOURG
Nittel a.d. Mosel
Kell
Wolfstein
Schillingen
N2
62
Bliesen
Mettlach
268
Bexbach
6
A31
Thionville
8
8
62
SAARBRÜCKEN
Zweibrücken
8
Pirmasens
Herbitzheim
A4
A32
METZ
Sarreguemines
N62
F R A N C E
A31
A4
Rhein
258
1
3
8
9
48
257
51
60
49
50
61
41
327
257
1
0 10 20 30 40 50 km.

Germany D 18

Germany D 19

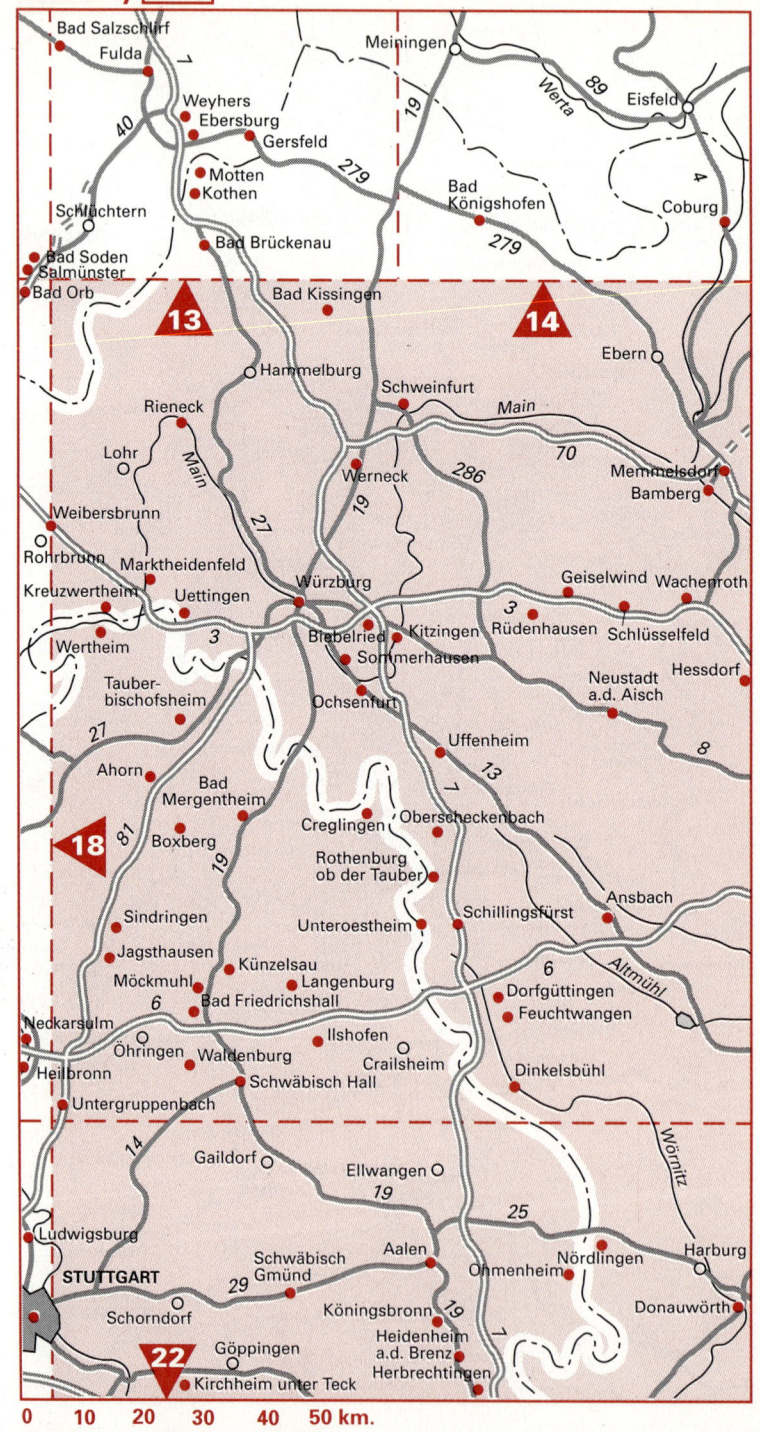

Germany D 20

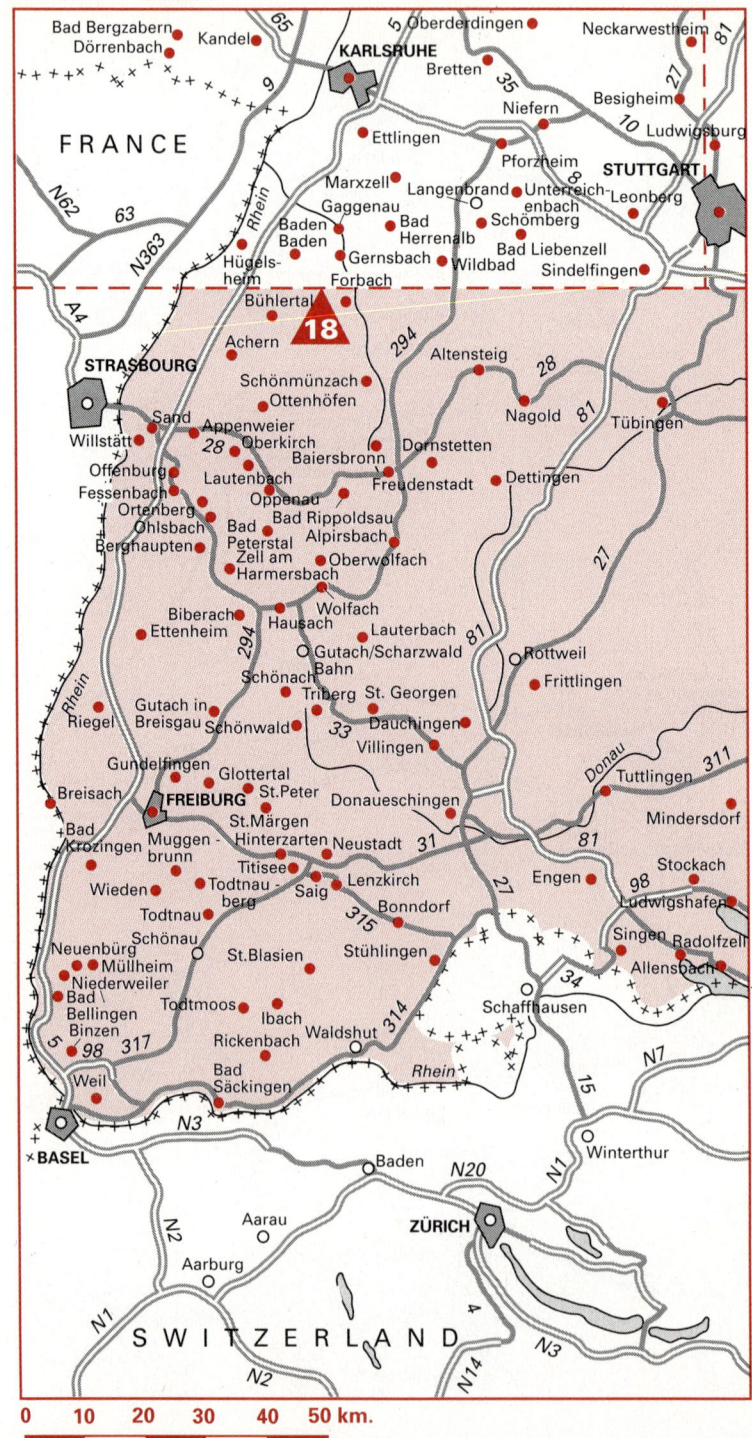

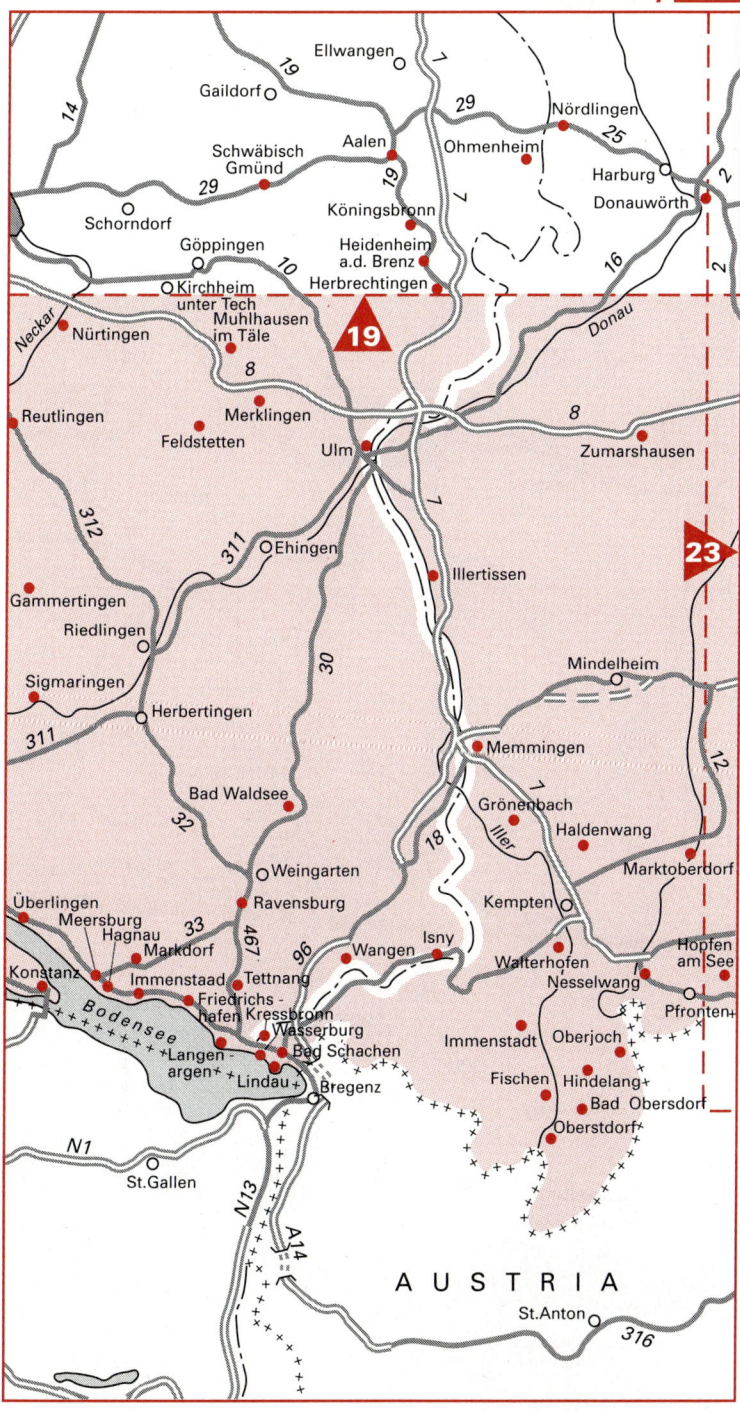

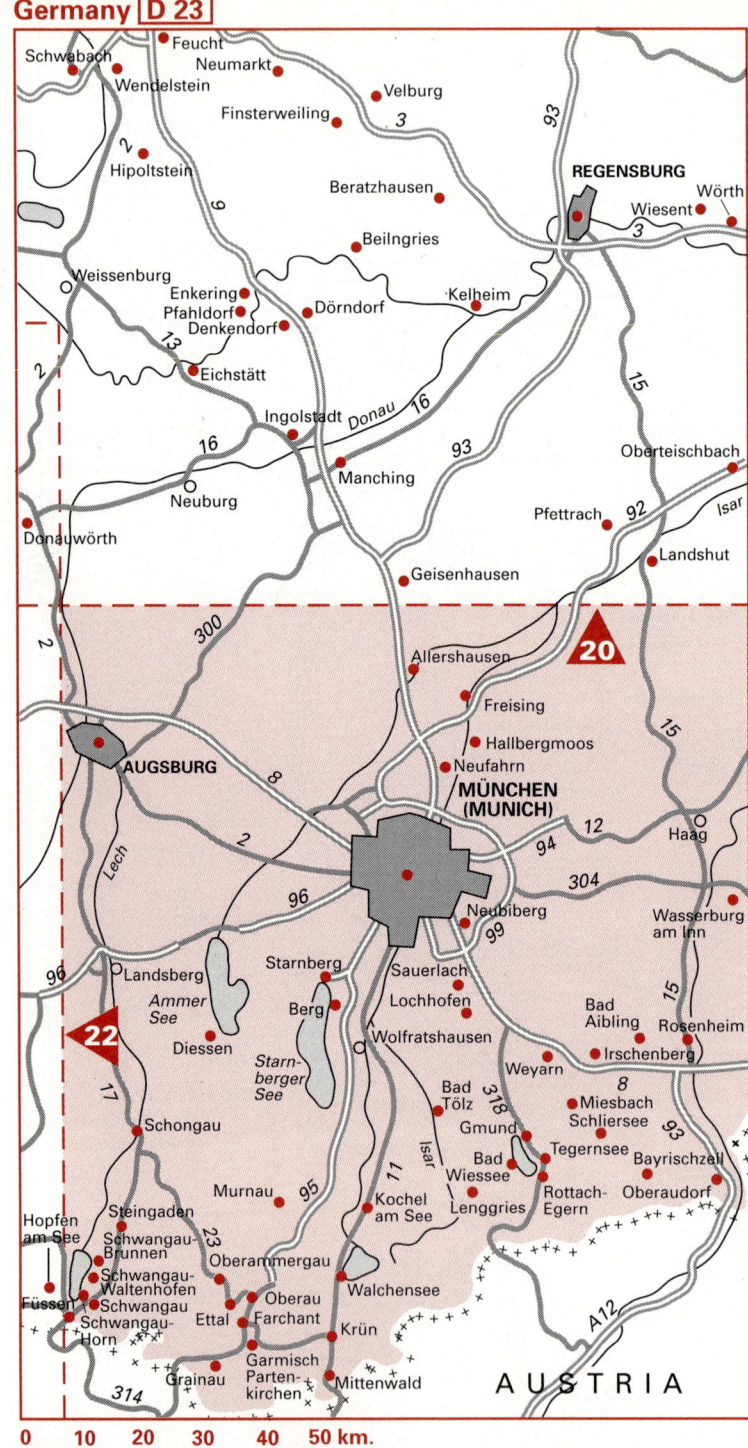

Austria A 1

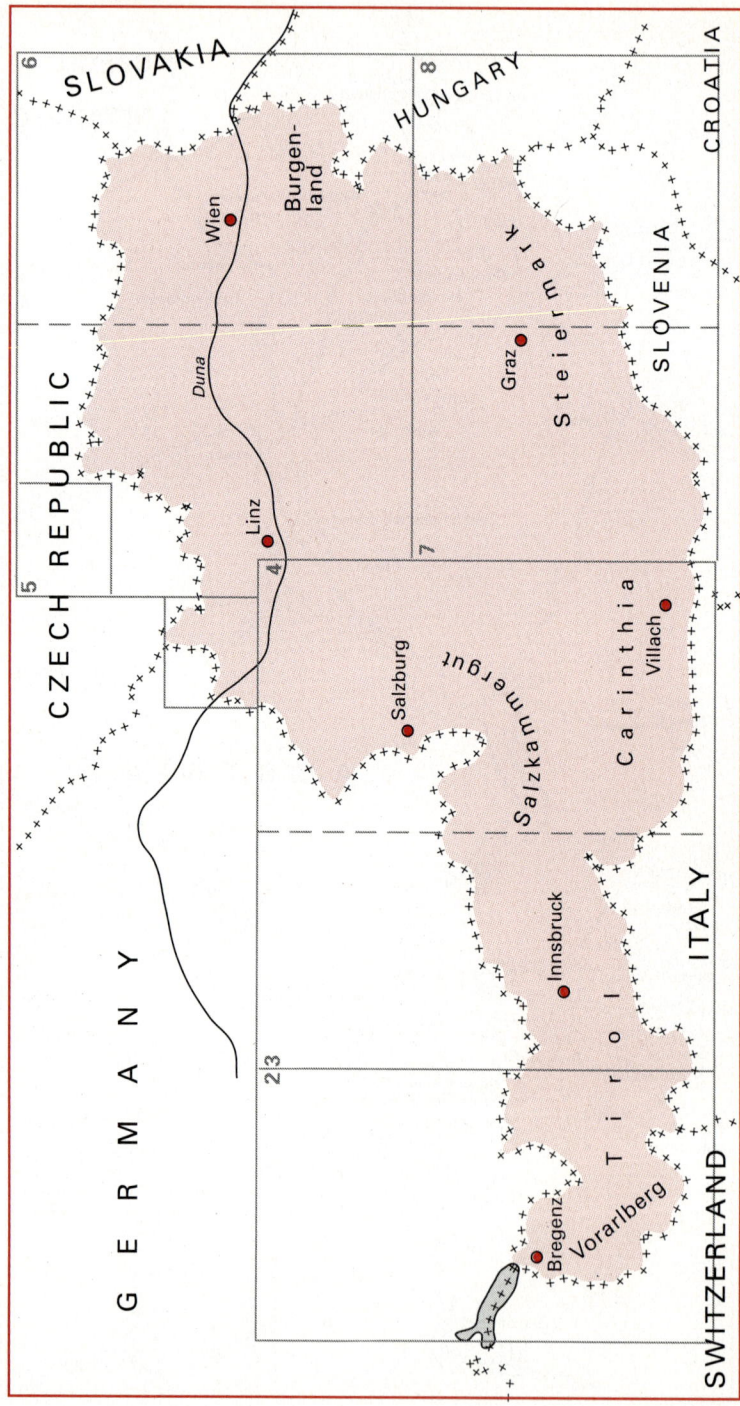

Austria A3

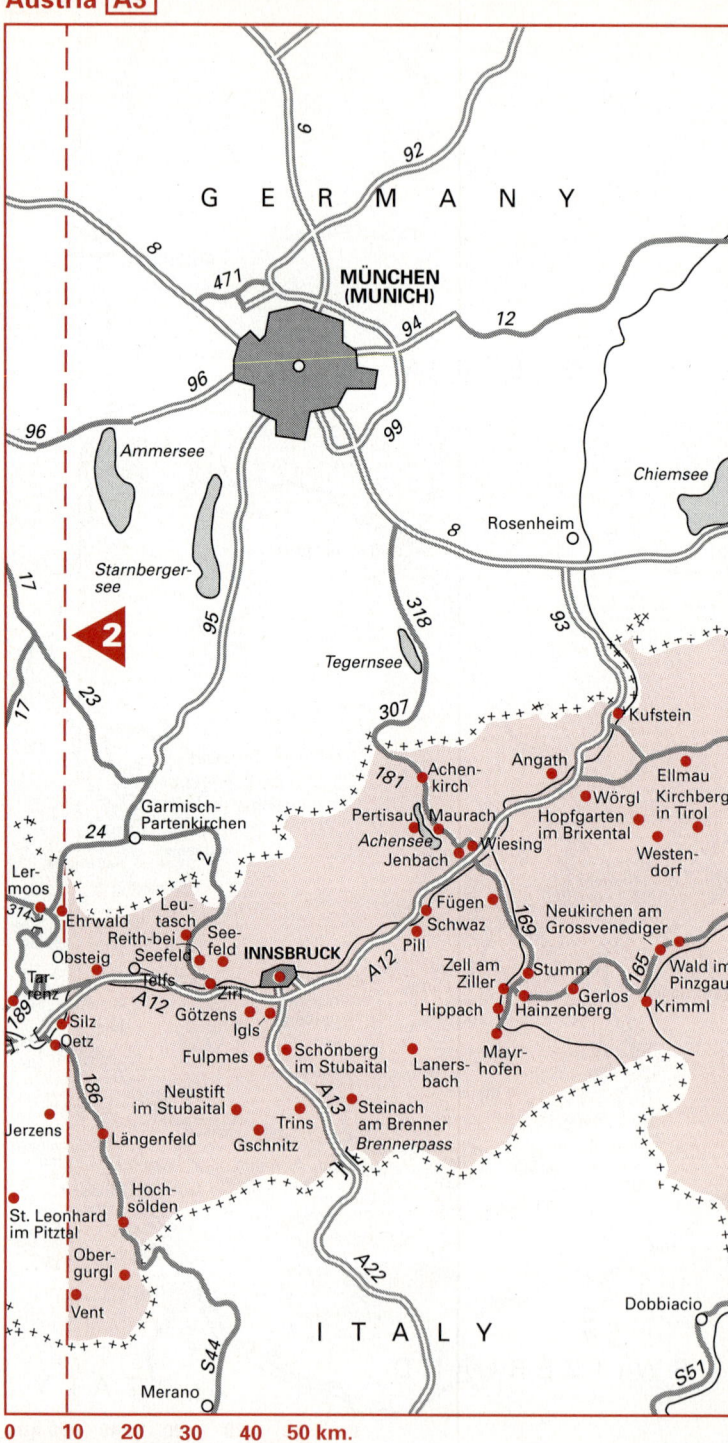

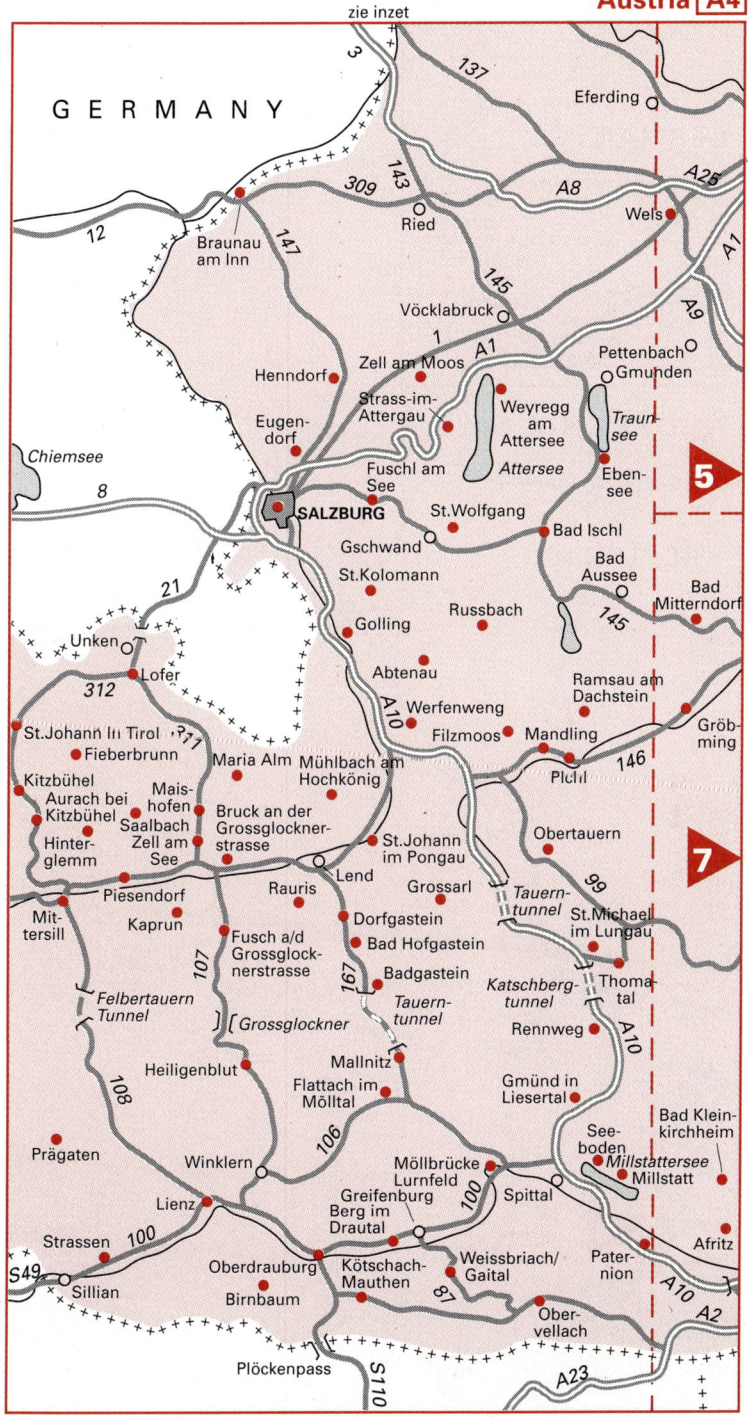

Austria A5

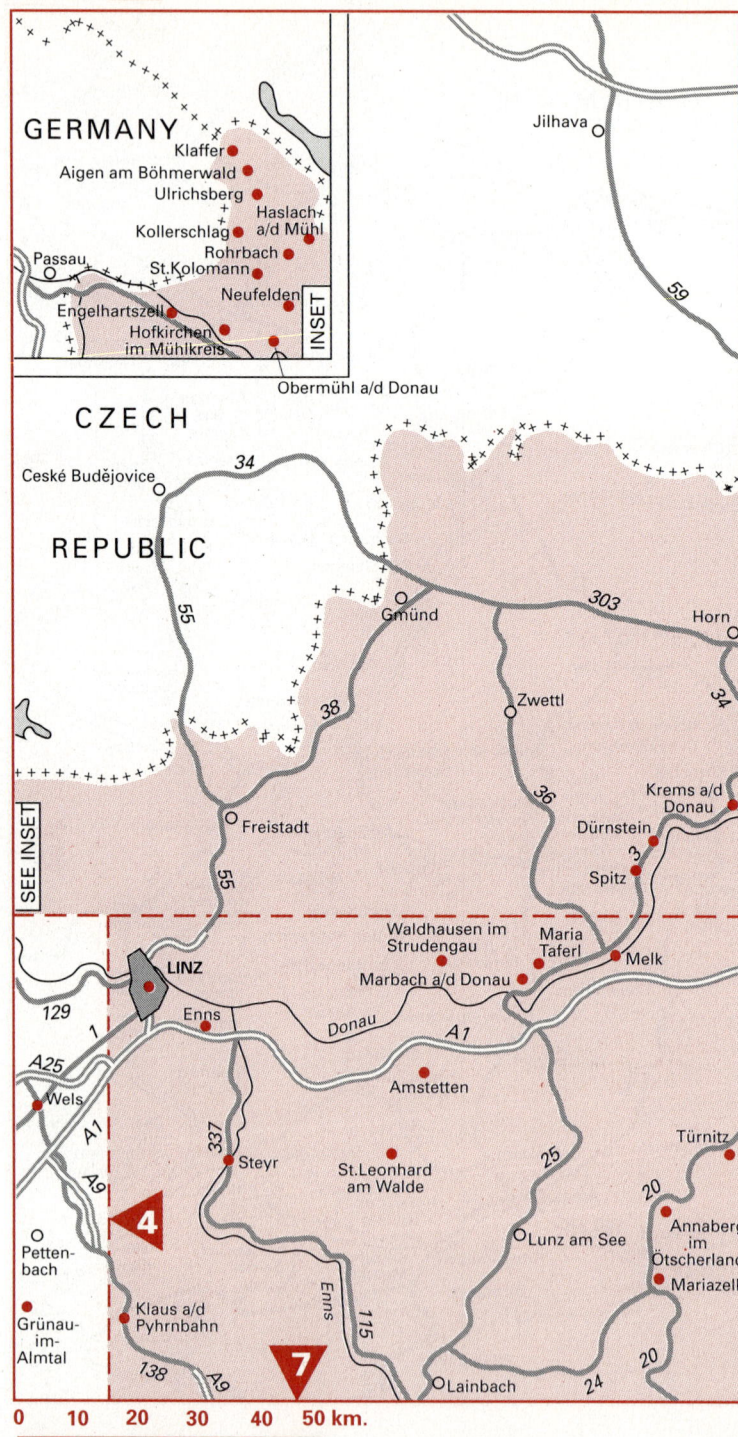

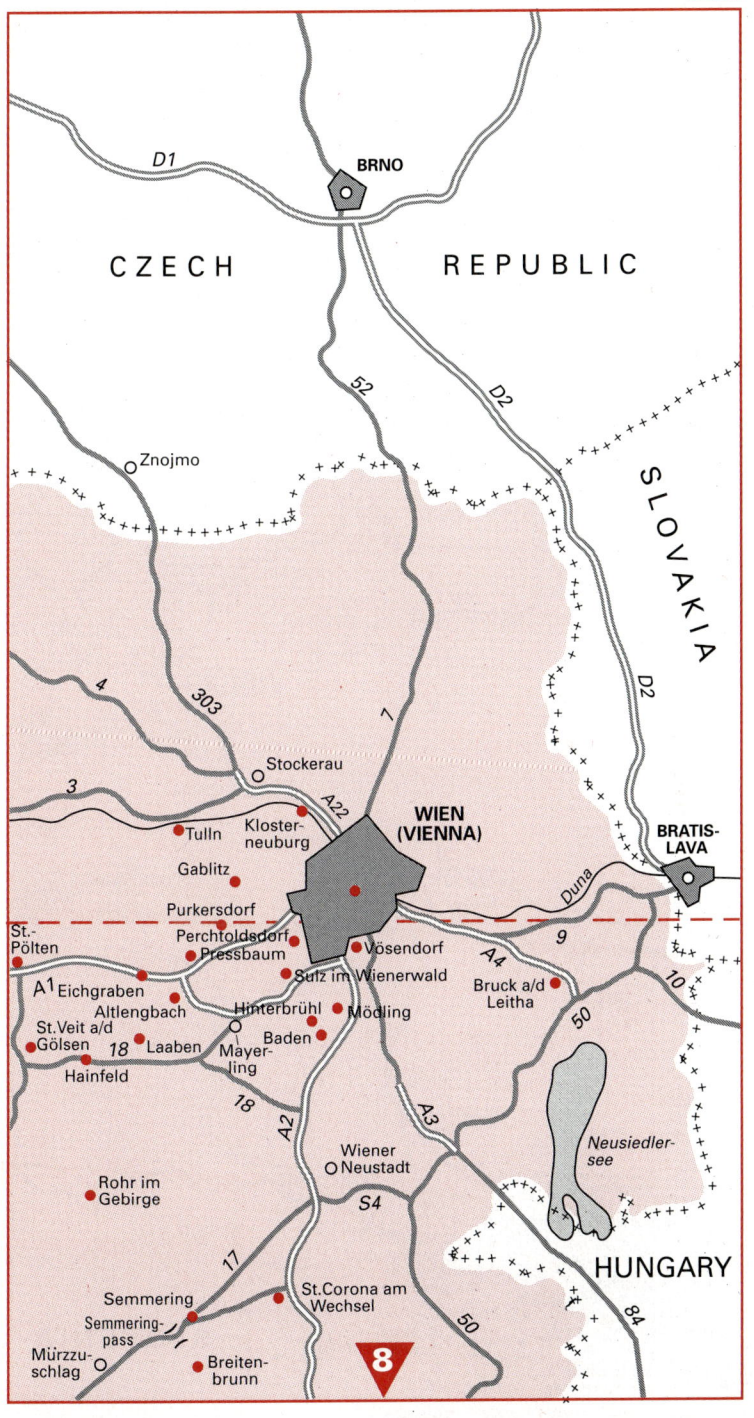

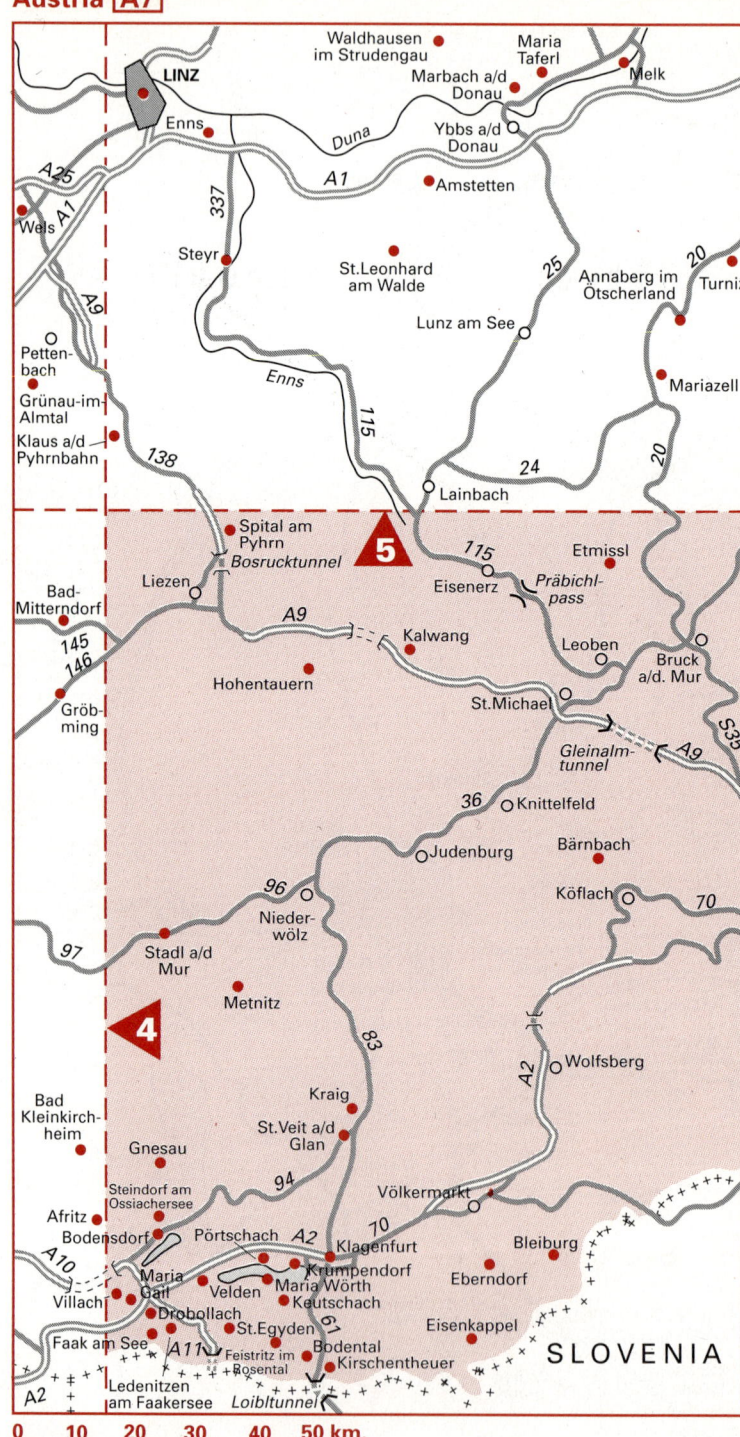

Austria A8

GERMANY

CAPITAL	Berlin
LANGUAGE	German
CURRENCY	Deutsche mark, divided into 100 pfennig UK £1 = DM2.41 US $1 = DM1.63
EMERGENCY NUMBERS	Fire, telephone 112; police and ambulance, telephone 110
TOURIST INFORMATION	*In Britain:* German National Tourist Office, Nightingale House, 65 Curzon Street, London W1Y 7PE, telephone 071 495 3990/1 *In USA:* German National Tourist Office, 122 East 42nd Street, Chanin Building, 52nd Floor, New York, NY 10168-0072, telephone 212 661 7200

MOTORING AND GENERAL INFORMATION ➢

For more information refer to the *Travellers' directory* on page IX.

Accidents   The police must be called in cases of injury or considerable damage. If you fail to give aid to anyone injured you could be fined. See also *Warning triangle* below.

Call boxes with two luminous red stripes contain a free emergency telephone; lift the receiver and pull the emergency lever and you will automatically be connected with the fire service or police.

Breakdown   If your car breaks down, try to move it so that it does not obstruct traffic flow. A warning triangle must be placed to the rear of the vehicle, and hazard warning lights, if fitted to the vehicle, must be used. See also *Warning triangle* below.

The German motoring club (ADAC) operates a breakdown service called the *Strassenwacht*. The Deutscher Touring Automobil Club (DTC), the Automobil Club of Germany (AvD) and the Auto Club Europa (ACE) also operate patrol services.

Children in cars   Children under 12 and/or less than 1.50 metres in height are not permitted to travel as front or rear-seat passengers unless using a suitable restraint system, if fitted.

Driving licence   A valid UK, Republic of Ireland or New Zealand licence is acceptable in Germany. An International Driving Permit is compulsory for holders of licences issued in Australia, Canada or USA. The minimum age at which a visitor may use a temporarily imported car or motorcycle is 17 years.

First-aid kit   German authorities recommend that visiting motorists carry a first-aid kit.

Fuel   Generally the major credit cards are accepted at all company-owned filling stations. Leaded petrol is available as *super benzin* (98 octane) grade. Unleaded petrol *(bleifrei)* is sold as *regular benzin* (91 octane), *premium benzin* (95 octane) and *super green benzin* (98 octane) grades. Unleaded fuel pumps are painted green. Only one grade of diesel *(diesel)* is sold for automotive use. Up to 10 litres of petrol or diesel fuel can be carried in a can in a vehicle.

Hotel classification   Hotels in Germany are not classified by a national rating system; price is the best indication of facilities and standards. Breakfast is usually included in the prices in this guide. We have specially selected a wide range of inexpensive accommodation *(Gasthöfe, Gaststätte)* close to German motorways.

A *Kurhotel* is a health resort or spa; these often have areas of garden *(Kurpark)* set aside for guests to sit or lie quietly, where no games or running around is permitted.

There is a wide range of accommodation in the former West Germany. Simple *Pensions* and *Fremdenzimmer* offer mainly bed and breakfast accommodation, there are hotels of all types, and the stylish *Schlosshotels* offer luxury accommodation in converted castles and palaces.

However in the former East Germany, because of its economic background, state-run hotels still form the main part of accommodation. These hotels tend to be somewhat neglected and impersonal; choice is relatively small and prices tend to be high. Since unification, the hotels are slowly being returned to the private sector and new hotels are being built to meet demands. This process is expected to take some years, and therefore for East Germany this guide lists only accommodation in Berlin. The shortage of reasonable hotel accommodation has led to people opening their homes to tourists, and pension rooms can be found everywhere. Addresses are available at local tourist information offices; we cannot assess the quality, but prices are low and usually include breakfast.

Lights Driving on parking lights or sidelights only is prohibited. When fog, falling snow or rain substantially affect driving conditions, dipped headlights and two fog-lamps must be used, even during daylight. However, rear fog lamps can only be used when visibility is less than 50 metres (55yds). Motorcyclists must use dipped headlights during the day. German authorities recommend that visiting motorists equip their vehicles with a spare set of vehicle bulbs.

Motoring club The principal German motoring clubs are the Allgemeiner Deutscher Automobil Club (ADAC) which has its headquarters at 81373 München, Am Westpark 8, telephone 089 76760, and the Deutscher Touring Automobil Club (DTC) whose headquarters is 881247 München, Amalienburgstrasse 23, telephone 089 8111048. Both clubs have offices in the larger towns; hours are 08.00 to 17.00 Monday to Friday. The ADAC also has offices at major frontier crossings.

Motorways A comprehensive motorway *(Autobahn)* network dominates the road system and takes most of the long-distance traffic. It is considered negligent to run out of fuel on a motorway, and the police can fine offending motorists up to DM75.

Parking Park in the direction of the traffic flow. Parking is forbidden in the following places: on a main road or one carrying fast-moving traffic; on or near tram lines; within 15 metres (50ft) of a bus or tram stop; above man-hole covers; on the left-hand side of the road (unless the road is one-way). A vehicle is considered to be parked if it cannot be immediately removed if required, or if it is stopped for more than three minutes. When stopping is prohibited under all circumstances, this is indicated by an international sign. Parking meters, and special areas where parking discs are used, are indicated by signs which also show the permitted duration of parking. Disabled drivers may be granted special parking concessions; application should be made to the local traffic authority. Spending the night in a vehicle is tolerated for one night, provided there are no signs to the contrary and the vehicle is lit and parked in a lay-by. The sign showing an eagle in a green triangle (indicating a wildlife reserve) prohibits parking outside designated areas.

Priority in traffic On pedestrian crossings pedestrians have the right of way over all vehicles except trams. Buses have priority when leaving public bus stops, and other vehicles must give way to a bus driver who has signalled an intention to leave the kerb.

Roads The *Bundesstrassen*, or state roads, vary in quality. In the north and west and in the touring areas of the Rhine valley, Schwarzwald and Bavaria, the roads are good and well graded. Traffic at weekends increases considerably during the school holidays, which are from July to mid-September. In order to ease congestion, heavy lorries are prohibited on all roads at weekends from about mid-June until the end of August, and generally on all Sundays and public holidays.

In the former East Germany the roads are generally poor and often rough and pot-holed. Roads in towns are also poor, many with uneven cobbled surfaces.

Public holidays 1994

Epiphany, Corpus Christi, Assumption and All Saints' Day are holidays only in certain areas.

January 1 New Year's Day	*May 23* Whit Monday	*November 17* Day of Prayer and Repentance
January 6 Epiphany	*June 2* Corpus Christi	
April 1 Good Friday	*August 15* Assumption	*December 25* Christmas Day
April 4 Easter Monday	*October 3* Reunification	*December 26* Second day of Christmas
May 1 Labour Day	*November 1* All Saints' Day	
May 12 Ascension Day		

Speed limits The speed limit in built-up areas is 50kph (31mph) unless otherwise indicated by signs. The beginning of a built-up area is indicated by the place name sign. Outside built-up areas the limit for private cars is 100kph (62mph). Motorways *(Autobahnen)*, dual-carriageways and roads with at least two marked lanes in each direction which are not specifically signposted, have a recommended speed limit of 130kph (80mph). Vehicles towing a caravan or trailer are limited to 80kph (49mph). All lower limits must be obeyed. Where indicated by a sign (circular with white figures on a blue background), vehicles cannot travel at a speed lower than that displayed. Outside built-up areas, motor vehicles to which a special speed limit applies, as well as vehicles with trailers with a combined length of more than 7 metres (23ft), must keep enough distance between vehicles in front to allow overtaking vehicles to pull in.

Telephone To make an international call from Germany, lift the receiver and then insert coins. Dial 00 and then the country code (see under *General and touring information* in the *Travellers' directory*), then the area code without the first 0 and the number. International call boxes have pay phones marked 'International'.

To call Germany from another country, the international code for Germany is 49; omit the first 0 of the area code.

German unification will result in changes to the telephone system, but at the time of going to press no details are available. Ask at a post office for further information.

Traffic lights At some intersections with several lanes going in different directions, there are lights for each lane; watch the light arrow for your lane. Occasionally there are traffic lights in rural areas which automatically change to green when an approaching vehicle passes a certain line, to enable vehicles from a secondary road to cross or turn into a priority road when there is heavy traffic.

In the former East Germany lights at some intersections may also feature a painted green arrow indicating that drivers may turn in the direction of the arrow provided they give way to all pedestrian and vehicular traffic, but these are being phased out.

Warning triangle The use of a warning triangle is compulsory in the event of accident or breakdown. The triangle must be placed on the road behind the vehicle to warn following traffic of any obstruction: 100 metres (110yds) on ordinary roads and 200 metres (220yds) on motorways. Vehicles over 2800kg (6173lbs) must also carry a yellow flashing light.

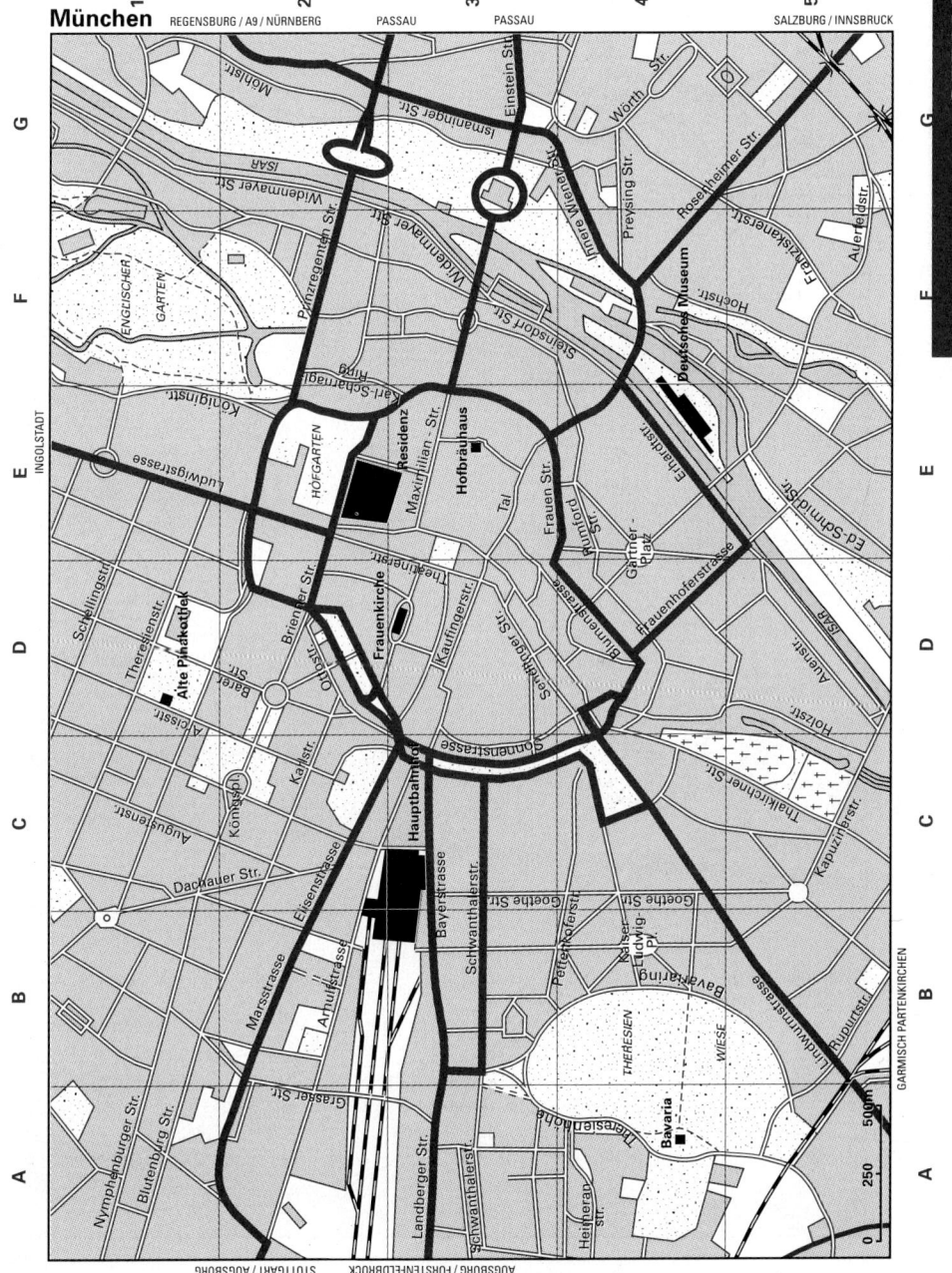

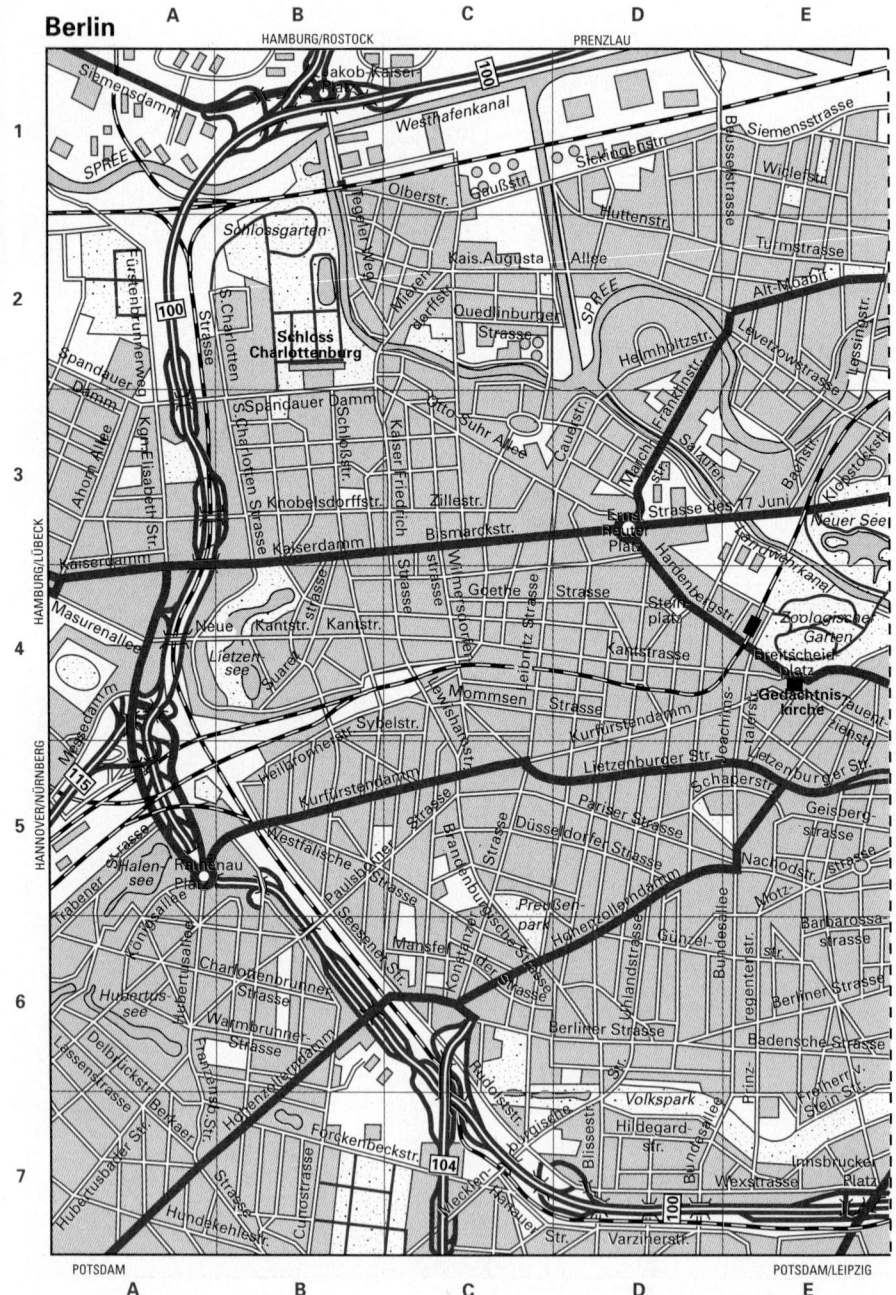

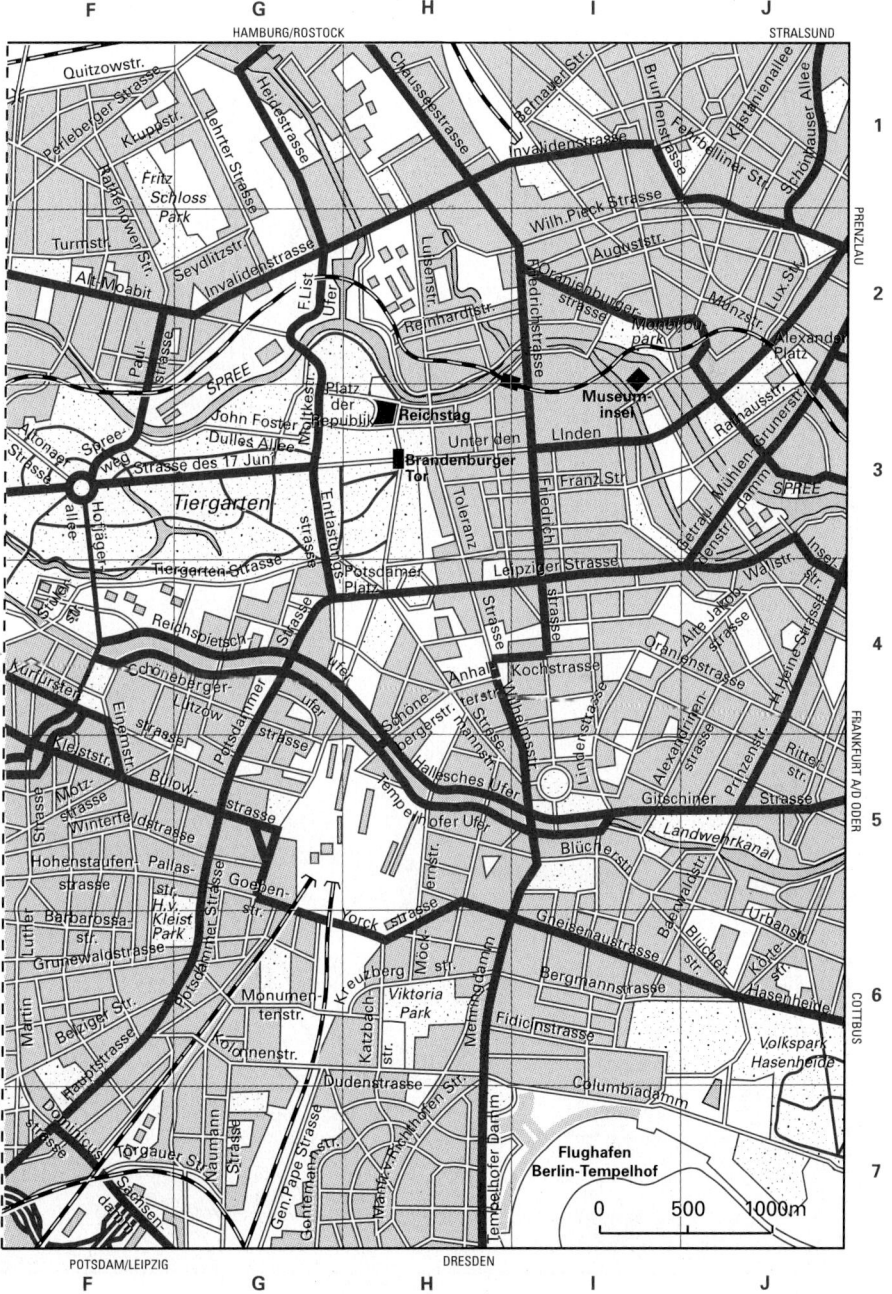

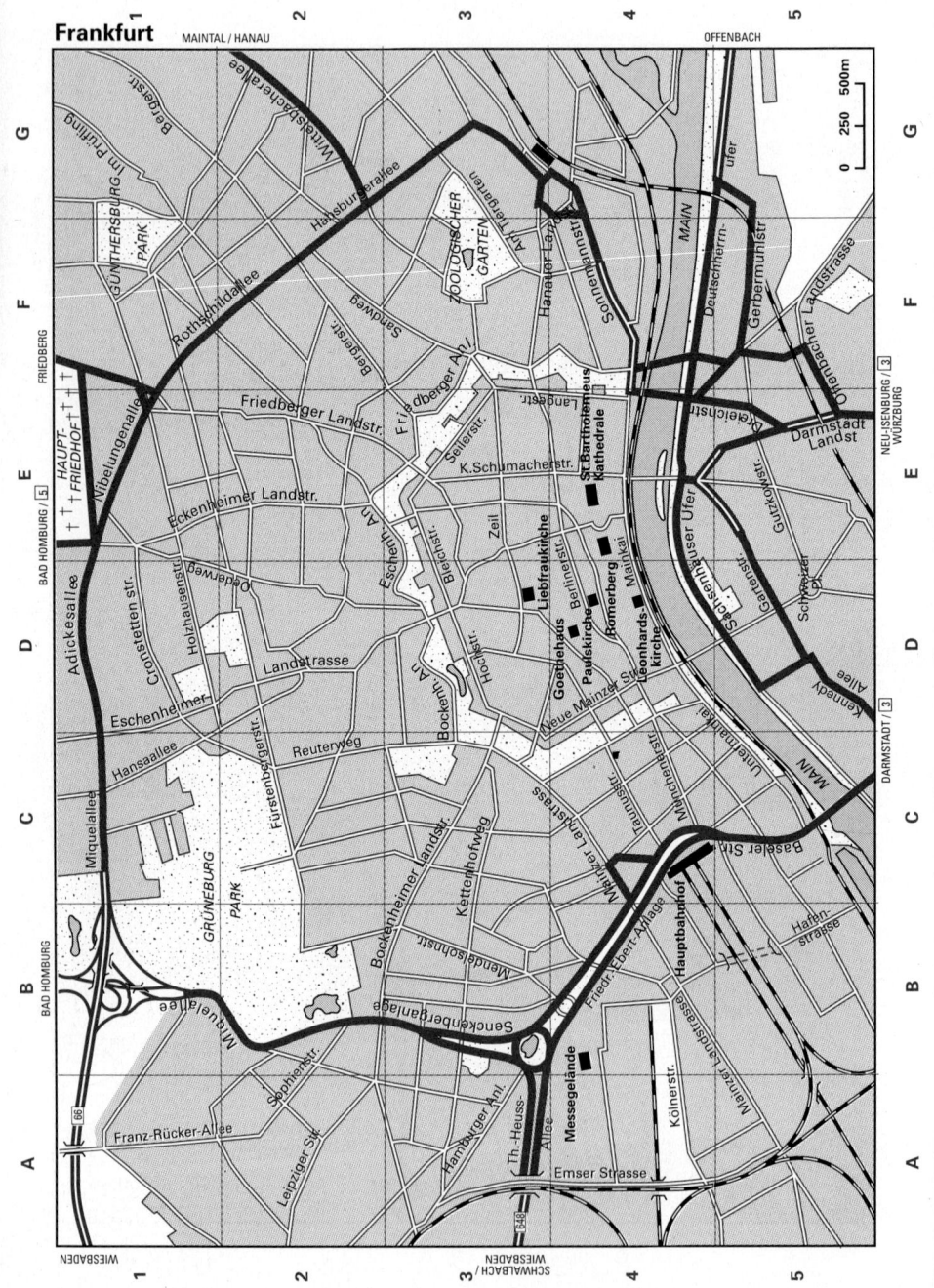

GERMANY 41

AACHEN Nordrhein-Westfalen 11

Holiday Inn Garden Court (HCR) AA ANWB
Krefelderstr 221
☎ 0241-18030 fax 0241-1803444
res nr 0130-815131
✉ 52070

The Holiday Inn Garden Court is a large, modern hotel easily accessible from the motorway. The bedrooms - some reserved for non-smokers - offer comfortable accommodation. It has a fitness centre and a cosy bar where guests can finish the day with a nightcap. The Dom and famous town hall are a few minutes' walk away.

* 48 ♦ 197/-
* 52 ♦ 219/-
AE ⓐ E ✕ ♦ ⬧ P ⛳ 🎾 ⇅ ⬜ ☐ WC TV 🍽

Regence (Best Western) (HCR)
Peterstr 71
☎ 0241-47870 fax 0241-39055
res nr 0130-4455
✉ 52062

* 30 ♦ 175/195
* 30 ♦ 205/280
AE ⓐ E ✕ ♦ ⬧ P ⛳ ⇅ ⬜ ☐ WC TV 🐕

Steigenberger Quellenhof (HCR) AA ANWB
Monheimsallee 52
☎ 0241-152081 fax 0241-154504
res nr 069-663080
✉ 52062

The luxury Steigenberger Quellenhof Hotel is situated in a Kurpark, only 5 minutes' walk from the town centre. The rooms and public lounges are attractively furnished and the smart restaurant has been awarded a Michelin star. The hotel has a swimming pool, and also offers conference facilities.

* 74 ♦ 175/260
* 86 ♦ 270/420
AE ⓐ E ✕ ♦ ⬧ ⛳ 🎾 ⇅ ⬜ ☐ WC TV 🍽

AALEN Baden-Württemberg 19

Ringhotel Kälber (HCR) AA ANWB
Behringstr 26
☎ 07361-8444 fax 07361-88264
✉ 73432

The Hotel Kälber offers a comfortable stay to both commercial travellers and tourists; the rooms have colour TV and minibar. There are splendid views of the hilly countryside from the cosy restaurant, where the large menu offers a range of both regional and international dishes. The nearby town of Aalen has thermal baths.

open 12.01 - 01.01
* 7 ♦ 80/98
* 13 ♦ 110/140
AE ⓐ E ✕ ♦ ⬧ ⓜ P ⛳ 🎾 ⇅ ⬜ ☐ WC TV 🍽

ACHERN Baden-Württemberg 21

Eintracht Götz Sonne (HR) AA ANWB
Hauptstr 112
☎ 07841-6450 fax 07841-645645
✉ 77855

The comfortable Hotel Eintracht Götz Sonne is situated in the centre of the wine and fruit producing region of Ortenau. Guests will receive a warm and friendly welcome here. The rooms have bath/shower, toilet, TV and telephone. The hotel offers conference facilities, a *Weinstube*, an indoor swimming pool with adjacent garden and parking facilities.

* 19 ♦ 89/179
* 36 ♦ 160/260
AE ⓐ E ✕ ♦ ⬧ P ⛳ 🎾 ⇅ ⬜ ☐ WC TV 🍽

Gasthaus Zum Lamm (HP)
Hauptstr 2
☎ 07841-21856
✉ 77855

* - ♦ 42/55
* 14 ♦ 80/105
AE ⓐ E ✕ ♦ ⬧ P ⛳ ☐ WC TV 🍽

42 GERMANY

AHORN Baden-Württemberg 19

Engel (HR)
Kirchbrunnenstr 3
☎ 06296-511
✉ 74744

4 ♦
5 ♦
[icons]

AHRWEILER Rheinland-Pfalz 11

Höhenzollern an der Ahr (HCR)
Silberberg
☎ 02641-4268
✉ 5483

2 ♦
18 ♦
[icons]

AITERHOFEN/STRAUBING Bayern 24

Murrerhof (HCR)   AA ANWB
Passauerstr 1
Straubing
☎ 07421-32740
✉ 94315

The holiday hotel Murrerhof can be found in rustic Aiterhofen, approximately 6km south of Straubing. Most rooms have their own washing facilities, some have TV. There is a restaurant and a terrace on the shady square. The hotel can be reached from the Regenburg - Passau motorway (A3), Straubing exit, direction Landa.

open 08.01 - 04.06 + 13.06 - 24.12
12 ♦ 46/68
13 ♦ 88/98
[icons]

ALF Rheinland-Pfalz 17

Mosel Hotel Alf (HCR)   AA ANWB
Moselstr 1
☎ 06542-2581 fax
06542-22963
✉ 56859

The traditional Mosel Hotel Alf is situated by the beautiful Mosel and is an ideal base for trips in the surrounding area. Most of the rooms have a bath, shower, telephone and a balcony. The restaurant is well known for its game dishes, and guests can relax on the Mosel terrace. There is a car park and

parking garage available.

open 01.03 - 14.11
* 2 ♦ 59/78
* 13 ♦ 88/132
[icons]

ALFELD/MARIENHAGEN Niedersachsen 8

Berghotel (HCR)   AA ANWB
Berliner Str 89748
Marienhagen
☎ 05185-6080 fax
05185-60833
✉ 31094

The Berghotel enjoys a pleasantly peaceful position in the town of Marienhagen, on the road from Afeld to Hamlyn. The rooms are attractively furnished and have en suite facilities, telephone and some have a balcony. The restaurant has a pretty décor and the menu offers a wide choice of good dishes. The open countryside of the surrounding area and plenty of fresh air make it an ideal spot for a weekend break or a short holiday.

26 ♦ 70/100
34 ♦ 100/140
[icons]

ALLENBACH Rheinland-Pfalz 17

Steuer (HCR)   AA ANWB
Hauptstr 10
☎ 06786-2089 fax
06786-2551
✉ 55758

Allenbach is a picturesque town in the German precious stone mining region, with plenty of opportunity for winter sports and walking. The family-run Hotel Steuer has a friendly and hospitable atmosphere, where the restaurant offers regional specialities. The rooms have en suite facilities and south-facing balconies with a fine view. As well as a sauna, fitness room and solarium, the hotel also has its own precious stone polishing centre and conference facilities.

* - ♦ 42/55
* 17 ♦ 63/84
[icons]

GERMANY

ALLENSBACH *Baden-Württemberg*   21

Haus Regina (HG)
☎ 07533-5091
✉ 78476

12 🛏
14 🛌

🅿 ⛱ ♨ 🍽 ⏰ WC 🐎 ✈

ALLERSHAUSEN *Bayern*   23

Huberhof (HG)
Freisingerstr 18
☎ 08166-8086 fax 08166-9298
✉ 85391

open 12.01 - 19.12
* 6 🛏 60/120
* 27 🛌 80/160

AE ⓘ E ⚡ ♨ 🅿 ⛱ ♨ 👥 🍽 ⏰ WC TV ☺

ALLMERSHAUSEN *Hessen*   18

Niedling (HG)
Neuensteiner Str 1
☎ 06621-75267
✉ 36251

1 🛏
5 🛌

⊙ 🅿 ⛱ ♨ WL TV

ALPIRSBACH *Baden-Württemberg*   21

Rössle (HR)
Aischbachstr 5
☎ 07444-2281 fax 07444-2368
✉ 72275

open 01.12 - 09.03 + 20.03 - 14.11
* 1 🛏 65/72
* 25 🛌 96/115

⊙ 🅿 ⛱ 🍴 ⏰ 🍽 ⏰ WC TV ☺

Waldhorn (HR)   AA ANWB
Kreuzstr 4
☎ 07444-2411 fax 07444-4469
✉ 72275

Situated in one of the most beautiful areas of Germany, the welcoming Hotel Waldhorn is in the centre of Alpirsbach. All the rooms are pleasantly furnished and have en suite facilities and a minibar. The lounge is tastefully decorated and is suitable for functions; the restaurant serves fine cuisine, and there are plenty of recreational facilities in the surrounding area of Alpirsbach.

* 2 🛏 56/66
* 18 🛌 98/124

AE ⓘ E ⊙ 🅿 ⛱ ♨ 🍽 ⏰ WC TV 🍴

ALSFELD *Hessen*   13

Krone (HR)
Schellengasse 2-4
☎ 06631-4041 fax 06631-4043
✉ 36304

* 18 🛏 65/75
* 26 🛌 105/115

AE ⓘ E ⚡ ♨ 🅿 ⛱ ♨ 🍽 ⏰ WC TV 🍴

ALSFELD/ROMROD *Hessen*   13

Sporthotel Vogelberg (HCR)
Kneippstr 1
Romrod
☎ 06636-890 fax 06636-89522
res nr 0130-4455
✉ 36329

* 23 🛏 90/110 excl. breakfast
* 86 🛌 170/210 excl. breakfast

AE ⓘ E ⚡ ♨ 🅿 ⛱ ♨ 🎾 🍴 🍽 ⏰ WC TV 🍴 ☺

ALTENAHR *Rheinland-Pfalz*   11

Zur Post (HCR)   AA ANWB
Brückenstr 2
☎ 02643-9310 fax 02643-931200
✉ 53505

The Hotel zur Post is situated in the 1000-year-old wine-producing region of Altenahr. There are over 100km of well marked footpaths and hiking trails in this area. The modern rooms all have a shower, toilet, telephone, minibar and TV. There are several restaurants in the hotel, plus a swimming pool (with children's area), sauna, solarium and gym.

open 19.12 - 14.11
* 8 🛏 60/85
* 47 🛌 110/150

AE ⓘ E ⚡ ♨ 🏊 ⊙ ♦ 🅿 ⛱ ♨ 🎾 🍴 🍽 ⏰ WC TV 🍴 ☺

ALTENKIRCHEN Rheinland-Pfalz 12

Glockenspitze (HCR) AA ANWB
Hochstr
☎ 02681-80050 fax 02681-800599
✉ 57610

The Hotel Glockenspitze is set in the heart of Germany - an oasis of peace and quiet. The comfortable rooms are bright and airy, both the Bistro and restaurant serve lunch and dinner, and the hotel has its own leisure park where 2 instructors are on hand for those who want to play tennis, squash or badminton. There is also an indoor swimming pool and fitness room.

* 6 ♋ 138/160
* 34 ♋ 187/209
AE ⊙ E ✕ ≿ ♠ ◊ ♦ P ⁂ ⋝ ⇃ ⋢ 🄿 WC TV IOI ⊚

Petershof (HR)
Wiedstr 84
☎ 02681-2983 fax 02681-70283
✉ 57610

* 3 ♋ -/60
* 4 ♋ -/100
AE E ≿ ♦ P ⁂ ⋢ 🄿 WC TV IOI ⊚

ALTENSTEIG Baden-Württemberg 21

Traube (HR)
Hauptstr 22
☎ 07453-8004 fax 07453-8006
✉ 72213

- ♋ 38/64
40 ♋ 61/110
E ≿ P ⁂ ⋝ ⇃ ⋢ 🄿 WC TV IOI ⊚

ALTENSTEIG/BERNECK Baden-Württemberg 21

Rössle (HP) AA ANWB
Altensteig
☎ 07453-8156
✉ 72213

The Hotel Rössle is a great place to enjoy the peace of the Schwarzwald. It is situated on the edge of a pine forest, overlooking Berneck and the Köllbachtal. All rooms have washing facilities, colour TV and balcony. The hotel has a friendly atmosphere, serves good food and has its own bakery. There is a garden terrace and plenty of parking space.

9 ♋ 50/75
18 ♋ 90/140
⊚ P ⁂ ⋝ ⋢ ⇃ 🄿 WC TV ⇑ ✕

ALZENAU Bayern 18

Krone Am Park (HG)
Hellersweg 1
☎ 06023-6052 fax 06023-8724
✉ 63755

* 8 ♋ 108/138 excl. breakfast
* 19 ♋ 164/224 excl. breakfast
P ⁂ ⇃ ⋢ 🄿 WC TV ⊚

ALZEY Rheinland-Pfalz 18

Krause (HR)
Gartenstr 2
☎ 06731-6181 fax 06731-45613
✉ 55232

open 15.01 - 31.12
* 5 ♋ 80/90
* 10 ♋ -/120
AE E ⊙ ♦ P ⁂ 🄿 WC TV IOI

Rheinhessen Treff (HR) AA ANWB
Industriestr 13
☎ 06731-4030 fax 06731-403106
✉ 55232

The Hotel Rheinhessen Treff is situated in the centre of Germany's largest wine-growing region. Its central location makes it a good base for trips in the surrounding area. The rooms have bath/shower, toilet, telephone, radio, TV and minibar. For the energetic there is a tennis court, squash court and skittle alley. The hotel has a pleasant *Weinstube*, and plenty of parking space is available.

* 27 ♋ 115/125
* 67 ♋ -/165
AE ⊙ E ✕ ≿ P ⁂ ⇃ ⋢ 🄿 WC TV IOI

Hotel-Gasthof
TRAUBE

Owner: Wurster family
D-72213 Altensteig 4-Berneck
Tel: 07453 - 8004/05, 8183
Fax: 07453 - 8006

Very modern rooms with bath/shower, toilet, bidet, telephone, television connection, balcony. Meeting rooms, room with a fireplace, café, pool table, skittle alley, swimming-pool, sauna, solarium, sunbathing area and fishing possibilities.

AMBERG *Bayern* 20

Goldenes Lamm (HCR)
Rathausstr 6
☎ 09621-21041
✉ 92224

* 10 🛏 48/85
* 14 🛏 80/150

**Industriestrasse 13
D-55232 ALZEY
Tel: 06731 - 4030
Fax: 06731 - 403106**

147 hotel rooms with bath/shower, toilet, direct-dial telephones, colour television with satellite connection, radio and mini-bar.

Room prices:
single room: DM 115,-   half board: DM 27,-
Studio: DM 125,- full board: DM 49,-
double room: DM 165,-

These prices include a generous buffet breakfast and telephone wake-up service. The sports facilities in our hotel are: 6 tennis courts, 3 squash courts and 4 official skittle alleys.

Gastronomy: one hotel restaurant, one sports restaurant and one wine bar.
The hotel also has seven conference/meeting rooms. The town of Alzey offers the following sports and recreational possibilities: training circuit, outdoor swimming-pool, museum, castle and miniature golf.

As an extra we can also offer you wine tasting at the nearby wine-producing estate, trips by covered wagon and sight-seeing in the vineyards.

GERMANY

AMECKE Nordrhein-Westfalen 12
Zum Wildpark (HCR)   AA ANWB
Seestr 26
☎ 02393-292
✉ 59846

The Hotel zum Wildpark is splendidly situated amid woods and mountains. The simple rooms are functionally furnished and some have en suite facilities. The hotel has a pleasant bar and restaurant and on-site parking. Recreational facilities in the immediate vicinity include a tennis court and a lake for fishing, swimming and surfing.

open 16.12 - 10.11
* 4 ♪ 40/-
* 6 ♬ 80/-
♫ ♠ ♣ ♦ P ♪ ♯ ♮ ♪

AMORBACH Bayern 18
Bayerischer Hof (HP)
Boxbrunn 8
☎ 09373-1435 fax 09373-3208
✉ 63916

* 3 ♪ 38/50
* 13 ♬ 76/92
♦ P ♪ ♯ ♮ WC ♪ ♪

Post (HR)
Schmiedsgasse 2
☎ 09373-410
✉ 63916

8 ♪
23 ♬
♠ ⊙ P ♪ ♯ ♮ ♪ WC TV ♪

ANDERNACH Rheinland-Pfalz 12
Alte Kanzlei (HG)
Steinweg 30
☎ 02632-44447 fax 02632-494865
✉ 56626

* - ♪ 95/98
* 10 ♬ 150/200
AE ⊙ E ≡ ♠ ⊙ P ♪ ♮ ♪ WC TV ♪ ♪

Urmersbach (HG)
Frankenstr 6
☎ 02632-45522
✉ 56626

11 ♪
17 ♬
♠ ⊙ P ♪ ♯ ♮ ♪ WC

ANHOLT Nordrhein-Westfalen 11
Parkhotel Wasserburg Anholt (HCR)   AA ANWB
Kleverstr
☎ 02874-4590 fax 02874-4035
✉ 46419

The oldest part of the moated Wasserburg Anholt castle dates from the 12th century, but additions date from the 17th century. It now houses a very luxurious hotel with well furnished rooms, a smart restaurant and a terrace by the water overlooking the park. The hotel can be reached from Arnhem via the A3, exit Bocholt-Rees.

open 25.01 - 02.01
7 ♪ 150/250
21 ♬ 200/360
⊙ E ≡ ♠ P ♪ ♯ ♮ ♪ ♪ ♪ WC TV

ANNWEILER Rheinland-Pfalz 18
Scharfeneck (HR)
Altenstr 17
☎ 06346-8392
✉ 76855

- ♪ 40/55
7 ♬ 80/90
⊙ ≡ ♠ ⊙ P ♪ ♯ ♮ ♪ ♪ WC ♪ ♪

ANSBACH Bayern 19
Am Drechselsgarten (Best Western) (HCR)
Am Drechselsgarten 1
☎ 0981-89020 fax 0981-8902605
res nr 0130-4455
✉ 8800

- ♪ 140/160
85 ♬ 180/205
AE ⊙ E ≡ ♠ ⊙ P ♪ ♯ ♮ ♪ WC TV ♪ ♪

Schwarzer Bock (HCR)
Pfarrerstr 31
☎ 0981-2148
✉ 8800

22 ♬
P ♪ WC

GERMANY

APPENWEIER Baden-Württemberg 21

Hanauer Hof (HCR) AA ANWB
Ortenauerstr 50
☎ 07805-2748 fax 07805-5365
✉ 77767

The Hotel Hanauer Hof is situated in the German wine-growing region and can be used as a good central point for making day trips. The hotel is well maintained and has a friendly atmosphere. The rooms have a shower, toilet and radio (TV and telephone can be provided on request). The restaurant serves well known local specialities.

* 4 ♉ 45/65
* 14 ♊ 75/110
AE ⓘ E ⊞ ♦ ⊙ P ⓟ ♨ ⑾ ⇅ ⊡ ☐ Ⓟ WC TV ⑩ ☺

Schwarzer Adler (HR)
Ortenauerstr 44
☎ 07805-2785 fax 07805-5216
✉ 77767

6 ♉
19 ♊
ⓘ E ⊞ ⊙ ♦ P ⓟ ☐ Ⓟ TV ⑩ ☺

ARNBRUCK Bayern 24

Landhotel Rappenhof (HR) AA ANWB
Rappendorf 5
☎ 09945-1374 fax 09945-2191
✉ 93471

The Landhotel Rappenhof is situated in the middle of beautiful scenery in the Bayerische Wald. This family-run hotel has rooms with en suite facilities. There is a farm which is especially appealing to children, and the hotel has an outdoor swimming pool.

open 15.12 - 15.11
* 6 ♉ 45/58
* 24 ♊ 78/106
ⓘ E ⊞ ♦ P ⓟ ♨ ⇄ ⑾ ⇅ ⊡ Ⓟ WC TV ⑩ ⇑ ⋈

ARNSBERG Nordrhein-Westfalen 12

Dorint Hotel Arnsberg Neheim (HCR)
Zu Den Drei Bänken
☎ 02932-2001 fax 02932-200228
res nr 0130-6605
✉ 59757

* 17 ♉ 157/270
* 148 ♊ 220/340
AE ⓘ E ⊞ ♦ ♠ P ⓟ ♨ ⇄ ⑾ ⇅ ⊡ Ⓟ WC TV ⑩ ☺

Menge (HR) AA ANWB
Ruhrstr 60
☎ 02932-4044 fax 02931-13556
✉ 59821

The Hotel Menge prides itself on tradition and comfort, as it has done for more than 7 generations. Its central location is good for making day trips and discovering the Sauerland area. All the modern rooms have washing facilities, telephone and TV. The cooking is good and makes use of fresh, seasonal products. The hotel also has a garden and full parking facilities.

* 5 ♉ 80/100
* 14 ♊ 140/170
E ♨ ⚲ ⊙ P ⓟ ⑾ ⊡ Ⓟ WC TV ⑩ ☺

AROLSEN Hessen 13

Treff Schloßhotel (HCR)
Große Allee 1
☎ 05691-8080 fax 05691-808529
✉ 34454

13 ♉ 119/140
43 ♊ 178/215
E ⊞ ♨ ♦ ♠ P ⓟ ♨ ⇄ ⑾ ⇅ ⊡ Ⓟ WC TV ⑩ ☺

ASCHAFFENBURG Bayern 18

Zum Goldenen Ochsen (HCR) AA ANWB
Karlstr 16
☎ 06021-23132 fax 06021-25785
✉ 63739

The Hotel zum Goldenen Ochsen is centrally situated in a beautiful part of Aschaffen and has views of Schloss Johannisburg, the Kapuziner church and the Schöntal. There has been an inn on this site since the year 1600; modern rooms have a shower, bath, toilet, TV and telephone. The restaurant serves lunch and dinner, and the hotel has conference facilities.

open 06.01 - 31.12
* - ♉ 85/95
* - ♊ 125/140
AE ⓘ E ⊞ ⊙ P ⓟ ♨ ⑾ ⊡ Ⓟ WC TV ⑩ ☺

Romantik Hotel Post (HR)
Goldbacherstr 19
☎ 06021-21333
✉ 63739

26 🛏 85/110
45 🛏 180/195
⊙ P 🅿 🍴 ♯ ■ 🏧 WC TV 🍽

ASSMANNSHAUSEN Hessen 18

Jungs Anker (HCR)
Rheinuferstr 5-7
☎ 06722-2912 fax 06722-48130
✉ 65385

7 🛏
41 🛏
🚗 P 🅿 🍴 ♯ ♨ 🏧 WC 🐾

ATTENDORN Nordrhein-Westfalen 12

Sporthotel Haus Platte (HCR)
Repetalstr 219
☎ 02721-1310 fax 02721-131455
✉ 57439

2 🛏
51 🛏
⊙ E ≈ ♿ 🏊 ⊖ P 🅿 🍴 🚲 ♨ ■ 🏧 WC TV 🍽 🐾

Waldhaus (HCR)
Innestr 11
☎ 02721-7254
✉ 5952

4 🛏
12 🛏
🏊 🚗 ⊖ 🏊 ♿ ♦ P 🅿 🍴 ♨ ■ 🏧 WC 🍽 🐾

AUDERATH Rheinland-Pfalz 17

Wilhelmshöhe (HCR)
An der B 259
☎ 02676-260 fax 02676-1527
✉ 56766

AA ANWB

The family-run hotel Wilhelmshöhe enjoys a central position - an ideal base for walking and car-excursions to the surrounding area. The rooms are spacious and well equipped; from the restaurant guests have pleasant views over the Volcano Eiffel, and the sunbathing lawn and terrace are peaceful places to relax.

open 01.02 - 31.12
3 🛏 45/50
10 🛏 80/90
🏊 ♿ ♦ P 🅿 🍴 🚲 ■ 🏧 WC 🍽

AUGSBURG Bayern 23

Drei Mohren (HCR)
Maximilianstr 40
☎ 0821-50360 fax 0821-157864
✉ 86150

30 🛏 195/225
70 🛏 284/354
AE ⊙ E ≈ ♿ ⊖ P 🅿 🍴 🚲 ♯ ■ 🏧 WC TV 🍽 🐾

BACHARACH Rheinland-Pfalz 18

Altkölnischer Hof (HR)
Blucherstr 2
☎ 06743-1339 fax 06743-2793
✉ 55422

open 01.04 - 05.11
3 🛏 65/95
18 🛏 95/140
AE ⊙ ≈ P 🅿 🍴 🚲 ♯ ■ 🏧 WC TV 🍽 ✈

Park Café (HCR)
Marktstr 8
☎ 06743-1422 fax 06743-1541
✉ 55420

open 01.03 - 15.11
* 7 🛏 75/120
* 15 🛏 105/200
E ≈ ♿ ⊖ P 🅿 🍴 🚲 ♯ ■ 🏧 WC TV 🍽 🐾

BAD AIBLING Bayern 23

Romantik Hotel Lindner (HCR)
Marienpl 5
☎ 08061-4050 fax 08061-30535
✉ 83043

AA ANWB

The peaceful, atmospheric Hotel Lindner - once known as Prantshausen castle - is in the centre of Bad Aibling. The hotel rooms are modern and have good amenities including bath, shower, toilet and TV. The public rooms contain beautiful antiques. The restaurant offers a wide choice of dishes, and the hotel has a magnificent garden.

* 10 🛏 60/150
* 23 🛏 110/220
AE ⊙ E ≈ ♿ ⊙ P 🅿 🍴 ♨ ■ 🏧 WC TV 🍽

BAD BELLINGEN Baden-Württemberg　21

Landgasthof Schwanen (HR)
Rheinstr 50
☎ 07635-1314 fax 07635-2331
✉ 79411

open 20.01 - 20.12
* 5 🛏 53/85
* 8 🛏 106/138
E P 🅿 ⛽ ♨ ⬜ WC TV 🍴 ☺

BAD BERGZABERN Rheinland-Pfalz　18

Park (HCR)
Kurtalstr 83
☎ 06343-2415
✉ 76887

17 🛏
25 🛏
🔵 E ⬜ ♨ ⬛ ⬤ P 🅿 ⛽ ♨ ⚓ ♨ 🍽 ⬜ WC TV 🍴

Pfälzerwald (HCR)
Kurtahl 77
☎ 06343-1056 fax 06343-4893
✉ 76887

open 01.03 - 31.12
12 🛏 50/65
14 🛏 100/130
AE E ⬜ ⬛ ♦ P 🅿 ⛽ ♨ 🍽 ⬜ WC TV 🍴 🦌

BAD BERLEBURG Nordrhein-Westfalen　12

Erholung (HCR)　　　　　AA ANWB
Laibach 1
☎ 02751-7218 fax
02751-2866
✉ 57319

The Hotel Erholung is 5km from the small town of Bad Berleburg. It enjoys a peaceful spot overlooking the mountains of the Sauerland. There are comfortable rooms with en suite facilities; the hotel has a terrace, large sunbathing lawn, parking places and garage, and is a suitable base for winter sports.

open 01.12 - 10.11
* 3 🛏 49/78
* 14 🛏 106/136
⬛ ⬤ P 🅿 ⛽ ♨ ⬜ WC TV 🍴 ☺

GERMANY　49

Westfälischer Hof (HCR)　　　AA ANWB
Astenbergstr 6
☎ 02751-494 fax 02751-2882
✉ 57319

A number of the rooms in the Hotel Westfälischer Hof are equipped with en suite facilities. The hotel is close to the station, and service buses stop at the hotel. There is a bar, a restaurant and a children's playground. Wooded countryside is only 5 minutes away and provides some beautiful walks.

* 18 🛏 50/85 excl. breakfast
* 30 🛏 99/160 excl. breakfast
P 🅿 ⛽ ⚓ 🍽 ⬜ WC TV 🍴

BAD BERTRICH Rheinland-Pfalz　17

Am Schwanenweiher (HG)
☎ 02674-669
✉ 56864

1 🛏
12 🛏
⬛ P 🅿 ⛽ ♨ ⚓ 🍽 ⬜ WC

BAD BRAMSTEDT Schleswig-Holstein　2

Köhlerhof (HCR)
Am Köhlerhof 4
☎ 04192-5050 fax 04192-505638
✉ 24576

* 11 🛏 174/-
* 121 🛏 -/247
⬛ ⬤ P 🅿 ⛽ ♨ ⚓ ♨ 🍽 ⬜ WC TV 🍴

BAD BREISIG Rheinland-Pfalz　17

Kurhaus (HR)
Koblenzerstr 35
☎ 02633-97311
✉ 53498

28 🛏 70/85
40 🛏 130/170
⬛ P 🅿 ⛽ ♨ ⚓ 🍽 ⬜ WC TV

Zur Mühle (HCR)
Rheinufer
☎ 02633-97061 fax 02633-96017
✉ 53498

open 05.03 - 04.01
* 10 🛏 75/85
* 30 🛏 120/150
AE 🔵 E ⬜ ⬛ ⬤ P 🅿 ⛽ ♨ ⚓ ♨ 🍽 ⬜ WC TV 🍴

GERMANY

BAD BRÜCKENAU *Bayern* 13

Deutsches Haus (HR)
Bahnhofstr 3
☎ 09741-5075
✉ 97769

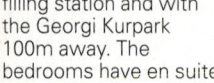

The Deutsches Haus can be found in the centre of Bad Brückenau, next to a filling station and with the Georgi Kurpark 100m away. The bedrooms have en suite toilet and shower facilities, telephone and TV. The friendly restaurant serves a range of good, value for money meals. There is a sauna, and on-site parking is available.

* 4 ♋ -/60
* 11 ♋ -/100
AE ⓘ E ⌶ ⊙ ◆ P ⛱ P WC TV ⑩

Dorint Hotel Bad Brückenau (HCR)
Heinrich V. Bibrastr 13
☎ 09741-850 fax 09741-85425
res nr 0130-6605
✉ 97769

* 27 ♋ 168/215
* 119 ♋ 240/290
AE ⓘ E ⌶ ⋏ ♨ ⊙ P ⛱ ⛱ ≋ ↕ ▬ P WC TV ⑩ ⊙

BAD CAMBERG *Hessen* 20

Camberg West (HCR)
☎ 06434-6066 fax 06434-7004
✉ 65520

9 ♋ 40/75 excl. breakfast
18 ♋ 60/115 excl. breakfast
E ◆ P ⛱ ⛱ ▬ P WC ⊙

BAD DÜRKHEIM *Rheinland-Pfalz* 18

Gartenhotel Heusser (HR)
Seebacherstr 50-52
☎ 06322-9300 fax 06322-930499
✉ 67098

* 35 ♋ 115/130
* 45 ♋ 165/195
AE ⓘ E ⌶ ⋏ ♨ P ⛱ ⛱ ≋ ↕ ▬ P WC TV ⑩ ⊙

BAD EMS *Rheinland-Pfalz* 17

Kurhotel Bad Ems (Best Western) (HCR)
Römerstr 1-3
☎ 02603-7990 fax 02603-799252
res nr 0130-4455
✉ 56119

* 38 ♋ 180/200
* 69 ♋ 220/500
AE ⓘ E ⌶ ⋏ ⊙ P ⛱ ⛱ ≋ ↕ ▬ P WC TV ⑩ ⊙

Park (HR)
Malbergstr 7
☎ 02603-2058
✉ 56119

10 ♋
20 ♋
♨ P ⛱ ≋ ↕ ▬ P WC ⑩

BADEN-BADEN *Baden-Württemberg* 18

Atlantic (HG)
Sophienstr 2 a
☎ 07221-24111
✉ 76530

23 ♋ 98/175
28 ♋ 190/289
⊙ P ⛱ ⛱ ↕ ▬ P WC TV

Badhotel Zum Hirsch (HR)
Hirschstr 1
☎ 07221-23896 fax 07221-38148
✉ 76530

9 ♋ 113/163
50 ♋ 198/268
P ⛱ ↕ ▬ P WC TV ⑩

Hollandhotel Sophienpark (HR)
Sophienstr 14
☎ 07221-3560 fax 07221-356121
✉ 76482

* 25 ♋ 170/-
* 48 ♋ 245/350
AE ⓘ E ⌶ ⊙ ⛱ ⛱ ↕ ▬ P WC TV ⊙

Löhr (HCR)
Lichtentalerstr 19
☎ 07221-31370
✉ 76530

1 ♋
20 ♋
⊙ ◆ ▬ P WC TV

Queens Hotel (HCR) 🅰🅰 ANWB
Falkenstr 2
☎ 07221-2190 fax 07221-219519
res nr 069-6090030
✉ 76530

The Queens Sport Hotel is peacefully situated in a beautiful park on the edge of the centre. The spacious rooms have en suite facilities, minibar, trouser-press and balcony. This hotel offers many recreational facilities, including a swimming pool, sauna, solarium, whirlpool and a fitness room. It also has a beauty and hair salon, a terrace, and meeting rooms. The intimate restaurant has a wide selection of culinary specialities available.

* 25 ♪ 160/240
* 96 ♫ 220/310

Der Quellenhof (Best Western) (HCR)
Sophienstr 27-29
☎ 07221-22134 fax 07221-28320
res nr 0130-4455
✉ 76530

1 ♪
50 ♫

Rasthaus Motel Baden Baden (HCR) 🅰🅰 ANWB
Am Rasthof 4
☎ 07221-65043 fax 07221-17661
✉ 76532

The well maintained Rasthaus Motel Baden Baden lies just a few kilometres away from the motorway. It features rooms with en suite facilities, a self-service restaurant, and for guests with more time, a traditional table-service restaurant. The reception area is open 24 hours and has a cashpoint machine.

* 9 ♪ 100/- excl. breakfast
* 30 ♫ 150/- excl. breakfast

Steigenberger Europäischer Hof (HR)
Kaiserallee 2
☎ 07221-93301 fax 07221-28831
res nr 069-663080
✉ 76530

* 55 ♪ 175/285
* 72 ♫ 270/470

Waldhotel Forellenhof (HCR) 🅰🅰 ANWB
Gaisbach 91
☎ 07221-9740 fax 07221-974299
✉ 76534

Waldhotel Forellenhof is a country hotel surrounded by woodland. All the rooms have a balcony, good modern facilities and offer comfortable accommodation. The restaurant is attractively furnished and offers a choice of excellent dishes. The small swimming pool with large lawn will please the younger guests. The hotel also has its own trout farm.

* 10 ♪ 85/130
* 15 ♫ 130/220

BAD FRIEDRICHSHALL Baden-Württemberg 19

Schöne Aussicht (HCR)
Deutschordenstr 2
☎ 07136-6057 fax 07136-8708
✉ 74177

open 20.01 - 26.12
* 5 ♪ 42/72
* 11 ♫ 74/98

BAD GANDERSHEIM Niedersachsen 8

Bartsch (HG)
Petristr 4
☎ 05382-4350
✉ 37581

* - ♪ -/50
* 5 ♫ -/90

GERMANY

BAD GRIESBACH IM ROTTAL Bayern 24

Birkenhof Therme (HCR)
Thermalbadstr 15-17
☎ 08532-7030 fax 08532-703169
✉ 94086

* 18 ♫ 110/120
* 137 ♫ 110/150
🅰 Ⓓ 🅴 ⚙ ⚓ Ⓟ ☎ ⚐ ⛵ 🍴 🛏 ▣ ▢ WC TV ⦿ 🐾 ☺

BAD GRUND Niedersachsen 13

Berlin (HP)
V Eichendorffstr 18
☎ 05327-2072 fax 05327-2618
✉ 37539

* 5 ♫ 64/-
* 17 ♫ 112/122
🏨 Ⓓ Ⓟ ☎ ⚐ ⛵ 🛏 ▣ ▢ WC TV ☺

Schönhofsblick Panorama Hotel (HCR) AA ANWB
Schönhofsblick 1
☎ 05327-2888 fax 05327-3015
✉ 37537

The family-run Schönhofsblick Panorama Hotel, set on a mountain, offers a marvellous view over the wonderful surroundings. The rooms are tidy and efficiently furnished; in the evening guests can relax by the fireplace in the lounge. The hotel is especially suitable as a base for walks and motoring excursions in the area.

* 3 ♫ 75/-
* 12 ♫ 150/-
🅰 Ⓓ 🅴 ⚙ ⚓ Ⓓ Ⓟ ☎ ⚐ ▣ ▢ WC TV

Haus Am Südhang (HG)
V. Eichendorffstr 37
☎ 05327-1576
✉ 37539

open 01.02 - 30.11
1 ♫ 42/45
8 ♫ 74/80
🏨 Ⓓ Ⓟ ☎ ⚐ 🛏 ▢ WC TV 🐾

BAD HARZBURG Niedersachsen 8

Appart (HCR) AA ANWB
Kurhausstr 18
☎ 05322-7840 fax 05322-78427
✉ 38667

The Hotel Appart is situated just a few hundred metres from the town centre. The bedrooms are comfortably furnished and some are situated on the ground floor. The attractively furnished restaurant has a menu with a selection of good value dishes. The immediate surroundings offer recreational facilities including golf and horse-riding. The Harzburg casino is directly opposite the hotel.

43 ♫
🅰 Ⓓ 🅴 ⚙ ⚓ 🏨 Ⓓ Ⓟ ☎ ⚐ ⛵ 🍴 🛏 ▣ ▢ WC TV ⦿

Breitenberg (HCR) AA ANWB
Am Breitenberg 54
☎ 05322-4041 fax 05322-2337
✉ 38667

The Hotel Breitenberg is situated in a health resort on the outskirts of the Harz. This well kept hotel has tidily furnished rooms with facilities including a safe and minibar; some rooms are on the ground floor. From the terrace there is a beautiful view over the surrounding area, which is wonderful for walking.

* 2 ♫ 85/90
* 12 ♫ 140/150
🅴 ⚓ 🏨 Ⓓ Ⓟ ☎ ⚐ 🛏 ▣ WC TV ☺

Landhaus Am Rodenberg (HG)
Am Rodenberg 20
☎ 05322-3058
✉ 38667

open 15.12 - 15.01 + 01.03 - 15.10
* 9 ♫ 47/59
* 6 ♫ 87/99
Ⓓ Ⓟ ☎ ⚐ 🛏 ▢ WC ☺

GERMANY 53

Seela (HCR)
Nordhäuserstr 5
☎ 05322-7011 fax 05322-796199
✉ 38667

10 🛏 107/215
110 🛏 174/390
⊙ⒺⓀ♦ⓅⓉ⚏≈⇅▬ⒻWC TV ⍟ ☺

BAD HERRENALB Baden-Württemberg 18

Harzer Am Kurpark (HCR) AA ANWB
Kurpromenade
☎ 07083-3021 fax 07083-8703
✉ 76332

The Hotel Harzer am Kurpark has a pleasant atmosphere and is situated in the centre of the spa town of Bad Herrenalb. The hotel is easily accessible by car and public transport, the rooms are modern with shower, toilet, telephone and colour TV; and the restaurant serves fine cuisine and has a comprehensive menu. Leisure facilities include an indoor swimming pool, and one can relax in the sauna afterwards. Parking facilities are available.

open 15.12 - 20.11
* 5 🛏 100/150
* 21 🛏 140/190
ⒶⒺⒺ⌬⊙Ⓟ⚏≈⇅▬ⒻWC TV ⍟ 🏠 ☺

Schwarzwald Kulm (HR)
Doblerstr 26
☎ 07083-7420 fax 07083-4071
✉ 76332

70 🛏 105/120
100 🛏 170/190
⊙Ⓟ⚏⇅▬ⒻWC TV ☺

BAD HOMBURG VOR DER HÖHE Hessen 18

Maritim Kurhaushotel (HCR)
Ludwigstr
Bad Homburg
☎ 06172-28051 fax 06172-24341
res nr 0221-219672
✉ 61348

* 63 🛏 249/399
* 75 🛏 298/490
ⒶⒺ⊙Ⓔ⌬⊙♦Ⓟ⚏≈⇅▬ⒻWC TV ⍟ ☺

Steigenberger Bad Homburg (HR)
K F Promenade 69-75
Bad Homburg
☎ 06172-1810 fax 06172-181630
res nr 069-663080
✉ 61348

* 70 🛏 245/295 excl. breakfast
* 100 🛏 290/340 excl. breakfast
ⒶⒺ⊙Ⓔ⌬⇅▬ TV

BAD IBURG Niedersachsen 6

Fischer Eymann (HCR) AA ANWB
Schloßstr 1
☎ 05403-311 fax 05403-5231
✉ 49186

The relaxed Hotel Fischer Eyman, originally a timber building, is situated in the town centre and just 10 minutes from the Teutoburgerwald; it is easily accessible by car and public transport. All the rooms are well furnished and have en suite facilities. One can enjoy peace and quiet in the garden, and there is a large parking place, bicycles for hire and table tennis.

* 4 🛏 40/60
* 10 🛏 75/115
Ⓔ♨⊙Ⓟ⚏≈▬ⒻWC TV

Zum Urberg (HCR) AA ANWB
Amtsweg 19
☎ 05403-2440 fax 05403-9452
✉ 49186

The Hotel Zum Urberg has a relaxed atmosphere and is situated at the foot of the 213m-high Urberg. Here you can have a complete rest and enjoy nature; there are marked walking routes in the area. The rooms are well kept and have en suite facilities. The well furnished restaurant offers good value for money. The hotel also has an indoor swimming pool, terrace and spacious parking facilities.

* 4 🛏 46/53
* 10 🛏 88/102
⊙Ⓔ♨⌬⊙Ⓟ⚏≈⇅ⒻWC ⍟ ☺

54 GERMANY

BAD KISSINGEN *Bayern* 19

Fürst Bismarck (HCR)
Euerdorferstr 4-6
☎ 0971-1277 fax 0971-68529
✉ 97688

11 ♂
18 ♋
[icons]

Steigenberger Kurhaus (HR)
Am Kurgarten 3
☎ 0971-80410 fax 0971-8041597
res nr 069-663080
✉ 97688

* 40 ♂ 180/225
* 60 ♋ 270/380
[icons]

BAD KÖNIGSHOFEN *Bayern* 14

Schlundhaus (HCR)
Marktpl 25
☎ 09761-1562
✉ 97631

2 ♂ 60/-
4 ♋ -/120
[icons]

BAD KREUZNACH *Rheinland-Pfalz* 18

Caravelle (HCR)
Im Oranienpark
☎ 0671-3740 fax 0671-374888
✉ 55543

50 ♂ 110/135
60 ♋ 180/195
[icons]

Oranienhof (HCR)
Priegerpromenade 5
☎ 0671-30071
✉ 55543

11 ♂
18 ♋
[icons]

Steigenberger Avance Kurhaus (HR)
Kurhausstr 28
☎ 0671-2061 fax 0671-35477
res nr 069-663080
✉ 55543

* 43 ♂ 149/199
* 65 ♋ 230/280
[icons]

Viktoria (HCR)
Kaiser Wilhelmstr 16
☎ 0671-2037
✉ 55543

15 ♂
18 ♋
[icons]

BAD KROZINGEN *Baden-Württemberg* 21

Pallotti (HCR)   *AA ANWB*
Theurachstr 3
☎ 07633-40060 fax 07633-400610
✉ 79184

The modern, comfortable Hotel Pallotti is situated in a *Kurpark* opposite the thermal baths. It is easily accessible by car or public transport. All the rooms have private facilities and some have telephone, TV and balcony. The à la carte restaurant serves fine cuisine and has a comprehensive menu. The hotel has a peaceful garden; on-site parking is available.

* - ♂ 60/85
* 64 ♋ 140/155
[icons]

BAD LAASPHE *Nordrhein-Westfalen* 12

Fasanerie (HR)
Lahnstr 55
☎ 02752-333 fax 02752-9685
✉ 57334

16 ♂
17 ♋
[icons]

GERMANY 55

BAD LAASPHE/FEUDINGEN
Nordrhein-Westfalen **12**

Landhotel Dörr (HCR) AA ANWB
Sieg Lahn Str 8-10
Feudingen
☎ 02754-3081 fax 02754-3084
✉ 57329

In the Landhotel Dörr guests are made welcome with comfort and first-class service. The rooms are equipped with modern amenities, drinks are served in the cosy bar, and the stylish and well furnished restaurant serves a range of high-quality dishes. The hotel has an indoor swimming pool and a sauna with solarium. The beautiful surroundings offer plenty of opportunities for walking, horse riding and cycling. On-site parking is available.

* 5 ♦ 92/115
* 30 ♦ 205/290

BAD LAUTERBERG *Niedersachsen* **14**

Panoramic Apartment (HA)
Dietrichstal 1
☎ 05524-841 fax 05524-84632
✉ 37431

- ♦ 79/125
306 ♦ 126/148

St Hubertusklause Kurhotel (HCR)
Wiesenberg 16
☎ 05524-2956
✉ 37431

7 ♦
24 ♦

BAD LIPPSPRINGE *Nordrhein-Westfalen* **12**

Park Hotel (Best Western) (HCR) AA ANWB
Peter Hartmann Allee 4
☎ 05252-2010 fax 05252-201111
res nr 0130-4455
✉ 33175

The spa town of Bad Lippspringe is on the edge of the Teutoburger Wald, and the Park Hotel can be found in one of the most beautiful *Kurparks* of the town. A number of the modern, comfortably furnished rooms have a balcony with views of the flower garden. The hotel has an indoor swimming pool, a sauna and solarium.

* 48 ♦ 120/188 excl. breakfast
* 52 ♦ 156/224 excl. breakfast

BAD MERGENTHEIM *Baden-Württemberg* **19**

Deutschmeister (HCR)
Ochsengasse 7
☎ 07931-7058 fax 07931-51725
✉ 97980

4 ♦ -/68
50 ♦ -/120

Kurhotel Steinmeyer (HR)
Wolfgangstr 2
☎ 07931-7220
✉ 97980

* 7 ♦ 70/75
* 8 ♦ 120/130

Parkhotel Maritim (HCR) AA ANWB
Lothar Daikerstr 6
☎ 07931-5390 fax 07931-539100
ros nr 0221-219672
✉ 97980

The luxury Parkhotel Maritim is beautifully situated near the *Kurpark*. It features elegant and graceful furnishings throughout and the rooms provide accommodation of a very high standard. The restaurant serves a wide choice of culinary specialities and there is a piano bar. Leisure facilities include a swimming pool with sauna and a health farm. The hotel is suitable for families with children.

* 42 ♦ 179/259
* 74 ♦ 248/328

Zum Wilden Mann (HR)
Reichengasse 4-6
☎ 07931-7638
✉ 97980

6 ♦
12 ♦

BAD MÜNDER AM DEISTER *Niedersachsen* 7

Terrassencafé (HCR)
Querlandweg 2
☎ 05042-6070 fax 05042-6303
✉ 31848

The comfortable Hotel Terrassencafé is just 30km from Hannover, and has rooms equipped with good amenities. The restaurant has a wide and varied choice of dishes on the menu, the hotel provides extensive fitness facilities for the energetic, and the splendid surroundings of this spa town offer plenty of opportunity for walking. The lift and entrance have been specially adapted for disabled guests.

* 11 ♦ 95/-
* 13 ♦ 180/-

BAD MÜNSTEREIFEL *Nordrhein-Westfalen* 11

Grünwald (HP)
Kettengasse 4
☎ 02253-8150
✉ 53902

4 ♦ 50/55
9 ♦ 84/96

BAD NAUHEIM *Hessen* 12

Gaudes (HR)
Hauptstr 6
☎ 06032-2508
✉ 61231

open 18.02 - 09.11 + 25.11 - 18.01
* 4 ♦ 40/42
* 4 ♦ 74/82

Parkhotel am Kurhaus (Best Western) (HCR)
Nordlicher Park 16
☎ 06032-3030 fax 06032-303419
res nr 0130-4455
✉ 61231

* 33 ♦ -/170
* 67 ♦ -/310

BAD NENNDORF *Niedersachsen* 7

Lindenhof (HG)
Bahnhofstr 29
☎ 05723-6245
✉ 31542

12 ♦

BAD NEUENAHR *Rheinland-Pfalz* 12

Steigenberger Bad Neuenahr (HCR)
Kurgartenstr 1
☎ 02641-9410 fax 02641-7001
res nr 069-663080
✉ 53474

* 90 ♦ 180/206
* 146 ♦ 286/340

BAD NEUENAHR/AHRWEILER *Rheinland-Pfalz* 12

Dorint (HCR)
Am Dahliengarten
Bad Neuenahr
☎ 02641-8950 fax 02641-895834
✉ 53474

Surrounded by greenery and overlooking the Ahr, the Dorint Hotel offers comfort combined with first-class service. All the rooms have a bath/shower, toilet, TV, radio, telephone, minibar and balcony. Along with a top-quality restaurant the hotel also offers a swimming pool, sauna, sun beds, table tennis, skittle alley and beauty parlour.

* 50 ♦ 194/-
* 130 ♦ 280/-

BAD OEYNHAUSEN *Nordrhein-Westfalen* 7

Bosse (HG)
Herforderstr 40
☎ 05731-28061 fax 05731-28063
✉ 32545

* 12 ♦ 85/120
* 20 ♦ 150/180

Stickdorn (HR)
Wilhelmstr 17
☎ 05731-21141 fax 05731-21142
✉ 32545

* 8 ♪ 95/125
* 20 ♭ 148/168
[AE] [E] ⚞ ⚲ ⊙ P 🍴 ⚓ ♨ ☐ [F] [WC] [TV]

Wittekind (HR)
Am Kurpark 10
☎ 05731-21096 fax 05731-3182
✉ 32545

* 1 ♪ 80/110
* 11 ♭ 150/190
⊙ [E] ⚞ ⚲ ⊙ P 🍴 ⚓ ♨ ☐ [F] [WC] [TV] ⫶ ✳

BAD OLDESLOE *Schleswig-Holstein* 3

Conti (HR)   [AA] [ANWB]
Bahnhofstr 51
☎ 04531-87796
✉ 25437

The Hotel Conti lies in the centre of Bad Oldesloe, just 500m from the station. The rooms are divided over 2 floors and have no en suite facilities. The hotel has a restaurant, TV lounge, a garden with terrace, and a children's playground. On-site parking is available.

* 7 ♪ -/40
* 10 ♭ -/80
⊙ P 🍴 ☺

BAD ORB *Hessen* 19

Hohenzollern (HCR)
Spessartstr 4
☎ 06052-80060 fax 06052-800647
✉ 63619

19 ♪ 95/105
25 ♭ 190/220
[AE] ⊙ [E] ⚞ ⊙ P ⚓ ♨ ☐ [F] [WC] ⫶ ☺

Steigenberger Kurhaus Bad Orb (HR)
Horststr 1
☎ 06052-880 fax 06052-88135
res nr 069-663080
✉ 63614

* 48 ♪ 150/185
* 64 ♭ 230/299
[AE] ⊙ [E] ⚞ ⊙ P 🍴 ⚓ ♨ [F] [WC] [TV] ⫶ ⫯ ☺

BAD PETERSTAL *Baden-Württemberg* 21

Adlerbad (HR)
Kniebisstr 55
☎ 07806-1071 fax 07806-8421
✉ 77740

* 10 ♪ 66/79
* 20 ♭ 112/128
⚲ P ⚓ ♨ ☐ [F] [WC] [TV] ⫶ ☺

Bärenwirtshof (HCR)
Schwimmbadstr 4
☎ 07806-1074
✉ 77740

8 ♪
16 ♭
⚲ ⊙ P ⚓ ♨ ☐ [F] [WC] [TV] ⫶

Waldhotel Palmspring (HCR)
Palmspring 1
☎ 07806-301 fax 07806-1282
✉ 77740

The comfortable Waldhotel Palmspring is situated in the middle of woods at an altitude of 600m; the area has natural springs and here one can enjoy the tranquillity and the scenery. The rooms have modern furnishings and are fitted with en suite facilities, telephone and balcony. The restaurant offers a comprehensive choice of dishes, and there is a fine view from the terrace. The hotel's leisure facilities include a tennis court, sauna and solarium.

open 29.01 - 09.01
* - ♪ 65/80
* 16 ♭ 110/130
⊙ [E] ⚞ ⚲ ♠ ⊙ P 🍴 ☐ [F] [WC] [TV] ⫶ ⫯ ☺

BAD PYRMONT *Niedersachsen* 7

Bergkurpark (HCR)
Ockelstr 11
☎ 05281-4001 fax 05281-4004
✉ 31812

* 12 ♪ 65/170
* 37 ♭ 175/380
[AE] [E] ⚞ ⊙ P 🍴 ⚓ ⚓ ♨ ☐ [F] [WC] [TV] ⫶ ☺

GERMANY

Schaumburg (HG)
Annenstr 1
☎ 05281-2554 fax 05281-2595
✉ 31812

open 20.03 - 31.01
* 9 ♨ 60/75
* 11 ♨ 125/145
🛇⊙PTΨ↟■⊡WC TV IOI ☺

Stiegenberger Bad Pyrmont (HCR)
Heiligenangerstr 2-4
☎ 05281-1502 fax 05281-152020
✉ 31812

* 40 ♨ 165/215
* 62 ♨ 252/292
🛇⊙PΨ↟WC TV IOI

BAD REICHENHALL Bayern 24

Aurora (HR)
Luitpoldstr 21
☎ 08651-2488 fax 08651-69335
✉ 83426

open 01.02 - 31.10 + 19.12 - 09.01
* 11 ♨ 57/75
* 15 ♨ 108/136
🛇PTΨ↟⊡WC TV IOI

Luisenbad (HCR)
Ludwigstr 33
☎ 08651-6040 fax 08651-62928
✉ 83435

open 20.12 - 31.10
* 35 ♨ 129/196
* 52 ♨ 214/363
⓪EΞ🛇⊙PTΨ↟⊡■⊡WC TV IOI

Residenz Bavaria (HR)
Am Munster 3
☎ 08651-7760 fax 08651-65780
✉ 83435

open 19.12 - 16.04 + 30.05 - 09.10
6 ♨ 53/67
21 ♨ 86/114
⊙↟⊡WC ☺

Steigenberger Axelmannstein (HR)
Salzburgerstr 2-6
☎ 08651-7770 fax 08651-5932
res nr 069-663080
✉ 83435

* 60 ♨ 175/275
* 83 ♨ 255/490
Æ⓪EΞ⊙◆PTΨ↟■WC TV IOI ⇪

Tivoli (HP)
Tivolistr 2
☎ 08651-5003
✉ 83435

9 ♨
14 ♨
🛇PTΨ↟⊡■⊡WC

BAD RIPPOLDSAU Baden-Württemberg 21

Zum Kranz (HCR)
Reichenbachstr 2
☎ 07440-725 fax 07440-511
✉ 77776

The Hotel zum Kranz enjoys a beautiful and quiet position on the outskirts of the centre in the wooded hills of the Schwarzwald. The rooms are well furnished. The restaurant serves fine cuisine with regional and international specialities. For health and fitness enthusiasts there are saunas, a fitness room, massage, swimming pool, tennis court, gymnastics and *Kneippkuren*..

open 07.02 - 10.01
* 8 ♨ 95/105
* 20 ♨ 170/190
🛇♨PTΨ≋↟■⊡WC IOI ☺

Ochsenwirtshof (HP)
Wolfacherstr 21
☎ 07839-223 fax 07839-1268
✉ 77776

The Hotel Ochsenwirthof is situated amid forests in the beautiful Wolftal - the area offers good spa, walking, and winter-sports amenities. The modern rooms are equipped with en suite facilities and balconies, the restaurant serves a wide choice of dishes, and there is a lounge with pleasant seating and open fire. The indoor swimming pool has a jet-stream, and parking facilities are available.

open 01.02 - 07.01
* 4 ♨ 57/67
* 17 ♨ 100/120
♨P≋⊡WC ⇪ ☺

BAD ROTHENFELDE Niedersachsen 6

Haus Deutsch Krone (HA)
Sonnenhang 15
☎ 05424-611 fax 05424-1459
✉ 49214

150 🛏
AE ⚿ ♨ P ♒ 🚞 🛗 ⊟ 🕐 WC TV 🍴

Zur Post (HCR) AA ANWB
Frankfurterstr 2
☎ 05424-1066 fax 05424-69540
✉ 49214

The *Kur* Hotel zur Post is in the centre of the peaceful village of Bad Rothenfelde. It features well kept and comfortable rooms, all with en suite facilities, colour TV and telephone. On the top floor is a roof terrace, sauna and solarium; the water in the indoor swimming pool is 28 degrees. The 2 restaurants have a good menu.

* 20 🛏 95/105
* 20 🛌 130/180
AE ⓓ E 🚞 ⚿ ⊙ P ♒ ⚓ 🚞 🛗 ⊟ 🕐 WC TV 🍴 🐕

BAD SACHSA Niedersachsen 14

Berghof Ravensberg (HR)
Einzeln
☎ 05523-2145
✉ 37441

5 🛌
AE ⓓ E 🚞 ♨ ⊙ P ♒ 🕐 WC

Lindenhof (HCR)
Hindenburgstr 4
☎ 05523-1053
✉ 37441

9 🛏
20 🛌
AE ⓓ E 🚞 ⊙ ⊛ P ♒ 🚞 🛗 🕐 WC TV 🍴

Romantischer Winkel (HCR)
Bismarckstr 23
☎ 05523-3040 fax 05523-304122
✉ 37437

open 19.12 - 14.11
* 30 🛏 105/150
* 40 🛌 180/345
AE E 🚞 ⚿ ♨ ⊙ P ♒ 🚞 🛗 ⊟ 🕐 WC TV 🍴 🐕

BAD SALZUFLEN Nordrhein-Westfalen 7

Maritim Staatsbadhotel (HCR)
Parkstr 53
☎ 05222-1810 fax 05222-15953
res nr 0221-219672
✉ 32105

* 100 🛏 197/283
* 106 🛌 292/358
AE ⓓ E 🚞 ⚙ ⊙ P ♒ 🚞 🛗 ⊟ 🕐 WC TV 🍴 🐕

BAD SASSENDORF Nordrhein-Westfalen 12

Maritim Schnitterhof (HCR)
Salzstr 5
☎ 02921-5990 fax 02921-52627
res nr 0221-219672
✉ 59505

17 🛏
125 🛌
AE ⓓ E 🚞 ⊙ P ♒ ⚓ 🚞 🛗 ⊟ 🕐 WC TV 🍴 🐕

BAD SCHÖNBORN Baden-Württemberg 18

Monica (HG)
Kirchbrändelring 42
☎ 07253-4016
✉ 76669

- 🛏 -/85
13 🛌 -/99
P ♒ ⚓ 🛗 🕐 WC TV 🐕

BAD SEGEBERG Schleswig-Holstein 3

B404 & Haus Stefanie (HCR)
An der B404
☎ 04551-3600 fax 04551-93343
✉ 23795

open 26.12 - 23.12
* - 🛏 25/60 excl. breakfast
* 37 🛌 42/80 excl. breakfast
AE ⓓ E 🚞 ♨ ⊛ P ♒ ⚓ 🛗 ⊟ 🕐 WC TV 🍴

BAD SODEN Hessen 18

Parkhotel (Best Western) (HCR)
Königsteinerstr 88
☎ 06196-2000 fax 06196-200153
res nr 0130-4455
✉ 63628

* 56 🛏 205/315
* 74 🛌 265/375
AE ⓓ E 🚞 ⊙ P ♒ 🛗 ⊟ 🕐 WC TV

GERMANY

BAD SODEN-SALMÜNSTER Hessen — 13

Landhotel Betz (HR)
Brüder Grimmstr 21
☎ 06056-7390 fax 06065-8080
✉ 63628

19 ♨
49 🛏

BAD TÖLZ Bayern — 23

Bellaria (HG)
Ludwigstr 22
☎ 08041-80080 fax 08041-800844
✉ 83646

8 ♨
16 🛏

Residenz Hotel König Ludwig (HCR)
Stef.-v. Strechinestr 16
☎ 08041-8010 fax 08041-801127
✉ 83646

* 16 ♨ 125/165
* 71 🛏 160/210

BAD WALDSEE Baden-Württemberg — 23

Kurhotel Post (HR)
Hauptstr 1
☎ 07524-1507
✉ 88339

13 ♨
15 🛏

Zum Ritter (HCR)
Wurzacher Str 90
☎ 07524-8018
✉ 88339

11 ♨
24 🛏

BAD WIESSEE Bayern — 23

Resi Von der Post (HR)
Zilcherstr 14
☎ 08022-82788 fax 08022-83216
✉ 83707

14 ♨
21 🛏

BAD WILDUNGEN Hessen — 13

Maritim Badehotel (HCR)   AA ANWB
Dr Marcstr 4
☎ 05621-7999 fax
05621-799799
res nr 0221-219672
✉ 34537

The fully renovated Maritim Badehotel is situated in a beautiful park. The bedrooms, and especially the suites, are spacious and tastefully furnished. There is an inviting restaurant with a good menu, complemented by a very comprehensive wine list. The luxurious swimming pool with sauna, solarium and beauty salon offers welcoming relaxation. The area around this *Kur* holiday hotel is ideal for walking.

* 73 ♨ 189/269
* 171 🛏 258/338

Schwarze (HCR)
Brunnenallee 42
☎ 05621-4064 fax 05621-74279
✉ 34537

* 10 ♨ 43/70
* 14 🛏 70/130

BAD WIMPFEN Baden-Württemberg — 19

Am Kurpark (HG)
Kirschenweg 16
☎ 07063-7091
✉ 74206

open 08.01 - 12.12
* 2 ♨ -/130
* 8 🛏 130/190

GERMANY

BAIERSBRONN Baden-Württemberg — 21

Talblick (HCR)   AA ANWB
Panoramaweg 111
☏ 07442-3318 fax 07442-7940
✉ 72270

The Hotel Talblick is situated in the Schwarzwald with beautiful views over the mountains and valleys. The hotel prides itself on its friendly atmosphere and hospitality and is a good base for summer day trips or winter sports excursions. The rooms are modern, most have a shower, toilet and balcony. The hotel has a large terrace and ample parking facilities.

open 01.12 - 20.10
* 6 ♗ 35/43
* 12 ⚏ 70/94

E ⌇ ♠ ⓢ P P ⚑ ⇐ ▭ ⒫ WC TV ☺

BAMBERG Bayern — 19

Die Alte Post (HCR)   AA ANWB
Heiliggrabstr 1
☏ 0951-27848 fax 0951-27014
✉ 96052

The Alte Post, built in typical regional style is situated in a peaceful side street about five minutes away from the town centre. The rooms are neatly furnished and many have private bathrooms. The restaurant offers a good range of regional specialities.

* 18 ♗ 83/87
* 22 ⚏ 105/140

AE ⓘ E ⌇ ♠ ⓢ P P ⇐ ▭ ⒫ WC TV ☺

BATTENBERG/EDER-DODENAU Hessen — 12

Berghotel Waidmannsheil (HR)   AA ANWB
Jahnstr 7
Battenberg
☏ 06452-6086 fax 06452-6086
✉ 35088

The Berghotel Waidmannsheil is a quietly situated, small, family-run hotel; offering guests a comfortable stay. The rooms are equipped with shower, toilet, telephone, radio and TV. The pleasantly furnished restaurant is especially known for its game specialities. The hotel has a swimming pool, solarium, sunbathing lawn, table tennis and ample parking space. There are plenty of winter sports opportunities.

* 3 ♗ 38/42
* 14 ⚏ 76/85

AE E ⌇ ⌇ ♠ ⓢ P P ⚑ ⇐ ▭ ⒫ WC TV ⌘ ☺

BAUNATAL Hessen — 13

Ambassador (Best Western) (HCR)
Friedrich Ebert Allee 1
☏ 0561-49930 fax 0561-4993500
res nr 0130-4455
✉ 34225

* 5 ♗ 150/170
* 115 ⚏ -/300

AE ⓘ E ⌇ ⓢ P P ⚑ ⇅ ⇐ ▭ ⒫ WC TV ⌘ ☺

BAYERISCH EISENSTEIN Bayern — 24

Maximilian (HCR)
Hafenbrädallee 17
☏ 09925-416
✉ 94252

1 ♗
13 ⚏

♠ ⓢ ◆ P P ⚑ ⇐ ▭ ⒫ WC ⌘ ☺

Sporthotel Brennes (HCR)
Brennes 14
☏ 09925-256 fax 09925-525
✉ 94252

2 ♗ 55/110
20 ⚏ 70/165

AE E ♠ ⓢ ◆ P P ⚑ ⌁ ▭ ⒫ WC TV ☺

GERMANY

BAYRISCHZELL *Bayern* 23

Annamirl (HG)
Schönbornweg 1
☎ 08023-647
✉ 83735

10 ⌥ 34/42
🏨 symbols

BEILNGRIES *Bayern* 20

Landgasthof Alberter (HR)
Haus 7
☎ 08461-9964
✉ 92339

1 ⌥
9 ⌥
symbols

Ringhotel Beilngries Die Gams (HCR) AA ANWB
Hauptstr 16
☎ 08461-256 fax 08461-7475
✉ 92339

The versatile Hotel Die Gams enjoys a central, yet peaceful position in the heart of the town. The well cared for rooms - many of which have recently been renovated - contain TV, telephone and radio. The cuisine is of a good standard and there is a pleasant bar and winter-garden. Leisure facilities include whirlpool, sauna, solarium, fitness room, table-tennis and a bicycle-hire service.

open 10.01 - 03.01
* 10 ⌥ 85/125
* 53 ⌥ 120/190
symbols

Fuchs Bräu (HCR) AA ANWB
Hauptstr 23
☎ 08461-295 fax 08461-8357
✉ 92339

The comfortable and family-run hotel Fuchs-Bräu can be found in the romantic *Altstadt*. The rooms are well maintained, with pleasant furnishings and modern amenities. It has a stylish restaurant with a wide choice of dishes, and has its own fish-pond for guests who enjoy angling; bikes are available for hire to explore the surrounding area.

* 16 ⌥ 80/95
* 51 ⌥ 120/140
symbols

Goldener Hahn (HR)
Hauptstr 44
☎ 08461-419 fax 08461-8447
✉ 92339

8 ⌥ 49/75
32 ⌥ 80/102
symbols

BEILSTEIN *Rheinland-Pfalz* 17

Haus Lipmann (HCR)
Marktpl 3
☎ 02673-1573
✉ 56814

open 01.04 - 31.10
* 1 ⌥ 100/130
* 28 ⌥ 120/150
symbols

BENSBERG *Nordrhein-Westfalen* 12

Goethehaus (HR)
Markt 3
☎ 02204-54031 fax 02204-56122
✉ 5060

4 ⌥ 85/165
10 ⌥ 140/210
symbols

BENSHEIM *Hessen* 20

Präzenzhof (HCR)
Bahnhofstr
☎ 06251-4256 fax 06251-38273
✉ 64625

8 ⌥
21 ⌥
symbols

BERATZHAUSEN *Bayern* 20

Pension Zum Schlossberg (HP)
Schloßbergstr 18
☎ 09493-823
✉ 93176

2 ⌥ 35/40
12 ⌥ 60/70
symbols

GERMANY 63

BERCHTESGADEN Bayern 24

Treff Alpenhotel Kronprinz (HR)
Am Brandholz
☎ 08652-6070 fax 08652-607120
✉ 83471

10 🛏 92/135
57 🛏 134/220

Vier Jahreszeiten (HR)
Maximilianstr 20
☎ 08652-5026 fax 08652-5029
✉ 83471

* 25 🛏 100/135
* 36 🛏 160/260

BERGHAUPTEN/SCHWARZWALD Baden-Württemberg 21

Brüderle (HP) AA ANWB
Schützenbergstr 21
Berghaupten
☎ 07803-2577
✉ 77791

The traditional Hotel Brüderie is situated in the Schwarzwald; there are many recommended walking routes in the densely wooded area. A number of the rooms in this hotel have en suite shower and toilet. There is a pleasant guest lounge and on-site parking is available.

* 2 🛏 50/55
* 4 🛏 70/80

BERGHAUSEN Rheinland-Pfalz 18

Berghof (HCR) AA ANWB
Bergstr 3
☎ 06486-7094 fax 06486-1837
✉ 5429

The traditional style Berghof is situated in the Taunus mountains; this region is ideal for walking. The hotel has well furnished bedrooms with shower, toilet and telephone, and TV sockets. The relaxed restaurant offers a good cuisine and serves both lunch and dinner. In addition, the hotel features a sunbathing lawn and a peaceful terrace, and there is on-site parking.

* 6 🛏 47/54
* 25 🛏 74/88

BERG KREIS STARNBERG Bayern 23

Dorint Starnburg Seehotel Leoni (HCR)
Assenbucher Str 4
☎ 08151-5060 fax 08151-506140
res nr 0130-6605
✉ 8137

15 🛏 175/205
52 🛏 260/290

BERLEBECK Nordrhein-Westfalen 12

Kanne (HCR)
Paderbornerstr 155
☎ 05231-47212
✉ 32760

1 🛏
18 🛏

BERLIN Berlin 10

Berlin is still a city struggling to become a whole from the two disparate parts which until recently were separate - one East and one West. The no-man's-land around the remains of the old wall still disfigures the city, marked in places by crosses of those killed trying to escape westwards. The area covered by the city is vast, contrasting with the intense urbanisation common in much of western Europe; huge areas consist of forest, lakes and even farmland.
What was West Berlin was virtually destroyed by the Allied armies in the final World War II conflicts and is almost entirely modern. Although frequently meretricious and ill-conceived, the best of the post-war city is stunning, with startling examples of art, architecture and design. East Berlin, also badly damaged in the war, has been reconstructed in two conflicting styles: drably functional on one hand, and painstakingly accurate reproductions of grandiose monuments on the other. Most cultural venues are duplicated on each side (two national galleries, two Egyptian museums, etc) and rationalisation is bound to occur. Some of the best museums are contained in two museum complexes: Museumsinsel on an island in the river Spree, including the fascinating Pergammuseum; and Museen-Dahlem, an important group of museums in the Arnimallee.
As befits its status as a world capital, Berlin has its own famous landmarks: the Brandenburger Tor was until recently stranded in no-man's-land, where →

64 GERMANY

passageways through the six Doric columns made a spectacular setting for Prussian military parades; the Brandenburger Tor overlooks the bronze statue of Frederick the Great, looking down on the swirling traffic of Unter den Linden and the monumental buildings of that famous thoroughfare; Alexanderplatz is hub of the historic centre of old Berlin, where one of Berlin's oldest parish churches, Marienkirche, is now dwarfed by the Fernsehnturm (Television Tower); the Haus am Checkpoint Charlie, where the East German guards kept watch, now displays a history of the wall with photographs and biographies of those who tried to escape to the west; the vast palace, Schloss Charlottenburg, contains sumptuous royal apartments and a fine collection of porcelain and boasts fine English-style gardens.

See city plan on page 38-9.

Ambassador Berlin (HR)
Bayreuther Str 42-43
☎ 030-219020 fax 030-21902380
res nr 030-21902354
✉ 10787
City Plan F4

* - ♪ 250/290
* 200 ♣ 310/350
AE ⓘ E ≡ ♪ ⊙ P ⛱ 🏊 ↕ 🛏 🚹 WC TV 🐾

Antares Hotel (HG)
Stresemannstr 97-10
☎ 030-2611444 fax 030-2615027
✉ 10963
City Plan H5

* 26 ♪ 170/195
* 47 ♣ 195/270
AE ⓘ E ≡ ♪ ⊙ P ↕ 🛏 🚹 WC TV 🐾

Bristol Hotel Kempinski (HCR)
Kurfürstendamm 27
☎ 030-884340 fax 030-8836075
res nr 0130-3339
✉ 10719
City Plan D4

* 9 ♪ 470/530 excl. breakfast
* 236 ♣ 940/1060 excl. breakfast
AE ⓘ E ≡ ⊙ 🏊 ≈ ↕ 🛏 WC TV 🍽 🐾

Palace Berlin (HCR)
Im Europa Center
☎ 030-25020 fax 030-2626577
✉ 10789
City Plan E4

- ♪ 290/450 excl. breakfast
350 ♣ 360/500 excl. breakfast
AE ⓘ E ≡ ⊙ P ≈ ≈ ↕ 🛏 🚹 WC TV 🍽 🐾

Queenshotel Berlin (HG)
Güntzelstr 14
☎ 030-870241 fax 030-8619326
res nr 0130-4433
✉ 10717
City Plan D6

* 7 ♪ 195/270
* 102 ♣ 250/300
AE ⓘ E ≡ ⊙ P ⛱ ↕ 🛏 🚹 WC TV 🐾

Savigny (HG)
Brandenburgischestr 21
☎ 030-8813001 fax 030-8825519
✉ 10707
City Plan C5

The Hotel Savigny offers a good bed and breakfast service and has a special breakfast area. It is in the centre of Berlin only 500m from the Kurfürstendam and is easily accessible by car and public transport. The rooms are well furnished, all have a telephone, and most have washing facilities.

* 28 ♪ 65/100
* 30 ♣ 120/160
E ♪ ⊙ ↕ 🔒 🛏 🚹 WC 🐾

Steiner (HG)
Albrecht-Achilles Str 58
☎ 030-8919016 fax 030-8928721
✉ 10709
City Plan C5

8 ♪
31 ♣
♪ ⊙ P ↕ 🚹 WC TV 🐾

Am Zoo (HCR)
Kurfürstendamm 25
☎ 030-884370 fax 030-88437714
✉ 10719
City Plan D4

* 54 ♪ 176/276
* 85 ♣ 316/386
⊙ ◆ P ⛱ ↕ 🛏 🚹 WC TV

GERMANY 65

BERNAU AM CHIEMSEE Bayern 24

Seiserhof (HCR)
Reit 5
Bernau a. Chiemsee
☎ 08051-7295
✉ 83233

2 ♦
25 ⚏
🚶 Ⓟ 🅿 🍴 ■ 🅿 WC TV 🍽

BERNKASTEL-KUES Rheinland-Pfalz 17

Kapuziner Stübchen (HR)
Römerstr 35
☎ 06531-2353
✉ 54470

3 ♦
8 ⚏
⊙ ◆ 🅿 WC

Moselpark (HCR)
Im Kurpark
☎ 06531-5080 fax 06531-508612
✉ 54470

* 25 ♦ 145/179
* 125 ⚏ 198/278
AE ⓄⒹ E ⌐ ♠ Ⓟ 🅿 🍴 ■ 🅿 WC TV 🍽

Zur Post (HR)
Gestade 17
☎ 06531-2022 fax 06531-2927
✉ 54463

open 04.02 - 02.01
2 ♦ 98/-
40 ⚏ 140/180
AE ⓄⒹ E ⌐ ⊙ Ⓟ 🅿 🍴 ■ 🅿 WC TV 🍽

BERNKASTEL/WEHLEN Rheinland-Pfalz 17

Mosel (HCR)
Uferallee 3
Wehlen
☎ 06531-8527 fax
06531-1546
✉ 54470

The Mosel Hotel, which is in the hands of the Leyendecker family, looks out over the river Mosel. It has a relaxed atmosphere, and all the rooms feature a shower and a toilet. The restaurant has earned a good reputation in the region, both because of the food, and also because of its fine Mosel wines.

---

open 01.03 - 15.11
* 2 ♦ 35/70
* 14 ⚏ 70/140
🚶 Ⓟ 🅿 🍴 ■ 🅿 WC TV 🍽

BERNRIED Bayern 24

Bernrieder Hof (HCR)
Bogenerstr 9
☎ 09905-8397 fax
09905-8400
✉ 94505

The Bernrieder Hof is a beautiful and versatile hotel in a quiet, rural atmosphere; it is close to the motorway and good for an overnight stop. All the rooms are well furnished and have en suite facilities, telephone, balcony and a TV connection. Leisure facilities include an outdoor swimming pool, sauna, solarium, skittle alley and table tennis.

open 15.01 - 31.12
7 ♦ 44/48
28 ⚏ 88/96
E 🚶 Ⓟ 🅿 🍴 ■ 🅿 WC TV 🍽 🐾

BESIGHEIM Baden-Württemberg 18

Röser (HR)
Woinstr 6
☎ 07143-35171
✉ 74354

8 ♦
14 ⚏
🚶 Ⓟ 🅿 🍴 ■ 🅿 WC 🍽

BESTWIG/VALME Nordrhein-Westfalen 12

Rüppel (HR)
Valme 4
Bestwig
☎ 02905-774
✉ 59909

Peace and quiet characterise Valmedal, where Gasthof Rüppel is situated. All the rooms have a private toilet and shower. Good beer is served in the Bierstube, and the restaurant serves a range of snacks and main meals. The surrounding area can be explored on bicycles, which can be hired

→

GERMANY

from the hotel. In winter this Gasthof is also an excellent venue for a winter-sports holiday.

2 🛏 42/46
10 🛏 84/92
🛐🏨🅿🍴🐕🖃🚾📺🍽☕

BEVERUNGEN Nordrhein-Westfalen 13

Stadt Bremen (HR)
Lange Str 13
☎ 05273-9030 fax 05273-21575
✉ 37688

* 20 🛏 70/100
* 30 🛏 130/180
🆎🅾🇪⚡☉◆🅿🍴🐕🔔🍴🖃🗜🚾📺🍽

BEXBACH Saarland 17

Hochwiesmühle (HR)
Hochwiesmühle 50-54
☎ 06826-8190 fax 06826-819147
✉ 66450

9 🛏
73 🛏
🆎🅾🇪⚡🅿🍴🐕🔔🍴🚾📺🍽☕

BIEBELRIED Bayern 19

Leicht (HR)
Würzburgerstr 3
☎ 09302-814 fax 09302-3163
✉ 97318

open 10.01 - 23.12
* 35 🛏 105/145
* 35 🛏 160/240
🆎🅾🇪⚡☉🅿🍴🍴🖃🗜🚾📺🍽☕

BIELEFELD Nordrhein-Westfalen 7

Landhotel Ummelner Mühle (HR) AA ANWB
Gütersloher Str 299
Bielefeld
☎ 0521-489070 fax 0521-488257
✉ 33649

Landhotel Ummelner Müle is situated on a trunk road outside the centre of Bielefeld near the Teutoburgerwald. It is a well maintained establishment, equally suited as a holiday hotel or for a night's stopover. There is a restaurant, and the rooms have en suite bathroom. For an extra fee, the facilities in the nearby leisure centre include badminton, squash, billiards, bowling and sauna.

20 🛏 45/85
30 🛏 100/150
🆎🅾🇪⚡☉◆🅿🍴🖃🗜🚾📺🍽

Mövenpick (HR) AA ANWB
Am Bahnhof 3
☎ 0521-52820 fax 0521-5282100
res nr 0130-852217
✉ 33602

* 19 🛏 135/450 excl. breakfast
* 143 🛏 230/450 excl. breakfast
🆎🅾🇪⚡🅿🍴🐕🔔🍴🖃🗜🚾📺🍽🏨☕

Peter Auf'm Berge (HCR)
Bergstr 45
☎ 0521-100037
✉ 33619

4 🛏 65/80
8 🛏 120/150
🇪🏨🅿🍴🐕🖃🚾📺🐎

Silencehotel Hoberger Landhaus (HCR) AA ANWB
Schäferdreesch 18
☎ 0521-101031 fax 0521-103927
✉ 33619

Hotel Hoberger Landhaus is situated on the edge of a forest, and is an ideal place to enjoy the peaceful Teutoburgwald. This cosy and well constructed hotel has very comfortable rooms and a pleasant restaurant which serves a range of good dishes. There are plenty of recreational facilities available nearby, including horse-riding, golf, tennis and swimming. Bielefeld is a 5-minute drive away.

13 🛏 120/152
18 🛏 190/-
🅾🇪⚡🛐☉🅿🍴🐕🔔🖃🗜🚾📺🍽

GERMANY 67

BIERSDORF Rheinland-Pfalz   17

Dorint Sporthotel Sudeifel (HCR)   AA ANWB
Am Stausee Bitburg
☎ 06569-990 fax
06569-7909
res nr 0130-6605
✉ 54636

The Dorint Sporthotel Sudeifel is a holiday hotel near the 35-hectare Bitburg reservoir with its splendid walking paths. Recreational facilities here include fishing, surfing, pedalos and rowing, and the area offers plenty of interesting excursions. All the rooms have en suite facilities, radio, TV, telephone and minibar. The hotel's leisure amenities include an indoor swimming pool, sauna, solarium, fitness room, table tennis, sunbathing lawn, skittle alley, tennis courts and mini golf.

* 8 ♊ 163/198
* 92 ⚏ 275/306
🅰🅔🅴🆉🐆🛏🅿️🏊🌊🍴🚻🔲📺📞☎

BINGEN Rheinland-Pfalz   18

Rheingau (HCR)
Am Rheinkai 8
☎ 06721-17496 fax 06721-17498
✉ 55411

open 15.01 - 20.12
* 1 ♊ 75/85
* 13 ⚏ 115/130
🅰🅴🆉⊙🅿️🔲📺🚻📺

BINZEN Baden-Württemberg   21

Ochsen (HR)   AA ANWB
Hauptstr 42
☎ 07621-62326 fax
07621-69257
✉ 79589

The cosy Hotel Ochsen is situated in the wine-producing village of Binzen, and is a good base for trips to the Schwarzwald, Alsace and Switzerland. The hotel has modern rooms with en suite facilities, radio, TV and telephone. The restaurant offers a wide choice of dishes and various seasonal specialities. There is a lounge with an open fire.

---

* 10 ♊ 70/85
* 10 ⚏ 120/140
⊙🅿️🏊🛏🔲📺🚻📺

BIRKENAU Hessen   18

Schimbacher Hof (HR)
☎ 06209-258
✉ 69488

6 ♊
16 ⚏
🐆🅿️🏊🌊🔲📺🚻🍴

BISCHOFSGRÜN Bayern   20

Sporthotel Kaiseralm (HR)
Fröbershammer 31
☎ 09276-800 fax 09276-8145
✉ 95493

* 41 ♊ 98/190
* 78 ⚏ 180/260
🅰🅔🅴🆉🐆🛏🅿️🏊🌊🍴🚻🔲📺📞☎

BISCHOFSWIESEN Bayern   24

Mooshausl (HP)
Postfach 44
☎ 08652-7261 fax 08652-7340
✉ 83483

open 01.01 - 25.10
7 ♊ 49/52
14 ⚏ 93/101
🐆🛏🅿️🏊🌊🍴🔲📺🚻📺🍴

BLANKENHEIM Nordrhein-Westfalen   11

Schloßblick (HCR)   AA ANWB
Nonnenbacherweg 4-6
☎ 02449-238 fax 02449-253
res nr 02449-238
✉ 53945

The Schlossblick is a traditional hotel situated in the Eifel, with a view of a castle and its lake. The rooms are comfortably furnished with en suite facilities, and some have a balcony, TV, telephone and minibar. The fine restaurant offers good value for money. Leisure facilities include an indoor swimming pool, sauna and solarium.

open 23.12 - 01.11
* 5 ♊ 70/100
* 28 ⚏ 88/130
🅰🅔🅴🆉⊙🅿️🏊🌊🍴🔲📺🚻📺🍴
See advertisement page 69

Violet (HCR)
Kölner Str 7
☎ 02449-1388 fax 02449-8098
✉ 53945

open 16.12 - 28.02 + 01.04 - 19.11
* - 🛏 62/-
* 9 🛌 98/105

BLIESEN Saarland   17

Zur Waldschenke (HCR)
Niederhofstr 53
☎ 06854-8649
✉ 66606

6 🛌

BOCHUM Nordrhein-Westfalen   12

Arcade (HR)
Universitätsstr 3
☎ 0234-33311 fax 0234-3331867
✉ 44789

* - 🛏 125/160
* 157 🛌 172/210

BODENMAIS Bayern   24

Hubertus (HCR)
Amselweg 2
☎ 09924-7026 fax 09924-831
✉ 94249

13 🛏
23 🛌

Neue Post (HCR)
Kötztinger Str 25
☎ 09924-7077 fax 09924-7269
✉ 94249

4 🛏
38 🛌

Waldeck (HCR)
Arberseestr 39
☎ 09924-1945
✉ 94249

4 🛏 -/52
36 🛌 80/102

Waldhotel Riederin (HR)
Riederin 1
☎ 09924-7760 fax 09924-7337
✉ 94249

6 🛏
50 🛌

BOLLENDORF Rheinland-Pfalz   17

Am Wehr (HCR)   AA ANWB
Laufenwehr
☎ 06526-242 fax 06526-298
✉ 54669

The Hotel am Wehr is quietly situated on the border and the river Sauer, close to a health resort. The hotel has a pleasant atmosphere and tasteful furnishings throughout. In addition there is a covered and open terrace, sunbathing lawn, children's playground, as well as a car park and individual lock-up garages. Half or full-board terms are available on request. The hotel offers substantial discounts for stays of more than 10 nights.

open 02.02 - 01.01
* - 🛏 52/67
* 16 🛌 84/134

Hauer (HCR)   AA ANWB
Sauerstaden 20
☎ 06526-323 fax 06526-314
✉ 54669

The rooms in the 3-storey Hotel Hauer all have a private shower, some of them also have a balcony. The hotel has a restaurant and a bar/café; there is lock-up storage for bicycles, and covered parking facilities are available.

* - 🛏 58/66
* 23 🛌 96/112

GERMANY 69

Hotel Schlossblick
Café - Restaurant

**A hotel where
you feel at home!**

- 60 beds, lift, telephone, balcony, minibar, television
- indoor swimming pool, sauna, solarium, fitness room
- restaurant accommodates 120, specialities from the Eifel
- recreation hall, parking space, ORIENTAL hotel bar
- inexpensive packages, hotel folder.

Nonnenbacherweg 2-6
D-53945 Blankenheim
Telephone 02449-238
Fax 02449/253

See entry page 67

Scheuerhof (HR)   AA ANWB
Sauerstaden 42
☎ 06526-395 fax 06526-8639
✉ 54669

The Hotel Scheuerhof enjoys a peaceful location about 500m from the town, and is a good base for trips to Trier, Luxembourg and Vianden. The hotel rooms are well furnished and have en suite facilities and a TV socket; a number also have a balcony and telephone. Two of the rooms have separate children's rooms with connecting door. From the sunbathing lawn there are beautiful views of the river Sauer.

open 15.01 - 15.12
* 2 ♋ 59/69
* 12 ♋ 106/126
⓪ E ⌇ ⚭ ⏀ ⓟ ⚲ ⓦⓒ ⓣⓥ ☺

BONN Nordrhein-Westfalen   **11**

Bonn, federal capital of the former West Germany, is situated in north Rhineland-Westphalia, 24km southsoutheast of Cologne, on the left bank of the Rhine. The archbishops of Cologne resided here from 1265 to 1794, and the town's beautiful Münster, dating from the 11th century, contrasts with extensive modern buildings of the federal parliament and ministries. The University of Bonn was re-established here in 1818 and is housed in the former electoral palace; in 1934 the agricultural college of Bonn-Poppelsdorf was incorporated with it. Beethoven was born in this city in 1770, at Bonngasse 20, now a museum, and Schumann spent his last years in Sebastianstrasse. Among Bonn's other attractions are the Baroque Jesu Church, 13th-century Remigius Church, the 18th-century castle, Poppelsdorfer Schloss, and the Alter Zoll, a bastion overlooking the Rhine.

Arcade Bonn (HR)
Vorgebirgsstr 33
☎ 0228-72660 fax 0228-7266405
✉ 53119

- ♋ -/135
147 ♋ -/185
AE E ⌇ ⊙ ⓟ ⓟ ⚲ ⓝ ⓒ ⓦⓒ ⓣⓥ ☺

Auerberg (HG)
Kölnstr 362
☎ 0228-671031 fax 0228-672933
✉ 53117

open 04.01 - 17.12
* 6 ♋ -/115
* 24 ♋ -/160
AE ⓪ E ⌇ ⚭ ◆ ⓟ ⓟ ⚲ ⓝ ⓒ ⓦⓒ ☺

Domicil (Best Western) (HCR)
Thomas Mannstr 24-26
☎ 0228-729090 fax 0228-691207
res nr 0130-4455
✉ 53111

open 03.01 - 22.12
* 15 ♋ 170/360 excl. breakfast
* 27 ♋ 265/410 excl. breakfast
AE ⓪ E ⌇ ⊙ ⓟ ⚲ ⓝ ⓒ ⓦⓒ ⓣⓥ ⓘⓞⓛ ☺

Jacobs (HG)
Bergstr 85
☎ 0228-232822
✉ 53129

11 ♋
24 ♋
ⓟ ⚲ ⓝ ⓒ ⓦⓒ

GERMANY

Kaiser Karl Hotel (HCR)
Vorgebirgsstr 56
☎ 0228-650933 fax 0228-637899
✉ 53119
18 🛏 190/250
24 🛏 250/350
[icons]

Maritim Hotel Bonn (HR)
Godesberger Allee
☎ 0228-81080 fax 0228-8108811
res nr 0221-219672
✉ 53175
* 115 🛏 249/419
* 254 🛏 294/484
[icons]

Pullman Königshof (HCR)
Adenauer Allee 9
☎ 0228-26010
✉ 53111
1 🛏
137 🛏
[icons]

BONN-BAD GODESBERG Nordrhein-Westfalen
11

Kaiserhof (HG)
Moltkestr 64
☎ 0228-362016 fax 0228-363825
✉ 53173
* 25 🛏 125/191
* 25 🛏 195/242
[icons]

Zum Löwen (HG)
Von Groote-Pl 1
☎ 0228-354951
✉ 53173
1 🛏
48 🛏
[icons]

BONNDORF Baden-Württemberg **21**

Schwarzwald Hotel (HR)   AA ANWB
Rothausstr 7
☎ 07703-421 fax 07703-442
✉ 79848

The Schwarzwald Hotel is a cosy hotel, situated just outside the centre of Bonndorf, and with a peaceful, relaxed and friendly atmosphere throughout. The rooms are well furnished and have en suite facilities, radio, colour TV and telephone. The restaurant serves both lunch and dinner. The hotel has an indoor swimming pool, sauna, table tennis, children's play area, sunbathing lawn, and sun-terrace.

*. 17 🛏 69/95
* 50 🛏 120/170
[icons]

BOPPARD Rheinland-Pfalz **17**

Bellevue Rheinhotel (Best Western)   AA ANWB
(HCR)
Rheinallee 41-42
☎ 06742-1020 fax 06742-102602
res nr 0130-4455
✉ 56154

The beautiful Art Nouveau façade of the Bellevue Rheinhotel is one of the sights of the town of Boppard. This luxurious hotel offers very comfortable accommodation. The rooms have en suite facilities, video, minibar and hairdryer. There is an excellent restaurant which serves a generous breakfast, a pleasant bar, and a well equipped gym.

* 12 🛏 120/210
* 83 🛏 180/320
[icons]
See advertisement page 73

GERMANY 71

Am Ebertor (HCR) [AA] [ANWB]
Heerstr 89
☎ 06742-2081 fax
06742-102602
✉ 56154

The pleasantly furnished Hotel am Ebertor is situated on the banks of the Rhine, close to the Ebertor and the 7500m nature park. It is easy accessible by car and public transport. The rooms feature modern furnishings and have en suite facilities, colour TV, radio and telephone. The Eberstube restaurant has a good menu, and weather permitting, meals are served in the garden restaurant with its view of the Rhine.

open 01.04 - 31.12
* - ♨ 91/111
* 66 ⚭ 116/156
[AE] [D] [E] [≡] [⅄] [⚙] [⊙] [P] [☂] [⚐] [⌂] [WC] [TV] [☺]
See advertisement page 73

Günther (HG) [AA] [ANWB]
Rheinallee 40
☎ 06742-2335 fax
06742-1557
✉ 56154

The Hotel Günther is centrally situated on the Rhine promenade and just 500m from the station. All the rooms have private facilities, radio, TV and telephone; those overlooking the Rhine have a balcony. Although the hotel has no restaurant, there is a lounge, TV room, and terrace. Parking facilities are available.

open 15.01 - 15.12
* 1 ♨ 59/120
* 18 ⚭ 79/148
[⚙] [⊙] [☂] [↑↓] [⚐] [⌂] [WC] [TV] [✈]

Haus Wilhelmsruh (HG)
Auf Sabel
☎ 06742-1771
✉ 56154

8 ⚭
[♨] [⚓] [P] [☂] [⚐] [⌂] [WC] [☺]

Hunsrücker Hof (HR)
Walburgergasse 3-5
☎ 06742-2433 fax 06742-4826
✉ 56154

* 2 ♨ 45/60
* 23 ⚭ 80/90
[AE] [E] [⚙] [⊙] [⚐] [⌂] [⌂] [WC] [☺]

BOSEN Saarland   17

Merker Bostal (HCR)
Bostalstr 46
☎ 06852-6770
✉ 66625

1 ♨
19 ⚭
[⚓] [P] [☂] [⌂] [⌂] [WC] [⌘]

BOXBERG Baden-Württemberg   19

Zur Kanne (HCR)
Frankendomstr 50
☎ 0793-6239
✉ 97944

4 ♨
4 ⚭
[P] [☂]

Zum Schwanen (HCR)
Bahnhofstr 7
☎ 0793-376
✉ 97944

4 ♨
10 ⚭
[⊙] [P] [⌂] [WC] [TV] [⌘]

BRAUNLAGE Niedersachsen   14

Berliner Hof (HCR)
Elbingeröderstr 12
☎ 05520-427
✉ 38700

open 20.12 - 31.10
* 12 ♨ 31/43
* 14 ⚭ 70/86
[⊙] [♦] [P] [☂] [☂] [⌂] [WC] [☺]

72 GERMANY

Maritim (HCR)
Pfaffenstieg
☎ 05520-8050 fax 05520-3620
res nr 0221-219672
✉ 38700

48 ♨ 189/309
261 ⚏ 272/368
[icons]

Rust (HCR) AA ANWB
Am Brande 5
☎ 05583-831 fax 05583-864
✉ 38700

The Hotel Rust is situated on the outskirts of Hohegleiss where the wooded surroundings are ideal for walking. The bedrooms are well furnished and equipped with bath, shower, toilet and telephone - some have a south-facing balcony. From the terrace are fine views of the southern mountain range of the Harz.

open 20.12 - 31.10
* 4 ♨ 60/65
* 11 ⚏ 114/130
[icons]

BRAUNSCHWEIG Niedersachsen   8

Deutsches Haus (HR)
Burgpl 1
☎ 0531-44422 fax 0531-44421
✉ 38015

* 37 ♨ 129/147
* 48 ⚏ 198/222
[icons]

Mercure Atrium (HCR)
Berliner Pl 3
☎ 0531-70080 fax 0531-7008125
res nr 0531-7008131
✉ 38102

* 65 ♨ 130/250
* 65 ⚏ 150/340
[icons]

Mövenpick (HR) AA ANWB
Jöddenstraße 3
☎ 0531-48170 fax 0531-4817551
res nr 0130/852217
✉ 38100

The Mövenpick Hotel Braunschweig is situated in the historic town centre. It offers comfortable standard and deluxe bedrooms, and a number of apartments. Meals are served in the Mövenpick restaurant, the Welfenstübli; the Pub serves drinks in a relaxed atmosphere and live music is played regularly. There is a cake shop, and recreational facilities include a sauna with whirlpool, a swimming pool, solarium, massage and bicycle hire. The hotel is suitable for guests in wheelchairs, and meeting rooms are available.

* 54 ♨ 250/260 excl. breakfast
* 67 ⚏ 290/300 excl. breakfast
[icons]

Nord (HR)
Robert Boschstr 7
☎ 0531-310860 fax 0531-3108686
✉ 38112

* 21 ♨ 89/130
* 29 ⚏ 120/190
[icons]

BRAUNSCHWEIG/WENDEN Niedersachsen 8

Sport & Seminar Hotel (HCR) AA ANWB
Hauptstr 48 B
Braunschweig
☎ 05307-2090 fax 05307-209400
✉ 38110

The Sport and Seminar Hotel offers its guests plenty of opportunities for an active holiday. The rooms have modern furnishings and are equipped with good amenities. In addition to the many sports facilities, it offers massage and gymnastics. The restaurant, which has a view of the large hotel terrace and outdoor tennis court, is attractively furnished and offers a good choice of dishes. This beautiful area is good for walks.

* 7 ♨ 154/230
* 59 ⚏ 198/295
[icons]

GERMANY

Two good hotels situated close to the most beautiful part of the Rhine in the romantic valley of Lorelei.
In Boppard, 20 kilometres from Koblenz, acces to motorway 61.
**** BEST WESTERN

Bellevue Rheinhotel

- 95 comfortable rooms
- 'Rivièra' pool, sauna, fitness center
- 'Pfeffermühle' restaurant with specialities of the house
- hotel bar en beer cellar
- 9 recreation rooms

(300 metres distance) ** PARKHOTEL

- 66 efficiently equipped rooms
- large room in Garden
- Eberstube restaurant
- a 700 year old restaurant in the monastery crypt
- a unique feature is the large garden

......and everything is surrounded by woods

Our reservations office will be happy to provide you with further details, fax 06742-102602 or telephone:
Bellevue 06742-1020, Ebertor: 06742-2081, Rheinallee, 56154 Boppard.

See entries page 70 + 71

BREISACH/HOCHSTETTEN Baden-Württemberg   21

Adler (HR)   AA ANWB
Hochstettenstr 11
Breisach
☎ 07667-93930 fax 07667-7096
✉ 79206

There is a relaxed atmosphere in the Hotel Adler, which is set in peaceful and rural surroundings, and is easily accessible by car.
The rooms are well furnished and have bath, shower and toilet, the restaurant has a good menu with reasonable prices, and one can enjoy plenty of peace and quiet on the hotel terrace. Covered parking facilities are available.

* 1 ♒ -/80
* 23 ⚏ 100/-
🅔♒🅟🍴♨⚔🛌🅟🆆🅃🍽☺

BREMEN Bremen   7

Maritim Hotel & Congress Zentrum (HR)
Hollerallee 99
☎ 0421-37890 fax 0421-3789600
res nr 0221-219672
✉ 28215

10 ♒ 239/389
251 ⚏ 288/496
🅐🅔🅞🅔🍴♨⊙🅟🍴♨⚔🛌🅟🆆🅃🍽☺

Mercure Columbus (HCR)
Bahnhofspl 5-7
☎ 0421-14161 fax 0421-15369
res nr 0421-14161
✉ 28195

* 24 ♒ 140/220
* 124 ⚏ 160/270
🅐🅔🅞🅔🍴♨⚬⬥🅟🍴♨⚔🛌🅟🆆🅃🍽☺

Munte Am Stadtwald (HCR)
Parkallee 299
☎ 0421-22020 fax 0421-219876
✉ 28213

- ♒ 150/210
122 ⚏ 180/240
🅐🅔🅞🅔🍴♨⚬⬥🅟🍴♨⚔🛌🅟🆆🅃🍽☺

Zur Post (Best Western) (HR)
Bahnhofspl 11
☎ 0421-30590 fax 0421-3059591
res nr 0130-4455
✉ 28195

* 87 ♒ 157/197 excl. breakfast
* 109 ⚏ 187/257 excl. breakfast
🅐🅔🅞🅔🍴♨⊙♦🅟🍴♨⚔🛌🅟🆆🅃🍽☺

BREMERHAVEN Bremen   7

Naber (Best Western) (HCR)
Theodor Heuss Pl 1
☎ 0471-48770 fax 0471-4877999
res nr 0130-4455
✉ 27568

* 42 ♒ 160/165
* 57 ⚏ 190/240
🅐🅔🅞🅔🍴♨⊙🅟🍴♨⚔🛌🅟🆆🅃☺

BRETTEN Baden-Württemberg   18

Krone (HCR)
☎ 07252-2041 fax 07252-80598
✉ 75015

20 ♒
25 ⚏
🅐🅔🅞🅔🍴♨⚬⬥🅟🍴♨⚔🛌🅟🆆🅃🍽⬆☺

GERMANY

BRILON Nordrhein-Westfalen　　　12

Quellenhof (HR)　　　AA ANWB
Strackestr 12
☎ 02961-2045 fax
02961-2047
✉ 59929

The Hotel Quellenhof is centrally but peacefully located. The rooms in this family hotel have washing facilities, radio, TV and telephone. The rustic wine bar has a very relaxed atmosphere and the hotel also offers a swimming pool with a jet stream, skittle alley, table tennis, a solarium, a sauna and a gym.

* 8 ♂ 73/95
* 14 ♋ 110/150

AE ⓘ E ⚒ ♠ ⊙ P ⤴ 🏊 ≈ ↕ ◻ ◨ WC TV ⦿ ⊚

Waldhotel Brilon (HCR)　　　AA ANWB
Am Holsterloh 1
☎ 02961-3473 fax
02961-50470
✉ 59929

The Waldhotel Brilon is situated at an altitude of 530m in the Hochsauerland region. The peaceful location and healthy climate make it an ideal holiday hotel. All the rooms have en suite facilities, TV and telephone; the hotel has a sauna and solarium. There is a large sunny terrace with views of the green countryside, the restaurant serves trout from the hotel's own lake, and the surrounding area offers opportunities for winter sports.

* 4 ♂ 58/64
* 10 ♋ 94/106

AE ⓘ E ⚒ ♠ ♣ P ⤴ 🏊 ≈ ↕ ◻ ◨ WC TV ⦿ ⊚

BRUCHSAL Baden-Württemberg　　　18

Autobahnhotel Bruchsal West (HG)
An Der A5
☎ 07251-3321 fax 07251-81359
✉ 76646

8 ♂
55 ♋

AE ⓘ E ⚒ ♠ ♦ P ⤴ ↕ ◻ ◨ WC ⊚

Forst (HCR)　　　AA ANWB
Gottlieb Daimler Str 6
☎ 07251-16058 fax
07251-83994
✉ 76646

The Forst is a modern hotel, just a short distance away from the Frankfurt - Basel motorway. It is situated on the banks of a small lake, with a terrace and a sunbathing lawn right beside the water. The restaurant always offers a choice of seasonal dishes, and all the rooms feature a shower, toilet, colour TV and telephone.

* 4 ♂ 98/150
* 21 ♋ 150/180

AE ⓘ E ⚒ ♠ ♣ P ⤴ 🏊 ≈ ↕ ◻ ◨ WC TV ⦿ ⊚

Garni Trautwein (HG)　　　AA ANWB
Amalienstr 6
☎ 07251-2138 fax 07251-82838
✉ 76646

Although the Garni Trautwein is situated in the centre of Bruchsal, it is a peaceful establishment. All the rooms in this bed and breakfast hotel have en suite facilities. The area is good for cycling, and bicycles can be rented from the hotel.

* 6 ♂ -/75
* 9 ♋ -/110

AE E ♠ ⊙ P ⤴ 🏊 ↕ ◻ ◨ WC ⊚

BRÜHL Nordrhein-Westfalen　　　11

Treff Hansa Hotel Brühl (HR)
Römerstr 1
☎ 02232-2040 fax 02232-204523
✉ 50321

* - ♂ 195/275
* 160 ♋ 269/349

AE ⓘ E ⚒ ⊙ ♦ P ⤴ 🏊 ↕ ◻ ◨ WC TV ⦿ ⊚

BRUNNEN/SCHWANGAU Bayern　　　23

Huber (HCR)
Seestr 67
Schwangau
☎ 08362-81362 fax 08362-81811
✉ 87645

2 ♂ 50/65
18 ♋ 80/110

♠ 🚲 P ⤴ 🏊 ↕ ◻ ◨ WC TV ⊚

GERMANY

Martini (HCR)
Seestr 65
Schwangau
☎ 08362-8257
✉ 87645

5 🛏
13 🛏

🚶 🅿 📞 🍴 🛏 📺 🍽

BÜHLERTAL Baden-Württemberg 21

Badischer Löwe (HR)
Sessgasse 3
☎ 07223-74266 fax 07223-75757
✉ 77830

* 1 🛏 80/110
* 20 🛏 140/170

💳 🚶 🅿 📞 🍴 🛏 📺

Villa Maria (HR)
Laubenstr 52
☎ 07223-72313 fax 07223-75757
✉ 77830

* 4 🛏 45/80
* 14 🛏 76/110

💳 🚶 🅿 📞 🍴 🛏 📺

BULLAY Rheinland-Pfalz 17

Andries Sonneck (HP)
Brautrockstr 16
☎ 06542-2675
✉ 56859

2 🛏
10 🛏

🚶 🅿 📞

BURBACH Nordrhein-Westfalen 12

Wasserscheide (HR)
Dillenburgerstr 66
☎ 02736-8068 fax 02736-8478
✉ 5909

* 7 🛏 40/75
* 8 🛏 80/120

🚶 🅿 📞 🛏 📺 🍽

BURGBROHL Rheinland-Pfalz 12

Haus Elisabeth (HG)
Ringstr 13
☎ 02636-2451
✉ 56659

The Haus Elisabeth enjoys a fairly quiet location in rural wooded surroundings. The rooms are simple but pleasantly furnished and are well maintained, and most of them have private facilities. There is a large, attractive breakfast room.

* 1 🛏 35/-
* 3 🛏 70/-

🚶 🅿 📞 🍴 🛏 📺

CELLE Niedersachsen 8

Caroline Mathilde (HG)
Bremer Weg 37-43
☎ 05141-32023 fax 05141-32026
✉ 29223

open 05.01 - 23.12
* 11 🛏 110/150
* 33 🛏 135/220

💳 🚶 🅿 📞 🍴 🛏 📺

Schifferkrug (HR)
Speicherstr 9
☎ 05141-7015 fax 05141-6350
✉ 29221

Hotel Schifferkrug is situated on the edge of the small historic town of Celle. The establishment was built in 1865 and has a pleasant atmosphere throughout. The rooms have romantic-style furnishings and are equipped with en suite bathroom, radio, telephone and TV. It has an intimate restaurant where the menu offers a varied choice of delightful dishes and good wines.

1 🛏 70/88
12 🛏 110/155

🚶 🅿 📞 🍴 🛏 📺 🍽

76 GERMANY

CHAM Bayern 24

Randsberger Hof (HR)
Randsbergerhofstr 15
☎ 09971-1266 fax 09971-20299
✉ 93413

14 ♨
71 ⛨
🅰🅾🅴🈂🅿🍴🚻🛗🆒🚾

Garni Ratskeller (HG)
Am Kirchpl
☎ 09971-1441 fax 09971-2578
✉ 93413

* 5 ♨ 50/-
* 6 ⛨ -/90
🅰🅾🅴🈂🅿🚻🆒🚾📺

COBBENRODE Nordrhein-Westfalen 12

Maria Köster (HP) ♪
Olperstr 43
☎ 02973-3157
✉ 59889

* - ♨ 28/31
* 7 ⛨ 50/56
🅴🅿🍴🚻🆒🚾📺

COBURG Bayern 14

Blankenburg (HR)
Rosenauer Str 30
☎ 09561-75005 fax 09561-75674
✉ 96450

16 ♨
20 ⛨
🅰🅾🅴🈂🅿🚻🛗🆒🚾📺

COCHEM Rheinland-Pfalz 17

Alte Thorschenke (HCR) *AA ANWB*
Brückenstr 3
☎ 02671-7059 fax 02671-4202
✉ 56812

This hotel's name, 'Thor's Old Inn', speaks for itself; it is a hotel in the old-fashioned German tradition. The building is medieval, and the hotel has a relaxed and welcoming atmosphere. The traditional feel is enhanced by the use of antiques and objets d'art in every room of the Alte Thorschenke. The restaurant offers Mosel wine and a choice of specialities, with game and trout on the menu. The rooms have warm, domestic-style furnishings, and most feature a bath or a shower.

open 15.03 - 03.01
5 ♨ 75/145
39 ⛨ 115/215
🅰🅾🅴🈂🅿🍴🚻🆒🚾📺

Burg (HCR) *AA ANWB*
Moselpromenade 23
☎ 02671-7117 fax 02671-8336
✉ 56812

The Hotel Burg is attractively situated on the boulevard along the Mosel in the centre of Cochem. All the rooms in this hotel have en suite facilities. Guests can enjoy an excellent dinner in the restaurant and the *Konditorei* (bakery) serves delicious home-baked cakes. The hotel amenities include a sauna and solarium.

open 01.04 - 01.12
6 ♨ 65/85
42 ⛨ 96/200
🅰🅾🅴🈂🅿🚻🆒🚾📺

Noss (HCR) *AA ANWB*
Moselpromenade 17
☎ 02671-3612 fax 02671-5366
✉ 56812

The Hotel Noss is situated on the banks of the river Mosel. Some of the rooms have washing facilities. The restaurant serves international specialities and good wines, and there is also a *Bierstube*. Parking facilities are available.

open 01.02 - 15.11
4 ♨ 70/85
30 ⛨ 110/160
🅰🅾🅴🈂🅿🍴🚻🆒🚾

Panorama (HCR) *AA ANWB*
Klostergartenstr 44
☎ 02671-8430 fax 02671-3064
✉ 56812

The family-run Hotel Panorama enjoys a quiet location 1.5km from the town centre, just across the road from the Mosel. The entire decor, including the rooms, is in an attractive romantic style. Some of the rooms have a balcony with a panoramic view. Hotel amenities include a *Hallenbad*, sauna, solarium, garden, sunbathing lawn, billiards and table tennis. There are modern meeting facilities for up to 150 people.

GERMANY 77

Burg Hotel D-5590 Cochem/Mosel

A friendly holiday hotel with the typical charm of the Mosel area. 100 beds with shower/wc, some with balcony and television, four-poster beds. Excellent restaurant, own bakery, lift, indoor swimming pool, sauna, solarium. Guest House shower/wc and breakfast from DM 30 per person.

Moselpromenade 23, D-56821 Cochem/Mosel. Tel.: 02671-7117 or 1317. Telex 869 432 bucod. Fax: 02671-8336. Exit motorway Kaisersesch A48.

* 10 ♦ 80/95
* 35 ♦ 135/190

Parkhotel Landenberg (HCR)
Sehler Anlagen 1
☎ 02671-7110 fax 02671-8379
✉ 56812

The beautiful views, vineyards and authentic architecture make the Mosel valley a popular area to visit. The Parkhotel Landenberg is only a short distance from the banks of the Mosel. The hotel has a well maintained appearance and is furnished in a classical style. Rooms are equipped with a bath or a shower and have central heating and a telephone; amenities include a heated swimming pool and a sauna.

open 15.03 - 05.01
5 ♦ 90/110
19 ♦ 150/210

Am Rosenhügel (HG)
Valwigerstr 57
☎ 02671-1396 fax 02671-8116
✉ 56812

The Hotel am Rosenhügel is a bed and breakfast hotel which enjoys a quiet and beautiful location and has well furnished rooms all with en suite facilities. The garden has a pleasant terrace and the hotel has a gym. There is a parking garage available.

open 16.02 - 30.11
* 2 ♦ 60/80
* 21 ♦ 110/140

Zur Schönen Aussicht (HR)
Sehler Anlagen 22
☎ 02671-7232
✉ 56812

The family-run Hotel zur Schönen Aussicht is close to the banks of the Mosel and easily accessible by car and public transport. It is an ideal base for trips to the Eifel and the Hünsruck. All the rooms are well furnished with a shower and toilet, and offer fine views of the Mosel and the vineyard-covered mountains. There is a good restaurant with an extensive menu - changed every day - and wine list. Parking facilities are available.

open 10.01 - 23.12
* 2 ♦ 55/65
* 13 ♦ 70/140

Thul (HCR)
Brauselaystr 27
☎ 02671-7134 fax 02671-5367
✉ 56812

The Hotel Thul is situated in the Mosel region and has beautiful bedrooms with en suite facilities. Good food is served in the restaurant and *Konditorei* (bakery). Cochem has many splendid walking routes and →

guests can also visit one of the many wine tastings. Bicycles can be hired in the hotel and parking facilities are available.

open 01.03 - 30.11
* 4 ♫ 70/80
* 20 ♫ 120/150

Zur Winnenburg (HCR)
Endertstr 141
☎ 02671-4527 fax 02671-4523
✉ 56812

The traditional Hotel Zur Winnenburg is situated at the edge of the Wilde Endert valley; this is a popular walking region. Because of its convenient location, the hotel is easily accessible by car, the rooms are well furnished with shower and a toilet, and the restaurant serves game and trout specialities. The hotel has a terrace and sunbathing lawns, and parking facilities are available.

open 02.03 - 04.01
* 1 ♫ 55/90
* 9 ♫ 70/120

CREGLINGEN Baden-Württemberg 19

Krone (HR)
Hauptstr 12
☎ 07933-558 fax 07933-1444
✉ 6993

open 08.02 - 12.12
* 3 ♫ 38/75
* 10 ♫ 70/115

CUXHAVEN Niedersachsen 2

Seepavillon Donner Ringhotel (HCR)
Bei Der Alten Liebe 5
☎ 04721-5660 fax 04721-566130
✉ 27472

* 21 ♫ 66/115
* 24 ♫ 150/208

DAHN Rheinland-Pfalz 18

Zum Jungfernsprung (HG)
Pirmasenserstr 9
☎ 06391-3211
✉ 66994

10 ♫
10 ♫

DARMSTADT Hessen 18

Darmstädterhof (HCR)
Heidelberger Landstr 249
☎ 06151-54222 fax 06151-54243
✉ 64297

6 ♫
10 ♫

Hawerkaste (HG)
Elisabethenstr 39
☎ 06151-21143
✉ 64283

15 ♫
18 ♫

Maritim Konferenzhotel (HCR)
Rheinstr 105
☎ 06151-8780 fax 06151-893194
res nr 0221-219672
✉ 64295

146 ♫ 209/319
206 ♫ 272/398

Maritim Rhein Main Hotel (HR)
Am Kavalleriesand 6
☎ 06151-3030 fax 06151-303111
res nr 0221-219672
✉ 64295

* 84 ♫ 245/405
* 164 ♫ 298/480

GERMANY

Hotel 'Zur Winneburg'

Endertstrasse 141
D-5590 Cochem
Tel.: 02671-4527

Attractive, quietly located family hotel on the edge of the woods. Large sunny verandah, large parking area, rooms with shower, wc and some with balconies.
Bed and breakfast from DEM 40 to 60.
Half board from DEM 60 to 80.
Full board from DEM 75 to 95.

DARSCHEID Rheinland-Pfalz   17

Kucher's Landhotel (HCR)   AA ANWB
Karl Kaufmann Str 2
☎ 06592-629 fax 06592-3677
✉ 54552

Kucher's Landhotel is an attractively furnished family-run hotel set in beautiful surroundings. The comfortable bedrooms - some with a balcony - feature en suite facilities, TV and telephone. There is a choice of 2 restaurants serving gourmet lunches and dinners, and the hotel prides itself on a large wine cellar with over 700 different wines. There are many tourist attractions in the region, and cross-country skiing is popular here in the winter.

open 01.02 - 31.12
* 3 ♋ 60/-
* 11 ☞ 120/-
AE E ♁ ⚘ ☉ P ♌ ☂ ⏚ WC TV ⏛

DAUCHINGEN Baden-Württemberg   21

Landgasthof Fleig (HR)
Villingerstr 17
☎ 07720-5909 fax 07720-65089
✉ 78083

5 ♋ 55/60
13 ☞ 80/95
E ⚘ ☉ P ♌ ☂ ⏚ WC TV ⏛

DAUN Rheinland-Pfalz   17

Hommes Ringhotel Daun (HCR)   AA ANWB
Wirichstr 9
☎ 06592-538 fax 06592-8126
✉ 54542

The Hommes Ringhotel Daun is a majestic hotel, centrally situated in the small town of Daun, and easily accessible by car and public transport. The rooms have modern furnishings and are equipped with en suite facilities, telephone, radio, colour TV and minibar. The cosy restaurant offers a good menu with international dishes. There is an indoor swimming pool and a sauna. The garden has outdoor chess, table tennis and children's playground, and on-site parking is available..

open 08.02 - 06.01
* 12 ♋ 77/93
* 30 ☞ 134/166
AE ⓓ E ⚘ ☉ P ♌ ☂ ⏚ ⏛ WC ⏛

Horten (HP)
Am Wiesenborn 7
☎ 06592-3917
✉ 54550

8 ☞
⚘ P ♌ ⏚ WC

Schloßhotel Kurfürstliches Amtshaus (HR)
Dauner Burg
☎ 06592-3031 fax 06592-4942
✉ 54550

open 30.01 - 06.01
* 17 ♋ 115/160
* 25 ☞ 200/260
ⓓ E ⚘ ☉ P ♌ ☂ ⏚ ⏛ WC TV ⏛

GERMANY

Stadt Daun (HCR)   AA ANWB
Leopoldstr 14
☏ 06592-3555 fax 06592-3556
✉ 54550

The internationally known Hotel Stadt Daun is situated in the heart of the Volcan-eifel in the centre of Daun. All the rooms have shower/bath/toilet, telephone, minibar and radio, and TV on request. The hotel has an indoor swimming pool, sauna and solarium; guests can go dancing in the Kurcafé. Air conditioned meeting rooms are available.

* 4 ♨ 70/80
* 23 ⚭ 130/140

Thielen (HR)   AA ANWB
Triererstr
☏ 06592-2580
✉ 54550

Surrounded by lakes and lying between the rivers Rhine, Mosel and Ahr; the town of Daun is an excellent place to stay. The Hotel Thielen is quietly situated on the outskirts of the town and is ideal for holiday-makers and *Kur* guests. The rooms have modern furnishings and shower, toilet, radio and TV. Meeting rooms for 20 to 50 people are available.

open 01.04 - 28.02
4 ♨ 38/45
7 ⚭ 84/90

DEIDISHEIM *Rheinland-Pfalz*   18

Hebinger (HG)
Bahnhofstr 21
Deidisheim
☏ 06326-387 fax 06326-7494
✉ 67146

open 07.01 - 22.12
* 2 ♨ -/80
* 10 ⚭ -/140

DELECKE *Nordrhein-Westfalen*   12

Haus Kleis (HCR)   AA ANWB
Linkstr 32
☏ 02924-1874 fax 02924-84117
✉ 59519

Haus Kleis is set in tranquil and rural surroundings on the borders of Sauerland. The bedrooms are well equipped and some of them have been renovated. There is a peaceful terrace with wonderful views over the Mohnesee. Swimming, golf and walking are among the many recreational facilities available in the area.

1 ♨ 40/70
14 ⚭ 70/120

DENKENDORF *Bayern*   20

Post (HCR)
Hauptstr 14
☏ 08466-236
✉ 85095

10 ♨
60 ⚭

DERNAU *Rheinland-Pfalz*   17

Poppelreuter (HR)
Friedensstr 4
☏ 02643-1738
✉ 53507

1 ♨
3 ⚭

DERNBACH *Rheinland-Pfalz*   12

Alt Dernbach (HR)
Mittlestr 4
☏ 02689-7765
✉ 76581

1 ♨ 43/48
7 ⚭ 80/90

Country (HCR)
Hauptstr
☏ 02689-2990 fax 02689-299322
✉ 76857

28 🛏
116 🛌

DETMOLD/HIDDESEN Nordrhein-Westfalen   7
See advertisement page 83

Römerhof (HCR)   AA ANWB
Maiweg 37
Detmold
☏ 05231-88238 fax 05231-8132
✉ 32760

The Hotel Römerhof is situated in the quiet Teutoburger wood which is well known for its walks. All the rooms have washing facilities and there is both a TV room and library provided for evening entertainment. There is a lift and ample parking facilities are available.

* 3 🛏 85/115
* 16 🛌 135/195

DIERDORF Rheinland-Pfalz   12

Waldhotel (HR)   AA ANWB
B 413
☏ 02689-2088 fax 02689-7881
✉ 56269

As the name suggests, the Waldhotel is situated in a beautiful wooded area; all the rooms have en suite facilities, and there are fine views of the peaceful surroundings from the garden-terrace. The restaurant has a wide choice of good dishes on the menu. Recreational facilities include a sauna, and horse-riding nearby.

* 5 🛏 -/57
* 12 🛌 -/90

DIESSEN AM AMMERSEE Bayern   23

Seefelderhof (HR)
Alexander-Kösterweg 6
☏ 08807-1022 fax 08807-1024
✉ 86911

open 20.02 - 22.12
4 🛏 44/99
17 🛌 82/156

Strandhotel Diessen (HCR)
Jahnstr 10
☏ 08807-5038 fax 08807-8958
✉ 86911

open 01.03 - 15.12
4 🛏 80/120
9 🛌 114/180

DILLENBURG Hessen   12

Oranien (HG)
Am Untertor 1-3
☏ 02771-7085
✉ 35683

10 🛏
15 🛌

Am Wilhelmsplatz (HR)
Am Wilhelmspl 2 a
☏ 02771-5507 fax 02771-23705
✉ 35683

5 🛏 55/65
5 🛌 100/-

DINKELSBÜHL Bayern   19

Deutsches Haus (HCR)
Weinmarkt 3
☏ 09851-2346
✉ 91550

3 🛏
10 🛌

82 GERMANY

DONAUESCHINGEN Baden-Württemberg 21

Linde (HR) [AA] [ANWB]
Karlstr 18
☎ 0771-3048 fax 0771-3040
✉ 78166

Donaueschingen is the source of the river Donau, a beautiful area with over 100km of marked walking trails available. All the rooms in the hospitable Linde hotel have a shower, toilet, telephone and colour TV, and most have a minibar. The relaxed restaurant offers a full range of food from the very simple to the sophisticated. Parking facilities are available.

open 25.01 - 19.12
* 10 ♪ 78/98
* 11 ⚏ 130/160
⓪ E ≖ ◉ P ⏰ ⇅ 🗐 WC TV |◉| ⚑

DONAUWÖRTH/PARKSTADT Bayern 19

Parkhotel Donauwörth (HCR)
Sternschanzenstr 1
Donauwörth
☎ 0906-6037 fax 0906-23283
✉ 86609

* 22 ♪ 95/110
* 26 ⚏ 140/170
Æ ⓪ E ≖ 🗝 P ⏰ ⚐ ⚑ ⚒ ⇆ 🗐 WC TV |◉| ⚑

DORFGÜTINGEN/FEUCHTWANGEN Bayern 19

Landgasthof Zum Ross (HP)
Dorfgütingen
☎ 09852-9933
✉ 91555

open 14.01 - 26.10 + 04.11 - 23.12
3 ♪ 58/-
10 ⚏ 83/100
P ⏰ ⚐ 🗐 WC TV ⚑

DÖRNDORF Bayern 20

Gasthof Jura Café (HCR) [AA] [ANWB]
Hauptstr 9
☎ 08466-312 fax 08466-1353
✉ 85095

Gasthof Jura Café is a friendly hotel overlooking extensive meadows, within easy reach of the Nürnberg-München motorway, junction Denkenhof. This family-run hotel is suitable either for a stopover or for a longer stay. The rooms are clean and tidy with en suite facilities. The wooded surroundings make this a popular venue for walks.

open 01.11 - 15.10
* 2 ♪ 36/-
* 5 ⚏ 70/-
E ⇣ 🗝 ◆ P ⚐ 🗐 WC TV ⚑

Sonnenhang (HCR) [AA] [ANWB]
Hauptstr 8
☎ 08466-476 fax 08466-1093
✉ 85095

The peaceful Hotel Sonnenhang enjoys a sunny location 1.5km from the Denkendorf junction of the München-Nürnberg motorway, and is situated in the Altmühltal nature park where Roman remains are on display. Recreational facilities include swimming, tennis, horse riding and fishing. It is a well kept, hospitable hotel where all the rooms have en suite facilities. The restaurant offers good value for money.

2 ♪ -/48
43 ⚏ -/78
Æ ⓪ E ≖ ◆ P ⏰ ⚐ ⇆ 🗐 WC TV |◉| ⚑

DORNSTETTEN Baden-Württemberg 21

Löwen (HR)
Hauptstr 3
☎ 07443-6481
✉ 72280

7 ♪
26 ⚏
⚒ ◉ ⏰ ⚐ 🗐 WC TV |◉|

GERMANY 83

LIPPE
DETMOLD
eine wunderschöne Stadt...

... in the Teutoburger Forest (up to 500m above sea level), has a suitable hotel, guest house or holiday home for you, too. The many objects of interest at Detmold, such as the famous monument of Hermann in the Kneipp health resort Detmold-Hiddesen, the bird and flower park at Heiligenkirchen, the largest eagle observatory at Berlebeck, the largest open-air museum in Germany, the Lippe Regional Museum, the romantic old town centre with the residential palace (the residence of the 'Prins zur Lippe') will astonish you. Naturally you can also book economical holiday programmes at Detmold, such as a walking or cycling holiday.

Information:
Fremdenverkehrsamt,
Rathaus am Markt,
Postfach 2761,
32754 Detmold.
Tel: 05231-977 327-8,
Fax: 977 299

See entry page 81

DÖRRENBACH Rheinland-Pfalz 18

Hubertus Klause (HCR)
Dörrenbach 42
☎ 06343-7544
✉ 76889

4 🛏
15 🛌
⊙ P 🅿 🛎 ⚐ 🚻 🍽

DORSTEN Nordrhein-Westfalen 11

Schloßhotel Lembeck (HCR)
Schloß 1
☎ 02369-7213 fax 02369-77370
✉ 46286

* 1 🛏 89/-
* 9 🛌 118/178
AE ⊙ E 🗺 🔑 🏧 P 🛎 🍽 🚻

DORTMUND Nordrhein-Westfalen 12

Esplanade (HG)
Bornstr 4-6
☎ 0231-528931 fax 0231-529536
✉ 44135

* 21 🛏 130/150
* 29 🛌 150/180
AE ⊙ E 🗺 ⊙ ◆ P 🚻 🍽 🅿 WC 🛎

Holiday Inn Römischer Kaiser (HCR)   AA ANWB
Olpe 2
☎ 0231-543200 fax 0231-574354
res nr 0130-815131
✉ 44135

The Holiday Inn Römischer Kaiser is situated in the centre of Dortmund. All the rooms and suites have en suite bathroom with hairdryer, a minibar, telephone with direct dialling facilities, cable TV, radio, safe and a trouser press. There is a floor for non-smoking guests, a VIP floor, and a room for disabled visitors. The hotel has a fitness room and a car-parking service.

* 76 🛏 235/295 excl. breakfast
* 50 🛌 295/355 excl. breakfast
AE ⊙ E 🗺 ⊙ P 🛎 🎿 🚻 🍽 🅿 WC TV 🍴 🛎

Königshof (HG)   AA ANWB
Königswall 4-6
☎ 0231-57041 fax 0231-57040
✉ 44137

The Hotel Königshof is located at the edge of the town centre, 250m from the station. All the rooms have en suite facilities, radio, TV and telephone. Whether you are a business traveller, a tourist, or in a group, the friendly family atmosphere remains the same. The hotel has meeting rooms for up to 40 people, and there is parking near the hotel.

* 18 🛏 145/155
* 27 🛌 168/178
AE ⊙ E 🗺 ⊙ ◆ P 🚻 🍽 🅿 WC TV 🛎

GERMANY — 84

Haus Mentler (HR)
Schneiderstr 1
☎ 0231-731788 fax 0231-730043
✉ 44229

8 ♌
8 ⌘
⊙ E ⌬ ⊙ ◆ P ♒ ⌨ ⌸ ▢ WC TV ⦿ ☏

DORTMUND/HOHENSYBURG Nordrhein-Westfalen   12

Landhaus Syburg (Best Western) (HR)   AA ANWB
Westhofenerstr 1
Dortmund
☎ 0231-77450 fax 0231-774421
res nr 0130-4455
✉ 4600

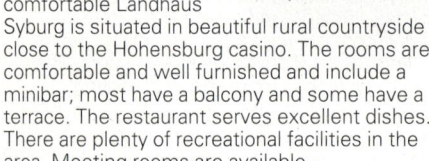

Hohensyburg is the southern-most suburb of Dortmund. The comfortable Landhaus Syburg is situated in beautiful rural countryside close to the Hohensburg casino. The rooms are comfortable and well furnished and include a minibar; most have a balcony and some have a terrace. The restaurant serves excellent dishes. There are plenty of recreational facilities in the area. Meeting rooms are available.

DREIEICH Hessen   18

Dorint Dreieich (HCR)
Eisenbahnstr 200
☎ 06103-6060 fax 06103-63019
res nr 0130-6605
✉ 63303

* 8 ♌ 193/310
* 84 ⌘ 250/390
AE ⊙ E ⌬ ⌨ ♄ ⊙ P ♒ ⌬ ⇄ ♉ ▢ ▢ WC TV ⦿ ☏

DROLSHAGEN Nordrhein-Westfalen   12

Auf dem Papenberg (HP)
Auf Dem Papenberg 15
☎ 02761-71210
✉ 57489

4 ♌
6 ⌘
E ♄ P ⌒ ♒ ▢ WC ⦿ ✕

DROLSHAGEN/ÖRINGSHAUSEN Nordrhein-Westfalen   12

Becker (HP)
Am Heliken 6
Drolshagen
☎ 02761-3174
✉ 57489

* - ♌ -/30
* 4 ⌘ -/60
AE ⊙ E ⌬ ♄ P ⌒ ♒ ⇄ ⌨ ▢ WC TV ⦿ ☏

DROLSHAGEN/SCHREIBERSHOF Nordrhein-Westfalen   12

Zur Alten Mühle (HCR)
Listerstr 1
Drolshagen
☎ 02761-6132
✉ 57489

2 ♌ -/36
10 ⌘ -/72
♠ ⊛ P ♒ ▢ ▢ WC

DUDELDORF Rheinland-Pfalz   17

Romantik Hotel Zum Alten Brauhaus (HR)   AA ANWB
D. Stadttor a/d Kirche
☎ 06565-2057 fax 06565-2125
✉ 54647

Dudeldorf is a historic 600 year-old medieval town in the Eifel. The Romantik Hotel Zum Alten Brauhaus is situated in the town centre and is easy accessible. The rooms are stylishly furnished and have all amenities. The pleasant restaurant offers a wide choice of dishes and various specialities. There is a historic pavilion in the hotel grounds, and parking facilities are available.

open 01.02 - 19.12
* 5 ♌ 120/140
* 10 ⌘ 180/240
AE ⊙ E ⌬ ♄ ⊙ P ♒ ▢ ▢ WC TV ⦿ ☏

DUDERSTADT Niedersachsen 13

Zum Löwen (HR)
Marktstr 30
☎ 05527-3072 fax 05527-72630
✉ 37115

open 10.01 - 31.12
* 8 ♦ 120/240
* 28 ♦ 220/340

DUISBURG Nordrhein-Westfalen 11

Sittardsberg (HR)
Sittardsberger Allee 10
☎ 0203-700001 fax 0203-701125
✉ 47249

* 11 ♦ 79/169
* 29 ♦ 109/215

Steigenberger Duisburger Hof (HR)
König Heinrich-Pl
☎ 0203-331021 fax 0203-339847
res nr 069-663080
✉ 47051

open 01.01 - 22.12
* 34 ♦ 190/290
* 77 ♦ 230/420

DÜLMEN Nordrhein-Westfalen 12

Am Markt (HCR)
Marktstr 21
☎ 02594-2388 fax 02594-85235
✉ 48249

open 03.01 - 17.12
* 10 ♦ 55/78
* 10 ♦ 95/125

Zum Wildpferd (HR)
Münsterstr 52
☎ 02594-5063 fax 02594-85235
✉ 48249

open 03.01 - 17.12
* 12 ♦ 55/135
* 25 ♦ 95/255

DÜSSELDORF Nordrhein-Westfalen 11

Capital of Nordrhein-Westfalen, Düsseldorf is a showcase of commercial wealth. Instead of old churches and monumental buildings, the skyline is a dazzling display of modern commerce like the elegant Thyssen skyscraper. Headquarters of many of the great Ruhr industries, Düsseldorf has also attracted many Japanese firms which have made it the base of their European operations, and the city's Japanese community is the largest in Europe. The many parks, gardens and pedestrian areas are a pleasant feature of the city, and visitors can stroll for hours across the city without crossing a road. Theatre, music, opera and cabaret all thrive in Düsseldorf, and the city's galleries are outstanding; the collection of Paul Klee paintings in the Kunstsammling Nordrhein-Westfalen is the biggest in the country.

Börsen (HG)
Kreuzstr 19 a
☎ 0211-363071 fax 0211-365338
res nr 0228-2697728
✉ 40210

* 25 ♦ 167/184
* 50 ♦ 238/265

Eden (Best Western) (HR)   AA ANWB
Adersstr 29-31
☎ 0211-38970 fax 0211-3897777
res nr 0130-4455
✉ 40215

The Hotel Eden is set in the centre of Düsseldorf, only 2 minutes' walk from the shopping street Königsallee. It has luxurious rooms equipped with modern facilities. The entrance and conference rooms have recently been renovated. The hotel has an inviting bar and restaurant, and there is also a crèche available.

open 04.01 - 21.12
* 62 ♦ 135/362 excl. breakfast
* 68 ♦ 135/412 excl. breakfast

Esplanade (HR)
Fürstenpl 17
☎ 0211-375010 fax 0211-374032
✉ 40215

* 24 ♦ 227/-
* 57 ♦ 268/-

86 GERMANY

Graf Adolf (Best Western) (HG) AA ANWB
Stresemannpl 1
℡ 0211-35540 fax
0211-354120
res nr 0130-4455
✉ 40210

Hotel Graf Adolf is in the centre of cosmopolitan Düsseldorf, only 5 minutes' walk from the famous Königsallee. It has well equipped rooms and serves a generous breakfast buffet. Guests can enjoy a apéritif and night cap in the pub, or have a meal in the pleasant bistro. The hotel has excellent function and conference facilities and its own parking garage.

* 58 ♬ 190/295
* 97 ♭ 260/395
AE ◉ E ⎓ ≿ ⊙ ⏿ ⇑ ⇅ ⊩ ▬ ⍗ WC TV ⦿ ⊗

Günnewig Savoy (HCR)
Oststr 128
℡ 0211-360336 fax 0211-356642
✉ 40211

* 30 ♬ 227/-
* 100 ♭ 313/-
AE ◉ E ⎓ ≿ ⊙ ⏿ ≘ ⇅ ⊩ ▬ WC TV ⦿ ⊗

Holiday Inn Düsseldorf Königsallee AA ANWB
(HCR)
Graf Adolf Pl 10
℡ 0211-38480 fax
0211-3848390
res nr 0130-815131
✉ 40213

This Holiday Inn is situated in the centre of Düsseldorf and stands on the famous Königsallee. Because of its position it is the ideal venue for both business people and tourists. The rooms are furnished to a high standard and equipped with modern amenities. The Düsseldorfer restaurant serves a range of regional and international dishes. Underground parking facilities are available.

* 79 ♬ 295/445 excl. breakfast
* 98 ♭ 340/495 excl. breakfast
AE ◉ E ⎓ ⊙ ⏿ ⇑ ⇅ ⊩ ▬ WC TV ⊗

Imperial (HG) AA ANWB
Venloerstr 9
℡ 0211-4921908 fax
0211-4982778
✉ 40477

The comfortable Hotel Imperial is situated within easy reach of the centre of Düsseldorf. The rooms have private toilet, shower/bath, telephone, and are fully sound proofed. Breakfast is served in the pleasant dining room. The hotel has an underground parking garage.

open 06.01 - 21.12
* 18 ♬ 104/164
* 22 ♭ 149/229
AE ◉ E ⎓ ⊙ ◆ P ⏿ ⇅ ⊩ ▬ ⍗ WC TV

DÜSSELDORF/RATINGEN Nordrhein-Westfalen
11

Holiday Inn (HR) AA ANWB
Broichhofstr 3
Ratingen
℡ 02102-4560 fax
02102-456444
res nr 0130-815131
✉ 40882

The Holiday Inn is near the airport and is suitable for both commercial travellers and tourists. The rooms are comfortably furnished and fully soundproof. It has a pleasant restaurant with good cuisine, and there are facilities for playing chess in the open air or relaxing in the swimming pool.

* 46 ♬ 295/350 excl. breakfast
* 153 ♭ 350/410 excl. breakfast
AE ◉ E ⎓ ≿ ◆ P ⏿ ⚓ ≘ ⊩ ▬ WC TV ⦿ ⊗

GERMANY 87

ECHTERNACHERBRÜCK Rheinland-Pfalz   17

Zum Golfstübchen (HP)   AA ANWB
Bitburgerstr 1
☎ 06525-210
✉ 54668

The comfortable hotel-pension Zum Golfstübchen is situated in the heart of the German/Luxembourg nature park, about 5 minutes' walk from the well known resort of Echternach. The rooms have en suite facilities, TV connection and a seating area. Hotel guests have 2 public lounges, children's playground and minigolf. During the holiday season the hotel organises special barbecue evenings.

* 2 ♦ 48/69
* 10 ♦ 76/118

EDENKOBEN Rheinland-Pfalz   18

Alte Kanzlei (HR)
Weinstr 120
☎ 06323-3983
✉ 67480

* - ♦ 50/60
* 4 ♦ 90/110

EDIGER-ELLER Rheinland-Pfalz   17

Moselromantik Zum Löwen (HCR)   AA ANWB
Moselweinstr 23
☎ 02675-208 fax 02675-214
✉ 56814

The Hotel Moselromantik Zum Löwen lies in the middle of the small wine-growing town of Ediger-Eller, on the road which runs alongside the Mosel. The terrace at the sunny front of the hotel offers fine views of the river and vineyards. The rooms are well maintained and have shower/bath and toilet; some have a balcony. The restaurant serves game specialities, complemented with wine from the hotel's own vineyard.

* 4 ♦ 58/95
* 26 ♦ 100/190

Weinhaus Oster (HR)   AA ANWB
Moselweinstr 61
☎ 02675-232 fax 02675-1570
✉ 56814

The comfortably furnished Weinhaus Oster is situated on the Mosel and has a fine view of the river. The hotel rooms have a bath, shower, toilet, radio and/or TV sockets. There is also a sun terrace. The hotel organises wine-tasting events in the 200-year old rough-stoned cellar. Spacious parking facilities for coaches and car are available.

open 15.03 - 30.11 + 26.12 - 03.01
* 1 ♦ 50/70
* 13 ♦ 84/120

EGESTORF Niedersachsen   8

Zu den Acht Linden (HCR)
Alte Dorfstr 1
☎ 04175-450 fax 04175-743
✉ 31848

* 8 ♦ -/85
* 23 ♦ 120/195

EHR Rheinland-Pfalz   17

Alter Posthof (HCR)
Hunsrückhöhenstr 3
☎ 06747-6276
✉ 56357

12 ♦

EICHSTATT Bayern   20

Adler (HG)
Marktpl 22-24
☎ 08421-6767 fax 08421-8283
✉ 85072

open 15.01 - 15.12
* 4 ♦ 110/140
* 28 ♦ 165/195

GERMANY

EISENSCHMITT Rheinland-Pfalz   17

Molitorsmühle (HR)   AA ANWB
☎ 06567-581 fax 06567-580
✉ 54533

The Hotel Molitorsmühle is beautifully situated by the shores of a lake, and there are plenty of opportunities to fish or walk in the nearby woods. The rooms have good facilities, and after a game of tennis, guests can relax in the sauna with solarium or swim in the hotel's pool. The hotel has a restaurant, and bicycles are available for hire.

open 16.02 - 09.01
* 10 ♪ 65/90
* 22 ♫ 120/210

EITORF Rheinland-Pfalz   12

Steffens (HR)   AA ANWB
Ottersbachtalstr 15
☎ 02243-6224
✉ 53783

The Haus Steffens is situated in Eitorf, which is well known for its timbered houses and surrounding woodlands. The hotel is well kept and the rooms are modern; all are equipped with a shower, toilet and telephone, and most have a balcony. The hotel has a skittle alley, sauna, solarium and a gym.

5 ♪ 45/50
9 ♫ 86/96

EMMELSHAUSEN Rheinland-Pfalz   17

Tannenhof (HP)   AA ANWB
Simmernerstr 21
☎ 06747-7654 fax 06747-8694
✉ 56281

The cosy Hotel Tannenhof is quietly situated on the edge of the woods and provides a pleasant stay throughout the year. The rooms are attractively furnished and have shower, toilet, telephone, minibar and TV socket. The hotel has a swimming pool and a sauna.

* - ♪ 75/80
* 15 ♫ 105/110

ENGEN Baden-Württemberg   21

Berggasthof Hegaublick (HR)
Hegaublick 4
☎ 07733-8754
✉ 78234

3 ♪
5 ♫

EPPSTEIN/VOCKENHAUSEN Hessen   18

Nassauer Hof (HR)   AA ANWB
Hauptstr 104
Vockenhausen
☎ 06198-1444 fax 06198-590222
res nr 06198-59020
✉ 65817

The Hotel Nassauerhof is situated on a fairly busy street in Vockenhausen. Some rooms have private toilet and shower; there is also a restaurant, TV lounge and a children's playground. Parking facilities are available.

open 17.01 - 01.01
* 4 ♪ 85/100
* 6 ♫ 120/140

GERMANY

ERLANGEN Bayern 20

Rangau (HR) AA ANWB
Röttenbacherstr 9
☎ 09135-8086
✉ 91056

Rangau is a hospitable family-run hotel, peacefully situated in the wooded Frankenland. Well marked walking routes and a beautiful lake make this a very attractive area for tourists. The hotel rooms are well furnished and have a shower and toilet; the restaurant has a good menu, and spacious parking facilities are available.

* 5 ♬ 45/60
* 35 ☎ 65/90

ESLOHE Nordrhein-Westfalen 12

Forellenhof Poggel (HCR)
Homertstr 21
☎ 02973-6721 fax 02973-6811
res nr 02973-6271
✉ 59889

* 4 ♬ 55/65
* 16 ☎ 110/120

ESLOHE/WENHOLTHAUSEN Nordrhein-Westfalen 12

Landhotel Sauerländerhof (HR) AA ANWB
Südstr 35
Wenholthausen
☎ 02973-777 fax 02973-2363
✉ 59889

The Landhotel Sauerlanderhof is situated in the nature park of Homert and is a comfortable base for seeing this beautiful area. It is a country hotel where all rooms have their own toilet and shower, half of them also have a TV. The restaurant offers a choice of Westphalian specialities, and there is a terrace with trees, a swimming pool and sauna.

open 22.03 - 21.12 + 26.12 - 28.02
* 4 ♬ 69/89
* 17 ☎ 128/190

ESSEN Nordrhein-Westfalen 11

Arcade Essen (HR)
Hollestr 50
☎ 0201-24280 fax 0201-2428600
res nr 06196-483800
✉ 45127

* 24 ♬ 120/150 excl. breakfast
* 120 ☎ 150/150 excl. breakfast

Mövenpick (HR) AA ANWB
Am Hauptbahnhof 2
☎ 0201-17081 fax 0201-1708173
res nr 0130-852217
✉ 45127

The Mövenpick Hotel Essen is situated in the city centre, opposite the station and 35 minutes from Düsseldorf airport. All the rooms are comfortably and fully furnished. The hotel has a choice of 2 restaurants: the Mövenpick restaurant Au Premier 'La Pêcherie', which specialises in seafood; and Le Bistro. Jimmy's Bar serves drinks. There are meeting rooms, and the hotel is suitable for guests in wheelchairs.

* 50 ♬ 200/250 excl. breakfast
* 141 ☎ 260/290 excl. breakfast

ESSEN/KETTWIG Nordrhein-Westfalen 11

Schloß Hugenpöt (HCR)
August Thyssenstr 51
Essen
☎ 0201-12040 fax 0201-120450
✉ 45127

* 5 ♬ 225/335
* 14 ☎ 285/435

ETTAL Bayern 23

Benediktenhof (HCR)
Zieglerstr 1
☎ 08822-4637
✉ 82488

1 ♬
16 ☎

GERMANY

ETTENHEIM Baden-Württemberg 21

Zum Ochsen (HR) AA ANWB
Kirschstr 3
☎ 07822-1333
✉ 77955

The Hotel zum Ochsen is situated in the historic baroque town of Ettenheim. It is well placed for walking excursions and day trips to the Schwarzwald and the Alsace region. The hotel is well furnished; some rooms have their own toilet and shower. The restaurant serves a range of good dishes, and ample parking facilities are available.

3 ♦ -/35
8 ♦ 70/92
⦿ P 🕭 🕭 WC TV ⦿ ⦿ ⦿

ETTLINGEN Baden-Württemberg 18

Holder (HR)
Bulacherstr./ Lindenstr
☎ 07243-16008 fax 07243-79595
✉ 76275

12 ♦
18 ♦
AE E ⦿ P 🕭 🕭 🕭 ⦿ 🕭 WC TV ⦿

EUTIN Schleswig-Holstein 3

Romantik Hotel Voss Haus (HCR)
Vosspl 6
☎ 04521-1797 fax 04521-1357
✉ 23701

1 ♦ 95/105
10 ♦ 170/190
AE ⦿ E ⥺ ⦿ ♦ P ⦿

Wittler (HCR)
Bahnhofstr 28
☎ 04521-2347
✉ 23701

9 ♦
20 ♦
AE ⦿ E ⥺ ⦿ P 🕭 🕭 🕭 🕭 WC TV ⦿ ⦿

FALLINGBOSTEL Niedersachsen 7

Sanssouci (HCR)
Tietlingen 4
☎ 05162-3048 fax 05162-6742
✉ 29664

open 01.03 - 31.01
* 2 ♦ 90/95
* 10 ♦ 130/140
AE E ⥺ ⦿ P 🕭 🕭 🕭 WC TV ⦿

FARCHANT Bayern 23

Föhrerhof (HR)
Frickenstr 2
☎ 08821-6640 fax 08821-61340
✉ 82490

open 01.02 - 14.01
* 10 ♦ 52/59
* 11 ♦ 94/158
⥺ P 🕭 🕭

FELSBERG Hessen 13

Ratskeller (HCR)
Markt 1
☎ 05662-2050
✉ 34587

6 ♦
⥺ ⦿ P 🕭 WC ⦿

FEUCHT Bayern 20

Rasthaus Nürnberg (MT)
☎ 09128-3444 fax 09128-12318
✉ 90537

18 ♦
36 ♦
⦿ P 🕭 🕭 🕭 🕭 WC

FEUCHTWANGEN Bayern 19

Romantikhotel Greifen Post (HR) AA ANWB
Marktpl 8
☎ 09852-2002 fax 09852-4841
✉ 91555

The atmospheric Romantik Hotel Greifen Post is situated on the Romantische Strasse and designed entirely in period style, including the public rooms with their open fireplaces. The rooms, some of which

are in Renaissance and Louis-XV style, are spacious and comfortable; they are equipped with colour TV, radio, telephone, minibar, hairdryer, and trouser press. The hotel serves a comprehensive breakfast buffet and has an excellent restaurant. There is a swimming pool, sauna and parking garage.

* 6 ♫ 129/155
* 35 ⚏ 185/250
🆎 ⓘ 🅴 ⚒ ♨ ⊙ 🍴 ⚓ 🍽 🛏 🚻 📺 🍽

FINNENTROP/FRETTER Nordrhein-Westfalen 12

Zur Post (HP)
Esloherstr 210
Finnentrop
☎ 02724-310 fax 02724-8552
✉ 57413

AA ANWB

The Hotel zur Post is a friendly hotel with a firm family tradition dating back to 1805. Facilities include a lounge, TV rooms, a sun terrace and a sauna. The south-facing rooms are quiet and have a bath, shower, toilet, seating area, telephone and TV connection.

* 4 ♫ 30/58
* 8 ⚏ 60/90
🅴 ♨ ⊙ 🅿 🍴 🍽 🚻 📺 🍽 ⤴ 🐕

See advertisement page 93

FINSTERWEILING Bayern 20

Schwarze Laaber (HP)
☎ 09182-440
✉ 8436

2 ♫ 35/38
8 ⚏ 56/60
🅴 ♨ 🅿 🍴 🍽 🚻 🍽 ⤴ 🐕

FISCHEN IM ALLGÄU Bayern 22

Burgmühle (HG)
Auf Der Insel 4
☎ 08326-1898 fax 08326-7352
✉ 87536

open 18.12 - 01.11
* 5 ♫ 65/106
* 20 ⚏ 118/280
♨ 🅿 🍴 🍽 🚻 📺 🍽 ⤴ 🐕

GERMANY 91

FLENSBURG Schleswig-Holstein 2

Am Rathaus (HG)
Rotestr 32-34
☎ 0461-17333 fax 0461-181382
✉ 24937

open 04.01 - 20.12
* 2 ♫ 83/96
* 40 ⚏ 135/145
🅴 ⊙ 🅿 🍴 🍽 🚻 🍽

FORBACH Baden-Württemberg 21

Löwen (HR)
Haubtstr 9
☎ 07228-2229 fax 07228-3633
✉ 76594

AA ANWB

An easy atmosphere pervades this comfortable, well kept, family-run hotel. Most of the rooms are furnished in the local traditional style and have a shower. There is a peaceful sunbathing terrace, as well as a skittle alley and table tennis. The Löwen Hotel is a good base for winter sports.

open 01.12 - 31.10
* 3 ♫ 26/37
* 17 ⚏ 53/73
🅴 ♨ 🅿 🍴 🍽 🚻 🍽

See advertisement page 93

Schwarzenbach (HR)
Schwarzenbachtalsperre
☎ 07228-2459
✉ 76594

8 ♫
25 ⚏
♨ 🅿 🍴 🍽 🚻 🍽

FRANKENTHAL IN DER PFALZ Rheinland-Pfalz 18

Post (HG)
Eisenbahnstr 2
☎ 06233-27217 fax 06233-27026
✉ 67227

* 6 ♫ 50/70 excl. breakfast
* 23 ⚏ 90/110 excl. breakfast
🆎 ♨ ⊙ ◆ 🅿 🍴 🍽 🚻 📺 ⤴

FRANKFURT AM MAIN Hessen 18

A trade centre since Roman times, Frankfurt today is Germany's financial capital, the home of the mighty Bundesbank, with a battalion of skyscrapers near the river Main. But this city is more than a financial centre: there is much to interest visitors, and the city's prosperity supports a wealth of culture, including fine opera, and commerce and literature join hands in the city's annual book fair - the largest in the world. Some of Frankfurt's central area was badly rebuilt after World War II, but there are many notable sights: the neo-classical opera house has been impressively restored (though operas are now staged elsewhere); the imposing 15th-century Eschenheimer Turm is one of the 42 towers that used to ring the city; nearby is the Börse, and the Goethehouse, the handsome family house where the poet Goethe was born and brought up, has been restored after wartime damage and now houses a museum. The lofty Gothic tower of the Dom overlooks a carefully restored cobbled square of half-timbered buildings, and just to the east is an interesting mix of ancient and modern - the ruins of a Carolignian palace and a Roman bath contrast with the new glass-walled Kultur-Schirn. Clustered around the river is a collection of interesting museums, including the new Jewish museum, a museum of sculpture, an important art museum, and a postal museum.

See city plan on page 40.

Altéa Hotel & Residenz (HCR)
Voltastr 29
Frankfurt
℡ 069-79260 fax 069-79261606
res nr 06196-483220
✉ 60486

1 ♪
425 ♫

Arcade Hotel Frankfurt (HR)
Speicherstr 3-6
Frankfurt
℡ 069-273030 fax 069-237024
✉ 60327
City Plan C5

20 ♪ 145/184
180 ♫ 190/238

Continental (HR)
Baselerstr 56
Frankfurt
℡ 069-230341 fax 069-232914
res nr 069-250840
✉ 60329
City Plan C5

* 39 ♪ 155/200
* 40 ♫ 220/270

Florentina (HG)
Westendstr 23
Frankfurt
℡ 069-746044 fax 069-747924
✉ 60325
City Plan B/C

open 06.01 - 21.12
* 17 ♪ 80/160
* 18 ♫ 200/300

Hessischer Hof (HR)
Friedrich Ebert Anlage 40
Frankfurt
℡ 069-75400 fax 069-7540924
res nr 069-7540911
✉ 60325
City Plan B4

* 50 ♪ 240/545 excl. breakfast
* 53 ♫ 300/605 excl. breakfast

Hoiday Inn Crowne Plaza (HCR)
Mailänderstr 1
Frankfurt
℡ 069-68020 fax 069-6802333
res nr 0130-815131
✉ 60598

* 154 ♪ 290/410 excl. breakfast
* 250 ♫ 380/520 excl. breakfast

Imperial am Palmgarten (Best Western) (HCR)
Sophienstr 40
Frankfurt
℡ 069-7930030 fax 069-79300388
res nr 0130-4455
✉ 60487
City Plan A2

The Imperial is a first-rate hotel, situated near the centre and the exhibition buildings. Together with excellent facilities and hospitality and spacious and comfortable rooms, it has all the necessary

GERMANY

Gasthof und Pension »Zur Post«

South-Sauerland in Homert scenic park close to Biggesee.

Gasthof und Pension Zur Post

Owner: Schulte family, since 1805
Renovated hotel and boarding house with friendly atmosphere. Rooms with shower and wc, balcony, all giving on to the garden. Sunbathing meadow, table tennis facilities, sauna, solarium, lounge with colour television, 300 metres from the woods and delightful walks. Bed and breakfast from DEM 30, half board from DEM 40.
Ask for our folder.
**Esloher Strasse 210, 57413 Finnentrop-Fretter
P.O.Box 522, 57408 Finnentrop-Fretter
Telephone 02724-310. Fax: 02724-8552**

See entry page 91

ingredients for a successful stay. The restaurant serves both French and international cuisine. The hotel also has a range of conference facilities available.

* - ♫ 150/-
* 60 ⌂ 190/480

Maingau (HR)
Schifferstr 38
Frankfurt
☎ 069-617001 fax 069-620790
✉ 60594
City Plan E5

The Hotel Maingau is situated 11km from Frankfurt's airport, and is ideal for both business travellers and visitors to the famous annual book fair. The rooms offer comfortable accommodation, and there is a restaurant on the premises - a good medium-class hotel.

* 45 ♫ 120/150
* 52 ⌂ 155/190

Meyn (HG)
Grüneburgweg 4
Frankfurt
☎ 069-590170 fax 069-555382
✉ 60322

The Hotel Meyn is a simple hotel situated in the centre of Frankfurt. The rooms are furnished in a functional style and have en suite facilities, TV, telephone and minibar. The hotel has a breakfast room, and there are plenty of good restaurants nearby. The listed prices are available only to AA and ANWB members.

* 5 ♫ 85/145
* 25 ⌂ 115/175

Gasthof · Pension
»Zum Löwen«

*Proprietor: G. Merkl and family
P.O.Box 1110, 76594 Forbach, Germany
Telephone: 07228-22 29. Fax: 07228-36 33*

Quiet location right next to the historic wooden bridge. Some rooms with shower/WC. Sunny terrace for sunbathing. Lift. 12 rooms with balcony. 40 beds. B&B DEM 26.50 - 35.50 per person. Cosy dining room. Lounge with television. Boat rental. Car park.

Send for our brochure.

See entry page 91

94 GERMANY

Mövenpick Parkhotel Frankfurt (HCR) AA ANWB
Wiesenhüttenpl 28-38
Frankfurt
☏ 069-26970 fax 069-2697884
res nr 0130-852217
✉ 60329
City Plan C4

Behind the imposing and historic frontage of the Mövenpick Parkhotel Frankfurt, guests are provided with comfort and service. The cosy rooms are prettily decorated and equipped with en suite facilities. The hotel has a fitness room, sauna, solarium and several restaurants. There is a happy hour in the nostalgic Casablanca bar from 17.00 until 19.00.

* 89 ♟ 298/548 excl. breakfast
* 210 ♟ 398/548 excl. breakfast

National (Best Western) (HR)
Baselerstr 50
Frankfurt
☏ 069-273940 fax 069-234460
res nr 0130-4455
✉ 60329
City Plan C5

* 27 ♟ 169/233
* 43 ♟ 283/394

Pullman Savigny (HR)
Savignystr 14-16
Frankfurt
☏ 069-75330 fax 069-7533175
✉ 60325
City Plan C4

53 ♟ 130/325 excl. breakfast
71 ♟ 170/380 excl. breakfast

Queens International (HCR)
Isenburger Schneise 40
Frankfurt
☏ 069-67840 fax 069-6702634
res nr 0130-4433
✉ 60528

* 132 ♟ 270/340 excl. breakfast
* 147 ♟ 350/420 excl. breakfast

Steigenberger Avance Frankfurt Airport (HCR)
Unterschweinstiege 16
Frankfurt
☏ 069-69750 fax 069-69752505
res nr 069-663080
✉ 60549

30 ♟ 345/455 excl. breakfast
349 ♟ 360/490 excl. breakfast

FRANKFURT AN DER ODER/LICHTENBERG
Brandenburg   **10**

Holiday Inn Garden Court (HCR) AA ANWB
Rosengartener Landstr
Frankfurt an der Oder
☏ 0335-55360 fax 0335-5536587
✉ 15234

This Holiday Inn Garden Court is right on the E30, ideal for an overnight stop on the way to eastern Europe. The rooms offer the usual modern amenities of a Holiday Inn; there are also a number of apartments. The hotel has 2 restaurants and a bar with a garden terrace. Facilities include a sauna, solarium and fitness centre. The hotel offers suitable accommodation for disabled guests. Meeting rooms are available.

2 ♟ 135/-
166 ♟ 150/-

FRANKFURT/BAD WEILBACH *Hessen*   **18**

Airport Country Hotel (HCR) AA ANWB
Alleestr 18
Bad Weilbach
☏ 06145-9300 fax 06145-930230
✉ 65439

The Airport Country Hotel lies in a rural area 18km from Frankfurt's airport. The rooms in this new hotel are tastefully furnished with light wood panelling. There is a friendly, welcoming atmosphere in the bar and restaurant, and there is a sauna and fitness room.

* 23 ♟ 205/265
* 34 ♟ 265/365

GERMANY

FRANKFURT/KARBEN Hessen 18

Stadt Karben (HCR)
St Egreve Str 25-27
Karben
☎ 06039-8010 fax 06039-801222
✉ 61184

AA ANWB

The Hotel Stadt Karben is a well kept establishment 18km from Frankfurt. This hotel has comfortable rooms with en suite facilities, colour TV and minibar. The pleasant bistro-restaurant serves excellent meals, and there are on-site parking and conference facilities. This is an excellent hotel for an overnight stop, ideal for Frankfurt trade fairs.

* 12 ♫ 95/155
* 24 ♫ 115/185

FRANKFURT/LANGEN Hessen 18

Holiday Inn Garden Court (HR)
Rheinstr 25-29
Langen
☎ 06103-5050 fax 06103-505100
res nr 0130-815131
✉ 63225

AA ANWB

The Holiday Inn Garden Court is centrally situated in the town centre of Langen. Frankfurt's conference facilities and city centre are 20km away, and the airport 15km. The rooms have comfortable, modern furnishings, and are fully equipped with a colour TV with video programme, trouser press and hairdryer. The hotel has a bar-bistro, fitness room with sauna and solarium, meeting rooms and an adapted room for disabled guests. There are floors exclusively for non-smokers.

* 40 ♫ 180/280 excl. breakfast
* 50 ♫ 360/560 excl. breakfast

FREDEBURG Nordrhein-Westfalen 12

Haus Waltraud (HCR)
Gartenstr 20
☎ 02974-287 fax 02974-1369
✉ 23909

open 15.12 - 15.11
* 2 ♫ 60/66
* 9 ♫ 116/128

FREIBURG Baden-Württemberg 21

Atlanta (HG)
Rheinstr 29
☎ 0761-272006 fax 0761-289090
✉ 79104

AA ANWB

Hotel Atlanta is a bed and breakfast hotel, situated in a quiet street on the outskirts of the attractive town of Freiburg. The station and the centre are just 5 minutes' walk away. This old town with its historic buildings is well worth visiting. There are a number of restaurants in the immediate vicinity.

* 15 ♫ 130/180
* 30 ♫ 165/200

Kolpinghaus (HR)
Karlstr 7
☎ 0761-31930 fax 0761-3193202
✉ 79104

AA ANWB

The traditional style Hotel Kolpinghaus is situated close to the town centre, its rooms are on 4 floors which are all accessible by lift. The rooms have modern furnishings and are equipped with bath/shower, toilet, radio, telephone and colour TV. The restaurant serves fine cuisine, including house specialities and special diet meals.

* 25 ♫ 98/105
* 52 ♫ 126/142

GERMANY

Panorama Hotel Mercure (HCR) AA ANWB
Wintererstr 89
☎ 0761-51030 fax 0761-5103300
res nr 0761-5103317
✉ 79104

The Panorama Hotel Mercure is situated in the middle of woods, and is suitable for both business people and holiday-makers. The rooms have modern furnishings and a south-facing balcony, and are equipped with good amenities. The restaurant and lounge with open fire are tastefully furnished. There is a swimming pool, and a sauna and solarium.

* 27 ♦ 170/225
* 60 ♦ 190/275

Senator Hotel Rheingold (Best Western) (HCR) AA ANWB
Eisenbahnstr 47
☎ 0761-28210 fax 0761-2821111
res nr 0130-4455
✉ 79098

The Senator Hotel Rheingold is built in post-modern style and is situated near the historic centre of Freiburg, 50m from the station. The rooms are comfortable and equipped with minibar and hairdryer. Excellent Chinese dishes are served in the Dynasty restaurant. Conference facilities are available and there is a public car park near the hotel.

* 3 ♦ 165/240
* 46 ♦ 220/320

Victoria (HR) AA ANWB

Eisenbahnstr 54
☎ 0761-31881 fax 0761-33229
✉ 79104

The Hotel Victoria is situated in the centre of Freiburg, just 200m from the station. The rooms have en suite facilities and a minibar, and there is a pleasant bar. There is a restaurant, and parking facilities are available.

30 ♦ 127/157
40 ♦ 182/237

FREILASSING Bayern 24

Gasthof Moosleitner (HR)
Wasserburgerstr 52
☎ 08654-63060 fax 08654-630699
✉ 83395

* 20 ♦ 98/130
* 25 ♦ 160/220

Rupertus (HR)
Am Kirchpl
☎ 08654-61010 fax 08654-66438
✉ 83395

open 01.02 - 31.12
10 ♦ 63/-
14 ♦ 96/106

FREINSHEIM Rheinland-Pfalz 18

Musikantenbuckel (HR)
In Den Bohnengärten 5
☎ 06353-3931
✉ 67251

open 16.08 - 19.07
2 ♦ 45/50
7 ♦ 80/85

FREISING Bayern 23

Bayerischer Hof (HR)
Untere Hauptstr 3
☎ 08161-3037
✉ 85354

* 48 ♦ 68/70
* 22 ♦ -/126

FREUDENBERG Nordrhein-Westfalen 12

Schreiber (HG)
Krottorferstr 116
☎ 02734-7196
✉ 57258

1 ♦
9 ♦

GERMANY

Haus Im Walde (HCR)
Schützenstr 31
☎ 02734-7057 fax 02734-20386
✉ 57258

10 🛏
40 🛌

AE E ⌸ ♿ ⓟ P 🅿 ♨ 🏊 🎾 ↕ ⛔ 🍽 🅼 WC TV 🍴 ⊛

FREUDENSTADT Baden-Württemberg   21

Kurhotel Sonne Am Kurpark (HR)   AA ANWB
Turnhallestr 63
☎ 07441-6044 fax 07441-6300
✉ 72250

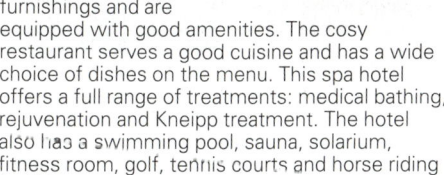

Guests will receive a very friendly and warm welcome in the first-class Kurhotel Sonne am Kurpark. The rooms have modern furnishings and are equipped with good amenities. The cosy restaurant serves a good cuisine and has a wide choice of dishes on the menu. This spa hotel offers a full range of treatments: medical bathing, rejuvenation and Kneipp treatment. The hotel also has a swimming pool, sauna, solarium, fitness room, golf, tennis courts and horse riding facilities.

* 15 🛏 115/169
* 45 🛌 198/288

AE ⓓ E ⌸ ♿ P 🅿 ♨ 🏊 🎾 ↕ ⛔ 🍽 WC TV 🍴 ✈

Schwanen (HR)
Forststr 6
☎ 07441-2267
✉ 72250

4 🛏 54/60
12 🛌 106/124

⊛ P 🅿 🍽 🅼 WC TV 🍴

FREYUNG Bayern   24

Bavaria Kur und Sporthotel (HR)
Solla 20
☎ 08551-899
✉ 94078

290 🛌

♨ ♿ P 🏊 ↕ ⛔ 🍴

Brodinger (HR)
Schulgasse 15
☎ 08551-4004 fax 08551-7283
✉ 94078

* 4 🛏 50/75
* 13 🛌 95/140

AE ⓓ E ⌸ ⊛ P 🅿 ♨ 🏊 ↕ ⛔ 🍽 WC TV 🍴 ⊛

FRIEDRICHSHAFEN Baden-Württemberg   22

Sieben Schwaben (HR)
Hauptstr 37
☎ 07541-55098 fax 07541-56953
✉ 88048

* 8 🛏 85/110
* 15 🛌 135/150

P ↕ ⛔ 🅼 WC TV 🍴

Zeppelin (HG)
Eugenstr 41
☎ 07541-25071
✉ 88045

2 🛏
16 🛌

♿ ⊛ P 🅿 ♨ ↕ 🅼 WC TV

FRITTLINGEN Baden-Württemberg   21

Felzen (HCR)
Schulstr 7
☎ 07426-7768
✉ 78665

4 🛏
5 🛌

♿ ⊛ P 🅿 ♨ 🅼 WC TV

FULDA Hessen   13

Holiday Inn Garden Court (HR)   AA ANWB
Lindenstr 45
☎ 0661-8330 fax 0661-8330555
res nr 0661-8330705
✉ 36037

This Holiday Inn Garden Court is a modern and comfortable hotel in the baroque town of Fulda, situated close to the historic centre. The rooms are suitable for business travellers, as well as those here for one night or a short holiday. The restaurant serves international dishes, and special diet meals are available on request. The hotel has a sauna, solarium, lounge, fitness room and meeting rooms.

→

GERMANY

* 28 ⌂ 145/210
* 106 ⌷ 170/231
AE ⓘ E ⚏ ⊙ ◆ P ↑↓ ■ ▣ WC TV |○| ☺

Keiper (HG)
Leipzigerstr 180
☏ 0661-69070
✉ 36039

5 ⌂
7 ⌷
◐ ◆ P ⌴ ⚐ ▣ WC

Maritim (HCR)
Pauluspromenade 2
☏ 0661-2820 fax 0661-78340
res nr 0221-219672
✉ 36037

10 ⌂ 189/273
95 ⌷ 248/348
AE ⓘ E ⚏ ⊙ P ⌴ ⚐ ⚒ ↑↓ ⌸ ■ ▣ WC TV |○| ⌂

FÜSSEN Bayern 23

Bergruh (HR)   AA ANWB
Alte Steige 16
☏ 08362-7742 fax 08362-39291
✉ 87629

Situated in the beautiful Allgaü, Hotel Bergruh looks out on the Weissensee and the mountains. Wood panelling is a feature in this hotel. Both bedrooms and bathrooms are comfortable and well equipped with modern amenities. The hotel offers a good restaurant, covered swimming pool, sauna, solarium and fitness facilities.

open 25.12 - 13.11
* 8 ⌂ 72/105
* 20 ⌷ 150/240
⌘ ◐ P ⌴ ⚐ ⚒ ↑↓ ■ ▣ WC TV |○| ☺

Seehof (HCR)
Gschrifterstr 5
☏ 08362-6822
✉ 87629

2 ⌂
12 ⌷
⌘ P ⚐ ⌸ ■ ▣ WC TV ⌘

FÜSSEN/HOPFEN AM SEE Bayern 23

Alpenblick (HCR)
Uferstr 10
Füssen
☏ 08362-50570 fax 08362-505773
✉ 87629

* 8 ⌂ 79/160
* 38 ⌷ 138/220
⌘ ⌂ ⌇ ◐ P ⌴ ⚐ ↑↓ ■ ▣ WC TV |○| ☺

GAGGENAU/SELBACH Baden-Württemberg 18

Zum Adler (HCR)   AA ANWB
Brunnerstr 39
Gaggenau
☏ 07225-5719
✉ 76571

The Hotel Zum Adler is situated between Baden-Baden and Gaggenau in the Murgtal. A proportion of the well furnished rooms in this family-run hotel have a bath, shower, toilet and telephone; and a good choice of dishes is served in the restaurant. There is horse-riding and a 12-hole golf course nearby. The hotel has its own parking facilities.

open 15.11 - 15.10
3 ⌂ 37/-
8 ⌷ 44/69
⌘ ⊙ P ⚐ ■ ▣ WC ⌂

GAMMERTINGEN Baden-Württemberg 22

Romantik Hotel Posthalterei (HR)   AA ANWB
Sigmaringer Str 4
☏ 07574-877 fax 07574-878
✉ 72501

Romantik Hotel Posthalterei is a family-run hotel situated on the Swäbische Alp, where the owners provide a very warm and hospitable atmosphere. The rooms feature country-style furnishings and en suite bathroom. The restaurant serves gourmet dishes, with fish from its own pond as a speciality. Conference rooms are available, and it is possible to hire bikes and ride in a horse-drawn carriage.

open 26.12 - 23.12
* 3 ♨ 85/150
* 30 ⚭ 138/195
AE ⓓ E ⚏ ⊙ ◆ P ⚑ ⇅ ⊟ ▬ F WC TV ⦿|

GARBSEN Niedersachsen 7

Bundesautobahn Rasthaus Motel (HCR)
Hannover-Garbsen-Nord
☏ 05137-72021 fax 05137-71819
✉ 30823

* 17 ♨ 80/150 excl. breakfast
* 23 ⚭ 140/250 excl. breakfast
E ⚏ ◆ P ⚑ ⇞ ⌘ ⇅ ⊟ F WC TV

GARMISCH-PARTENKIRCHEN Bayern 23

Aschenbrenner (HG) AA ANWB
Loisachstr 46
☏ 08821-58029 fax
08821-4805
✉ 82467

Hotel Aschenbrenner is peacefully situated in beautiful surroundings, yet only a 4-minute walk from the town centre. The hotel's furnishings are comfortable, partly dating back to the days of the royal house of Reuss. The rooms are tastefully decorated and feature bath, toilet, radio, telephone and colour TV. The attractive garden has a terrace with a view over the Zugspitze.

* 7 ♨ 70/100
* 18 ⚭ 120/190
AE ⓓ E ⚏ ⋋ ⊙ P ⚑ ⇅ ⊟ ▬ F WC TV

Bellevue (HG)
Riesserseestr 9
☏ 08821-58008
✉ 82467

9 ♨
15 ⚭
⋋ P ⚑ ⇅ ⊟ ▬ F WC

Obermühle (Best Western) (HR) AA ANWB
Muhlstr 22
☏ 08821-7040 fax
08821-704112
res nr 0130-4455
✉ 82467

The Hotel Obermühle is situated within 5 minutes' walk of the centre, and is distinctive because of its architectural design, as well as the tasteful furniture and decor inside. The rooms are spacious and comfortable, with balconies overlooking the beautiful countryside. The restaurant serves a choice of excellent dishes, and the leisure facilities include a swimming pool, sauna, tennis and squash courts and a golf course.

6 ♨ 195/240
91 ⚭ 270/340
AE ⓓ E ⚏ ⋋ ⚓ ⓑ P ⚑ ⇞ ⇅ ⊟ ▬ F WC TV ⦿|

Reindl's Partenkirchner Hof (HR)
Bahnhofstr 15
☏ 08821-58025 fax 08821-73401
✉ 82454

open 15.12 - 15.11
* 25 ♨ 55/145 excl. breakfast
* 50 ⚭ 120/174 excl. breakfast
AE ⓓ E ⚏ ⋋ P ⚑ ⇞ ⌘ ⇅ ⊟ ▬ F WC TV ⦿|

Grand Hotel Sonnenbichl (HCR)
Burgstr 97
☏ 08821-7020 fax 08821-702131
✉ 82467

* 12 ♨ 100/200
* 78 ⚭ 175/300
AE ⓓ E ⚏ ⌂ ⓑ ◆ P ⚐ ⇞ ⇅ ⊟ F WC TV ⦿|

GAU-BICKELHEIM Rheinland-Pfalz 18

Huster (HR)
Max Planck Str 8
☏ 06701-7344
✉ 55599

5 ⚭
⋋ P ⚑ ⊟ F TV ⦿|

GEILENKIRCHEN Nordrhein-Westfalen 11

Jabusch (HR) AA ANWB
Markt 3
☎ 02451-2725 fax 02451-64687
✉ 52511

The town of Geilenkirchen lies just across the Dutch border from Brunssum, and the Hotel Jabusch is situated in the town centre on the marketplace. It is a traditional hotel where all the rooms have a telephone, and some have a private toilet, shower and colour TV. The hotel has a large, pleasant terrace.

* 5 ≠ 49/62
* 10 ≠ 80/104
AE ◐ E ✕ ⅄ ⊙ P ☂ ♨ ⌷ WC TV ☺

GEISELWIND Bayern 19

Hannelore Müller (HP) AA ANWB
Fischhausstr 7
☎ 09556-243
✉ 96160

* 2 ≠ 35/65
* 6 ≠ 60/90
⅄ ⊙ P ☂ ♨ ⌷ WC

Gasthof Krone (HR)
Kirchpl 2
☎ 09556-244 fax 09556-400
✉ 96160

* 12 ≠ 38/65 excl. breakfast
* 48 ≠ 64/86 excl. breakfast
AE ◐ E ✕ ⊙ ◆ P ☂ ♨ ⌷ ▬ ⌷ WC TV ☺

GEISENHAUSEN Bayern 20

Pfannenstiel (MT) AA ANWB
Kysosstr.21 9
☎ 08441-84144
✉ 84144

All the rooms in Hotel Pfannenstiel have shower and toilet facilities. Because of its roadside location it is suitable for an overnight stop. There is a restaurant and a parking garage.

* 4 ≠ -/50
* 6 ≠ 65/70
AE ◐ E ✕ P ☂ ♨ ⌷ WC ☺

GELSENKIRCHEN Nordrhein-Westfalen 11

Maritim (HCR)
Am Stadtgarten 1
☎ 0209-1760 fax 0209-207075
res nr 0221-219672
✉ 45879

110 ≠
113 ≠
AE ◐ E ✕ ⅄ ⊙ P ☂ ♨ ⌷ ▬ ⌷ WC TV ☺

GERNSBACH Baden-Württemberg 18

Lautenfelsen (HCR)
Lautenfelsenstr 1
☎ 07224-2784 fax 07224-68183
✉ 76593

open 02.02 - 02.01
* 10 ≠ 40/42
* 24 ≠ 75/80
⅄ ♨ ⊙ P ☂ ♨ ⌷ WC ☺

GEROLSTEIN Rheinland-Pfalz 17

Seehotel (HCR)
Am Stausee 2
☎ 06591-222 fax 06591-81114
✉ 54568

open 06.02 - 19.11
* 3 ≠ 46/60
* 33 ≠ 74/94
AE ◐ E ✕ ⅄ ♨ ⊙ P ☂ ♨ ⌷ ▬ ⌷ WC TV ☺

Landhaus Tannenfels (HCR) AA ANWB
Lindenstr 68
☎ 06591-4123 fax 06591-4104
✉ 54568

The Hotel Tannenfels is in a tranquil location on the edge of Gerolstein, in an area that is good for walking. The rooms are well furnished; some have a balcony, and all have both a toilet and a shower. The hotel has a sunbathing lawn, a garden and terrace. Parking facilities are available.

* 3 ≠ 46/60
* 9 ≠ 88/106
⅄ ⊙ P ☂ ♨ ▬ ⌷ WC TV ☺

GERMANY 101

Z I M M E R F R E I
Guest house
HANNELORE MÜLLER

Fischhausstr. 7
96160 GEISELWIND/Bavaria
STEIGERWALD

Telephone: 09556-243

600 m from motorway exit
(behind ARAL filling station)

GERSFELD/RHÖN Hessen — 13

Sonne (HR)
Amelungstr 1
Gersfeld
☎ 06654-303 fax 06654-7649
✉ 36125

open 29.01 - 09.01
* 3 ♙ 41/47
* 22 ♞ 72/80
⊙ P ⛽ P WC TV ⚑ ☺

GILLENFELD Rheinland-Pfalz — 17

Zur Post (HR)   AA ANWB
Pulvernaarstr 8
☎ 06573-533 fax 06573-9202
✉ 54558

The Hotel zur Post is long established and well maintained. This peaceful hotel, situated in the centre of Gillenfeld, has rooms with en suite shower and toilet - some also have a balcony. The hotel's terrace and garden are quiet places to relax. The Hotel zur Post has a bowling alley and private parking facilities.
* 3 ♙ 32/-
* 12 ♞ 62/-
⊙ P ⛽ P WC ⚑ ☺

GLOTTERTAL Baden-Württemberg — 21

Landgasthof Zum Kreuz (HR)
Landstr 14
☎ 07684-80080 fax 07684-800839
✉ 79286

* 11 ♙ 60/110
* 25 ♞ 100/180
AE ⊙ E ⚡ ♙ P ⚑ ⛽ P WC TV ☺

GMUND AM TEG Bayern — 24

Oberströger (HR)   AA ANWB
Tölzerstr 4
Gmund
☎ 08022-7019 fax 08022-74816
✉ 83701

The Hotel Oberströger is situated on the sunny side of Gmund and has views of the Tegernsee. The country-style furnishings give the hotel a rural atmosphere, the rooms are well furnished - some have en suite facilities and a telephone - and the south-facing rooms have a balcony with sun-loungers. The hotel has a parking place and garage available.

open 11.12 - 31.10
* 7 ♙ 60/65
* 21 ♞ 102/112
⊙ E ⚡ ⊙ ◆ P ⛽ P WC ☺

GONDORF Rheinland-Pfalz — 7

ESH Eifel Sport Hotel (HCR)   AA ANWB
Philippsheimerstr 8
☎ 06565-2051 fax 06565-2296
✉ 54647

The ESH Eifel Sport Hotel is situated in the small town of Gondorf, where you will also find the popular Hochwildschutzpark Eifel. It offers a range of

→

102 GERMANY

leisure facilities, including a swimming pool with water chute, tennis court, a bowling and a skittle alley, sauna, thermal mud-bath and solarium. The rooms feature modern-style furnishings, and have en suite facilities, TV, telephone and minibar.

* 11 ♫ 75/101
* 56 ♬ 120/172
🆎 ⓘ 🇪 ≖ ⅄ ⓞ 🅿 🎯 💈 ≈ 🕯 ⌘ 🅿 🅒 WC TV ⅠⅠ ☺

GOSLAR Niedersachsen 8

Der Achtermann (HCR) AA ANWB
Rosentorstr 20
☏ 05321-21001 fax 05321-42748
✉ 38640

Hotel der Achtermann stands in the heart of Goslar, the rooms providing a high standard of comfortable accommodation. There is an extensive self-service breakfast buffet, and in the evening the cosy restaurant has a romantic atmosphere. There are splendid meeting and conference facilities, and the location is an ideal base for excursions to the mountainous countryside of the Harz.

* 56 ♫ 119/219
* 100 ♬ 238/348
🆎 ⓘ 🇪 ≖ ⅄ ⓞ 🅿 🎯 💈 ≈ 🍴 ⌘ 🅿 🅒 WC TV ⅠⅠ ☺

Brothanhof (HCR) AA ANWB
Bleicheweg 16
☏ 05321-22524
✉ 38640

The Hotel Brothanhof lies in open countryside, at the foot of the Rammelsberg, just a few minutes' walk from the centre. Most of the modern rooms have en suite facilities. The restaurant with its antler-lamps, coffee terrace and garden make this a suitable venue for a relaxing stay. On-site parking is available.

* 2 ♫ 40/75
* 7 ♬ 80/120
🆎 ⅄ 🎯 ⓞ 🅿 💈 ⌘ 🅒 WC ⅠⅠ ☺

Schwarzer Adler (HCR)
Rosentorstr 25
☏ 05321-24001 fax 05321-24192
✉ 38640

4 ♫
23 ♬
⅄ ⓞ 🅿 🎯 💈 ⌘ 🅿 🅒 WC TV ⅠⅠ ☺

Zur Tanne (HR) AA ANWB
Bäringestr 10
☏ 05321-21131 fax 05321-40999
✉ 38640

The Hotel zur Tanne is situated in the 1000-year-old imperial town of Goslar. The well kept rooms in this hotel have en suite toilet and shower, and a telephone. There is a good restaurant where special-diet meals are available on request. Full parking facilities are available.

* 6 ♫ 45/90
* 18 ♬ 100/160
⅄ ⓞ 🅿 🎯 ⌘ 🅒 WC ⅠⅠ ☺

Victoria Luise (HCR)
Bockswieserstr 2
☏ 05325-70389
✉ 38644

6 ♫
8 ♬
⅄ 🎯 ⓞ 🅿 🎯 💈 🅒 WC TV ⅠⅠ

GOSLAR/HAHNENKLEE Niedersachsen 8

Dorint Hotel Kreuzeck (HCR) AA ANWB
Am Kreuzeck 1
Goslar
☏ 05325-740 fax 05325-74839
res nr 0130-6605
✉ 38644

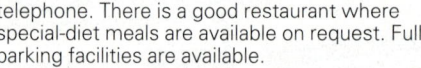

Situated in peaceful surroundings with a lake nearby, the Dorinthotel Kreuzeck has a cosy atmosphere and modern facilities. The rooms, most with balconies, provide comfortable accommodation. The hotel is equipped with a fitness room, sauna, solarium and swimming pool. Bicycles are available for hire.

* 7 ♫ 163/210
* 90 ♬ 240/310
🆎 ⓘ 🇪 ≖ 🎯 ⓞ ♦ 🅿 🎯 💈 ≈ 🍴 ⌘ 🅿 🅒 WC TV ⅠⅠ ☺

GRABEN-NEUDORF Baden-Württemberg 18

Löwen (HR)   AA ANWB
Karlsruherstr 19
☎ 07255-9342
✉ 76106

The Hotel Löwen is a small hotel situated in the centre of Graben-Neudorf. Most of the rooms have en suite facilities, there is a TV lounge and a restaurant, and private parking facilities are available.

open 25.12 - 23.12
* 3 ♦ 33/50
* 11 ♦ 55/80

Neudorfer Mühle (HR)
An Der B 36
☎ 07255-9310
✉ 76676

2 ♦
5 ♦

GRAINAU Bayern 23

Garni Sonneneck (HG)   AA ANWB
Waxensteinstr 17
☎ 08821-8940 fax 08821-82838
✉ 82491

The bed and breakfast Hotel Sonneneck has a frontage covered by colourful flowers in summer. The rooms here are very comfortable; those with a balcony or terrace enjoy splendid views over the mountains. The surrounding area offers plenty of opportunity for pleasant walks, and the less energetic can relax on the terrace.

open 11.12 - 14.11
* 2 ♦ 75/85
* 16 ♦ 140/160

Wetterstein (HG)
Waxensteinstr 14 C
☎ 08821-8004
✉ 82491

3 ♦
12 ♦

GRASSAU Bayern 24

Astron Sporthotel Achental (HCR)
Mietenkamerstr 65
☎ 08641-4010 fax 08641-1758
✉ 83224

* 21 ♦ 150/-
* 186 ♦ 190/-

GRÖNENBACH Bayern 22

Zur Tanne (HCR)
Mozartstr 2
☎ 08334-832 fax 08334-9354
✉ 87730

* 7 ♦ 50/-
* 23 ♦ 80/-

GROSS GERAU Hessen 18

Adler (HR)
Frankfurter Str 11
☎ 06152-8090
✉ 64521

27 ♦
36 ♦

GROSS REKEN Nordrhein-Westfalen 11

Vogelwiesche (HR)
Hauptstr 31
☎ 02864-1069
✉ 48734

2 ♦
16 ♦

GRÜNSTADT/ASSELHEIM Rheinland-Pfalz 18

Pfalzhotel Asselheim (HCR)
Holzweg 6
Grünstadt
☎ 06359-80030 fax 06359-800399
✉ 83257

open 10.01 - 31.12
3 ♦ 78/140
23 ♦ 140/250

GERMANY

GULDENTAL Rheinland-Pfalz   18

Guldentaler Hof (HR)
Naheweinstr 63-65
☎ 06707-9150 fax
06707-1033
✉ 55452

The Guldentaler Hof can be found in the Guldenbach Valley lying amid vineyard-covered hills. All the rooms have en suite facilities, telephone, radio, TV and minibar. The restaurant serves a choice of excellent dishes, complemented with a variety of good regional wines. The hotel also features its own bowling alley.

* 3 ♫ 65/75
* 14 ⚏ 110/150
AE ① E ⚏ ⊙ P ⚓ ⛁ ⛄ WC TV ⦿ ☺

GUMMERSBACH/LIEBERHAUSEN
Nordrhein-Westfalen   12

Akzent Hotel Landgasthof Reinhold AA ANWB
(HCR)
Kirchpl 2
Gummersbach
☎ 02354-5273 fax
02354-5873
✉ 51647

Landgasthof Reinhold enjoys a peaceful and beautiful position in the village of Gummersbach. This well maintained hotel has comfortably appointed rooms; some have a balcony. The restaurant has a relaxed atmosphere, and there is a terrace and a pleasant garden.

open 01.04 - 15.03
* - ♫ 65/75
* 17 ⚏ 110/140
AE ① E ⚏ ⛁ ⛄ ⊙ P ⚓ ⛁ ⛄ WC TV ⦿ ☺

GUNDELFINGEN Baden-Württemberg   21

Regina (HR) AA ANWB
Bundesstr 82
☎ 0761-581704
✉ 79194

The Hotel Regina is situated near the point where France, Switzerland and Germany meet; the nearest town is Freiburg. It is a modest hotel, conveniently close to the Karlsruhe - Basel motorway.

* 5 ♫ 42/60
* 8 ⚏ 80/90
AE ① E ⊙ P ⚓ ⛁ ⛄ WC ⦿ ☺

GÜTENBACH/FURTWANGEN Baden-
Württemberg   21

Parkhotel Neu Eck (HCR)   AA ANWB
Vordertalstr 53-55
Furtwangen
☎ 07723-2083 fax
07723-5361
✉ 78120

The Parkhotel Neu Eck is at an altitude of 1000m in the heart of the Schwarzwald. It is extremely suitable as a base for day trips to Switzerland, Alsace and Bodermeer. The rooms are well furnished and a number of them have a shower, toilet, telephone, radio, TV and balcony. The restaurant's specialities are delicious. Covered parking facilities are available.

* 11 ♫ 55/82
* 50 ⚏ 84/136
AE ① E ⚏ ◆ P ⚓ ⛁ ⛄ ⛁ ⛄ WC TV ⦿ ⌂ ☺

GERMANY

HAAN Nordrhein-Westfalen   11

Friedrich Eugen Engels (HCR)   AA ANWB
Hermann Lönsweg 14
☏ 02129-32010 fax 02129-32070
✉ 42781

The Hotel Friedrich Eugen Engels is situated on the edge of Hildener Moor, which is overlooked by the hotel's spacious rooms. The rooms are well furnished and have a shower, toilet, radio and telephone; some also have a balcony. The hotel has an indoor swimming pool, sauna and garden with terrace.

open 06.01 - 15.07 + 15.08 - 23.12
* 8 ♪ 75/100
* 10 ⚭ 130/160
AE ① E ⚞ ⚒ ♠ P ⛻ ⚲ ✈ ⛔ ▣ P WC TV ⛷ ⊕

HAGEN Nordrhein-Westfalen   12

Dresel (HR)
Rummenohler Str 31
☏ 02337-1318 fax 02337-8981
✉ 58091

open 01.08 - 30.06
* 8 ♪ 68/106
* 11 ⚭ 143/168
AE ① E ⚞ ♠ P ⛻ ⚲ ▣ P WC TV

HAGNAU Baden-Württemberg   22

Löwen (HCR)
Hans Jakobstr 2
Hagnau
☏ 07532-6241 fax 07532-9048
✉ 88709

open 16.04 - 31.10
* 4 ♪ 65/100
* 11 ⚭ 130/180
⚒ ⚞ ⊕ P ⛻ ⚲ ▣ P WC TV ⛷

Steible (HR)
Seestr 17
☏ 07532-5900
✉ 88709

1 ♪
6 ⚭
⚒ ⊕ P ⛻ P WC

HALDENWANG Bayern   22

Landgasthof Höhenblick (HCR)
Am Schwimmbad 4
☏ 08374-8604
✉ 87490

1 ♪
7 ⚭
⚒ P ⛻ P WC ⛷

HALLENBERG/HESBORN Nordrhein-Westfalen   12

Zum Hesborner Kuckuck (HCR)   AA ANWB
Ölfestr 22
Hesborn
☏ 02984-475 fax 02984-573
✉ 59969

This comfortably furnished hotel is situated in the Sauerland region. All the rooms in the Zum Hesborner Kuckuck have a shower/toilet and balcony; the atmospheric restaurant offers a menu with a wide choice of appetising specialities. The woods and mountains of the Sauerland provide many long walks and in winter there are good skiing facilities.

open 04.12 - 18.11
* - ♪ 71/86
* 27 ⚭ 118/148
⚒ ⚞ P ⛻ ⚲ ⇅ ✈ ▣ P WC TV ⛷ ⊕

HALTERN Nordrhein-Westfalen   11

Jägerhof Zum Stift (HCR)   AA ANWB
Fläsheimerstr 360
☏ 02364-2327
✉ 45721

The simple but well maintained Jägerhof zum Stift has rooms with good facilities. Special-diet meals are available in the restaurant on request. This is a good area to explore by bicycle, and these can be hired in the hotel. There is a skittle alley, a terrace and on-site parking.

* - ♪ 58/-
* 13 ⚭ 110/-
⊙ P ⛻ ⚲ ▣ P WC TV ⛷

GERMANY

Seestern (HCR)
Hullernerstr 42
☎ 02364-3642 fax 02364-169964
✉ 45721

25 ♨ 40/60
20 ♨♨ 80/100
AE ⓓ E ⌧ ⅄ ⊛ ⇌ ⓑ P 🅿 ♨ ▤ ⊟ WC TV ⓘ ⊙

HAMBURG Hamburg 3

Germany's second largest city and major port is the proud heir of a great merchant seafaring tradition dating from Hanseatic days. As a city of merchants, Hamburg has few grand monuments, and after massive wartime bombing it was rebuilt mostly in a sympathetic redbrick style, and there are no skyscrapers to spoil the elegant skyline of green-copper spires on the banks of the Alster. A guided boat tour of the port - the fourth largest in Europe - is a good introduction to the city, with its 68km of quays and the 4km Kihlbrand suspension bridge. Nearby is what remains of old Hamburg, the *Altstadt*, after destructive fires in 1842 and 1943. Here, church towers and spires are interspersed with gabled warehouses and merchants houses. Along the broad inner ringway is an area of new stylish and luxurious shopping arcades, and there is an imposing neo-Renaissance style Rathouse. Beyond the ringway looms the glass vaulted roof of the Hauptbahnhof (station), the Museum für Kunst und Gewerbe, and the city's main art museum, the Kunsthalle.
The large outer lake of the Ausenalster is a shimmering focus of recreation and further on, in the gardens of Planten und Blomen and the Alter Botanischer Garten, illuminated fountains play on summer nights.
The St Pauli district, best known for its main street, the notorious Reeperbahn, is now waning as the city's red-light district, and is becoming more respectable with the opening of some smart restaurants. The big suburb of Altona, Danish until 1864, has stately white patrician houses, and its Nord-Deutches Landesmuseum is Hamburg's nicest museum, with old ship's figureheads, and fishing boats, local costumes and paintings of Schleswig scenes.

Alsterkrug (Best Western) (HCR)
Alsterkrugchaussee 277
☎ 040-513030 fax 040-51303403
res nr 0130-4455
✉ 22297

* 38 ♨ 155/180 excl. breakfast
* 42 ♨♨ 189/207 excl. breakfast
AE ⓓ E ⌧ P 🅿 ♨ ▤ ⇌ ⊟ WC TV ⊙

Atlantic Hotel Kempinski Hamburg AA ANWB (HCR)
An Der Alster 12357
☎ 040-28880 fax 040-247129
res nr 0130-3339
✉ 20099

The luxury Atlantic Hotel Kempinski, distinctive because of its beautiful architecture, is a hotel with a luxurious and refined atmosphere throughout. There are rooms and suites offering extensive amenities, various restaurants (each with their own culinary speciality) and a tastefully furnished cocktail bar with live music. The hotel offers a wide choice of healthy leisure facilities, including a heated swimming pool, sauna, solarium and body massage.

* 53 ♨ 320/430 excl. breakfast
* 203 ♨♨ 370/480 excl. breakfast
AE ⓓ E ⌧ ⌇ ⊙ ◆ 🅿 ♨ ⌇ ▤ ⊟ WC TV ⓘ ⊙

Europäischer Hof (HR)
Kirchenallee 45
☎ 040-248248 fax 040-24824799
✉ 20099

120 ♨ 180/340
200 ♨♨ 240/420
AE ⓓ E ⌧ ⊙ ◆ 🅿 ♨ ⌇ ▤ ⊟ WC TV ⓘ ⊙

Holiday Inn Crowne Plaza (HR)
Graumannsweg 10
☎ 040-228060 fax 040-2208704
res nr 0130-815131
✉ 22087

* 77 ♨ 295/330 excl. breakfast
* 207 ♨♨ 335/370 excl. breakfast
AE ⓓ E ⌧ ⊙ P 🅿 ⌇ ▤ ⊟ WC TV ⓘ ⊙

Ibis Königstrasse (HCR)
Königstr 4
☎ 040-311870 fax 040-31187304
✉ 22767

* 19 ♨ -/155
* 129 ♨♨ -/196
AE E ⌧ ⊙ P ▤ ⊟ TV ⓘ

GERMANY 107

HOTEL IBIS HAMBURG Altona

Königstrasse 4, D-22767 HAMBURG
Tel: 040-31187-0. Fax: 040-31187.304
Tlx: 2166089 arca d

◆ ◆ ◆ ◆

Your Ibis hotel is close to the Exchange, the fish market in the harbour, the Reeperbahn and the musicals 'Cats' and 'The Phantom of the Opera'.

single room .... DM **150,-**
double room .... DM **196,-**
including buffet breakfast.

All rooms have shower, toilet, telephone and cable television.

Maritimhotel Reichshof (HR)
Kirchenallee 34-36
℡ 040-248330 fax 040-24833588
res nr 0221-219672
✉ 20099

140 ♦ 238/358
163 ♦ 288/438

Norge (HR)
Schäferskampsallee 49
℡ 040-441150 fax
040-44115577
✉ 20357

The Hotel Norge is 5 minutes' walk from the town centre. All the rooms in this business hotel have en suite facilities, telephone, radio, colour TV and minibar. The restaurant has Norwegian-style furnishings and serves its own Norwegian specialities. The hotel has its own swimming pool, and on-site parking is available.

* 60 ♦ 180/225 excl. breakfast
* 65 ♦ 220/290 excl. breakfast

St Raphael (Best Western) (HCR)
Adenauerallee 41
℡ 040-248200 fax 040-24820333
res nr 0130-4455
✉ 20097

* 60 ♦ 180/230
* 70 ♦ 230/280

Vier Jahreszeiten (HCR)
Neuer Jungfernstieg 9-14
℡ 040-34940 fax 040-3494602
✉ 20354

* 82 ♦ 375/455 excl. breakfast
* 90 ♦ 465/595 excl. breakfast

HAMELN Niedersachsen   7

Zur Börse (HR)
Osterstr 41 a
℡ 05151-7080 fax 05151-25485
✉ 31762

The Hotel zur Börse is situated in the centre of the historic town of the Pied Piper. The rooms in this peaceful hotel are split over 3 floors and have a balcony, en suite facilities and telephone. There is a good restaurant, a lift, covered parking facilities and lockable bicycle storage.

open 08.01 - 15.12
* 13 ♦ -/66
* 21 ♦ -/124

Dorint Hotel Hameln (HCR)
164-er Ring 3
℡ 05151-7920 fax 05151-792191
res nr 0130-6605
✉ 31785

* 49 ♦ 177/290
* 56 ♦ 280/390

GERMANY

Zur Krone (HCR)
Osterstr 30
☎ 05151-9070 fax 05151-907217
✉ 31785

6 ♟ 150/240 excl. breakfast
28 ⚐ 190/380 excl. breakfast
AE ⓘ E ≡ ⅄ ◉ P 🅟 ≈ ↕ 🚾 TV IOI

HANAU/STEINHEIM Hessen   18

Villa Stokkum (HCR)   AA ANWB
Steinheimer Vorstadt 70
Steinheim
☎ 06181-6640 fax
06181-661580
✉ 63401

The Hotel Villa Stokkum lies within reach of the Steinheimer *Altstadt* has fine views over the city ramparts. This historic building is tastefully furnished throughout and is an equally good choice for a business or holiday visit. The rooms have air conditioning, king-size beds, and elegant en suite bathrooms with marble bath. There is a Mediterranean atmosphere in the Atrium restaurant, and for small meals and cocktails there is the Bar-Bistro. The hotel has excellent meeting and conference facilities.

* 72 ♟ 190/240 excl. breakfast
* 65 ⚐ 240/290 excl. breakfast
AE ⓘ E ≡ ⅄ ♨ ◉ ◆ P 🅟 ≈ ↕ 🚾 TV IOI

HANNOVER Niedersachsen   7

City (HG)
Limburgstr 3
☎ 0511-360759 fax 0511-360777
✉ 30159

* 14 ♟ 90/110
* 22 ⚐ -/180
P ↕ 🚾 TV

Congresshotel am Stadtpark (HR)
Clausewitzstr 6
☎ 0511-28050 fax 0511-814652
✉ 30175

* 107 ♟ 170/350
* 141 ⚐ 305/455
AE ⓘ E ≡ ⅄ ◉ P 🅟 ≈ ↕ 🚾 TV IOI

Eden (HP)
Waldhausenstr 30
☎ 0511-830430 fax 0511-833094
✉ 30519

* 3 ♟ 60/85
* 20 ⚐ 90/130
⅄ ≈ 🚾

Föhrenhof (Best Western) (HCR)
Kirchhorsterstr 22
☎ 0511-61721 fax 0511-619719
res nr 0130-4455
✉ 30659

* 36 ♟ 150/240
* 41 ⚐ 230/340
AE ⓘ E ≡ ⅄ ◉ P 🅟 ≈ ↕ 🚾 TV IOI

Holiday Inn Garden Court (HCR)   AA ANWB
Oldenburger Allee 1
☎ 0511-61550 fax
0511-6155555
res nr 0130-8151310
✉ 30659

The Holiday Inn Garden Court Hannover is especially suitable for business people, but tourists on short breaks will have a pleasant stay. The hotel has comfortable and modern furnishings and rooms throughout. They offer extensive amenities including a trouser press and a minibar. During the summer specially priced breaks are available on request. The hotel is centrally situated for trips to the Harz mountains. Meeting rooms and free parking spaces are available.

* 14 ♟ 135/-
* 136 ⚐ 150/-
AE ⓘ E ≡ ⅄ ◉ ◆ P 🅟 ≈ ↕ 🚾 TV IOI

Holiday Inn Hannover Airport (HCR)
Petzelstr 60
☎ 0511-77070 fax 0511-737781
res nr 0130-815131
✉ 30159

65 ♟
145 ⚐
AE ⓘ E ≡ ◉ P ≈ ≋ ↕ 🚾 TV IOI

GERMANY 109

Inter Continental (HCR)
Friedrichswal 11
☏ 0511-36770 fax 0511-325195
res nr 0511-3677107
✉ 30159

* 122 ♦ 255/495 excl. breakfast
* 163 ♦ 305/545 excl. breakfast
AE ⦿ E ⌸ ⦿ P ⛵ ⇅ ⊟ ⊡ WC TV ⚬

Kastens Luisenhof (HCR)
Luisenstr 1-3
☏ 0511-30440 fax 0511-3044807
✉ 30159

* 70 ♦ 199/395
* 90 ♦ 248/578
AE ⦿ E ⌸ ⦿ P ⛵ ⇅ ⊟ ⊡ WC TV ⚬

Maritim Stadthotel (HCR)   AA ANWB
Hildesheimerstr 34-40
☏ 0511-16531 fax
0511-9805105
res nr 0221-219672
✉ 30169

The Maritim Stadthotel is beautifully situated in the centre of Hannover. This first class business hotel, which is part of the Maritim Hotelgesellschaft, is pleasantly furnished with spacious rooms and good amenities. The restaurant with its comprehensive menu, the bar, terrace, swimming pool and sauna, all ensure a pleasant stay. On-site parking is available.

* 40 ♦ 245/429
* 253 ♦ 298/588
AE ⦿ E ⌸ ⦿ ♦ P ⛵ ⇅ ⊟ ⊡ WC TV ⚬

Grandhotel Mussmann (HG)
Ernst Augustpl 7
☏ 0511-327971 fax 0511-324325
✉ 30159

* 40 ♦ 168/498
* 62 ♦ 218/498
AE ⦿ E ⌸ ⦿ ⇅ ⊟ ⊡ WC TV

Parkhotel Kronsberg (Best Western) (HCR)
Laatzenerstr 18
☏ 0511-861086 fax 0511-867112
res nr 0130-4455
✉ 30539

* 73 ♦ 160/260
* 101 ♦ 230/380
AE ⦿ E ⌸ ⦿ ♦ P ⛵ ⇅ ⊟ ⊡ WC TV ⚬

Queens am Tiergarten (HCR)
Tiergartenstr 117
☏ 0511-51030 fax 0511-526924
✉ 3000

65 ♦ 230/370 excl. breakfast
111 ♦ 290/454 excl. breakfast
AE ⦿ E ⌸ ⦿ P ⛵ ⇅ ⊟ ⊡ WC TV ⚬

Zentral Kaiserhof (HCR)
Ernst Augustpl 4
☏ 0511-36830 fax 0511-3683114
✉ 30159

32 ♦
49 ♦
AE ⦿ E ⌸ ⦿ ♦ P ⇅ ⊟ ⊡ WC TV ⚬

HANNOVERSCH-MÜNDEN Niedersachsen 13

Schmucker Jäger (HR)
Wilhelmshäuserstr 45
☏ 05541-98100 fax 05541-2901
✉ 34346

open 17.01 - 31.12
* 2 ♦ 52/90
* 28 ♦ 88/140
AE ⦿ E ⌸ ⦿ ♦ P ⛵ ⋈ ⊟ ⊡ WC TV ⚬

HASBORN Rheinland-Pfalz 17

Thomas (HR)   AA ANWB
Hauptstr 10
☏ 06574-341
✉ 54533

The small town of Hasborn lies one km from the Trier to Koblenz motorway, Hasborn exit. The Hotel Thomas is pleasantly situated in this rustic village and has well furnished rooms with private toilet and shower, radio, colour TV, and telephone. The hotel offers a comprehensive choice of recreational facilities including a tennis court, skittle alley, sauna and solarium. On-site parking is available.

* 2 ♦ 37/-
* 12 ♦ 74/-
♦ P ⛵ ⊡ WC TV ⚬

110 GERMANY

HASSLOCH Rheinland-Pfalz   18

Pfalz (HR)   AA ANWB
Lindenstr 50
☎ 06324-4047 fax 06324-82503
✉ 67454

The Hotel Pfalz is centrally situated near the Hassloch exit of the Koblenz - Ludwigshafen motorway. It is within easy reach of the Deutsche Weinstrasse and the nature park of Pfalzerwald. The rooms are modern and comfortable, and the hotel also has a swimming pool, sauna and solarium.

13 ♪ 86/96
22 ♫ 150/-
⦿ E ≡ P 🅿 🏊 ↕ 🔲 🔳 WC TV ☼

Silencehotel Sägmühle (HCR)
Sägmühlweg 140
☎ 06324-1031 fax 06324-1034
✉ 67454

* 4 ♪ 80/120
* 16 ♫ 130/170
AE ⦿ E ≡ ♨ ⚓ P 🅿 🏊 ↕ 🔲 🔳 WC TV ⍟ ☼

HAUSACH Baden-Württemberg   21

Zur Eiche (HP)   AA ANWB
Wilhelm Zangenstr 30
☎ 07831-229 fax 07831-8947
✉ 77756

The rooms in Hotel zur Eiche are comfortable, and all have a splendid view over the mountains. The Hausach area is especially suitable for exploring the Schwarzwald. The restaurant's speciality is trout, complemented by some excellent wines. Swimming pools, tennis courts and minigolf are available nearby.

* 2 ♪ 37/56
* 10 ♫ 70/92
AE ⦿ E ≡ ⦿ P 🅿 ↕ 🔲 🔳 WC TV ☼

HEEDE Niedersachsen   6

Van Eiken (HCR)
Haupstr 8
☎ 04963-721
✉ 49356

2 ♪
8 ♫
AE ⦿ E ≡ ⦿ P 🅿 🏊 🔳 WC TV ⍟ ☼

HEIDELBERG Baden-Württemberg   18

Alt Heidelberg (Best Western) (HR)
Rohrbacherstr 29
☎ 06221-9150 fax 06221-164272
res nr 0130-4455
✉ 69115

* 24 ♪ 195/210
* 56 ♫ 230/250
AE ⦿ E ≡ ⦿ P 🅿 🏊 ↕ 🔲 🔳 WC TV ☼

Arcade Intercity (HCR)
Lessingstr 3
☎ 06221-9130 fax 06221-913300
✉ 69115

* - ♪ 120/140 excl. breakfast
* 170 ♫ 150/170 excl. breakfast
AE ⦿ E ≡ ⦿ P 🅿 ↕ 🔲 🔳 WC TV ☼

Holiday Inn Crowne Plaza (HR)
Kurfürstenanlage 1
☎ 06621-9170 fax 06621-21007
res nr 0130-815131
✉ 69115

* 89 ♪ 275/310 excl. breakfast
* 143 ♫ 305/340 excl. breakfast
AE ⦿ E ≡ ⦿ ♦ P 🅿 🏊 ↕ 🔲 🔳 WC TV ☼

Queens Moat House (HCR)
Pleikartsfösterstr 101
☎ 06221-7880 fax 06221-788499
✉ 69115

55 ♪ 172/192 excl. breakfast
56 ♫ 214/234 excl. breakfast
AE ⦿ E ≡ ⦿ P 🅿 🏨 🔲 🔳 WC TV ☼

Regahotel Heidelberg (Best Western) (HR)
Bergheimerstr 63
☎ 06221-5080 fax 06221-508500
res nr 0130-4455
✉ 69115

* 11 ♪ 220/250
* 113 ♫ 260/280
AE ⦿ E ≡ ⦿ P 🅿 ↕ 🔲 🔳 WC TV ☼

Romantik Hotel Zum Ritter (HCR)
Hauptstr 178
☎ 06221-24272 fax 06221-12683
✉ 69117

* 8 ♪ 98/225
* 32 ♫ 245/325
AE ⦿ E ≡ ♨ ⦿ 🅿 ↕ 🔲 🔳 WC TV ⍟ ☼

GERMANY

Mentioned in the annals in the 13th century, this old mill has been romantically and lovingly restored to create the Sägmühle Hotel.

D-67454 Hassloch/Pfalz, Sägmühlweg 140
Fam. H. Marneth.
Tel.: 06324-1031, fax: 06324-1034.

Here, in the middle of nature, you can really feel at home and relax properly. The charm of the past, the stylish setting, the comfortably furnished rooms as well as the exquisite cuisine lend our hotel a special touch.

HEIDELBERG/WALLDORF Baden-Württemberg **18**

Holiday Inn Heidelberg Walldorf (HR)
Roterstr
Walldorf
☏ 06227-360 fax 06227-36504
res nr 0130-815131
✉ 69190

* 45 ♊ 250/360 excl. breakfast
* 102 ⚭ 295/415 excl. breakfast
🆎 ⓞ E ⛁ ⓢ P ☂ ♒ ⛵ ▬ ⌂ WC TV 🍴 ✈

HEIDENHEIM AN DER BRENZ
Baden-Württemberg **19**

Ottilienhof (HR)
Schnaitheimerstr 19
☏ 07321-41077
✉ 89520

7 ♊
10 ⚭
⊙ ♦ P ♒ ⌂ WC TV 🍴

Senator Hotel Aquarena (Best Western) (HCR) AA ANWB
Friedrich Pfenning Str 30
☏ 07321-0980 fax 07321-980100
res nr 0130-4455
✉ 89518

The modern Senator Hotel Aquarena is quietly situated on a hill on the outskirts of the town, and has a beautiful view of Heidenheim. The station is one km away, and the *Autobahn* is about 2km. The rooms are luxuriously furnished and fully equipped with minibar, hairdryer, and trouser press. German and international dishes are served in the modern Dolce Vita restaurant, and there is a cocktail bar with a dance floor. The hotel has a swimming pool, sauna, solarium and meeting rooms. There are parking facilities for 200 cars.

* 12 ♊ 155/165
* 72 ⚭ 195/240
🆎 ⓞ E ⛁ P ♒ ♒ ▬ ⌂ WC TV 🍴

HEILBRONN/FLEIN Baden-Württemberg **18**

Wo der Hahn kräht (HR)
Altenbergweg 11
Heilbronn
☏ 07131-50810 fax 07131-508166
✉ 74520

* 20 ♊ 105/125
* 30 ⚭ 140/180
♒ ♿ P ☂ ♒ ⛵ ▬ ⌂ WC TV 🍴 ⊙

HEILIGENROTH Rheinland-Pfalz **20**

Raststätte Heiligenroth (HCR)
☏ 02602-1030 fax 02602-103450
✉ 56412

* 15 ♊ 110/- excl. breakfast
* 15 ⚭ 145/210 excl. breakfast
🆎 ⓞ E ⛁ ♿ P ☂ ♒ ⛵ ▬ ⌂ WC TV ⊙

HEIMBACH/HERGARTEN Nordrhein-Westfalen 11

Ritterstuben (HCR) AA ANWB
Kermeterstasse 36
Hergarten
☏ 02446-3555
✉ 52396

The Hotel Ritterstuben has modern rooms, all with en suite facilities. The restaurant serves dishes prepared with produce from the hotel's own bakery and butcher; apéritifs are served in the bar. The hotel's central location makes it an excellent base for trips in the surrounding area. There is a terrace and a pleasant sunbathing lawn.

open 01.03 - 21.03
1 ⌂ 32/48
6 ⌂ 64/96

HELMSTEDT Niedersachsen 8

Senator Hotel Helmstedt (Best Western) (HG) AA ANWB
Chardstr 2
☏ 05351-1280 fax 05351-128128
res nr 0130-4455
✉ 38350

The recently-opened Senator Hotel Helmstedt is ideal for business travellers, as well as visitors to eastern Europe. All the modern rooms are comfortably and fully furnished, including colour TV with video, fax-socket, hairdryer, minibar and trouser press. The cosy hotel bar also serves small snacks. The hotel has meeting rooms, sauna, solarium, a parking garage and is directly situated on the A2 Hannover/Berlin motorway.

* 22 ⌂ 150/195
* 42 ⌂ 170/245

HENGERSBERG Bayern 24

Erika (HCR)
Am Ohewehr 13
☏ 09901-6001 fax 09901-6762
✉ 94491

* 2 ⌂ 55/65
* 23 ⌂ 80/98

Niederalteicher Hof (HCR)
Marktpl 9
☏ 09901-6112
✉ 94491

10 ⌂
28 ⌂

HEPPENHEIM Hessen 18

Starkenburger Hof (HCR)
Kalterer Str 7
☏ 06252-6061 fax 06252-68183
✉ 64646

open 20.01 - 15.12
* 11 ⌂ 68/80
* 26 ⌂ 98/115

HERBITZHEIM Saarland 17

Bliesbrück (HCR) AA ANWB
Rubenheimer Str
☏ 06843-1881 fax 06843-8731
✉ 66453

The Hotel Bliesbrück is a peacefully situated, easily accessible hotel. There is a nature reserve in the area where more than 30 different species of orchids can be seen. All the rooms have en suite washing facilities and a hairdryer, and some also have a balcony. The hotel's own home-made ice cream is served on the terrace. There is a sauna and bicycle hire.

* 3 ⌂ 55/89
* 27 ⌂ 90/140

GERMANY 113

HERBORN/BÜRG Hessen 12

Engelbert (HG) AA ANWB
Hauptstr 50
Herborn
☏ 02772-3562 fax 02772-3556
✉ 35745

The Hotel Engelbert is situated in the centre of the 1000-year-old town of Herborn. It is very suitable for a stopover during a long journey and provides parking spaces and a garage. All the rooms have a shower and toilet, and a TV can be provided on request.

4 ♪ 48/50
11 ⚏ 78/80
E ♨ ⊙ P 🍽 ♨ ⚒ 🔲 WC TV ☺

HERBRECHTINGEN Baden-Württemberg 19

May (HG)
Ostpreussenstr 1
☏ 07324-2049 fax 07324-42359
✉ 89545

open 07.01 - 20.12
9 ♪
11 ⚏
E ♨ ⊙ P 🍽 ♨ ⚒ 🔲 WC TV

HERDORF Rheinland-Pfalz 12

Hair (HP)
Guldenhardt 6
☏ 02744-5248
✉ 57562

3 ♪
9 ⚏
♨ ⚒ ⊙ P 🔲 WC ☺

HERFORD Nordrhein-Westfalen 7

Winkelmann (HR)
Mindenerstr 1
☏ 05221-9800 fax 05221-980162
✉ 32049

12 ♪
24 ⚏
AE ⓓ E ⚒ ⊙ ◆ P ↕ 🔲 WC TV ☺

HERSCHEID Nordrhein-Westfalen 12

Pension Zur Hardt (HP) AA ANWB
Hardt 4
☏ 02357-2203
✉ 58849

The Pension zur Hardt is situated in the Sauerland region, a wooded area which is peaceful and has plenty of walking trails. This pension is ideal for both lazy and active holidays.
The rooms are well furnished and have a shower and toilet. Features of the hotel include an indoor swimming pool, sunbathing lawn and sun terrace.

3 ♪ 38/48
5 ⚏ 68/78
♨ ⚒ P 🍽 ♨ ⚒ 🔲 WC ☺

Jagdhaus Weber (HCR)
Reblin 11
☏ 02357-90900 fax 02357-909090
✉ 58849

open 27.12 - 23.12
* 2 ♪ 75/110
* 11 ⚏ 130/160
ⓓ E ♨ ⊙ P 🍽 🔲 🔲 WC TV ⓘ ☺

HERZBERG Niedersachsen 13

Englischerhof (HCR)
Vorstadt 10
☏ 05521-5032 fax 05521-71839
✉ 37412

* 3 ♪ 76/92
* 41 ⚏ 128/152
AE ⓓ E ⚒ ⊙ ◆ P 🍽 ♨ 🔲 🔲 WC ☺

HERZBERG/SIEBER Niedersachsen 13

Haus Iris (HG) AA ANWB
An Der Sieber 102 b
Sieber
☏ 05585-355
✉ 37412

Haus Iris enjoys a sunny location in the attractive little village of Sieber in the Harz. It is a comfortable bed and breakfast hotel, where all the rooms have en suite facilities, and some also have a spacious

→

balcony. Guests can relax in the large garden with terrace, and in the sauna and solarium. The surrounding woods and mountains form the ideal setting for walking and cross-country skiing.

open 16.12 - 14.11
* 5 ♬ 37/54
* 13 ☞ 72/180

Zur Krone (HCR)
An Der Sieber 102
Herzberg
☏ 05585-336 fax 05585-1222
✉ 37412

7 ♬
27 ☞

HERZOGENAURACH Bayern 20

Auracher Hof (HR)
Welkenbacher Kirchweg 2
☏ 09132-2080
✉ 91074

6 ♬
7 ☞

HESSDORF Bayern 19

Zur Post (HR)
Im Zollstock 13
☏ 09135-915 fax 09135-2887
✉ 97783

12 ♬ 70/115
16 ☞ 90/150

HILCHENBACH Nordrhein-Westfalen 12

Haus Am Sonnenhang (HR)   AA ANWB
Wilhelm Münkerstr 21
☏ 02733-7004 fax 02733-4260
✉ 57121

Haus Am Sonnenhang is situated in the middle of the woods and is an ideal holiday spot for any time of the year. Hilchenbach and the surrounding area offer plenty of recreational facilities - swimming pool, tennis courts, minigolf and horse riding. The modern rooms have a shower, toilet, telephone and most have a balcony. The restaurant has become well known for its traditional dishes.

* 10 ♬ 88/115
* 10 ☞ 130/180

HILCHENBACH/LÜTZEL Nordrhein-Westfalen 12

Ginsberger Heide (HCR)
Hof Ginsberg 2
Lützel
☏ 02733-3224 fax 02733-3253
✉ 57271

open 15.11 - 31.10
2 ♬
14 ☞

HILPOLTSTEIN Bayern 20

Waldmüller (HCR)
Jahrsdorf 4
☏ 09174-845 fax 09174-2734
✉ 91161

open 24.11 - 31.10
5 ♬ 48/50
22 ☞ 82/95

HINDELANG Bayern 22

Ferienhotel Bären Kur (HP)
Bärengasse 1
☏ 08324-2001
✉ 87541

open 01.12 - 31.10
13 ♬ -/78
17 ☞ -/156

Kur Und Sporthotel (KH)
Zillenbachstr 50
☏ 08324-840 fax 08324-84728
✉ 87541

100 ♬
100 ☞

Sonneck (HR)
Rosengasse 10
☏ 08324-2278
✉ 87541

12 ♬ -/75
14 ☞ 150/180

GERMANY

HINTERZARTEN Baden-Württemberg 21

Lafette (HCR)   AA ANWB
Heiligbrunnenstr 10
☎ 07652-360 fax 07652-5906
✉ 79856

The Hotel Lafette is situated in Hinterzarten, 3km from the Titisee. The area is famous for its sunshine, clean air, woods, and winter-sports facilities. The rooms are well furnished and have en suite shower and toilet. The hotel has a south-facing sun terrace with a sunbathing lawn.

open 21.12 - 04.11
* 6 ♬ 47/54
* 16 ♬ 92/106
▒ ◆ P ⛽ ♨ ▬ ▣ WC ☺

HÖCHSTADT/WACHENROTH Bayern 19

Steigerwald Süd (MT)
Wachenroth
☎ 09548-433 fax 09548-435
✉ 96193

* 2 ♬ 95/105 excl. breakfast
* 44 ♬ 120/130 excl. breakfast
◆ P ♨ ↑↓ ▣ WC

HOCKENHEIM Baden-Württemberg 18

Akzenthotel Motodrom (HCR)
Hockenheimring
☎ 06205-2980 fax 06205-298222
✉ 68766

open 01.02 - 31.12
* 24 ♬ 119/149
* 32 ♬ 149/179
AE ◐ E ✳ ♨ ◆ P ⛽ ♨ ↑↓ ▬ ▣ WC TV ☺

Rheinhotel Luxhof (HCR)
A D Speyerer Rheinbrucke
☎ 06205-3030 fax 06205-30325
✉ 68766

10 ♬
33 ♬
AE ◐ E ✳ ♨ P ⛽ ♨ ▬ ▣ WC TV ◉

HOFKIRCHEN Bayern 24

Waldhotel Grübhof (HCR)
Grübhof
☎ 08545-515
✉ 94544

10 ♬ 40/45
30 ♬ 65/80
▒ ♨ P ⛽ ♨ ▬ ▣ WC TV

HOHEGEISS Niedersachsen 14

Estenfelder (HR)   AA ANWB
Kirchstr 20
☎ 05583-847
✉ 38700

The Hotel Estenfelder is situated at an altitude of 642m, in the small *Kur* resort of Hohegeiss, which is the ideal base for walking trips in this beautiful area. All the rooms of this comfortable hotel have private toilet and shower facilities and a colour TV - some also have a balcony. The hotel has an inviting, traditional German *Bierstube* where fine beers are served.

4 ♬ -/68
17 ♬ 130/150
E ♨ ◉ P ⛽ ♨ ▬ ▣ WC TV ↑ ☺

HOHENAU Bayern 24

Romantikhotel die Bierhütte (HCR)
Bierhutte 10
☎ 08558-315 fax 08558-2387
✉ 94545

* 3 ♬ 95/139
* 40 ♬ 146/210
AE ◐ E ✳ ♨ ♨ ◐ P ⛽ ♨ ▬ ▣ WC TV ◉

HÖHR-GRENZHAUSEN Rheinland-Pfalz 12

Heinz (HCR)   AA ANWB
Bergstr 77
☎ 02624-3033 fax 02624-5974
✉ 56203

Hotel Heinz caters for business travellers and tourists alike. This peaceful hotel is surrounded by greenery, the rooms have up-to-date modern amenities. There are 2 restaurants both serving their own specialities. The hotel is conveniently situated for excursions to the Rhine and Mosel. Recreational facilities such as horse-riding and

→

golf are available nearby, and there is a beauty salon on the premises.

open 27.12 - 22.12
* 14 ♬ 90/155
* 50 ⚬ 150/280
AE ⓞ E ⚙ ♣ ♠ ⓟ P ⌐ ⚐ ♨ ╫ ▬ ▭ WC TV ⦿ ⊙

HOMBERG Hessen 13

Stadt Cassel (HR)   AA ANWB
Westheimerstr 25
☎ 05681-7061 fax 05681-7064
✉ 34576

The Hotel Stadt Cassel is very comfortable and well furnished. The rooms range in size from normal to very spacious, and include a minibar. The hotel has a bar and restaurant. Meeting rooms and conference facilities are available.

* 2 ♬ 90/-
* 10 ⚘ 150/-
AE ⓞ E ⚙ ⦿ ♦ P ⌐ ⚐ ▬ ▭ WC TV ⦿ ⊙

HORB/DETTINGEN Baden-Württemberg 21

Adler (HR)
Alte Str 3
Horb
☎ 07482-230
✉ 72160

* 5 ♬ 38/43
* 9 ⚘ 64/76
♣ ⦿ P ⚐ ▭ WC ⦿ ⊙

HÖSBACH Bayern 18

Zur Sonne (HR)
Haibacher Str 108
☎ 06021-69972 fax 06021-60201
✉ 63768

open 31.08 - 01.08
2 ♬ 70/90
9 ⚘ 120/130
P ⚐ ▬ ▭ WC ⦿ ⌂ ⊙

HÖXTER Nordrhein-Westfalen 13

Niedersachsen Ringhotel Höxter (HR)
Möllingerstr 4
☎ 05271-6880 fax 05271-688444
✉ 37671

* 23 ♬ 89/118
* 42 ⚘ 158/178
ⓞ E ⚙ ♣ ⦿ P ⌐ ⚐ ♨ ╫ ▬ ▭ WC TV ⦿

Weserberghof (HCR)   AA ANWB
Godelheimerstr 16
☎ 05271-1087 fax 05271-3921
✉ 37671

The Hotel Weserberghof is a more mature but well maintained establishment; rooms have en suite bathroom and telephone, some have colour TV. It is an excellent base for day trips in the surrounding area, and bicycles can be hired from the hotel.

* 10 ♬ 65/95
* 15 ⚘ 110/130
♣ ⦿ P ⌐ ⚐ ♨ ⚑ ▬ ▭ WC ⦿ ⊙ ✈

HÜGELSHEIM Baden-Württemberg 21

Zum Schwan (HR)
Haupstr 45
☎ 07229-30690 fax 07229-306969
✉ 76549

* 2 ♬ 62/68 excl. breakfast
* 19 ⚘ 98/102 excl. breakfast
⦿ P ⌐ ⚑ ▭ WC ⦿

HÜRTGENWALD/VOSSENACK
Nordrhein-Westfalen 11

Zum Alten Forsthaus (HCR)
Germeter 49
Hürtgenwald
☎ 02429-7822 fax 02429-2104
✉ 52393

* 7 ♬ 98/128
* 63 ⚘ 150/190
ⓞ E ⚙ ♣ ♠ P ⌐ ⚐ ▬ WC TV ⊙

IBBENBÜREN Nordrhein-Westfalen 6

Hubertushof (HCR)
Münsterstr 222
☎ 05451-3410 fax 05451-45074
✉ 49479

open 25.01 - 22.12
* 5 ♬ 75/120
* 10 ⚘ 130/180
AE ⓞ ⚙ ⚬ ♦ P ⌐ ⚐ ▬ ▭ WC TV ⦿ ⊙

GERMANY 117

Leischulte (HCR)
Rheiner Str 10
☏ 05451-4088 fax 05451-1080
✉ 49479

16 🛏 53/95
25 🛌 130/160
AE ⓘ E ≡ ⓢ ♦ P 🍴 ♋ ♒ ⇅ ⊟ 🅿 WC TV ⓘ ⊙

IDAR-OBERSTEIN Rheinland-Pfalz   17

Handelshof (HCR)   AA ANWB
Tiefensteinerstr 235
☏ 06781-31011 fax 06781-31057
✉ 55743

The Hotel Handelshof enjoys a beautiful location 2km from the centre of Idar-Oberstein. All the rooms have en suite facilities and most also have a TV. There is a bar and a pleasant restaurant, and private parking facilities are available.

8 🛏 50/68
9 🛌 80/110
ⓢ P 🍴 ⇅ ⊟ 🅿 WC TV ⓘ⊙

IDSTEIN Hessen   18

Kern (HCR)
Am Dorfbrunnen 6
☏ 06126-8474
✉ 65510

4 🛏
16 🛌
♋ ⓢ P 🅿 WC ⓘ⊙

IGGENSBACH Bayern   24

Linsmeier (HCR)   AA ANWB
Hauptstr 5
☏ 09903-8407 fax 09903-2407
✉ 94547

The Hotel Linsmeier is situated in the Bayern woods and is ideal for an overnight stop. The rooms are well furnished and have a shower and toilet. The restaurant serves Bayern specialities, and parking facilities are available.

* - 🛏 40/55
* 45 🛌 70/80
E ♋ ⓢ P 🍴 ♒ ⇅ ⊟ 🅿 TV ⓘ⊙

ILLERTISSEN Bayern   22

Am Schloß (HR)
Lindenweg 6
☏ 07303-3040
✉ 89257

5 🛏
12 🛌
♋ P 🍴 ♒ ⇅ ⊟ 🅿 WC TV

Sonnenhof (HR)   AA ANWB
☏ 07303-3635
✉ 89257

The Hotel Sonnenhof is approximately 2km outside the centre of Illertissen. The rooms are well furnished, and most have a shower and toilet. For youngsters there is a recreation ground and skittle alley, and there is also a sunny terrace.

* 7 🛏 40/45
* 8 🛌 76/86
♋ ⓢ P ♒ ⊟ 🅿 WC ⊙

ILSHOFEN Baden-Württemberg   19

Brauereigasthof Post (HR)
Hauptstr 5
☏ 07904-1012
✉ 74532

10 🛌
ⓢ P ⇅ 🅿 WC 🐕

IMMENSTAAD Baden-Württemberg   22

Seehof (HR)
Bachstr 15
☏ 07545-784 fax 07545-786
✉ 88090

open 01.03 - 31.12
12 🛏 85/125
22 🛌 140/175
AE E ≡ ♋ ⓢ ⓐ P 🍴 ♒ ♒ ⇄ 🅿 WC TV ⓘ⊙ 🐕

IMMENSTADT Bayern 22

Goldener Adler (HCR)
Marienpl 14
☎ 08323-8549 fax 08323-4665
✉ 87509

The Goldener Adler is situated in a town renowned for its art, culture and richly decorated houses. The nearby Alpsee offers windsurfing and swimming. The well decorated rooms have a pleasant atmosphere and all have a shower and toilet. The restaurant offers international and local specialities and parking facilities are available.

6 ♦ 45/50 excl. breakfast
17 ♦ 90/100 excl. breakfast
E ⊙ P ⚲ ♨ ⊟ ⊡ WC

Hirsch (HR)
Hirschstr 11
☎ 08323-6218 fax 08323-80965
✉ 87509

* 8 ♦ 60/70
* 16 ♦ 115/130
AE ⊙ E ⚌ ⚹ ⊙ P ⚲ ↕ ⊟ ⊡ WC TV

INGELHEIM AM RHEIN Rheinland-Pfalz 18

Multatuli (HR)
Mainzerstr 255
☎ 06132-73183 fax 06132-76363
✉ 55218

* 2 ♦ 90/-
* 16 ♦ 140/-
⚹ P ⚲ ⊡ WC TV

INGOLSTADT Bayern 20

Rasthaus Gabel (HR)
An Der Bundesstr 13/16
☎ 08458-8482
✉ 91484

4 ♦
11 ♦
♠ ◆ P ⚲ ⊡

INZELL Bayern 24

Binderhausl (HCR)
Bichlstr 43
☎ 08665-461
✉ 83331

3 ♦
9 ♦
⚹ ⊙ P ⚲ ⊟ ⊡ WC TV ⎌ ☺

Chiemgauer Hof (HA)
Lärchenstr 5
☎ 08665-6700 fax 08665-67070
✉ 83331

* 38 ♦ 90/125
* 50 ♦ 140/210
⚌ ⚹ ⊙ P ⚲ ⚐ ↕ ⟵ ⊟ ⊡ WC TV ⎌ ☺

IRSCHENBERG Bayern 23

Landhotel Irschenberg (HCR)
Loiderdinger Str 12
☎ 08062-1516 fax 08062-5250
✉ 83737

Landhotel Irschenberg is quietly situated just 2 minutes away from the A8 München-Salzburg motorway. This attractively furnished hotel is equally suited to tourists and business people; rooms are well kept and have a private toilet and shower. The terrace is a pleasant place to relax, and there are plenty of recreational facilities available in the immediate vicinity.

open 01.12 - 31.10
* 3 ♦ 100/120
* 25 ♦ 140/160
E ⚌ ♠ ⊙ ◆ P ⚲ ⟵ ⊟ ⊡ WC TV

ISENBURG Rheinland-Pfalz 12

Haus Maria (HCR)
Caanerstr 6
☎ 02601-2980
✉ 72160

Haus Maria is situated in the woods but is well signposted and easy to find. Most rooms have washing facilities and their own terrace. There is a lounge with seating areas and an open fire.

The restaurant offers a varied choice of food, and the hotel also has conference facilities.

open 10.01 - 27.12
* 4 ♪ 45/60
* 10 ⚐ 85/110

ISNY Baden-Württemberg 22

Berghotel Jägerhof (Best Western) (HR)
☏ 07562-770 fax 07562-77252
res nr 0130-4455
✉ 88316

* 8 ♪ 155/205
* 61 ⚐ 220/290

Hohe Linde (HR)
Lindauerstr 75
☏ 07562-4046
✉ 88316

12 ♪
18 ⚐

JAGSTHAUSEN Baden-Württemberg 19

Krone (HR)
Brückenstr 1
☏ 07943-2397
✉ 74249

4 ♪
6 ⚐

JENA Thuringen 14

Holiday Inn Jena (HCR)
☏ 03641-3010 fax 03641-334575
res nr 0130-815131
✉ 07747

This new Holiday Inn is one km from the *Autobahn* Jena-Lobeda and 16km from the Hemsdorfer Kreuz (A9/A4). It is a pleasant hotel for both business travellers and tourists. The rooms and suites are comfortable, fully furnished and spacious. There is a special VIP floor and a room with facilities for disabled guests. The Panorama roof restaurant has splendid views of the Saaletal and the Thüringer mountains. The hotel offers a *Schillerbar, Biergarten,* terrace, fitness centre,

sauna and solarium.
* - ♪ 160/200 excl. breakfast
* 172 ⚐ 200/240 excl. breakfast

KAISERSLAUTERN Rheinland-Pfalz 18

Blechhammer (HCR)
Am Hammerweiher 1
☏ 0631-70071 fax 0631-70075
✉ 67659

6 ♪ 58/115
27 ⚐ 90/175

Dorint Hotel Kaiserslautern (HCR)
St Quentin Ring 1
☏ 0631-20150 fax 0631-27640
res nr 0130-6605
✉ 67663

* 75 ♪ 175/205
* 75 ⚐ 220/260

Pommerscherhof (HG)
Stahlstr 12
☏ 0631-40180 fax 0631-40180
✉ 67655

* 8 ♪ 38/67
* 8 ⚐ 60/95

KAISERSLAUTERN/HOHENECKEN Rheinland-Pfalz 18

Seehotel Gelterswoog (HCR)
Hohenecken
☏ 0631-54011 fax 0631-5811 /
✉ 67661

* 10 ♪ 90/130
* 38 ⚐ 130/170

KALLSTADT Rheinland-Pfalz 18

Gästehaus Keck (HG)
Freinsheimerstr 69
☏ 06322-1606
✉ 67169

2 ♪
5 ⚐

Weincastel zum Weissen Roß (HR)
Weinstr 80-82
☏ 06322-5033 fax 06322-8640
✉ 67169

open 15.02 - 05.01
* - ♪ 95/120
* 13 ♪ 140/180
AE E ⊙ ⛁ ⛴ WC ¶⊘¦

KANDEL Rheinland-Pfalz 18

Zur Pfalz (HCR)
Marktstr 57
☏ 07275-5021 fax 07275-8268
✉ 76870

* 16 ♪ 95/120
* 28 ♪ 136/154
AE ⓘ E ⛴ ⊙ ◆ P ♇ ↑↓ ⛁ WC TV ¶⊘¦

KARLSRUHE Baden-Württemberg 18

Queens Hotel Karlsruhe (HCR)   AA ANWB
Ettlinger Str 23
☏ 0721-37270 fax 0721-3727170
res nr 0130-4433
✉ 76137

Queens Hotel Karlsruhe is a modern hotel, situated 500m from the station and town centre, with the conference centre nearby. All the rooms are spacious and offer comfortable accommodation. There is a cosy, and relaxed atmosphere in the En Vogue bar. The hotel also features a stylish restaurant which has an extensive choice of dishes on the menu.

* 48 ♪ -/245
* 99 ♪ 245/285
AE E ⛴ ⊙ ◆ P ♇ ⛁ WC TV ¶⊘¦

Landgasthof Hotel Sonne (HCR)
Kleinsteinbacherstr 2
☏ 0721-472239 fax 0721-474728
✉ 76228

open 13.01 - 23.05
* 14 ♪ 50/71
* 32 ♪ 86/105
E ⊙ ◆ P ♇ ⛁ WC TV ⊘

KASSEL Hessen 13

Dorinthotel Reiss (HCR)
Werner Hilpertstr 24
☏ 0561-78830 fax 0561-7883777
res nr 0130-6605
✉ 34117

* 26 ♪ -/170
* 75 ♪ -/215
⊙ ◆ P ♇ ↑↓ ⛁ WC TV ¶⊘¦

Mövenpick Kassel (HCR)   AA ANWB
Spohrstr 4
☏ 0561-72850 fax 0561-7285118
res nr 0561-7285104
✉ 34117

The Mövenpick Kassel is in the centre of the Kurfürsten-Galerie, the new shopping centre of Kassel. The rooms and suites have extensive facilities. The well known Mövenpick restaurant, serves good quality food, and the Tchin Tchin bar is open until late. There are facilities for disabled visitors and meeting rooms. The hotel can be reached from the A7 (junction Kassel-Ost) and from the A44 to Dortmund (junction Kassel-Südkreuz).

* 44 ♪ 175/300 excl. breakfast
* 84 ♪ 230/340 excl. breakfast
AE ⓘ E ⛴ ↑↓ ⛁ WC TV ¶⊘¦

Queens Hotel Kassel (HCR)
Heiligenröderstr 61
☏ 0561-52050 fax 0561-527400
✉ 34123

15 ♪
127 ♪
AE ⓘ E ⛴ ⊙ P ♇ ↑↓ ⛁ WC TV ¶⊘¦ ⊘

Schloßhotel Willemshöhe (HCR)
Am Schlosspark 2
☏ 0561-30880 fax 0561-3088428
✉ 34131

30 ♪
82 ♪
AE ⓘ E ⛴ ♠ ◆ P ♇ ☂ ⚓ ↑↓ ⇥ ⛁ WC TV ¶⊘¦

GERMANY 121

KASSEL/LOHFELDEN Hessen　　　　　　13

Autobahn Rasthaus (HR)
Ab-Ausfahrt Kasselmitte
Lohfelden
☎ 0561-583031
✉ 34253

10 🛏
32 🛌
⛔ 🔘 🇪 🛒 ◆ 🅿 🏠 ♨ ↑↓ 🛏 🛋 🚾 📺 🍴

KASSEL/NIEDERZWEHREN Hessen　　　　　　13

Gude (HR)
Frankfurterstr 299
Kassel
☎ 0561-48050 fax 0561-4805101
✉ 34134

* 14 🛏 130/200
* 48 🛌 170/260
🇪 🛒 🔘 ◆ 🅿 🏠 ♨ 🎣 ↑↓ 🛏 🛋 🚾 📺 🍴

KASSEL/WILHELMSHÖHE Hessen　　　　　　13

Schweizer Hof (HCR)
Am Schloßpark 2
Kassel
☎ 0561-34048
✉ 34131

20 🛏
40 🛌
⛔ 🔘 🇪 🛒 🔘 ◆ 🅿 🏠 ♨ ↑↓ 🛋 🚾 📺

KAUB Rheinland-Pfalz　　　　　　18

Goldner Stern (HR)
Metzgergasse 4
☎ 06774-221
✉ 56349

2 🛏
9 🛌
🔘 🅿

KELHEIM Bayern　　　　　　20

Ehrnthaller (HR)
Donaustr 22
☎ 09441-3333 fax 09441-21420
✉ 93309

open 27.12 - 21.12
15 🛏 55/75
45 🛌 88/120
⛔ 🇪 🛒 🔘 🅿 🏠 ↑↓ 🛋 🚾 📺 ⊛

KELL Rheinland-Pfalz　　　　　　17

Zur Post (HR)
Hochwaldstr 2
☎ 06589-1600 fax 06589-2235
✉ 54427

1 🛏 48/54
8 🛌 86/92
🇪 🔘 🅿 🏠 ♨ 🛋 📺 🍴 ✈

KERPEN/SINDORF Nordrhein-Westfalen　　　11

Park Hotel (HG)　　　　　　AA ANWB
Kerpener Str 183
Sindorf
☎ 02273-570094 fax 02273-54985
✉ 50170

Park Hotel is set in a favourable position just a short distance from the centre and the motorway. This hotel is especially suitable for a stopover during a long journey. The rooms are well equipped and the restaurant serves good quality dishes. There are ample covered and open parking facilities.

* 7 🛏 75/100
* 18 🛌 110/150
⛔ 🔘 🇪 🛒 🔘 ◆ 🅿 🏠 ♨ ↑↓ 🛋 🚾 ⊛

KIEL Schleswig-Holstein　　　　　　3

Astor (HCR)
Am Holstenpl
☎ 0431-93017 fax 0431-96378
✉ 24103

* 12 🛏 80/125
* 47 🛌 160/170
⛔ 🔘 🇪 🛒 🔘 🏠 ↑↓ 🛋 🚾 📺 ⊛

Avance Conti Hansa (HCR)　　　AA ANWB
Schlossgarten 7
☎ 0431-51150 fax 0431-5115444
✉ 24103

This first-class Steigenberger hotel is situated by the Kieler Förde just outside the centre of Kiel, on the outskirts of the Schlossgarten. The comfortable, tastefully furnished rooms on the first floor of the Avance Conti Hansa hotel offer

→

fine views of the harbour. The hall with its abundance of glass and flowers and the restaurant have the peaceful atmosphere of a winter-garden.

* 40 ♫ 215/245
* 124 ⚭ 260/310

AE ⓘ E ⚒ ⚓ ⊙ P ⥮ ⚒ ⚐ 🖥 🅿 WC TV 🍴 ☺

Erkenhof (HG)
Dänische Str 12-16
☏ 0431-95008 fax 0431-978965
✉ 24103

4 ♫
23 ⚭

AE ⓘ E ⚒ ⚓ ⊙ P ⥮ 🖥 🅿 TV

Maritim (HCR)
Bismarckallee 2
☏ 0431-38940 fax 0431-338490
res nr 0221-219672
✉ 24063

* 19 ♫ 195/325
* 70 ⚭ 285/420

AE ⓘ E ⚒ ⚓ ⚒ ⊙ P ⥮ ⚒ ⚓ ⚒ ⥮ 🖥 🅿 WC TV 🍴 ☺

KINDING/ENKERING Bayern 24

Heckl (HCR) AA ANWB
Hauptstr 25
Enkering
☏ 08467-321 fax 08467-764
✉ 85125

Hotel Heckl is situated in the small town of Kinding, not far from the Nürnberg-München motorway, and is the ideal venue for an overnight stop. It has views over the wooded slopes in the Altmütal. The bedrooms are well kept and the restaurant offers a choice of good value meals.

* 10 ♫ 45/55
* 26 ⚭ 75/85

E ⊙ ◆ P 🅿 ⚒ 🅿 WC 🍴

KIPFENBERG/PFAHLDORF Bayern 20

Geyer (HCR) AA ANWB
Alte Hauptstr 10
Pfahldorf
☏ 08465-501 fax 08465-3396
✉ 85110

The Hotel Geyer is situated in a nature reserve close to Eichstatt, where various ruins and museums can be found, appealing particularly to nature and culture enthusiasts. The rooms are well kept and fully equipped; and the restaurant offers a rich and varied menu, following the tradition of German hotels. The hotel has bicycles for hire.

* 5 ♫ 35/50
* 30 ⚭ 60/85

E ⚓ P 🅿 ⚒ ⥮ ⚓ 🖥 🅿 WC TV 🍴 ☺

KIRCHEN/KATZENBACH Rheinland-Pfalz 12

Zum Weissen Stein (HCR) AA ANWB
Kirchen
☏ 02741-62085 fax 02741-62581
✉ 89584

The Hotel zum Weissen Stein is a modern, comfortable hotel just outside Kirchen. It has views over the valley, a beautiful walking area and the 1000- year-old Castle Freusburg nearby. The hotel, an inn until 1968, consists of two joined buildings; in one part there are several restaurants, and in the other the bedrooms. The rooms are large, with a seating area, balcony, minibar, safe, toilet and TV.

* 8 ♫ 82/88
* 23 ⚭ 139/159

AE ⓘ E ⚒ ⚓ ⚓ P 🅿 ⚒ ⚓ 🖥 🅿 WC TV 🍴 ☺

KIRCHHEIM Hessen 13

Eydt (HCR)
Hauptstr 19
☏ 06625-7001 fax 06625-5333
✉ 36273

11 ♫
45 ⚭

E ⚓ ⊙ P 🅿 ⥮ ⚓ 🖥 🅿 WC TV 🍴

GERMANY 123

KIRCHHEIMBOLANDEN Rheinland-Pfalz   18

Braun (HR)
Uhlandsstr 1
☎ 06352-2343 fax 06352-6228
✉ 67292

12 🛏
23 🛌
🌿 ⊙ P 🅿 ⛱ ↨ 🚻 WC TV 🍽

KIRCHHEIM/HESSEN Hessen   13

Center Kirchheim (MT)   AA ANWB
Kirchheim
☎ 06625-1080 fax
06625-8656
✉ 36273

This large motel is situated on a hillside in northern Hessen. The rooms have washing facilities, radio, TV, telephone and a minibar. The Center Kirchheim has 2 restaurants, both with their own specialities. There is a swimming pool, solarium and an 18-hole golf course.

* 64 🛏 90/125 excl. breakfast
* 76 🛌 125/145 excl. breakfast
AE ⓪ E ≡ ◆ P 🅿 ⛱ 🏊 🛏 🍴 🗄 WC TV 🍽
See advertisement page 125

KIRCHHUNDEM Nordrhein-Westfalen   12

Zur Post (HR)   AA ANWB
Selbecke 21
☎ 02723-72744
✉ 57399

The Hotel zur Post is a family-run country hotel just outside Kirchhundem, in the small village of Selbecke, an area which is suitable for summer and winter holidays. The rooms are large and have shower and toilet. There is an excellent restaurant, a separate TV room, a sunbathing lawn and plenty of parking spaces.

open 01.12 - 31.10
* 2 🛏 35/45
* 9 🛌 70/90
🌿 🛏 P 🅿 🗄 WC 🍽 ⊙

KIRN Rheinland-Pfalz   17

Parkhotel (HR)   AA ANWB
Kallenfelser Str 40
☎ 06752-3666 fax
06752-3667
✉ 55606

The Parkhotel is set in a small park in Kirn, surrounded by a romantic landscape. It offers first-class cuisine, friendly service, comfort and relaxation. Special dishes are prepared on an open wood fire on the vine-covered terrace. Most of the rooms have a shower, toilet and telephone. There is plenty of opportunity in the surrounding area for walking, climbing and searching for precious stones.

open 01.03 - 31.01
* 2 🛏 50/75
* 16 🛌 80/125
🌿 ⊙ P 🅿 ⛱ 🗄 WC TV 🍽 ⊙

KITZINGEN Bayern   19

Deutsches Haus (HR)
Bismarckstr 8-10
☎ 09321-91690 fax 09321-916955
✉ 97318

* 9 🛏 60/105
* 31 🛌 95/140
AE ⓪ E ≡ 🌿 ⊙ P 🅿 🍴 🗄 🗄 WC

KLEINICH Rheinland-Pfalz   17

Landhaus Arnoth (HCR)   AA ANWB
Auf dem Pütz
☎ 06536-286 fax
06536-1217
✉ 54483

Landhaus Arnoth is a comfortably furnished hotel, set in the Hunsrück. The comfortable rooms - some situated on the ground floor - are spacious, and have toilet and shower. The hotel has a games room, a garden and a sauna. The restaurant serves home-cooking, as well as international dishes. Use of bicycles is free.

open 20.08 - 24.07
* - 🛏 80/110
* 15 🛌 120/150
🏠 ⊙ ◆ P 🅿 ⛱ 🍴 🗄 🗄 WC 🍽

KOBLENZ *Rheinland-Pfalz* 17

Cityhotel Metropol (HCR)   AA ANWB
Altstadt-Münzpl
☎ 0261-35060 fax 0261-160366
✉ 56068

The Cityhotel Metropol lies in the centre of ancient Koblenz close to the Deutsches Eck, and is an ideal base for making day trips. The hotel is well appointed throughout, and well maintained, while the rooms provide comfortable accommodation. Guests can enjoy a glass of wine in the pleasant bistro and pub. A swimming pool and fitness room are only 50m from the hotel.

* 8 ♂ 100/190
* 42 ⚭ 140/290
AE ⓪ E ☰ ♃ ⊙ P ⇥ ⇅ ⊟ ⌐ WC TV ⑩ ⓥ

Continental Pfälzerhof (HR)   AA ANWB
Bahnhofstr 1
☎ 0261-33073 fax 0261-12390
✉ 56068

The Hotel Continental Pfälzerhof is situated opposite the station, and has double glazing throughout to ensure its guests a peaceful stay. The well kept rooms feature en suite facilities, telephone and radio. The hotel offers a range of function and conference facilities, and covered parking is available.

9 ♂ 85/130
28 ⚭ 130/200
AE ⓪ E ☰ ♃ ⊙ P ⇥ ⇅ ⊟ ⌐ WC TV ⓥ

Hamm (HG)   AA ANWB
St Josephstr 32
☎ 0261-34546 fax 0261-160972
✉ 56068

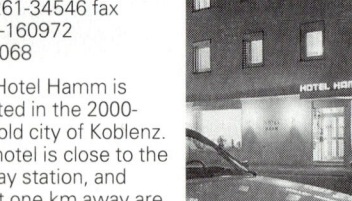

The Hotel Hamm is situated in the 2000-year-old city of Koblenz. The hotel is close to the railway station, and about one km away are the moorings for the Rhine ships. The rooms all have a shower, toilet, telephone and radio, and TV is available on request. The rooms can all be reached by lift. Parking facilities are available.

* 6 ♂ 65/95
* 24 ⚭ 130/170
AE ⓪ E ☰ ♃ ⊙ P ⇥ ⇅ ⊟ ⌐ WC TV ⓥ

KOCHEL AM SEE *Bayern* 23

Zum Lutzhof (HR)
Altjoch 12
☎ 08851-263 fax 08851-1625
✉ 82431

open 11.02 - 09.01
* 2 ♂ 68/95
* 18 ⚭ 105/150
♃ P ⇥ ⚓ ⊟ ⌐ WC

Zur Post (HCR)
Schmied V Kochek Pl 6
☎ 08851-209
✉ 82431

5 ♂
25 ⚭
♃ ⊙ P ⇥ ⚓ ⌐

Schmied Von Kochel (HR)
Schlehdorferstr 6
☎ 08851-216
✉ 82431

8 ♂
26 ⚭
♃ ⊙ P ⇥ ⚓ ⇅ ⇥ ⊟ ⌐ WC TV ⑩

KOCHEL AM SEE/RIED *Bayern* 23

Rabenkopf (HCR)
Kochelstr 23
Kochel am See
☎ 08851-208 fax 08851-9167
✉ 82431

5 ♂ 48/68
13 ⚭ 116/136
AE ⓪ E ☰ ⊙ ♦ P ⇥ ⇥ ⊟ ⌐ WC TV ⑩ ⌂ ⓥ

KÖLN *Nordrhein-Westfalen* 11

With the twin spires of its glorious cathedral visible far away across the surrounding plain, Cologne is one of Germany's great metropolitan cities, a centre of culture, arts and learning as well as industry and commerce. Centrepiece of the city, the Dom, begun in the 13th century, was only completed in the 19th, still faithful to the original drawings of the medieval architects. Lace-like masonry decorates the exterior mass, and inside are many important works of art as well as superb stained glass. A stiff climb up the south tower is rewarded by a fine panorama over the city.

GERMANY

WELCOME

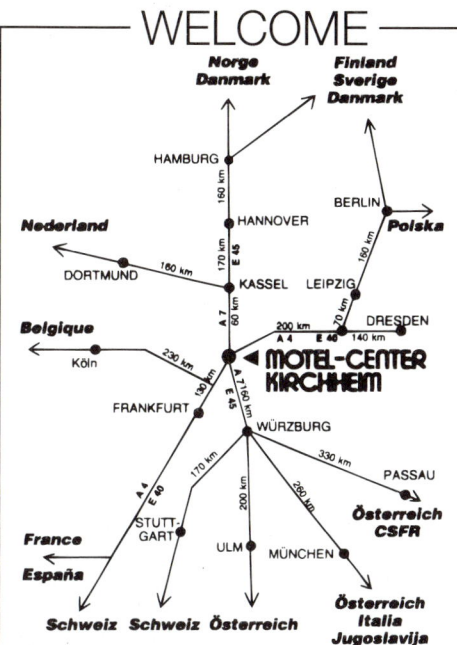

to Germany's biggest motel. Your stopover during your trip south. 140 rooms with every comfort you require. Baby beds, family rooms, rooms for the handicapped and non-smoking rooms. Well-organised parking space, free of charge for each room ● outdoor swimming pool ● fitness club and indoor swimming pool, sauna, solarium and keep-fit room ● gaming hall ● newspaper stand ● family and grill restaurant ● verandahs ● bistro ● family playground. Charge per night per person double room NLG 69, three-person room NLG 55, four-person room NLG 47, single room NLG 109.

10% discount for members with valid membership card.

Credit cards, VISA, EG, DC, AE.

Motorway Dortmund-Kassel-Würzburg, Exit: Kirchheim, kilometre 368, A7, follow the blue signs to the MOTEL.

GERMANY'S LARGEST MOTEL

D-36275 KIRCHEIM, Hess.
Telephone: 06625-108-0
Fax: 06625-8656

See entry page 123

Southeast of the cathedral is the splendid Römansch-Germanisches Museum; the modern complex housing the concert hall, Philharmonie; and the Wallraf-Richard and Ludwig museums, with their major collections of German and international art. Southwards again is the Hohe Strasse, the city's main shopping street; other streets and passages lead towards the Rhine into old Cologne, the *Altstadt*, centred on the Alter Markt and the 14th century Gothic Rathaus, with its Renaissance loggia.

Euro Garden Cologne (HCR)
Domstr 10-16
☎ 0221-16490 fax 0221-1649333
res nr 0221-123051
✉ 50668

* 1 ♦ 95/350 excl. breakfast
* 89 ♦ 125/410 excl. breakfast

Euro Plaza Cologne (HCR)
Breslauer Pl 2
☎ 0221-16510 fax 0221-1651333
res nr 0221-123051
✉ 50668

* 41 ♦ 105/390 excl. breakfast
* 67 ♦ 135/460 excl. breakfast

Holiday Inn Crowne Plaza Köln (HCR)
Habsburgerring 9-13
☎ 0221-20950 fax 0221-251206
res nr 0130-815131
✉ 50674

* 118 ♦ 330/550 excl. breakfast
* 181 ♦ 375/600 excl. breakfast

Lenz (HR)
Ursulapl 9-11
☎ 0221-120055 fax 0221-132845
✉ 50668

25 ♦
65 ♦

Maritim (HCR)
Heumarkt 20
☎ 0221-20270 fax 0221-2027826
res nr 0221-924080
✉ 50667

* 115 ♦ 245/423
* 305 ♦ 298/488

GERMANY

Mercure Severinshof (HCR)
Severinstr 199
☎ 0221-20130 fax 0221-2013666
✉ 50676

* 39 ♪ 148/295
* 213 ♫ 178/395

Pullman Hotel Mondial (HCR)
Kurt Hackenberg Pl 1
☎ 0221-20630 fax 0221-2063522
res nr 0221-2063519
✉ 50667

* 60 ♪ 193/330 excl. breakfast
* 144 ♫ 214/355 excl. breakfast

Queens Hotel Köln (HCR)
Dürener Str 287
☎ 0221-46760 fax 0221-433765
✉ 50935

* 45 ♪ 155/-
* 102 ♫ 185/-

Regent International (Best Western) (HR)
Melatengürtel 15
☎ 0221-54990 fax 0221-5499998
res nr 0130-4455
✉ 50933

* 74 ♪ 199/359 excl. breakfast
* 100 ♫ 229/399 excl. breakfast

Rema Hotel Europa am Dom (HR)
Am Hof 38-46
☎ 0221-20580 fax 0221-211021
res nr 0130-3633
✉ 50667

open 02.01 - 22.12
* 40 ♪ 150/290
* 52 ♫ 240/390

KÖLN-MÜHLHEIM Nordrhein-Westfalen 11

Kaiser (HG)   AA ANWB
Genovevastr 10
Köln-Mühlheim
☎ 0221-623057 fax 0221-623050
✉ 51065

The bed and breakfast hotel Kaiser has rooms with en suite facilities, colour TV and telephone. Guests can enjoy an apéritif in the bar before going out to dinner in one of Köln's many restaurants. It is the ideal venue for business people, as well as for tourists wishing to explore the city. The hotel has parking facilities available.

* 7 ♪ 110/-
* 40 ♫ 155/-

KÖLN-PORZ Nordrhein-Westfalen 11

Holiday Inn Köln/Bonn Airport (HR)   AA ANWB
Waldstr 255
Köln-Porz
☎ 02203-5610 fax 02203-5619
res nr 0130-815131
✉ 51147

The Holiday Inn Köln is only 500m from the airport, and 20 minutes by car to the centres of Bonn and Köln. It is a good base for both business travellers and holiday-makers alike; luxury rooms all have washing facilities, radio, TV, air conditioning, minibar and sound insulation. Drinks are served in the Munchhausen Bar.

* 101 ♪ 240/380 excl. breakfast
* 140 ♫ 300/440 excl. breakfast

KÖNIGSTEIN IM TAUNUS Hessen 18

Grüner Baum (HP)
Hauptstr 12
☎ 06174-7346
✉ 61462

8 ♪
10 ♫

GERMANY

Sonnenhof (HCR)
Falkensteinerstr 9
☎ 06174-29080 fax 06174-290875
✉ 61462

* 19 ♦ 160/190
* 25 ♦ 230/310
AE ⓘ E 🕀 P 🍴 🐕 🛏 ⏐ 📺

KÖNIGSWINTER Nordrhein-Westfalen   12

Maritim (HCR)
Rheinallee 3
☎ 02223-7070 fax 02223-707811
res nr 0221-219672
✉ 53639

40 ♦ 207/357
176 ♦ 274/474
AE ⓘ E 🕀 ♦ ⊙ P 🍴 🐕 🛏 ⏐ 📺 🍽

Rheingold (HCR) AA ANWB
Drachenfelsstr 36
☎ 02223-92020 fax 02223-920220
✉ 53639

The town of Königswinter lies near the river Rhine, in the Zeven mountains, at the foot of the Drachenfels, scene of many old folk tales. The Hotel Rheingold is quite a large tourist hotel in the town centre, close to the railway station. All the rooms have a bathroom or shower and toilet. The restaurant, conference rooms and café/garden terrace seat approximately 500 people, and a dance orchestra plays every day.

* 2 ♦ 70/100
* 21 ♦ 130/160
AE ⓘ E 🕀 ♦ ⊙ P 🍴 🛏 ⏐ 📺 🍽

Siebengebirge (HR) AA ANWB
Hauptstr 342
☎ 02223-21359 fax 02223-1803
✉ 53639

The Hotel Siebengebirge offers modern rooms, well prepared food and drink and hospitality at a very reasonable price. In addition to the various function rooms, there is a café and a restaurant which prepares local and international dishes. The hotel is family run, is centrally located and has secure garages which can be locked.

open 01.02 - 14.12
* 1 ♦ 55/75
* 9 ♦ 90/130
AE ⓘ E 🕀 ⊙ P 🍴 🐕 ⏐ ✈
See advertisement page 129

KÖNINGSBRONN Bayern   19

Weisses Rössl (HR)
Zangerstr 1
☎ 07328-6282
✉ 89551

open 18.04 - 04.04
6 ♦ 50/-
7 ♦ 85/-
ⓘ E 🕀 ♦ P 🍴 ⏐ 🍽

KONSTANZ Baden-Württemberg   22

Graf Zepplin (HCR)
St Stefanspl 15
☎ 07531-23780 fax 07531-17226
✉ 78462

* - ♦ 60/80
* 25 ♦ 110/150
⊙ ⏐

Mago (HG)
Bahnhofpl 4
☎ 07531-27001 fax 07531-27003
✉ 78462

* 10 ♦ 120/130
* 19 ♦ 150/190
AE E 🕀 ♦ ⊙ P 🍴 🛏 ⏐ 📺 ⊙

Steigenberger Inselhotel (HR)
Auf Der Insel 1
☎ 07531-1250 fax 07531-26402
res nr 069-663080
✉ 78462

* 31 ♦ 215/265
* 72 ♦ 300/480
AE ⓘ E 🕀 P 🍴 🛏 ⏐ 📺 🍽 ⊙

128 GERMANY

KORDEL Rheinland-Pfalz   17

Raach (HR)   AA ANWB
Kreuzfeld 1
☎ 06505-598 fax 06505-509
✉ 54306

The Hotel Raach is a comfortable hotel situated in a wooded area which is good for walking. The modern rooms all have a shower and toilet, and the hotel has a grill restaurant and a terrace. Parking facilities are available.

open 05.03 - 31.10 + 01.12 - 31.12
* 4 ♂ 40/59
* 13 ₪ 64/108
AE ⊙ P ⚐ ↑↓ C WC TV ☺

KOTHEN Bayern   13

Rhonperle (HCR)
Zum Schmelzhof 32
☎ 09748-515
✉ 8781

4 ♂
13 ₪
◆ P ⚐ ⌂ C WC ⎈

KOTHEN-RHÖN Bayern   13

Gästehaus Möller (HP)
Auersbergstr 26
Kothen
☎ 09748-333 fax 09748-333
✉ 97786

* 1 ♂ 22/28
* 7 ₪ 44/56
E ♣ P ⚐ ☂ ⌂ C WC ⎈

KREFELD Nordrhein-Westfalen   11

Parkhotel Krefelderhof (Best Western) (HCR)   AA ANWB
Ürdingerstr 245
☎ 02151-5840 fax 02151-58435
res nr 0130-4455
✉ 47800

The Parkhotel Krefelderhof is situated in a large park containing beautiful old trees, just a short distance from the town centre and the major motorways. The rooms and suites have luxurious furnishings, and there are 3 different pleasantly furnished restaurants, each serving its own specialities. Excellent meeting and conference facilities are available.

* 63 ♂ 210/295
* 87 ₪ 300/400
AE ⓞ E ⚐ P ⚐ ↑↓ ⌂ C WC TV ⎈ ☺

Treff Hansa Hotel Krefeld (HR)
Am Hauptbahnhof 2
☎ 02151-8290 fax 02151-829150
res nr 0130-858282
✉ 47798

* - ♂ 195/275
* 107 ₪ 219/349
AE ⓞ E ⚐ ⊙ ◆ P ⚐ ↑↓ ⌂ C WC TV ⎈ ☺

KREKEL Nordrhein-Westfalen   11

Schönblick (HCR)   AA ANWB
Ahrstr 9
☎ 02447-1447
✉ 53925

The Hotel Schonblick gets its name ('beautiful view') because of its location. All rooms are comfortable and have hot and cold running water. The restaurant's speciality is game.

open 01.11 - 15.10
* 2 ♂ 35/40
* 5 ₪ 70/78
♣ P ⚐ ⚐ ⌂ C WC TV ⎈ ☺

KRESSBRONN Baden-Württemberg   23

Seehof (HP)
Seestr 25
☎ 07543-6480
✉ 97892

2 ♂
18 ₪
♣ P ⚐ ⚐ ☂ ⌂ C WC TV ⎈ ⬆ ⎈

GERMANY 129

Hauptstrasse 342
(Pedestrian-only area)
D-53639 Königswinter
Owner:
Theo Münchrath
Tel.: 02223 - 21359
Fax: 02223 - 1803

Family property since 75 years

Hotel-Restaurant **SIEBENGEBIRGE**

Excellent regional cuisine, marvellous wines. Modern rooms with shower/wc, bath on each floor, telephone and television connection, tv-lounge and terrace giving onto inner courtyard. Garage and indoor parking area.

Apartments (up to 4 persons) on request. Half-board on request.

Prices:
single room 55 to 75 DEM
double room 45 to 65 DEM per person

Special prices!
Ask for our special prices and the folder.

See entry page 127

KREUZWERTHEIM Bayern 19

In den Herrnwiesen (HR)   AA ANWB
In den Herrnwiesen 4
☎ 09342-37031 fax 09342-22863
✉ 97892

The In den Herrnwiesen is a completely renovated, hospitable hotel situated on the wooded outskirts of the small town of Kreuzwertheim. It is an ideal base for walking trips and car excursions. The hotel has a comfortable atmosphere, and rooms vary from simple and functional to very comfortable with en suite bathroom. During the summer, the garden with its renovated terrace is a pleasant place to relax.

* 3 ♦ 85/110
* 18 ⚏ 130/180

Lindenhof (HCR)   AA ANWB
Lindenstr
☎ 09342-1041 fax 09342-4353
✉ 82494

The Hotel Lindenhof is surrounded by woods and hills and is easily accessible from the Spessart motorway. This is a business and holiday hotel; facilities include a swimming pool, tennis courts, bowling alley and riding.

open 15.01 - 23.12
5 ♦ 80/120
9 ⚏ 120/210

KRÜN Bayern 23

Schönblick (HG)
Soiernstr 1
☎ 08825-228
✉ 8108

13 ♦
14 ⚏

KULMBACH Bayern 20

Hansa (HG)
Weltrichstr 2 a
☎ 09221-7995 fax 09221-66787
✉ 95326

open 06.01 - 22.12
* 4 ♦ 100/130 excl. breakfast
* 20 ⚏ 170/210 excl. breakfast

Kronprinz (HG)
Fischergasse 4-6
☎ 09221-84031 fax 09221-1585
✉ 95326

* 7 ♦ 95/120
* 12 ⚏ 130/160

Senator Parkhotel (Best Western) (HCR) AA ANWB
Luitpoldstr 2
☎ 09221-6030 fax 09221-603100
res nr 0130-4455
✉ 95309

The Senator Parkhotel enjoys an idyllic location, not far from the centre of Kulmbach. The modern and comfortable rooms have exceptionally wide beds, a minibar, trouser press and hairdryer. Both in the restaurant Dolce Vita and the bistro Siesta guests are served excellent fish and regional dishes. During the week the hotel's leisure and massage centre, in a pleasant cave decor, is open and offers sauna, solarium, Turkish bath and whirlpool. The hotel has meeting rooms and free parking space for 100 vehicles.

* 6 ♫ 145/187
* 97 ⚘ 196/229
AE ⓘ E ☰ P ⚒ ⇅ ▬ ☐ WC TV ⌂

KÜNZELSAU Baden-Württemberg 19

Gasthof Comburgstuben (HR)
Comburgstr 12
☎ 0794-3570
✉ 74653

open 06.01 - 22.12
* 6 ♫ 48/75
* 8 ⚘ 90/115
⚘ P ⌂ ⚒ ▬ ☐ WC TV ⎈ ⌾

Frankenbach (HR)
Bahnhofstr 10
☎ 0794-2333
✉ 74653

* 5 ♫ 38/52
* 7 ⚘ 75/95
⚘ P ⌂ ☐ WC

KYLLBURG Rheinland-Pfalz 17

Haus Wehr Büsch (HCR)
Wilseckerstr
☎ 06563-2666
✉ 54655

7 ♫
14 ⚘
⚑ P ⌂ ⚒ ⇅ ▬ ☐ WC ⎈

LACKENHÄUSER/NEUREICHENAU Bayern 24

Bergland Hof (HP) AA ANWB
Lackenhäuser 5
Neureichenau
☎ 08583-1286 fax 08583-2586
✉ 94089

The Hotel Bergland Hof has a typical southern German atmosphere and is situated on the south side of the Dreisesselberg. All the bedrooms have washing facilities and colour TV, and the hotel also has 2 apartments. The restaurant offers panoramic views; there is a swimming pool, sauna, solarium, tennis court, garden chessboard and children's playground.

open 16.12 - 30.10
* 6 ♫ 59/79
* 24 ⚘ 98/138
E ⚑ ⚘ P ⌂ ⚒ ⇅ ▬ ☐ WC TV ⎈ ⌂ ⌾

LAGE/HÖRSTE Nordrhein-Westfalen 7

Haus Berkenkamp (HP)
Hesskamp J H 50
Hörste
☎ 05232-71178
✉ 32791

* 8 ♫ 48/54
* 10 ⚘ 92/100
⚘ P ⌂ ⚒ ▬ ☐ WC ⎈

LAICHINGEN/FELDSTETTEN
Baden-Württemberg 22

Zur Post (HCR) AA ANWB
Langestr 60
Feldstetten
☎ 07333-5118 fax 07333-21151
✉ 89150

The Hotel zur Post is a peaceful, sunny and attractively situated hotel just 100m from the woods. It consists of a main renovated building, and an annexe. The rooms in the main building are bright and airy and equipped with en suite facilities, TV and telephone. The restaurant offers a wide choice of various specialities and serves an extensive breakfast buffet.

* 6 ♦ 55/60
* 10 ♦ 96/110
🆎 🔣 ♦ ⬧ 🅿 ☂ ♨ ↑⬜ ⬛ 🆎 🆎 🍽 ☺

LAMSPRINGE Niedersachsen 8

Lindenhof (HR)
Bergstr 10
☎ 05183-1041
✉ 31195

4 ♦
11 ♦
🆎 🔣 ♦ ⬧ 🅿 ☂ ♨ ↑⬜ 🆎 🆎 🍽

LANDAU IN DER PFALZ Rheinland-Pfalz 18

Brenner (HR)
Linienstr 16
☎ 06341-20039
✉ 76829

* 10 ♦ 80/90
* 15 ♦ 135/160
🆎 🔣 ♦ 🅿 ☂ 🆎 ☺

Parkhotel Landau (Best Western) AA ANWB
(HCR)
Mahlastr 1
☎ 06341-1450 fax 06341-145444
res nr 0130-4455
✉ 76807

Park Hotel Landau lies on the edge of a park containing a small lake, within walking distance of the centre. The rooms in this first class hotel have en suite facilities, video, hairdryer and trouser-press. The restaurant serves a wide range of dishes and has a well chosen wine list. Guests can relax in the swimming pool (with jet-stream), the fitness room, sauna, solarium or in the bowling alley.

* 4 ♦ 145/-
* 74 ♦ 190/220
🆎 🔣 ♦ 🅿 ☂ ♨ ↑⬜ ⬛ 🆎 🆎 🍽

LANDSHUT Bayern 20

Luitpold (HR)
Luitpoldstr 43
☎ 0871-61538
✉ 84034

6 ♦ 45/80
9 ♦ 75/110
🆎 🔣 ♦ 🅿 ☂ ⬛ 🆎 🆎

LANGENARGEN Baden-Württemberg 22

Strand Café (HCR)
Obere Seestr 32
☎ 07543-2434 fax 07543-49426
✉ 88085

open 01.02 - 31.12
6 ♦ -/75
6 ♦ -/150
🔣 🅿 ☂ ♨ ↑⬜ 🆎 🆎 ☺

LANGENBURG Baden-Württemberg 19

Post (HR)
Hauptstr 55
☎ 07905-352
✉ 74595

5 ♦
9 ♦
🔣 🅿 ☂ ⬛ 🆎 🆎 ☺

LANGSCHEID Nordrhein-Westfalen 12

Seegarten (HCR)
Zum Sorpedam 21
☎ 02935-1579
✉ 59846

2 ♦
21 ♦
🆎 🔣 ♦ 🅿 ☂ ♨ ↑⬜ 🆎 🆎 🍽 ☺

Volmert (HCR) AA ANWB
Langscheiderstr 46
☎ 02935-2500 fax 02935-7647
✉ 59846

One of the main attractions of this family-run hotel is its location, overlooking the Sorpesee. The rooms are well furnished and have a shower and toilet. There is a separate lounge with an open fire and TV. The food is excellent and special-diet meals are available on request. There is plenty of parking space.

open 16.11 - 31.10
* 2 ♦ 43/50
* 9 ♦ 78/88
🔣 ♦ 🅿 ☂ ♨ 🆎 🆎 🍽 ☺

LAUTENBACH Baden-Württemberg 21

Sternen (HCR) [AA] [ANWB]
Hauptstr 47
☎ 07802-3538 fax 07802-700161
✉ 77794

The Hotel Sternen is situated in the well known spa town of Lautenbach. This is a summer and winter hotel where all the rooms are accessible by lift, and most have en suite facilities. The restaurant serves a range of regional German specialities. Ample on-site parking is available.

open 15.12 - 15.11
* 7 ♫ 52/60
* 30 ☎ 94/116
⓪ 🅴 🖃 ⊙ ◆ 🅿 ⏚ ♒ ↕ ▮ ☏ 🆆🅲 📺 🍽

LAUTERBACH Baden-Württemberg 21

Holzschuh (HR)
Siebenlinden
☎ 07422-4440 fax 07422-21815
✉ 78730

open 16.11 - 14.10
* 2 ♫ 50/60
* 8 ☎ 95/120
🅴 🖃 ♒ 🛎 🅿 ⏚ ♒ ≈ ☏ 🆆🅲 📺 🍽 ⊙

LAUTERECKEN Rheinland-Pfalz 17

Pfälzer Hof (HR)
Hauptstr 12
☎ 06382-7338 fax 06382-6652
✉ 67742

open 08.01 - 15.07 + 10.08 - 31.12
7 ♫ 48/58
15 ☎ 80/90
[AE] ⓪ 🅴 ♒ ⊙ 🅿 ⏚ ♒ ▮ ☏ 🆆🅲 📺 🍽 ✈

LEIWEN Rheinland-Pfalz 17

Zummethof (HCR)
Panoramaweg 1
☎ 06507-93550 fax 06507-935544
✉ 54340

open 15.03 - 15.01
2 ♫ 53/70
22 ☎ 90/120
🅴 ♒ 🛎 🅿 ⏚ ♒ ☏ 🆆🅲 🍽

LEIWEN/MOSEL Rheinland-Pfalz 17

Weinhaus Weis (HCR)
Römerstr 10
Leiwen
☎ 06507-3048 fax 06507-8232
✉ 54340

4 ♫ 53/60
14 ☎ 85/95
[AE] ⓪ 🅴 🖃 ⊙ 🅿 ⏚ ♒ ↕ ▮ ☏ 🆆🅲 📺

LENGGRIES Bayern 23

Altwirt (HR)
Marktstr 13
☎ 08042-8085 fax 08042-5357
✉ 83661

open 18.12 - 14.11
* 5 ♫ 50/60
* 15 ☎ 80/100
⊙ 🅿 ⏚ ♒ ▮ ☏ 🆆🅲 📺 🍽 ⊙

Arabella Brauneck (HR)
Münchenerstr 25
☎ 08042-5020 fax 08042-4224
res nr 089-92324444
✉ 83661

* - ♫ 135/155
* 105 ☎ 179/199
[AE] ⓪ 🅴 🖃 🛎 🅿 ⏚ ♒ ≈ ↕ ▮ ☏ 🆆🅲 📺 🍽 ⊙

LENNESTADT Nordrhein-Westfalen 12

Haus Buckmann (HR)
Rosenweg 10
☎ 02725-251 fax 02725-7340
✉ 57368

* 3 ♫ 60/68
* 10 ☎ 110/126
🅴 🛎 ⊙ 🅿 ⏚ ♒ ≈ ☏ 🆆🅲 📺 ⊙

LENSAHN Schleswig-Holstein 3

Wehde (MT)
Birkenallee 4
☎ 04363-611
✉ 23738

2 ♫
8 ☎
🅿 ⏚ 🛏 ☏ 🆆🅲

GERMANY 133

LEONBERG Baden-Württemberg 18

Eiss (Best Western) (HCR)
Neue Ramtelstr 28
☎ 07152-20041 fax 07152-42134
res nr 0130-4455
✉ 71229

* 40 ♂ 148/220
* 40 ⚭ 180/300
AE ⓘ E ≡ P ⚑ ⚐ ↕ ⚑ ⚑ WC 🍴 ⚑

LICH Hessen 13

Holländischer Hof (HR)
Braugasse 8
☎ 06404-2376
✉ 35423

10 ♂
11 ⚭
⚐ P ⚑ ⚑ ⚑ ⚑ WC 🍴

LIESENICH Rheinland-Pfalz 17

Wellems (HP) AA ANWB
Hauptstr 14
☎ 06545-6789
✉ 56858

The Hotel Wellems is situated in the wooded Hunsrück area, which has many well marked walking trails. It is a good base for trips to the Mosel and Rhine. All the rooms have a shower, most have a toilet and balcony. The garden has a terrace and barbecue. Parking facilities are available nearby.

open 28.12 - 19.12
* 3 ♂ 27/30
* 9 ⚭ 54/60
E ⚐ P ⚑ ⚑ WC ⚑ ⚑

LIMBACH Baden-Württemberg 18

Volk (HCR)
Baumgartenstr 3
☎ 06287-1811 fax 06287-1488
✉ 74838

* 4 ♂ 85/90
* 19 ⚭ 100/140
ⓘ E ≡ ⚑ ⚑ P ⚑ ⚑ ⚑ ⚑ WC TV 🍴 ⚑

LIMBURG AN DER LAHN Hessen 12

Dom Hotel (HR) AA ANWB
Grabenstr 57
☎ 06431-24077 fax 06431-6856
✉ 65549

The Dom Hotel is situated in the centre of the old town within a picturesque area that is good for day trips. The rooms all have a bath/shower, toilet, telephone and radio and the restaurant is well known for its national and international dishes. Conference and parking facilities are available.

open 02.01 - 24.12
* 16 ♂ 99/150
* 34 ⚭ 160/250
AE ⓘ E ≡ ⚑ ⚐ P ↕ ⚑ ⚑ WC TV 🍴 ⚑

Huss (HCR) AA ANWB
Bahnhofpl 3
☎ 06431-278087 fax 06431-25136
✉ 65549

Huss is a modern, hospitable hotel in the town centre, offering comfortable rooms with private bathroom facilities (colour TV is available on request). There is an idyllic garden with fountain and sunbathing lawn, and an attractive Chinese restaurant is linked to the hotel. The hotel has conference rooms.

8 ♂ 95/100
24 ⚭ 145/155
AE ⓘ E ≡ ⚐ P ⚑ ↕ ⚑ ⚑ WC TV ⚑

LINDAU Bayern 22

Goldenes Lamm (HR)
Schafgasse 3
☎ 08382-5732
✉ 88131

12 ♂
28 ⚭
⚐ P ⚑ ⚑ ⚑ WC 🍴

Peterhof (HCR)
Schafgasse 10
☎ 08382-5700
✉ 88131

9 🛏
20 🛌

LINDENFELS Hessen 18

Bellevue (HCR)
Buchenstr 17-20
☎ 06255-2031
✉ 64678

5 🛏
17 🛌

Odenwald (HCR)
Nibelungenstr 73
☎ 06255-2008
✉ 64678

20 🛏
22 🛌

LINDENHOLZHAUSEN Hessen 17

Zum Goldenen Grund (HR)
Frankfurterstr 1
☎ 06431-73128 fax 06431-74509
✉ 65551

4 🛏
5 🛌

LINDLAR Nordrhein-Westfalen 12

Schloß Georghausen (HR)
Hommerich 8
☎ 02207-2561 fax 02207-2683
✉ 51789

14 🛌

LINZ Rheinland-Pfalz 12

Weinstock (HCR)
Linzhausenstr 38
☎ 02644-2459
✉ 53545

6 🛏
26 🛌

LOHMAR/WAHLSCHEID Nordrhein-Westfalen 12

Schloß Auel (HCR)
Lohmar
☎ 02206-2041 fax 02206-2316
✉ 53797

4 🛏 110/160 excl. breakfast
19 🛌 160/220 excl. breakfast

Haus Seemann (HCR)
Am Alten Rathaus 17
Wahlscheid
☎ 02206-7787 fax 02206-83017
✉ 53797

4 🛏
7 🛌

LORSCH Hessen 18

Jäger (HCR)
Bahnhofstr 79
☎ 06251-52244
✉ 64653

14 🛏
16 🛌

LÜBECK Schleswig-Holstein 3

Bahnhof (HG)
Am Bahnhof 21
☎ 0451-83883
✉ 23558

6 🛏
22 🛌

Mövenpick Hotel (HR)   AA ANWB
Auf der Wallhalbinsel 1-3
☎ 0451-15040 fax 0451-1504111
res nr 0130-852217
✉ 23554

The Mövenpick Hotel Lübeck stands a short distance from the Holstentor, near the entrance to this historic town. The rooms are comfortably and fully furnished. The Mövenpick Restaurant also has a terrace and guests can enjoy a drink in the Duell Pub. Meeting rooms are available. To get to the hotel from the A1, take the Lübeck-Mitte junction.

* 57 ♫ 155/195 excl. breakfast
* 140 ⚭ 235/275 excl. breakfast
🅿 ✱ ⇅ 🗐 🄵 🆆🅲 🆃🆅 🍽 ⬆ ☺

LÜBECK/TRAVEMÜNDE Schleswig-Holstein 3

Strandhotel Maritim (HCR)
Trelleborgallee 2
Lübeck
☏ 04502-890 fax 04502-74439
res nr 0221-219672
✉ 23570

10 ♫ 187/307
230 ⚭ 242/418
🅰🅴 ⓞ 🄴 ⌸ ⚲ ⓓ 🅿 ☏ ✱ ⇅ 🗐 🄵 🆆🅲 🆃🆅 🍽 ☺

LÜDENSCHEID Nordrhein-Westfalen 12

Queens Hotel Lüdenscheid (HCR)
Parkstr 66
☏ 02351-1560 fax 02351-39157
✉ 58509

* 43 ♫ 190/210
* 122 ⚭ 270/290
🅰🅴 ⓞ 🄴 ⌸ ⚲ ⓓ 🅿 ☏ ✱ ⇅ 🗐 🄵 🆆🅲 🆃🆅 🍽 ☺

LUDWIGSBURG Baden-Württemberg 18

Schloßhotel Monrepos (Best Western) (HCR)
Postfach 543
☏ 07141-3020 fax 07141-302200
res nr 0130 4455
✉ 71605

open 07.01 - 23.12
37 ♫ 230/260
42 ⚭ 260/280
🅰🅴 ⓞ 🄴 ⌸ ⚲ ⓓ 🅿 ☏ ✱ ⇅ 🗐 🄵 🆆🅲 🆃🆅 🍽 ☺

LUDWIGSHAFEN Rheinland-Pfalz 18

Excelsior (Best Western) (HCR)
Lorientallee 16
☏ 0621-59850 fax 0621-5985500
res nr 0130-4455
✉ 67059

* 81 ♫ 170/190
* 81 ⚭ 195/240
🅰🅴 ⓞ 🄴 ⌸ ⚲ 🅿 ☏ ⚓ ⇅ 🗐 🄵 🆆🅲 🆃🆅

Viktoria (HR)
Bahnhofstr 1 b
☏ 0621-515087
✉ 67059

26 ♫ 38/65
36 ⚭ 65/115
🅰🅴 ⓞ 🄴 ⌸ ⓓ ✱ ⇅ 🗐 🆆🅲 🆃🆅 ☺

MAINZ Rheinland-Pfalz 18

Hammer (HR)
Bahnhofspl 6
☏ 06131-611061 fax 06131-611065
✉ 55116

* 20 ♫ 135/160
* 20 ⚭ 165/200
🅰🅴 ⓞ 🄴 ⌸ ⚲ ⓓ 🅿 ☏ ✱ ⇅ 🗐 🄵 🆆🅲 🆃🆅 ☺

Stiftswingert (HG)
Am Stiftswingert 4
☏ 06131-82441 fax 06131-832478
✉ 55131

open 27.12 - 23.12
* 12 ♫ 128/138
* 18 ⚭ 196/210
🅰🅴 ⓞ 🄴 ⌸ ⚲ 🅿 ☏ ✱ ⇅ 🗐 🆆🅲 🆃🆅

MAINZ/NIERSTEIN Rheinland-Pfalz 18

Rheinhotel (HCR)   AA ANWB
Mainzerstr 16
Nierstein
☏ 06133-97970 fax 06133-979797
✉ 55283

The Rheinhotel is splendidly situated between Mainz and Worms. The cities of Heidelberg, Frankfurt and Rüdesheim are all only an hour's drive away. The hotel is pleasantly furnished throughout, and the rooms have a private toilet and bath, telephone, colour TV, minibar and safe. The restaurant has an extensive menu and wine list. Wine tastings are held in the candlelit cellar.

open 15.01 - 15.12
* 1 ♫ 129/275
* 14 ⚭ 159/375
🅰🅴 ⓞ 🄴 ⌸ ⚓ ◆ 🅿 ☏ ✱ ⚓ 🗐 🄵 🆆🅲 🆃🆅 🍽

MALSFELD/BEISEFÖRTH Hessen 13

Parkcafé (HR) AA ANWB
Bahnhofstr 19
Malsfeld
☎ 05664-466
✉ 34323

The Hotel Parkcafé is situated on the outskirts of the town of Beiseförth and has fine views over the Fulda valley. The rooms are well kept and have a private toilet, shower and TV. The restaurant serves good cuisine with the emphasis on regional specialities. The recreational facilities include a tennis court, skittle alley and a sauna. From the sun terrace there is a splendid view of the Fulda valley.

* 3 ♪ 77/82
* 11 ⚭ 120/-
AE ① E ≡ ✓ ⓑ P ⚑ ⊨ ▣ Ⓕ WC TV ⓘ ⊙

MANCHING Bayern 20

Sandner (HCR) AA ANWB
Ingolstädterstr 31
☎ 08459-925
✉ 85077

The Hotel Sandner is situated in the centre of Manching and most of its rooms have en suite facilities. Guests can relax in the TV lounge or in the hotel's sauna. Special-diet meals are available in the restaurant on request. The hotel has on-site parking.

* 6 ♪ 50/55
* 23 ⚭ 75/80
✓ ⓞ P ⚑ ▣ Ⓕ WC ⓘ ⊙

MANDERSCHEID Rheinland-Pfalz 17

Zens (HR) AA ANWB
Kurfürstenstr 35
☎ 06572-768 fax 06572-1365
✉ 54531

The Hotel Zens is surrounded by woods and lakes and can be reached via the A48, by taking the Manderscheid exit. All the rooms have washing facilities and telephone, and the hotel has a swimming pool, sauna, solarium and massage facilities. The garden behind the hotel gives access to the *Kurpark*.

open 15.02 - 07.11
13 ♪ 55/88
18 ⚭ 110/170
E ✓ ⊙ P ⚑ ⊨ ▣ Ⓕ WC ⓘ ⊙

MANNHEIM Baden-Württemberg 18

Augusta Hotel Mannheim (HCR)
Augusta Anlage 43-45
☎ 0621-42070 fax 0621-4207199
✉ 68165

* 53 ♪ 162/-
* 53 ⚭ 203/-
AE ① E ≡ ⓑ ◆ P ⚑ ⊨ ▣ Ⓕ WC TV ⓘ ⊙

Avance Mannheimer Hof (HCR)
Augustaanlage 4-8
☎ 0621-40050 fax 0621-4005190
res nr 069-663080
✉ 68165

* 35 ♪ 175/245
* 130 ⚭ 260/290
AE ① E ≡ ✓ ⊙ P ⚑ ⊨ ▣ WC ⊙

Basler Hof (HG) AA ANWB
Tattersallstr 27
☎ 0621-28816 fax 0621-153292
✉ 68165

The 5-storey Hotel Basler Hof lies in the centre of Mannheim. Some rooms have en suite facilities. The hotel only serves breakfast, but there are many good restaurants in Mannheim. Half-board is an option for large parties.

open 07.01 - 23.12
30 ♪ 45/90
30 ⚭ 85/130
AE ① E ≡ ✓ ⊙ P ⚑ ⊨ ▣ Ⓕ WC TV

Delta Park Hotel (Best Western)
(HCR)
Keplerstr 24
☎ 0621-44510 fax 0621-4451-888
res nr 0130-4455
✉ 68165

The Delta Park Hotel is a new, modern hotel situated near the centre of Mannheim. The spacious rooms have en suite facilities, hair dryer, fax and PC sockets, and minibar. There is an attractive restaurant with a choice of international dishes, and an inviting bar. The hotel has extensive conference facilities and a parking garage.

* - ♪ 212/290
* 130 ⚏ 280/360
AE ⓘ E ⚏ ◆ P ♨ ⇅ ▬ 🆔 WC TV 🍴

Holiday Inn (HR)
Kurfüstenarkade N6 3
☎ 0621-10710 fax 0621-1071167
res nr 0130-815131
✉ 68015

* - ♪ 252/350
* 126 ⚏ 327/425
AE ⓘ E ⚏ ⊙ P ♨ ⇄ ⇅ ▬ 🆔 WC TV 🍽 🍴

Holländerhof (HG)
Breitestr 11-12
☎ 0621-16095 fax 0621-101546
✉ 62161

* - ♪ 75/95
* 37 ⚏ 100/140
AE ⓘ E ⚏ ⓘ P ⇄ 🆔 WC TV

Maritim Parkhotel (HR)
Friedrichspl 2
☎ 0621-45071 fax 0621-152424
res nr 0221-219672
✉ 68165

The Maritim Parkhotel is situated in the centre of the town just 5 minutes from the motorway. It is a luxury hotel with a splendid Renaissance façade, and the bedrooms provide extensive facilities. The cosy restaurant serves a wide choice of dishes and features an extensive wine list. There is a range of leisure facilities including a swimming pool, Turkish bath, solarium and sauna. During the months of July and August this magnificent hotel offers a very competitively priced stopover package.

76 ♪ 209/349
111 ⚏ 268/448
AE ⓘ E ⚏ ⊙ ◆ P ⇄ ⇅ ▬ 🆔 WC TV 🍽 🍴

MARBURG Hessen 12

Waldecker Hof (HCR)
Bahnhofstr 23
☎ 06421-60090 fax 06421-600959
✉ 35037

* 20 ♪ 130/165
* 20 ⚏ 165/250
AE ⓘ E ⚏ ⊙ ◆ P ⇄ ⇅ ▬ 🆔 WC TV 🐕

MARKDORF Baden-Württemberg 22

Zum Rebstock (HR)
Hauptstr 40
☎ 07544-2333
✉ 7778

8 ♪
15 ⚏
◆ P ⇄ ▬ WC 🍽 🍴

MARKTHEIDENFELD Bayern 19

Zum Löwen (HCR)
Marktpl 3
☎ 09391-1571 fax 09391-1721
✉ 97828

The Hotel zum Löwen is situated on the picturesque market square of Marktheidenfeld. The hotel is centuries old, but there is a new extension, and the renovated monastery farm on the nearby banks of the river Maine serves as an annexe. The rooms are very well furnished and have good facilities, and some have 4-poster beds. Wine tastings can be organised on request.

* 8 ♪ 60/75
* 36 ⚏ 98/128
⚑ ⊙ P ⇄ ♨ ▬ 🆔 WC TV 🍽

Zur Schönen Aussicht (HCR)
Brückenstr 8
☎ 09391-3055 fax 09391-3722
✉ 97828

The Hotel zur Schönen Aussicht enjoys a beautiful location on the edge of the small town of Marktheidenfeld. This traditional hotel has well furnished rooms, most with a private toilet and shower. There are two skittle alleys and the attractive 'swim-paradise' is nearby.

* 6 ♦ 75/100
* 43 ✦ 120/150

AE ⓘ E ♦ P ⚑ ¶ ■ □ WC TV ⊙

MARKTLEUGAST Bayern 20

Landgasthof Haueis (HR)
Gasthofbesitzer Hermes
☎ 09255-245 fax 09255-7263
✉ 95352

This hotel makes a peaceful and relaxing place to stay; the village is remotely situated and the surroundings invite long walks in the open countryside. The rooms in the Landgasthof Haueis are tidy and modestly furnished, and trout from the hotel's own trout farm features on the restaurant menu. The hotel is open in winter for skiers.

open 10.03 - 10.01
* 8 ♦ 30/50
* 27 ✦ 60/100

AE ⓘ E ♦ P ⚑ ¶ ⌂ □ WC ⊙ ⊙

MARKTOBERDORF Bayern 22

Sepp (HCR)
Poststr 13
☎ 08342-2048 fax 08342-2040
✉ 87616

The Hotel Sepp, located in the Allgau, makes an excellent centre for excursions to such nearby attractions as Newschwanstein, Oberammergau and the Bodensee. All its rooms have modern en suite facilities and some have a balcony. There is an attractive restaurant serving good food, and there are parking facilities.

18 ♦ 80/90
41 ✦ 125/150

E ♦ ⓘ P ⚑ ¶ ■ □ WC TV ⊙ ⋈

MARQUARTSTEIN Bayern 24

Prinzregent (HCR)
Loitshauserstr 5
☎ 08641-8256 fax 08641-8710
✉ 83250

* 2 ♦ 55/60
* 12 ✦ 90/110

⊙ ♦ P ⚑ ¶ ■ □ WC TV ⊙

MARSBERG Nordrhein-Westfalen 12

Haus Wegener (HCR)
Stobkeweg 8
☎ 02992-2629
✉ 34431

1 ♦
6 ✦

♦ P ⚑ ¶ □ WC ⊙

MAYEN Rheinland-Pfalz 17

Traube (HG)
Bäckerstr 3-6
☎ 02651-3018 fax 02651-72187
✉ 56725

The Hotel Traube is situated in the heart of Mayen, on the historic market square. This family hotel has comfortable rooms with washing facilities, telephone and TV. There is a good breakfast room, and full parking facilities are available nearby.

8 🛏 45/65
12 🛏 85/95
AE E 🗲 ☉ ☏ 🏊 P WC TV ☺

MAYSCHOSS Rheinland-Pfalz 12

Lochmühle (HCR)
☏ 02643-8080 fax
02643-808445
✉ 53508

The Hotel Lochmühle is situated in the well known Ahrdal area, and can easily be reached via the Köln-Koblenz motorway (exit Altenahr-Meckenheimer). The rooms are well furnished and have washing facilities. There is a restaurant, bar, swimming pool, sauna and solarium.

* 22 🛏 101/139
* 42 🛏 179/214
AE ⓓ E 🗲 ☉ P ☏ 🏊 ≈ ✝ 🛏 🚻 P WC TV ☺

Gasthof Zur Saffenburg (HCR) AA ANWB
Bundesstr 43
☏ 02643-8392 fax
02643-8100
✉ 53508

The Hotel zur Saffenburg is situated in the Ahrdal area. It has been completely renovated and now offers a combination of traditional German atmosphere and modern comfort. The rooms have a shower and toilet, and the windows have double glazing. Parking facilities are available.

open 01.02 - 30.11
* 4 🛏 55/60
* 15 🛏 110/120
E ☉ ♦ P ☏ 🏊 🚻 🛏 P WC ☺

MEERSBURG Baden-Württemberg 22

Zum Schiff (HR)
Bismarckpl
☏ 07532-6025
✉ 88709

4 🛏
33 🛏
🏊 P ☏ 🛏 P WC 🐕

Villa Bellevue (HG)
Am Rosenhag 5
☏ 07532-9770
✉ 88709

1 🛏
8 🛏
🏊 P ☏ 🏊 🚻 🛏 P WC TV

MELLE Niedersachsen 7

Berghotel Menzel (HCR)
Walter Sudtfieldweg 6
☏ 05422-94940 fax 05422-949494
✉ 49324

* 10 🛏 75/90
* 22 🛏 130/150
AE ⓓ E 🗲 ☉ P ☏ 🏊 ≈ ✝ 🛏 P WC TV ☺

Lumme (HR) AA ANWB
Haferstr 7
☏ 05422-3364 fax
05422-45402
✉ 49324

The Hotel Lumme is situated in the centre of Melle. This well kept establishment serves both as a stopover for travelling tourists and as a holiday hotel. Most of the rooms have washing facilities and the restaurant offers a good choice of dishes. Parking facilities are available.

open 06.01 - 23.12
* 5 🛏 55/80
* 6 🛏 85/125
☉ P ☏ P WC TV 🐕

MEMMELSDORF Bayern 19

Drei Kronen (HR)
Hauptstr 19
☎ 0951-43001 fax 0951-43869
✉ 96117

* 4 ♦ 49/80
* 26 ♦ 85/130
[icons]

MEMMINGEN Bayern 22

Weisses Ross (HCR)
Salzstr 12
☎ 08331-2020 fax 08331-84057
res nr 08331-84056
✉ 87700

Memmingen is situated in the Allgäu region where the A7 crosses the A96 and B18. The Hotel Weisses Ross is in the centre of the old town. Some of the rooms are in the old part of the hotel, and some in the new part; all have washing facilities, telephone and TV. The old cellar with its magnificent cross-vaults is now being used as a wine bar.

* 10 ♦ 77/95
* 30 ♦ 120/150
[icons]

MENDEN Nordrhein-Westfalen 12

Central (HG)
Unnaer Str 33
☎ 02373-5045 fax 02373-5531
✉ 58681

open 04.01 - 22.12
* 4 ♦ -/90
* 12 ♦ 120/180
[icons]

MENDIG/MARIA LAACH Rheinland-Pfalz 17

Felsenkeller (HR)
Bahnstr 35
Mendig
☎ 02652-1272 fax 02652-51398
✉ 56743

7 ♦ 44/80
21 ♦ 85/130
[icons]

Hansa (HR)
Laacher See Str 11/13
Mendig
☎ 02652-4410 fax 02652-2316
✉ 56743

The family-run Hotel Hansa is situated between the Rhine, Mosel and Ahr, close to the largest lake in this area, the Laacher See. The hotel is well maintained with well equipped rooms featuring, bath, shower, bidet, toilet, radio and TV sockets. The restaurant offers a good menu with fondues and *flambé* specialities. There is a children's playground and a large sunbathing lawn. Covered parking facilities are available.

open 02.03 - 19.12
* 4 ♦ 44/70
* 19 ♦ 72/105
[icons]

MERKLINGEN Bayern 22

Ochsen (HR)
Hauptstr 12
☎ 07337-283
✉ 71263

Merklingen is one km from the Stuttgart to München motorway and 25km from the highest church steeple in the world, the tower of Ulm. Hotel Ochsen is a well maintained hotel and all the rooms have en suite facilities. The attractively furnished restaurant has a good choice of dishes, including local specialities. Full parking facilities are available.

4 ♦ 88/-
11 ♦ 130/-
[icons]

MESCHEDE Nordrhein-Westfalen 12

Holländer Hof (HR)
Ohlstr 4
☎ 02934-260
✉ 59872

1 ♦
14 ♦
[icons]

GERMANY 141

MESCHEDE/FREIENOHL Nordrhein-Westfalen
12

Haus Luckai (HCR)   AA ANWB
Chr Kochstr 11
Meschede
☎ 02903-7752 fax
02903-18369
✉ 59872

Haus Luckai is quietly situated in the countryside, at the edge of the holiday village of Freienohl. The surrounding mountains and woods offer plenty of recreational facilities in both summer and winter. Most of the rooms have a shower/bath and balcony, along with a beautiful view over the area and the Arnsberger wood. There is also a garden, a sun terrace and a garage and parking places.

* 5 ♦ 55/65
* 7 ♦ 110/120
♦ ♦ ♦ ♦ P ♦ ♦ ♦ ♦ WC TV ♦ ♦

Teehaus (HCR)   AA ANWB
Auf'm Hahn 2
Freienohl
☎ 02903-539
✉ 59872

The family-run Hotel Teehaus is situated in very quiet surroundings. The bedrooms have a privet shower and toilet. The hotel has its own *Konditorei*, parking place, parking garage, sunbathing lawn and terraces.

open 01.02 - 15.01
* 3 ♦ 50/70
* 6 ♦ 104/120
♦ E ♦ ♦ ♦ P ♦ ♦ ♦ ♦ WC ♦ ♦

METTENDORF Rheinland-Pfalz
17

Fronhof (HR)
Im Fronhof 12
☎ 06522-289
✉ 54675

2 ♦
16 ♦
♦ ♦ P ♦ ♦ ♦ WC ♦

METTLACH/ORSCHOLZ Saarland
17

Zur Saarschleife (HCR)   AA ANWB
Clöfstr 44
Mettlach
☎ 06865-1790 fax
06865-17930
✉ 66693

Hotel zur Saarschleife is a family-run hotel, comfortably furnished throughout, and situated at the point where the borders of France, Luxembourg and Germany meet. The rooms have a private toilet and shower, colour TV and telephone. There is an indoor swimming pool, sauna, solarium, bowling alley and a tennis court. There are special prices for weekend breaks and holidays. Parking facilities are available near the hotel.

open 15.01 - 31.12
* 5 ♦ 85/125
* 48 ♦ 125/190
AE ♦ E ♦ ♦ ♦ ♦ P ♦ ♦ ♦ ♦ ♦ ♦ P WC TV ♦ ♦

MIESBACH Bayern
23

Sonnenhof Harzberg (HCR)
Heckenweg 8
☎ 08025-4248
✉ 83714

4 ♦
19 ♦
♦ ♦ P ♦ ♦ ♦ P WC ♦

MINDEN Nordrhein-Westfalen
7

Exquisit (HCR)
In Den Bärenkämpen 2 a
☎ 0571-43055 fax 0571-49799
✉ 32425

38 ♦
85 ♦
AE ♦ E ♦ ♦ ♦ ♦ P ♦ ♦ ♦ P WC TV ♦

MINDERSDORF Baden-Württemberg
21

Landgasthof Adler (HCR)
Adlergasse 4
☎ 07775-1031 fax 07775-7403
✉ 78355

6 ♦
♦ P ♦ P WC TV ♦

142 GERMANY

MITTENWALD Bayern 23

Alpenrose Bichlerhof (HP)
Obermarkt 1
☎ 08823-5055 fax 08823-3720
✉ 82477

* 5 ♂ 67/92
* 13 ⚭ 121/185
AE ⓘ E ⚏ ♾ ⊙ P 🍴 🛏 👔 🛁 ✉ WC TV ℗ 🛎

Jägerhof (HCR) AA ANWB
Partenkirchnerstr 35
☎ 08823-1041 fax 08823-8582
✉ 82481

The Hotel Jägerhof is a modern and comfortable hotel overlooking the Karwendel and Wetterstein mountains. The rooms are well furnished and have washing facilities, radio and telephone; some have a south-facing balcony. The restaurant offers 200 different dishes. Parking facilities are available.

open 15.12 - 01.11
12 ♂ 66/88
38 ⚭ 109/160
AE ⓘ E ⚏ ♦ P 🍴 🛏 👔 🛁 ✉ WC

Post (HCR)
Obermarkt 9
☎ 08823-1094
✉ 82481

28 ♂ 60/110
68 ⚭ 110/190
🛁 ⊙ P 🍴 🛏 👔 🛁 ✉ WC TV ℗

Tonihof (HR)
Brunnental 3
☎ 08823-5031
✉ 8102

5 ♂ 39/93
17 ⚭ 78/166
P 🍴 🛏 👔 ✉ WC

MITTERFIRMIANSREUTH Bayern 24

Almberg (HCR)
☎ 08557-138
✉ 94158

40 ⚭
🛁 P 🍴 🛏 WC TV ℗ 🛎

MÖCKMÜHL Baden-Württemberg 19

Württemberger Hof (HR)
Bahnhofstr 11
☎ 06298-5002 fax 06298-7779
✉ 74215

open 21.01 - 15.12
* 5 ♂ 46/60
* 11 ⚭ 98/-
AE ⓘ E ⚏ ⊙ P 🍴 🛏 👔 WC ℗

MOHRWEILER Rheinland-Pfalz 17

Rink Berghotel (HCR)
Höhen 14
☎ 06563-2444
✉ 54655

The spa resort of Mohrweiler boasts of its healthy clean air, and offers plenty of opportunity for walks and sightseeing. All rooms at the Rink Berghotel have washing facilities. The restaurant serves appetising dishes and seasonal specialities. The hotel also has a swimming pool and a sauna.

- ♂ 60/75
15 ⚭ 90/140
E 🛁 ♦ P 🍴 🛏 👔 🛁 ✉ WC TV ℗ 🛎 ⊕

MÖLLN Schleswig-Holstein 3

Parkhotel Am Kurgarten (HCR)
Auf Dem Klüschenberg 9
☎ 04542-3930
✉ 35085

14 ♂
23 ⚭
🛁 ♦ P 👔 🛁 ✉ WC TV

MÖNCHENGLADBACH Nordrhein-Westfalen 11

Dorinthotel (HCR)
Hohenzollerstr 5
☎ 02161-8930 fax 02161-87231
res nr 0130-6605
✉ 41061

67 ♂ 185/245 excl. breakfast
79 ⚭ 215/265 excl. breakfast
AE ⓘ E ⚏ ⊙ ♦ P 🍴 🛏 👔 🛁 ✉ WC TV ℗ 🛎 ⊕

Queens Hotel Mönchengladbach (HCR)
Speickerstr 49
☎ 02161-3070 fax 02161-30719
✉ 41061

17 ♦ 198/268 excl. breakfast
109 ♦ 246/306 excl. breakfast

MONSCHAU Nordrhein-Westfalen 11

Aquarium (HP)
Heidgen 34
☎ 02472-4193 fax 02472-7199
✉ 52156

The Hotel Aquarium is situated in the foothills of the Monschauer Forest, within walking distance of the centre of Monschau. The rooms in this relatively new hotel, furnished in Biedermeier style, have a bath, shower, toilet, radio, TV and telephone. The hotel also has a swimming pool, sauna, solarium and gym.

* 1 ♦ 75/90
* 12 ♦ 90/136

Burghotel Monschau (HP)
Laufenstr 1
☎ 02472-2332
✉ 52156

The Burghotel Monschau is situated in the centre of Monschau, a medieval town with narrow streets. This family-run hotel is well appointed, and most of the rooms have a private toilet and shower. The restaurant menu offers a good choice of international dishes and regional Eifel specialities. Parking facilities are available.

open 15.02 - 31.12
* 2 ♦ 40/45
* 13 ♦ 62/95

Lindenhof (HCR)
Laufenstr 77
☎ 02472-4186 fax 02472-3134
✉ 52156

The medieval town of Monschau is surrounded by mountains and woods in the Rur valley, an area that is ideal for winter and summer holidays. A quietly situated family hotel, Lindenhof has comfortable rooms with washing facilities. The bar, only open to residents, serves good beer.

* 2 ♦ 65/75
* 6 ♦ 84/110

Haus Vennblick (HG)
Hauptstr 24
☎ 02472-2295
✉ 52156

Haus Vennblick is situated in the centre of Monschau in the Nordeifel nature park. It is ideally placed either for making day trips in Germany and the surrounding countries, or as a stopover for travelling tourists. The hotel is well furnished and the rooms are clean. There is a skittle alley, and parking facilities are available.

* - ♦ 40/-
* 4 ♦ 75/-

MONSCHAU/HÖFEN Nordrhein-Westfalen 11

Sporthotel Prümmer (HCR)
Hauptstr 88
Monschau
☎ 02472-2298 fax 02472-7957
✉ 52156

The Sporthotel Prümmer is situated on a mountain slope overlooking the Rur valley close to the town of Monschau and the surrounding woods. Near the hotel are game reserves and the Eifelart open-air museum. All the rooms have washing facilities, and the hotel also offers an indoor pool, sauna, solarium and 4 →

tennis courts. Parking facilities are available.
* 2 🛏 45/55
* 12 🛌 84/100
🆎 🌀 🇪 🔣 ♦ 🅿 🍽 🐾 🚞 🔚 📺 🇼🇨 📺 🍴 ☺

MOSBACH Baden-Württemberg 18

Lamm (HR)
Haupstr 59
☏ 06261-2415
✉ 74821

21 🛏
31 🛌
🍴 ⊙ 🅿 🍽 ↕ 🔚 📺 🇼🇨 🍴 🏠

MOSELKERN Rheinland-Pfalz 17

Anker Pitt (HCR)   AA ANWB
Moselstr 41-42
☏ 02672-1303 fax
02672-8944
✉ 56254

The old wine village of Moselkern is just south of Koblenz, in the Eifel and Hünsrück mountains. The Anker Pitt is an ideal base for making day trips to Cochem, Koblenz and Trier. All the rooms of this family hotel have a shower, toilet and balcony overlooking the surroundings. There is a sauna and skittle alley.

open 01.02 - 23.12
* - 🛏 45/60
* 25 🛌 80/110
🍴 ⊙ 🅿 🍽 🐾 ↕ 🇪 🇼🇨 📺 🍴 🏠 ☺

MOTTEN Bayern 13

Will Braü (HCR)
Brückenauerstr 8
☏ 09748-261 fax 09748-1282
✉ 97786

* 5 🛏 43/-
* 10 🛌 75/-
🌀 🇪 🔣 ⊙ ♦ 🅿 🔚 🇪 🇼🇨 🍴 ☺

MÜGGENBRUNN Baden-Württemberg 21

Adler (HCR)   AA ANWB
Schau-Ins Land Str 13
☏ 07671-783 fax
07671-8268
✉ 7868

The Hotel Adler is situated in one of the most beautiful regions of the Schwarzwald at an altitude of about 1000m. This area has plenty to offer for both summer and winter holidays. The rooms in this hotel are very well kept, and have en suite facilities and telephone; some also have a minibar and TV. The restaurant provides a lovely view and serves a good choice of national and international specialities.

* 4 🛏 56/-
* 27 🛌 90/98
🆎 🌀 🇪 🔣 🅿 🍽 🐾 🚞 🔚 🇪 🇼🇨 📺 🍴 ☺

MÜHLHAUSEN IM TÄLE Baden-Württemberg
22

Eseleck (HR)
Gosbacherstr 15
☏ 07335-5275 fax 07335-7925
✉ 73347

2 🛏
4 🛌
🆎 🌀 🇪 🔣 ♦ 🅿 🍽 🐾 🇪 🇼🇨 🍴

MÜLLHEIM Baden-Württemberg 21

Bad (HR)
Badstr 40
☏ 07631-3885 fax 07631-4326
✉ 79379

1 🛏 50/60
8 🛌 -/94
🅿 🍽 🐾 🇪 🇼🇨 📺 🍴 ☺

Kaiserhof (HR)
Goethestr 10
☏ 07631-2739 fax 07631-15848
✉ 78379

* 1 🛏 40/50
* 14 🛌 70/95
🍴 ⊙ 🅿 🍽 🔚 🇪 🇼🇨 📺 🍴 ☺

GERMANY   145

MÜLLHEIM/NIEDERWEILER Baden-Württemberg   21

Pension Weilertal (HP)   AA ANWB
Weilertalstr 15
Niederweiler
☏ 07631-5794 fax 07631-14826
✉ 79379

The friendly family-run hotel Pension Weilertal is set in peaceful surroundings 30km from the Swiss border. The rooms and apartments are simply furnished, but well kept and equipped with en suite facilities. The hotel has a large and attractive garden with terrace where fishing is available, and bicycles can be hired. There is a limited restaurant menu, and grill/barbecue evenings are held occasionally.

open 20.02 - 25.11 + 15.12 - 10.01
* 2 ♫ 55/90
* 5 ⚏ 98/150
🅴 ⊙ 🅿 ⚐ 🚾 📺

MÜNCHEN Bayern   23

Munich is a city of exuberant atmosphere and vitality: one of the great cultural centres of Europe, with an array of museums unrivalled in the country. Central Munich is easy to see on foot. The city is an attractive prospect for visitors, with tree-lined boulevards, fountains, parks, pavement cafés, beer-halls and beer-gardens. The main pedestrianised street running from the Karlstor near the main station, to Marienplatz dominated by the Gothic Neues Rathaus, bustles with shoppers, buskers and tourists. This is the heart of the city, and near here are the Frauenkirche with its huge onion- domed towers, the Renaissance church of St Michael, and just south of Marienplatz is the cheerful food market, the Viktualienmarkt, with high quality regional produce and matching prices. A short distance southwest are two of the city's finest churches, the Damenstiftskirche and the astonishing rococo Asamkirche.
In the north-central area, the Max-Joseph Platz is overlooked by the Nationaltheater and the southern end of the huge Residenze. This is the western end of Maximilianstrasse, a tree-lined thoroughfare of high-class boutiques and galleries, punctuated at its far end by the towering Maximilaneum, the Bavarian Parliament and Senate.
Northwest of the centre is the main museum quarter: major museums here include the Alte and Neue Pinakothek, together forming one of the world's great art galleries; the Deutsches Museum, a leading world museum of science and technology; and the Residenzmuseum, with dazzling collections of riches dating from the 11th century; and the Staatsmuseum,

housed in a former arsenal. In the western suburbs is the incomparable Nymphenburg, summer residence of the former rulers of Bavaria, with a wonderful baroque interior and a lovely park of canals, lake, hunting lodges and pavilions.

See city plan on page 37.

Alfa (HG)   AA ANWB
Hirtenstr 22
☏ 089-598461 fax 089-592301
✉ 80335
City Plan B2

The Hotel Alfa is situated in a quiet street in the heart of the town, close to the station and within walking distance of the shopping centre and tourist sights. All the rooms have a bathroom, and most have TV. The hotel has a bar, and parking facilities are available.

* 37 ♫ 85/175
* 42 ⚏ 120/270
🆎 ⊙ 🅴 ⚒ ⚒ ⊙ 🅿 ⚑ ⚓ 🍽 🅲 🚾 📺

Atrium (Best Western) (HCR)
Landwehrstr 59
☏ 089-514190 fax 089-598491
res nr 0130-4455
✉ 80336
City Plan B3

* 1 ♫ 206/246
* 163 ⚏ 256/296
🆎 ⊙ 🅴 ⚒ 🅿 🍽 🅲

Austrotel (HCR)
Arnulfstr 2
☏ 089-54530 fax 089-54532255
✉ 80335
City Plan B2

40 ♫ 205/270
134 ⚏ 300/370
🆎 ⊙ 🅴 ⚒ ⊙ ♦ 🅿 ⚑ ⚐ ⚓ ↔ 🍽 🅲 🚾 📺 🍴

Hotel Drei Löwen (HCR)
Schillerstr 8
☏ 089-551040 fax 089-55104905
✉ 80336

* 60 ♫ 182/190
* 70 ⚏ 230/250
🆎 ⊙ 🅴 ⚒ ⊙ 🅿 ⚑ 🅲 🚾 📺 📺

See advertisement page 147

GERMANY

Grandhotel Continental (Best Western) (HCR)
Max Josephstr 5
☎ 089-551570 fax 089-55157500
res nr 0130-4455
✉ 80333
City Plan D2

* 40 ♦ 295/375 excl. breakfast
* 109 ♦ 350/490 excl. breakfast

Holiday Inn (HR)
Leopoldstr 194
☎ 089-381790 fax 089-38179888
res nr 0130-815131
✉ 80804

* 70 ♦ 250/420 excl. breakfast
* 294 ♦ 330/450 excl. breakfast

Holiday Inn München Süd (HR)
Kistlerhofstr 142
☎ 089-780020 fax 089-78002672
res nr 0130-815131
✉ 81379

* 26 ♦ 255/325 excl. breakfast
* 280 ♦ 315/385 excl. breakfast

Krone (HG)
Theresienhöhe 8
☎ 089-504052 fax 089-506706
✉ 80339
City Plan A3

* - ♦ 140/195
* 30 ♦ 260/280

König Ludwig (Best Western) (HG)
Hohenzollernstr 3
☎ 089-335995 fax 089-394658
res nr 0130-4455
✉ 80801

* 3 ♦ 180/350
* 43 ♦ 190/350

Maritim Hotel (HR)
Goethestr 7
☎ 089-552350 fax 089-55235900
res nr 0221-219672
✉ 80036
City Plan B4

* 50 ♦ 245/423
* 302 ♦ 298/488

Queens Hotel München (HCR)
Effnerstr 99
☎ 089-927980 fax 089-983813
res nr 0130-4433
✉ 81925

* 3 ♦ 185/320 excl. breakfast
* 149 ♦ 235/370 excl. breakfast

Stachus (HCR)
Bayerstr 7
☎ 089-592881 fax 089-8232133
✉ 80335
City Plan C3

The Hotel Stachus is situated between the station and the Karlsplatz, known locally as Stachus. The Karlstor leads to the old town centre with its many sights. This hotel, popular with both business guests and tourists, has well furnished rooms, some with en suite facilities. The cosy breakfast room is a pleasant place to start the day, and the hotel has full parking facilities.

* 26 ♦ 120/155
* 40 ♦ 165/225

Tourotel (HR)
Domagkstr 26
☎ 089-360010 fax 089-36001340
✉ 80807

87 ♦ 159/189
143 ♦ 199/229

Vier Jahreszeiten Kempinski (HR)
Maximilianstr 17
☎ 089-230390 fax 089-39693
res nr 0130-3339
✉ 80539
City Plan E3

* 106 ♦ 320/465
* 208 ♦ 465/730

GERMANY

HOTEL DREI LÖWEN

CENTRAL AND PEACEFUL LOCATION

At three minutes' walking distance from the Central Station, the bus to the airport and the pedestrian area. A first-class hotel with 130 rooms with bath, radio, colour television and mini-bar. Bistro, bar, café, conference room, garages and parking places.

Schillerstrasse 8, D-80336 Munich
Tel : 089 - 551040
Tlx : 532 867 loew d
Fax : 089 - 55104.905

See entry page 145

MÜNCHEN AIRPORT/HALLBERGMOOS
Bayern 23

Cadett Hotel Mövenpick München Airport (HR)
Ludwigstr 43
Hallbergmoos
☎ 0811-8000 fax 0811-888444
res nr 0130-852217
✉ 85399

The Cadett Hotel Mövenpick has attractive furnishings and offers modern, comfortable rooms. A number of rooms are especially equipped for guests on an extended stay. There is a Mövenpick restaurant, a snack bar and a lounge; the sauna and fitness rooms are free to guests. Coffee and croissants are served every morning between 05.00 and 06.00. The hotel is suitable for disabled guests, and meeting rooms are available. The airport is 10 minutes away.

* - ♦ 135/180 excl. breakfast
* 144 ♦ 270/360 excl. breakfast

MÜNCHEN/NEUBIBERG *Bayern* 23

Rheingoldhof (HG)
Rheingoldstr 4
Neubiberg
☎ 089-6600440 fax 089-660044-55
✉ 85579

The Hotel Rheingoldhof lies 12km from München in the small town of Neubiberg and is very well suited as a stopover during a long car journey. Despite being only a short distance from the motorway it is pleasantly peaceful. The rooms have basic furnishings, but all are equipped with en suite facilities, telephone, TV and minibar. The hotel has ample parking facilities.

open 16.01 - 19.12
* 5 ♦ 84/88
* 13 ♦ 135/142

MÜNSTER *Nordrhein-Westfalen* 12

Conti (HR)
Berliner Pl 2 A
☎ 0251-40444 fax 0251-51711
✉ 48143

* 26 ♦ 69/189
* 30 ♦ 109/229

Europa (HCR)
Kaiser Wilhelm-ring 26
☎ 0251-37062 fax 0251-394339
✉ 48145

* 27 ♦ 189/-
* 32 ♦ 229/269

Kaiserhof (HG)
Bahnhofstr 14
☎ 0251-41780 fax 0251-4178666
✉ 48143

* 34 ♦ 148/232
* 75 ♦ 203/248

Mövenpick Hotel Münster (HR) AA ANWB

Kardinal Von Galen Ring 65
☏ 0251-89020 fax 0251-8902616
✉ 48149

The Mövenpick Hotel Münster is situated on the banks of the Aasee, 15 minutes' walk from the centre. The rooms and suites are comfortably and fully furnished. The Mövenpick restaurant and the Rössli both specialise in international dishes, and the Tucano bar serves drinks. Bicycles are available for hire; meeting rooms are available. The hotel has facilities for disabled visitors. To reach the hotel take the A11/E3 junction Münster-Nord or Süd, in the direction of the Zoo.

* 44 ♫ 220/250 excl. breakfast
* 72 ⚏ 260/290 excl. breakfast
🆎 ⓘ 🅴 ⚒ ⓢ ◆ 🅿 ⚓ ⇅ 🔲 🆎 🆆🅲 🆃🆅 🍽

Schloß Wilkinghege (HR)
Steinfurterstr 374
☏ 0251-213045 fax 0251-212898
✉ 48159

* 7 ♫ 170/230
* 31 ⚏ 265/390
🆎 ⓘ 🅴 ⚒ ⓢ ◆ 🅿 ⚓ ⇅ 🔲 🆎 🆆🅲 🆃🆅 🍽 🐕

MÜRLENBACH Rheinland-Pfalz 17

Eifeler Hof (HCR) AA ANWB

Schöneckerstr 1
☏ 06594-226 fax 06594-321
✉ 54570

The Hotel Eifeler Hof is the oldest and most traditional hotel in Mürlenbach. It is situated in the valley of the Kyll River, which is very popular with anglers, and where there are many marked walking trails. The rooms are clean and have a shower, toilet and TV. The restaurant offers a good choice of dishes.

open 25.12 - 14.11
* 2 ♫ 50/55
* 10 ⚏ 80/90
🅴 ⚒ ⓢ ◆ 🅿 ⚓ ⇅ 🆎 🆆🅲 🆃🆅 🍽 🐕

MURNAU AM STAFFELSEE Bayern 23

Post (HG)
Obermarkt 1
☏ 08841-1861 fax 08841-99411
✉ 82418

open 07.12 - 07.11
* 8 ♫ -/80
* 14 ⚏ -/140
🅴 ⚒ ⓢ ◆ 🅿 ⚓ ⇅ 🔲 🆎 🆆🅲 🐕

MUTTERSTADT Rheinland-Pfalz 20

Ebnet (HR)
Neustadter Str 53
☏ 06234-1731 fax 06234-50845
✉ 67112

open 06.01 - 22.12
* 9 ♫ 50/65
* 13 ⚏ 100/105
ⓢ ◆ 🅿 ⚓ ⇅ 🔲 🆎 🆆🅲 🐕

NECKARGEMÜND Baden-Württemberg 18

Kredell (HCR) AA ANWB
Hauptstr 67
☏ 06223-2633 fax 06223-6228
✉ 69151

The Hotel Kredell is situated in the centre of Neckargemünd, only 12 minutes' drive from Heidelberg. The rooms in this well maintained hotel have a bath, shower and toilet. Breakfast is served in the comfortable lounge, and on the terrace there is a bar service. Close to the hotel is a swimming pool, golf course and tennis courts.

open 15.02 - 15.12
* 2 ♫ 50/75
* 11 ⚏ 90/100
🅴 ⚒ ⓢ 🅿 ⚓ ⇅ 🔲 🆎 🆆🅲

NECKARSULM Baden-Württemberg 18

Neckarsulmer Hof (HP)
Marktstr 35
☏ 07132-2031
✉ 74172

26 ♫
30 ⚏
ⓢ ◆ 🅿 🔲 🆎 🆆🅲 🐕

NECKARWESTHEIM Baden-Württemberg 18

Schloßhotel Liebenstein (HCR)
☎ 07133-6041 fax 07133-6045
✉ 74382

open 01.02 - 31.12
5 ♪ 165/180
19 ♨ 240/280
AE ⓘ E ⚞ ♠ P ⚞ ╫ ▬ ▫ WC ☻

NESSELWANG Bayern 22

Alpspitz (HCR)
Badeseeweg 10
☎ 08361-255
✉ 87484

4 ♪ 59/65
34 ♨ 108/128
♠ P ⚞ ⚞ ╫ ▬ ▫ WC ☼

Brauerei & Hotel Post (HR)
Hauptstr 25
☎ 08361-30910 fax
08361-30973
✉ 87484

The Hotel Brauerei and Post is situated in the Allgäu at an altitude of 1100m. It is a traditional family-run hotel with stylish furnishings throughout. The rooms have private toilet, bath/shower, TV and telephone. The restaurant serves a choice of specialities from the Allgäu, complemented with beer from the 100-year-old brewery.

* 6 ♪ 80/90
* 16 ♨ 140/160
E ⚞ ⓘ ◆ P ⚞ ⚞ ▬ ▫ WC TV ⏷ ☻

Marianne (HCR) AA ANWB
Römerstr 11
☎ 08361-3218 fax
08361-1091
✉ 87484

The Hotel Marianne is quietly situated a couple of minutes' walk from the town centre, with the Alpspitze mountain directly opposite - in summer good for walking, and in the winter ideal for skiing. The hotel has been furnished in typically southern German style, and most of the rooms have en suite facilities and a balcony. In summer, meals are served from the barbecue on the terrace.

open 22.12 - 31.10
5 ♪ 40/48
26 ♨ 108/120
♠ ⓘ P ⚞ ▬ ▫ WC ☼

NETPHEN/SOHLBACH Nordrhein-Westfalen 12

Waldhaus (HCR) AA ANWB
Netphen
☎ 02738-1284 fax
02738-8050
✉ 57250

The Hotel Waldhaus is situated in a remote spot in the Siegerland area, overlooking a valley. It is easily accessible via the Sauerland motorway, B62 and Afholderbach exit. The hotel is well cared for and has rooms with washing facilities and telephone. There is an indoor swimming pool, sauna and solarium. The restaurant offers international dishes.

open 25.12 - 15.11
* 2 ♪ 53/75
* 9 ♨ 100/130
AE E ⚞ ⓘ P ⚞ ⚞ ⚞ ▬ ▫ WC TV ⏷ ☻

NEUENBÜRG Baden-Württemberg 21

Touristik (HG)
Basler Str 2
☎ 07631-7876
✉ 75305

14 ♨
ⓘ P ⚞ ▫ WC TV ☼

NEUERBURG Rheinland-Pfalz 17

Berghof (HR)
Am Plascheider Berg
☎ 06564-2550
✉ 54673

4 ♪
11 ♨
AE E ⚞ P ⚞ ⚞ ▬ ▫ WC TV ⏷ ☻

NEUFAHRN BEI FREISING Bayern — 23

Krone (HCR)
Echinger Str 23
Neufahrn
☎ 08165-4081 fax 08165-3821
✉ 85375

* 18 ♪ 50/80
* 18 ♫ 90/120
🇪 🔥 ♦ 🅿 🍴 ⛽ 📞 WC TV

NEUKIRCHEN/KNÜLLGEBIRGE Hessen — 13

Kur und Sporthotel Combecher (HCR)
Kurhessenstr 32
Neukirchen
☎ 06694-6048 fax 06694-6116
✉ 34626

* 6 ♪ 63/98
* 33 ♫ 100/150
AE ① 🇪 🔥 ♦ ⊙ 🅿 🍴 ⛽ ≈ 📞 WC TV 🏠 ⬆ ⊙

NEUMARKT Bayern — 23

Mehl (HR)
Am Viehmarkt
☎ 09181-1366 fax
09181-6296
✉ 92318

AA ANWB

The central location of the Hotel Mehl makes it an ideal base for visiting the sights of Neumarkt, including the churches of Hofkirche and St Johanneskirche and the Pfalzgrafenschloss castle. It is a comfortable hotel with well kept rooms, equipped with private toilet and shower, radio, colour TV and telephone. Parking facilities are available.

open 14.01 - 22.12
* 10 ♪ 48/90
* 13 ♫ 85/130
① 🇪 🔥 ⊙ 🅿 🍴 ⛽ 📞 WC TV 🍽 ⊙

NEUSTADT AN DER AISCH Bayern — 19

Burckshof (HR)
Herzogstr 56
☎ 09161-66016 fax 09161-66017
✉ 91413

2 ♪
19 ♫
🔥 ⊙ 🅿 🍴 ⛽ 📞 WC TV 🍽 ⊙

Römerhof (HR)

Richard Wagnerstr 15
☎ 09161-3011 fax
09161-2498
✉ 91413

AA ANWB

The Hotel Römerhof is situated in Neustadt an der Aisch, surrounded by greenery. The rooms are modern and have a bath, shower, toilet and telephone. The Forum restaurant has a large garden terrace and offers a good choice. There is a children's playground and parking facilities are available.

open 11.01 - 19.12
* 6 ♪ 60/80
* 16 ♫ 115/130
AE ① 🇪 🔥 ⊙ 🅿 🍴 ⛽ 📞 WC 🍽 ⊙

NEUSTADT AN DER WEINSTRASSE Rheinland-Pfalz — 18

Kurfürst (HR)
Mussbacher Landstr 2
☎ 06321-7441 fax 06321-32151
✉ 67433

* 20 ♪ -/100
* 20 ♫ 150/170
AE ① 🇪 🔥 ♦ 🅿 🍴 ⛽ 📞 WC TV

NEU-ULM Bayern — 22

Mövenpick (HCR)
Silcherstr 40
☎ 0731-80110 fax
0731-85967
res nr 013085-2217
✉ 89231

AA ANWB

This Mövenpick Hotel is part of the Edwin Scharff Haus conference centre, and is situated in a park on the banks of the Donau, a 10-minute walk from the centre. The rooms have comfortable and modern furnishings; one floor is allocated to business guests, with appropriate facilities including PC sockets. Drinks are served in the Bayernstube or Münster bar, excellent meals are served in the Mövenpick restaurant which has a cosy winter garden. The hotel has a swimming pool, solarium and bicycles for hire and and has adapted facilities for disabled guests.

GERMANY 151

* 26 ♨ 180/240 excl. breakfast
* 109 ⚃ 220/280 excl. breakfast
AE ⓘ E ⚡ P 🅿 🎿 🍴 ▬ WC TV 🍽

NICKENICH Rheinland-Pfalz 12

Burgklause (HCR)   AA ANWB
Hauptstr 78
☎ 02632-82993 fax 02632-83545
✉ 56645

The Hotel Burgklause is conveniently situated close to a walking area and the motorway. This well maintained hotel has clean, well appointed rooms with en suite facilities. The restaurant specialises in Greek dishes. Hotel guests can use the swimming pool in Nickenich free of charge.

* - ♨ 45/-
* 7 ⚃ 78/-
AE ⓘ E ⚡ ⊙ ♦ P 🅿 P WC TV

NIDEGGEN Nordrhein-Westfalen 11

Ratskeller (HCR)
Markt 1
☎ 02427-218
✉ 52385

8 ⚃
⊙ P 🅿 ▬ P WC TV 🍽 ⊙

NIEDERDÜRENBACH Rheinland-Pfalz 12

Maarheide (HCR)
Maarheiderweg
☎ 02636-6335
✉ 56651

23 ⚃
⤴ P P 🎿 ⚓ ☎ P WC TV

NIEDERKALL Rheinland-Pfalz 17

Lamberty Eifel (HR)
Brückenstr 10
☎ 06575-4286
✉ 5565

2 ♨ 50/55
20 ⚃ 100/110
AE ⤴ ⊙ P P P WC TV 🍽 🐎

NIEDERZISSEN Rheinland-Pfalz 12

Am Bowenberg (HCR)
Am Bowenberg
☎ 02636-6217 fax 02636-8217
✉ 56651

- ♨ 50/60
14 ⚃ 90/98
⤴ ⚘ ⊙ P ▬ WC TV 🍽 ⊙

NIEFERN Baden-Württemberg 18

Krone (HCR)   AA ANWB
Schlosstr 1
☎ 07233-7070 fax 07233-70799
res nr 07233-70711
✉ 75223

The beautiful Hotel Krone is situated in Niefern, which lies between Pforzheim and Mühlacker. The hotel has modern furnishings and a high standard of housekeeping throughout. The rooms are spacious and have en suite facilities, colour TV, radio and telephone. The pleasant, cosy restaurant offers a choice of Badische and Scwäbische specialities.

open 09.01 - 25.12
* 24 ♨ 109/138
* 31 ⚃ 138/188
AE ⓘ E ⚡ ⤴ P 🅿 🎿 🍴 ▬ P WC TV 🍽 ⊙

NIEFERN/ÖSCHELBRONN Baden-Württemberg 18

Kirnbachtal (HR)   AA ANWB
Hauptstr 123
Niefern
☎ 07233-3111 fax 07233-4846
✉ 75223

The Hotel Kirnbachtal is a small, pleasant family-run hotel, situated on the A8 motorway between Karlsruhe and Stuttgart. The rooms offer a good standard of comfortable accommodation, and the restaurant serves a range of well prepared dishes. This is a hotel where personal service and attention are given a high priority.

open 21.02 - 04.02
* 5 ♨ 48/100
* 10 ⚃ 84/125
E ⊙ ♦ P P P WC TV

GERMANY

NITTEL AN DER MOSEL Rheinland-Pfalz 17

Zum Mühlengarten (HCR) 🅰🅰 *ANWB*
Uferstr 5
Nittel
☏ 06584-387 fax 06584-837
✉ 54453

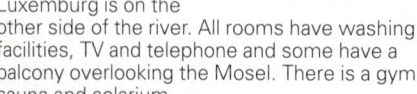

The modern Hotel zum Muhlengarten is situated on the bank of the Mosel at Nittel. The Grand Duchy of Luxemburg is on the other side of the river. All rooms have washing facilities, TV and telephone and some have a balcony overlooking the Mosel. There is a gym, sauna and solarium.

3 ♙ -/50
21 ♘ -/90
🆎 🅴 ⊙ 🅿 🅿 🌂 ♨ 📧 🆎 🆎 🛏 ☺

NÖRDLINGEN Bayern 19

Am Ring (HCR)
Bürgermeister Reigerstr
☏ 09081-4029
✉ 86720

13 ♙
26 ♘
🅿 🌂 📧 🆎 🆎 🍽 🛏

NÜRNBERG Bayern 20

Altéa Hotel Carlton (HCR)
Eilgutstr 13-15
☏ 0911-20030 fax 0911-2003532
res nr 069-230858
✉ 90443

* 59 ♙ 130/255
* 71 ♘ 150/355
🆎 🅾 🅴 ⊜ ⊙ 🅿 ♨ ♨ 📧 🆎 🆎 🍽

Arvena Park (Best Western) (HCR)
Görlitzerstr 51
☏ 0911-89220 fax 0911-8922115
res nr 0130-4455
✉ 90473

open 06.01 - 23.12
120 ♙ 209/330
122 ♘ 259/390
🆎 🅾 🅴 ⊜ 🅾 🅿 🌂 ♨ ♨ 📧 🆎 🆎

Käferstein (HG)
Reutleserstr 65-67
☏ 0911-30905
✉ 90427

10 ♙
38 ♘
☘ 🅿 🌂 ♨ 🌂 📧 🆎 🆎 🆎

Landhotel Schindlerhof (HR)
Steinacher Str 6-8
☏ 0911-93020 fax 0911-9302620
✉ 90427

* 14 ♙ 180/210
* 57 ♘ 230/270
🆎 🅾 🅴 ⊜ 🅾 🅿 🌂 ♨ ♨ 📧 🆎 🆎 🆎

Maritim (HCR)
Frauentorgraben 11
☏ 0911-23630 fax 0911-2363836
res nr 0221-219672
✉ 90443

* 113 ♙ 227/429
* 203 ♘ 308/492
🆎 🅾 🅴 ⊜ ⊙ 🅿 🌂 ♨ 📧 🆎 🆎

Garni Peter Henlein (HG) 🅰🅰 *ANWB*
Peter Henleinstr 15
☏ 0911-412912 fax 0911-417242
✉ 90443

The Hotel Peter Henlein is named after the inventor of the Nürnberger Ei, the world's first pocket watch, in 1510. The hotel is within walking distance of the old town, close to the famous Verkehrsmuseum and the station. The rooms are simple but clean, and a number have bathrooms. There is limited parking available.

* 10 ♙ 90/-
* 18 ♘ 160/-
☘ 🌂 📧 🆎 🆎 🆎 ☺

Queens Hotel Nürnberg (HCR) 🅰🅰 *ANWB*
Münchenerstr 283
☏ 0911-94650 fax 0911-468865
res nr 0130-4433
✉ 90471

The Queens Hotel Nürnberg is quietly situated in the southern part of the town, near the exhibition buildings. The spacious, brightly decorated rooms offer a good standard of accommodation. In the Nudelstube a range of pasta dishes is served, while the Puppenstube offers a choice of international dishes. The hotel has a pleasant cocktail bar, and also a gym, sauna, solarium and children's play corner.

* 69 ♪ 198/228 excl. breakfast
* 72 ⬭ 246/296 excl. breakfast
AE ⦿ E ⚏ ⦸ ◆ ⚘ ⚐ ⬧ ▬ ▭ WC TV |◎|

Am Sterntor (HR)
Tafelhofstr 8-14
☎ 0911-23581 fax 0911-203101
✉ 90443

AA ANWB

The Hotel am Sterntor is well placed for a visit to this medieval town and is situated between the station and the Opernhaus. Most rooms in this tourist and business hotel have a shower or bath and a toilet, and a large number have a TV. The restaurant and breakfast room are traditionally furnished.

* 6 ♪ 60/150
* 110 ⬭ 90/220
⚘ ⦿ P ⚐ ⬧ ▬ ▭ WC TV

NÜRTINGEN Baden-Württemberg 22

Am Schlossberg (Best Western) (HCR)
Europastr 13
☎ 07022-7040 fax 07022-704343
res nr 0130-4455
✉ 72622

* 42 ♪ 180/200
* 129 ⬭ 235/265
AE ⦿ E ⚏ ⦸ ◆ ⚐ ⚘ ⚐ ⬧ ▬ ▭ WC TV |◎|

OBERAMMERGAU Bayern 23

Alois Lang (HCR)
St Lukasstr 15
☎ 08822-4141
✉ 82487

13 ♪
30 ⬭
⚘ P ⚘ ⬧ ▭ WC TV

Wittelsbach (HR)
Dorfstr 21
☎ 08822-1011 fax 08822-6688
✉ 82487

open 20.12 - 05.11
* 6 ♪ 85/95
* 40 ⬭ 140/180
AE ⦿ E ⚏ ⦿ ⬧ ▬ ▭ WC TV |◎|

OBERAU Bayern 23

Forsthaus (HCR)
Hauptstr 1
☎ 08824-212 fax 08824-212
✉ 83471

AA ANWB

The Hotel Forsthaus is situated in the beautiful Loisach valley close to the Zugspitze, and is the ideal for exploring the area by car or on foot - Garmisch-Partenkirchen is 8km away. All the rooms in this comfortable hotel have en suite facilities and TV, and some also have telephone. The restaurant serves a range of regional Bavarian specialities.

open 20.12 - 30.10
8 ♪ 75/85
28 ⬭ 110/150
AE ⦿ E ⚏ ⦿ ◆ P ⚐ ⚘ ▬ ▭ WC TV ⦿

OBERAUDORF Bayern 24

Der Bayerische Hof (HCR)
Sudelfeldstr 12
☎ 08033-1084 fax 08033-4391
✉ 03080

open 15.12 - 15.11
* 2 ♪ 50/62
* 11 ⬭ 84/110
E ⚘ ⦿ P ⚘ ⦿

OBERDERDINGEN Baden-Württemberg 18

Landhotel Gillardon (HR)
Im Hemrich 7
☎ 07045-573 fax 07045-8907
res nr 07045-573
✉ 75038

* 14 ♪ 90/115 excl. breakfast
* 14 ⬭ 120/160 excl. breakfast
AE ⦿ E ⚏ ⦿ P ⚘ ⬧ ▬ ▭ WC TV |◎| ⬥ ⦿

GERMANY 153

OBERHAUSEN *Nordrhein-Westfalen* 11

Parkhotel zur Bockmühle (Best Western) (HCR)
Teutoburger Str 156
☎ 0208-69020 fax 0208-6902158
res nr 0130-4455
✉ 82386

open 04.01 - 22.12
38 ♦ 135/214
47 ♦ 198/318
AE ⓘ E ≈ ⊙ ◆ P ☂ ¶ ■ ⊏ WC TV ⎮⊙⎮ ☺

OBERJOCH *Bayern* 23

Alpengasthof Löwen (HCR)
Passstr 17
☎ 08324-7600 fax 08324-7515
✉ 87541

open 01.05 - 01.11 + 20.12 - 10.04
* 5 ♦ 60/75
* 19 ♦ 104/140
E ♦ ⊙ P ☂ ¶ ■ ⊏ WC TV ⎮⊙⎮ ☺

OBERKIRCH *Baden-Württemberg* 21

Lamm (HR)
Gaisbach 1
☎ 07802-3346 fax 07802-5966
✉ 77704

* 5 ♦ 85/95
* 12 ♦ 130/148
♦ P ¶ ■ ⊏ WC TV

Pflug (HP)   *AA ANWB*
Fernacher Pl
☎ 07802-4081 fax 07802-50322
✉ 77704

Oberkirch is the wine-producing town of the Ortenau area and is ideal as a base for walking holidays. The Hotel Pflug is a modern hotel with spacious rooms. All have a bath, shower, toilet and telephone, and some have a balcony. The restaurant offers national and international dishes. Full parking facilities are available.

open 28.01 - 05.01
* 5 ♦ 82/108
* 30 ♦ 116/150
E ≈ ⊙ P ☂ ¶ ■ ⊏ WC TV ⎮⊙⎮

OBERLEICHTERSBACH/BREITENBACH *Bayern* 13

Ferienhaus Sieglinde (HR)
Langerweg 16-18
Oberleichtersbach
☎ 09741-2753
✉ 97789

6 ♦
17 ♦
AE ≈ ♦ P ☂ ⊏ WC TV ⎮⊙⎮

OBERSTDORF *Bayern* 22

Mohren (HCR)
Marktpl 6
☎ 08322-3005 fax 08322-4480
✉ 87561

open 29.11 - 31.10
20 ♦ 28/80
35 ♦ 90/130
♦ ⊙ P ■ ⊏ WC TV

Sporthotel Menning (HG)
Öschlesweg 18
☎ 08322-3029 fax 08322-8532
✉ 87561

2 ♦ 75/85
20 ♦ 124/190
AE ♦ ⊙ P ☂ ¶ ≈ ¶ ⊡ ■ ⊏ WC TV ✈

Steinacker (HP)
Am Ottorrohr 3
☎ 08322-2146
✉ 87561

open 22.05 - 10.10 + 20.12 - 04.04
* 8 ♦ 65/75
* 10 ♦ 120/140
E ♦ ⊙ P ☂ ⊡ ■ ⊏ WC TV ⎮⊙⎮ ⬆ ☺

Traube (HP)
Hauptstr 6
☎ 08322-4648 fax 08322-3168
✉ 87561

open 01.05 - 31.10 + 18.12 - 09.04
* 7 ♦ 70/110
* 12 ♦ 140/240
P ■ ⊏ WC

GERMANY

Weller (HG)
Fellhornstr 22
☎ 08322-3008
✉ 87561

6 🛏
12 🛌
🅿 ⚡ ♨ 🍴 📺 WC TV

Wittelsbacher Hof (HCR)
Prinzenstr 24
☎ 08322-6050 fax 08322-605300
✉ 87561

open 08.12 - 04.04 + 13.05 - 29.10
* 40 🛏 90/126
* 46 🛌 144/220
AE ⓘ 🅴 ⚡ 🅿 ♨ 🍴 📺 WC 🛗 ⛰ 🐾

OBERTEISCHBACH Bayern 20

Raucherhansl (HCR)
☎ 08731-3025
✉ 8311

56 🛌
🅿 ⚡ 🍴 WC 🍽

OBERWEIS Rheinland-Pfalz 17

Landhaus Wirtz (HCR)   AA ANWB
Bitburger Str 4-6
☎ 06527-362
✉ 54636

The holiday town of Oberweis is in the Prümtal area, close to the beer- producing town of Bitburg. This family hotel has comfortable rooms with shower and toilet, and some also have a balcony. Landhaus Wirtz has a 4000-square- metre sunbathing lawn with a playground and a skittle alley. Facilities for walking, swimming, fishing, rowing, horse riding and windsurfing are all close by.

* - 🛏 44/47
* 15 🛌 74/77
🅴 ♦ 🅿 ♨ 📺 WC 🐾

OBERWESEL Rheinland-Pfalz 17

Rheingoldschänke (HP)
Damscheiderstr
☎ 06744-508
✉ 55430

5 🛌
🅿 ⚡ ♨ 🍴 📺 WC

OBERWOLFACH Baden-Württemberg 21

Hirschen (HR)   AA ANWB
Scharzwaldstr 2
☎ 07834-4962 fax 07834-6775
✉ 77709

The Hotel Hirschen is one of the oldest hotels in the Schwarzwald, and is situated in the idyllic setting of the Wolftal with its well marked walking trails. Much use is made of wood in the rooms, which are modern and pleasantly furnished; all have en suite facilities, colour TV and telephone, and some also have a balcony. The attractively furnished restaurant offers a wide choice of dishes. Recreational facilities include sauna, solarium and a skittle alley.

open 29.01 - 06.01
* 7 🛏 65/90
* 36 🛌 104/150
AE ⓘ 🅴 ⚡ 🅿 ♨ 🍴 🛗 🍽 📺 WC TV 🐾

OCHSENFURT Bayern 19

Bären (HR)   AA ANWB
Hauptstr 74
☎ 09331-2282
✉ 97199

The Hotel Bären is situated by a major road junction in Ochsenfurt. This old town has historic buildings, including the well known town hall which is worth visiting. The hotel has well maintained rooms, most equipped with toilet and shower facilities and colour TV; the restaurant serves a choice of national and international dishes, and there is a terrace and parking facilities.

open 02.03 - 14.01
* 6 ♪ 60/85
* 22 ⚭ 85/160
🛆 🄴 ⊙ ◆ 🄿 ⏏ 🜨 🗐 🄵 🆆🅲 🆃🆅 🍽

OCHTRUP Nordrhein-Westfalen 6

Münsterländer Hof (HR)   AA ANWB
Bahnhofstr 7-9
☏ 02553-93930 fax
02553-939378
✉ 48607

The Hotel Münsterländerhof is situated in the centre of Ochtrup. Close by are the Wasserburg, the Gildehauser Venn nature reserve and the Vogelpark. The rooms in this well maintained hotel have a shower, toilet, radio, telephone and colour TV. The hotel has bicycles for rent and parking facilities are available.

* 5 ♪ 95/110
* 14 ⚭ 150/180
🄰🄴 🛆 🄴 ⚒ 🜨 ⊙ 🄿 ⏏ 🜨 🗐 🄵 🍽 ☺

OFFENBURG Baden-Württemberg 21

Drei Könige (HG)   AA ANWB
Klosterstr 9
☏ 0781-24390 fax
0781-71244
✉ 77652

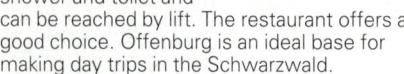

The Hotel Drei Könige is situated in a quiet street in the centre of the town, close to the Neptun springs. Most of the rooms have a shower and toilet and can be reached by lift. The restaurant offers a good choice. Offenburg is an ideal base for making day trips in the Schwarzwald.

* 8 ♪ 69/89
* 14 ⚭ 98/119
🄴 ⚒ 🜨 ⊙ ⏏ ↕ 🗐 🄵 🆆🅲 🆃🆅 ☺

Sonne (HR)   AA ANWB
Hauptstr 94
☏ 0781-71039 fax
0781-71033
✉ 77652

The Hotel Sonne is situated next to the baroque town hall in the centre of Offenburg. The pedestrian area starts in front of the hotel. This is an ideal base for making day trips to the Voges mountains and Baden-Baden. All the rooms have a bath, shower, toilet and colour TV. The rooms in the old part of the hotel are furnished in the Empire or Biedermeister style. The hotel has 15 parking places.

16 ♪ 55/75
18 ⚭ 78/100
🄰🄴 🄴 ⚒ 🜨 ⊙ 🄿 ⏏ 🜨 🗐 🄵 🆆🅲 🆃🆅 ☺

OFFENBURG/FESSENBACH
Baden-Württemberg 21

Traube Fessenbach (HR)   AA ANWB
Fessenbacherstr 115
Offenburg
☏ 0781-4690 fax
0781-46969
✉ 77654

The Hotel Traube is delightfully situated among fruit trees and vineyards. This very comfortable hotel has modern rooms, all with washing facilities, TV, telephone and minibar. The restaurant serves various specialities, and special-diet meals are available on request. Parking facilities are available.

* - ♪ 80/145
* 23 ⚭ 115/150
🄰🄴 🛆 🄴 ⚒ 🜨 ⊙ 🄿 ⏏ ↕🗐 🄵 🆆🅲 🆃🆅 🍽 ☺

OHLSBACH Baden-Württemberg 21

Landgasthof Kranz (HR)
Hauptstr 28
☎ 07803-3312
✉ 77797

This family-run hotel, situated in the town centre, makes a suitable base for excursions to the Schwarzwald. The rooms are modern and comfortably furnished, the atmospheric restaurant serves seasonal specialities from Baden and the Alsace, and the surrounding area has many signposted footpaths. The Hotel Landgasthof Kranz is 8km from the Frankfurt/Basel motorway.

- ♪ 58/75
14 ♫ 98/120
E ♪ P ♫ ⇔ ₣ WC TV IOI ⊙

OHMENHEIM Baden-Württemberg 19

Zur Kanne (HR)
Brühlstr 2
☎ 07326-7088 fax 07326-6343
✉ 73450

6 ♪
44 ♫
◐ E ⇌ ♪ P ₣ WC

OHRENBACH/OBERSCHECKENBACH Bayern 19

Gasthof Jägerstube (HR)
Oberscheckenbach 30
Ohrenbach
☎ 09865-324
✉ 91620

* 8 ♪ 28/45
* 10 ♫ 56/90
Æ ◐ E ⇌ ♪ ◐ P ₣ ♫ ⇔ ₣ WC TV IOI ⊙

OLPE/DROLSHAGEN Nordrhein-Westfalen 12

Zur Schönen Aussicht (HCR)
Frenkhausen-höhe
Drolshagen
☎ 02761-2583 fax 02761-5124
✉ 57489

The Zur Schönen Ausssicht is a peaceful family-run hotel with a welcoming atmosphere, situated near woods with views of the Biggesee. The hotel offers rooms - of which some are south-facing - equipped with shower and toilet. There is a terrace overlooking the Biggesee and a shady garden. The hotel has skittle alley.

3 ♪ 48/52
8 ♫ 90/98
E ♣ ⊙ ◆ P ₣ ♫ ⇔ ₣ WC TV IOI ⚕

OLSBERG Nordrhein-Westfalen 12

Olsberg Parkhotel (HCR)
Stehestr 23
☎ 02962-8040 fax 02962-5889
✉ 59939

The Hotel Olsberg is situated in the *Kurpark* and offers a beautiful view over the 704m-high Olsberg mountain itself. The rooms are comfortable with shower, toilet, telephone and a seating area. The hotel has a bar, café, restaurant, pub and disco, a swimming pool, solarium, sauna, tennis court and skittle alley. Conference facilities are also available.

- ♪ -/120
114 ♫ -/160
Æ ◐ E ♪ ◐ P ♫ ⇌ ↑↓ ₣ WC TV IOI ⊙

Schloß Gevelinghausen (HR)
Schoßstr 1
☎ 02962-8030 fax 02962-1243
✉ 59939

19 ♪ 90/-
31 ♫ 180/-
Æ ◐ E ♪ ♣ P ♫ ⇌ ↑↓ ₣ WC IOI ⊙

158 GERMANY

OLSBERG/WIEMERINGHAUSEN Nordrhein-Westfalen 12

Zur Mühle (HP) [AA] [ANWB]
Zur Mühle 7
Wiemeringhausen
☎ 02985-224
✉ 59939

The simple Hotel zur Mühle is beautifully situated on the edge of the Naturpark Diemelsee in a vast walking area, and is ideal for winter-sports enthusiasts because of its convenient position between the winter-sports areas of Winterberg, Willingen and Olsberg. The hotel has private parking spaces.

* 1 ♫ 28/30 excl. breakfast
* 5 ☎ 56/60 excl. breakfast
🛇 🅿 📠 🅾 🛇

OPPENAU/LÖCHERBERG Baden-Württemberg 21

Schwarzwaldhotel Erdrichshof (HR) [AA] [ANWB]
Schwarzwaldstr 57
Oppenau
☎ 07804-97980 fax 07804-979898
✉ 77728

The Schwarzwaldhotel Erdrichshof is situated in the beautiful Rench valley, close to the well known spa town of Bad Peterstal; it is an area suitable for winter-sports. This pleasant hotel, furnished in country style, has comfortable rooms equipped with a private toilet, bath/shower, TV, telephone, minibar and balcony. Facilities include a swimming pool, sauna and solarium.

2 ♫ 70/90
12 ☎ 140/180
🆎 ⓪ 🅴 ⚒ 🔑 ♦ 🅿 🐕 🏊 🌊 📠 ▭ 🅿 🆆🅲 🆃🆅 🍽 🏠 ❄

ORTENBERG Baden-Württemberg 21

Glattfelder (HR) [AA] [ANWB]
Kinzigtalstr 20
☎ 0781-31219
✉ 77799

The family-run Hotel Glattfelder is situated in a well known holiday resort on the Badische Weinstrasse. It is a well maintained and peaceful hotel; all the rooms have en suite shower facilities and most also have a toilet and telephone. There is a stylish restaurant which serves a range of international specialities. Good beer is served on the sunny terrace.

open 11.03 - 24.02
* 6 ♫ 45/65
* 8 ☎ 85/95
🆎 ⓪ 🅴 ⚒ 🔑 🅾 🅿 🐕 🎿 🅿 🆆🅲 ❄

OSNABRÜCK Niedersachsen 6

Hohenzollern (HR)
Heinrich Heinestr 17
☎ 0541-33170 fax 0541-3317351
✉ 49074

* - ♫ 135/310
* 98 ☎ 160/460
🆎 ⓪ 🅴 ⚒ 🅾 🅿 🏊 ↕ ▭ 🅿 🆆🅲 🆃🆅 🍽 🏠

Neustadt (HG) [AA] [ANWB]
Miquelstr 34
☎ 0541-51200
✉ 49074

The Hotel Neustadt is situated in the centre of Osnabrück. Some of the bedrooms have en suite facilities; breakfast is the only meal served. There is a TV lounge and a garden, and plenty of parking facilities.

8 ♫ 43/72
17 ☎ 80/95
🆎 ⓪ 🅴 ⚒ 🔑 🅾 🅿 🐕 📠 🅿 🆆🅲 🆃🆅 ❄

GERMANY 159

OSNABRÜCK/HARDERBERG Niedersachsen 6

Waldesruh (HCR) AA ANWB
Zur Waldesruh 30
Harderberg
☎ 0541-54323 fax
0541-54376
✉ 49124

The Hotel Waldesruh is on the outskirts of Osnabrück on the edge of the Teutoburgerwald. The rooms have en suite facilities, the restaurant offers hot and cold meals, and the bar serves good wine and beer. There are plenty of opportunities for day trips, including a visit to Osnabrück and many marked walking routes. The hotel has ample parking space.

open 01.03 - 31.01
* 13 ♦ 42/75
* 15 ♦ 85/120
🆎 ⓘ 🇪 ⚙ ♦ 🅿 🍴 ♨ 🛁 🛏 🚻 📺 🍽 ☺

OSTERODE/LERBACH Niedersachsen 13

Sauerbrey (HCR) AA ANWB
Friedrich-Ebert-Str 129
Osterode
☎ 05522-50930 fax
05522-509350
✉ 37520

The Hotel Sauerbrey is an attractive holiday hotel situated in a beautiful hilly area. The rooms are comfortably furnished and have good facilities. The *Stube*-style decorated restaurant has a good menu with a wide choice of dishes, and there is an attractive bar. There is a play-garden for children.

* 1 ♦ 98/160
* 30 ♦ 140/210
🆎 ⓘ 🇪 ⚙ ♦ 🅿 🍴 ♨ 🛁 🛏 🚻 📺 ☺

PADERBORN Nordrhein-Westfalen 12

Arosa (Best Western) (HR) AA ANWB
Westermauer 38
☎ 05251-1280 fax
05251-128806
res nr 0130-4455
✉ 33098

Paderborn is a 1200-year-old Westphalian town with many interesting sights. The Hotel Arosa is a first class hotel with a wide range of amenities. There are rooms with modern furnishings equipped with bath, shower, toilet, TV, telephone and minibar. The fashionable Walliser Stube restaurant serves international cuisine.

* 29 ♦ 150/260
* 73 ♦ 260/320
🆎 ⓘ 🇪 ⚙ ♦ 🅿 🍴 ♨ 🛁 🛏 🚻 📺 ☺

PARSBERG Bayern 20

Flair Hotel zum Hirschen (HCR) AA ANWB
Dr.schrettenbrunnerstr 1
☎ 09492-6060 fax
09492-606222
✉ 92331

The Flair Hotel zum Hirschen is suitable as a comfortable stopover, and is situated on the road from Nürnberg to Regensburg, near the Parsberg junction. The hotel is furnished in modern style and has spacious, stylish rooms, offering a high standard of comfortable accommodation. The attractive restaurant serves a range of national and international dishes. There is a fitness room, sauna and solarium.

open 11.01 - 22.12 + 27.12 - 01.01
* 28 ♦ 65/98
* 50 ♦ 96/140
🇪 ⚙ ⊙ 🅿 🍴 ♨ 🛁 🛏 🚻 📺 🍽 ☺

PASSAU *Bayern* 24

Abrahamhof (HCR)
Abraham 1
☏ 0851-6788
✉ 94032

4 ♻ 38/48
23 ♻ 85/95

Holiday Inn (HCR)
Bahnhofstr 24 a
☏ 0851-59000 fax 0851-5900514
res nr 0130-815131
✉ 94032

49 ♻ 192/-
80 ♻ 264/-

Pell (HR)
Steinbachstr 60
☏ 0851-81501 fax 0851-89340
✉ 94036

* - ♻ 60/-
* 30 ♻ 96/-

Weisser Hase (HR)   AA ANWB
Ludwigstr 23
☏ 0851-92110 fax
0851-92211100
✉ 94032

The Hotel Weisser Hase is situated in Passau, overlooking 3 rivers which converge in the town:– the Danube, the Inn and the Ilz. This comfortable hotel has a good restaurant and halls which are used for large parties and conferences. Most of the rooms have washing facilities, and the hotel has full parking facilities.

open 29.02 - 31.12
* 17 ♻ 100/130
* 100 ♻ 170/200

PFETTRACH *Bayern* 20

Linden (HR)
Linden 8
☏ 08704-250
✉ 84032

10 ♻
11 ♻

PFORZHEIM *Baden-Württemberg* 21

Maritimhotel Goldene Pforte (HCR)
Hohenstaufenstr 6
☏ 07231-37920 fax 07231-3792144
res nr 0221-219672
✉ 75177

20 ♻ 189/275
120 ♻ 248/344

PFUNGSTADT *Hessen* 20

Autobahn Hotel Pfungstadt (MT)
An der A67
☏ 06157-3031 fax 06157-2426
✉ 64319

* 18 ♻ 69/79
* 33 ♻ 116/136

PIRMASENS *Rheinland-Pfalz* 17

Wasgauland (HG)
Bahnhofstr 35
☏ 06331-5310 fax 06331-531144
✉ 66953

22 ♻ 55/65
22 ♻ 90/108

PLAIDT Rheinland-Pfalz   12

Geromont (HR)   *AA ANWB*
Römerstr 3 a
☎ 02632-6056 fax 02632-6066
✉ 56637

The Hotel Geromont is a very comfortable hotel with spacious rooms, all with washing facilities, telephone and TV. Breakfast is an extensive buffet, and snacks can be ordered in the evening. Parking facilities are available.

open 04.01 - 22.12
* 19 ♫ 65/68
* 27 ♫ 95/110
🚶 ☉ P 🕐 🛎 ⬜ ■ 🗝 WC TV ⎘ ☺

PÖLICH Rheinland-Pfalz   17

Pölicher Held (HCR)   *AA ANWB*
Hauptstr 5
☎ 06507-3317
✉ 54340

The Hotel Pölicher Held is situated on a peninsula formed by the Mosel; it is surrounded by fruit trees and vineyard-covered mountains. Swimming, fishing, motor boating, canoeing and walking are just a few of the many recreational facilities on offer in the area. The hotel is well maintained and a number of the rooms have a private shower and toilet. Parking facilities are available.

open 15.01 - 23.12
* - ♫ 38/44
* 13 ♫ 70/85
🚶 P 🕐 🛎 WC ⎘ 🛏

PRÜM Rheinland-Pfalz   17

Wenzelbach (HCR)
Kreuzerweg 30
☎ 06551-557 fax 06551-3602
✉ 54595

3 ♫
13 ♫
E ☉ P 🕐 🛎 ⬜ ■ 🗝 WC TV ⎘ ☺

PRÜM/BASELT Rheinland-Pfalz   17

Baselter Hof (HR)   *AA ANWB*
B 410 nr 7
Baselt
☎ 06558-548 fax 06558-8542
✉ 54597

The Hotel Baselter Hof is near Prüm and features modern rooms with private shower and toilet. There is a restaurant serving grilled dishes, pleasant public rooms, skittle alleys, sunbathing lawns, horse riding, and cross-country skiing in winter. The hotel has ample parking facilities.

- ♫ 80/100
24 ♫ 120/140
AE ① E ⚙ 🛎 ♦ P 🕐 🛎 ⛵ ↕ ■ 🗝 WC TV ⎘ ☺

PRÜMZURLAY Rheinland-Pfalz   17

Haus Am Berg (HCR)   *AA ANWB*
Kapellenstr 15
☎ 06523-534 fax 06523-1228
✉ 54668

The Haus am Berg enjoys a quiet location and provides views of the beautiful Prümtal. The surrounding area with its marked trails offers beautiful walks. All the rooms in this well kept hotel have a shower and toilet; some also have a balcony. For sunny days there is a sunbathing lawn. Parking facilities are available.

open 07.02 - 03.01
* 1 ♫ 34/39
* 8 ♫ 56/68
🚶 P 🕐 WC 🛏 ☺

Ringhotel Haller (HCR)   *AA ANWB*
Michelstr 1-3
☎ 06523-692 fax 06523-1368
✉ 54668

The Ringhotel Haller is situated in the village of Prümzurlay on the River Prüm overlooking rock gardens. The modern hotel rooms all have a shower and toilet, some

GERMANY

have colour TV, telephone and a balcony. There are additional rooms, a sauna and solarium in the recently added extension, some 120m away. Parking facilities are available.

open 19.03 - 31.12
* 3 ♪ 44/66
* 22 ♫ 88/138

RADOLFZELL Baden-Württemberg 21

Braun (HP)
Schaferhalde 16
☎ 07732-3730
✉ 78315

7 ♪
10 ♫

RAESFELD Nordrhein-Westfalen 11

Haus Epping (HCR)
Weseler 5
☎ 02865-7021 fax 02685-1723
✉ 46348

2 ♪ 60/-
10 ♫ 100/-

RAHDEN Nordrhein-Westfalen 7

Bohne (HR)
Lübeckerstr 38
☎ 05771-2039
✉ 32369

Rahden is a good area for pleasant day trips; there are numerous marshes. The traditional Bohne Hotel is well furnished throughout, and many rooms have bath, shower, toilet and colour TV; all have telephone. There are 2 large bowling alleys and a spacious car park.

* 5 ♪ 38/58
* 13 ♫ 72/95

RAMSAU Bayern 24

Oberwirt (HP)
Im Tal 86
☎ 08657-225
✉ 84437

open 20.12 - 31.10
1 ♪
27 ♫ 98/108

Rehlegg (HCR)
Holzengasse 16
☎ 08657-1214 fax 08657-501
✉ 84437

12 ♪ 116/127
48 ♫ 187/253

RATHSMANNSDORF Bayern 24

Zur Alten Post (HCR)
Schloßpl 5
☎ 08546-1037 fax 08546-2483
✉ 94565

* 7 ♪ 45/71
* 22 ♫ 90/142

RAVENSBURG Baden-Württemberg 22

Waldhorn (HR)
Marienpl 15
☎ 0751-36120 fax 0751-3612100
✉ 88212

The Hotel Waldhorn is situated in the centre of the historic town of Ravensburg, 20km from the Bodensee. This is an ideal base for making trips to Austria and Switzerland. The hotel is well furnished and has modern rooms with all facilities. The restaurant has a different menu each day.

open 01.12 - 24.12
* 30 ♪ 110/155
* 10 ♫ 155/245

GERMANY 163

REGEN *Bayern* 24

Panorama (HP)
Johannesfeldstr 27
☎ 09921-2356 fax 09921-2356
✉ 94209

3 🛏 44/56
14 🛏 88/112
[icons]

Wieshof (HP)
Poschetsriederstr 2
☎ 09921-4312
✉ 94209

3 🛏
14 🛏
[icons]

REGENSBURG *Bayern* 20

Kaiserhof (HR)
Kramgasse 10-12
☎ 0941-54027 fax 0941-54025
✉ 93047

11 🛏 80/100
20 🛏 120/130
[icons]

Münchner Hof (HR) AA ANWB
Taendlergasse 9
☎ 0941-58440 fax 0941-561709
✉ 93047

The Hotel Munchner Hof is situated in a small, colourful street in the heart of the historic town centre, close to the impressive St Peter's cathedral and the medieval Steinerne Brücke - the oldest bridge in Germany. The rooms are well cared for and have en suite bathroom and TV. The lounges and dining rooms are attractively furnished in the traditional, Bayern style. There is a parking garage nearby.

* 16 🛏 90/120
* 25 🛏 135/170
[icons]

RELLINGEN/KRUPUNDER *Schleswig-Holstein* 2

Fuchsbau (HR)
Altonaerstr 355-3
Rellingen
☎ 04101-31031 fax 04101-33952
✉ 25462

20 🛏
30 🛏
[icons]

REMAGEN/KRIPP *Rheinland-Pfalz* 12

Rhein Ahr (HCR)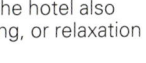
Quellenstr 67-69
Remagen
☎ 02642-44112 fax 02642-46319
✉ 53424

The Hotel Rhein Ahr is situated at the spot where the small River Ahr flows into the Rhine. Because of the vineyards on both banks of the river, there is an extensive choice of wines, and this is reflected, naturally enough, in the hotel's wine cellar. The restaurant offers a variety of good-quality dishes every day. All the rooms feature a shower, toilet and TV. The hotel also offers bowling facilities, swimming, or relaxation in the sauna.

open 16.01 - 22.12
* 2 🛏 70/85
* 12 🛏 100/120
[icons]

REMSCHEID *Nordrhein-Westfalen* 12

Remscheider Hof (HR)
Bismarckstr 39
☎ 02191-4320 fax 02191-432158
✉ 42804

* 47 🛏 180/260 excl. breakfast
* 59 🛏 261/360 excl. breakfast
[icons]

GERMANY

RENDSBURG *Schleswig-Holstein*   **2**

Coventgarden (HCR)
Hindenburgstr 38-42
☎ 04331-59050 fax 04331-59050
✉ 24751

* 17 ♦ -/95
* 39 ♦ -/150
AE ① E ≡ ♦ ⊙ P ⌂ ♨ ⇅ ⊟ ➀ WC TV |◎|

Hansen (HR)
Bismarckstr 29
☎ 04331-22550 fax 04331-21647
✉ 24751

13 ♦
14 ♦
♦ P ⌂ ➀ WC TV ⊙

RHEDA-WIEDENBRÜCK *Nordrhein-Westfalen* **12**

Ratskeller Wiedenbrück (HR)   AA ANWB
Langestr Am Marktpl
☎ 05242-7051 fax 05242-7256
✉ 33378

The luxury Romantikhotel Ratskeller Wiedenbrück is a historic timbered building. The rooms are fully equipped and are furnished with either classical or rustic furniture. The restaurant has beautiful wainscots, and the bar serves a good beer. The attic has a sauna and opens on to a roof terrace.

open 26.12 - 22.12
* 14 ♦ 100/142
* 23 ♦ 175/240
AE ① E ≡ ⊙ P ⌂ ♨ ⇅ ⊟ ➀ WC TV |◎|

RHEINBÖLLEN *Rheinland-Pfalz*   **17**

Am Markt (HCR)
Marktstr 16
☎ 06764-2014
✉ 55494

2 ♦ 55/60
5 ♦ 85/90
AE E ♦ ⊙ P ⌂ ⇌ ➀ WC TV ⊙

RIEGEL *Baden-Württemberg*   **21**

Zum Rebstock (HCR)
Haupstr 37
☎ 07642-1026 fax 07642-3766
✉ 79359

* 5 ♦ 80/90
* 10 ♦ 120/140
E ⊙ P ➀ WC |◎|

RIENECK *Bayern*   **19**

Spessarthotel Gut Dürnhof (HR)
Burgsinnerstr 3
☎ 09354-1001 fax 09354-1512
✉ 97794

* - ♦ 90/125
* 30 ♦ 140/170
AE ① E ≡ ♠ ⊙ P ⌂ ♨ ⇌ ⊟ ➀ WC TV ⊙

RIMSTING *Bayern*   **24**

Gasthof Seehof (HP)
Schafwaschen 4
☎ 08051-1697
✉ 83253

open 01.11 - 08.10
* 3 ♦ 40/44
* 14 ♦ 68/104
♦ ⊙ ≈ ⊙ P ♨ ➀ WC ⊙

RINTELN *Niedersachsen*   **7**

Stadt Kassel (HR)
Klosterstr 42
☎ 05751-44064 fax 05751-44066
✉ 31737

8 ♦ 60/80
14 ♦ 95/120
AE ① E ≡ ⊙ ♦ P ➀ WC TV |◎| ⊙

ROCKENHAUSEN *Rheinland-Pfalz*   **18**

Pfälzer Hof (HR)   AA ANWB
Kreuznacherstr 30
☎ 06361-7968 fax 06361-3733
✉ 67806

The Hotel Pfälzer Hof is quietly situated in rural Rockenhausen. All the rooms have a shower, and most have a TV. The restaurant serves regional specialities.

The garden has a pond, and the wooded Nordpfälzer Bergland is good for walks.

open 16.01 - 21.12
* 5 ♪ 70/-
* 11 ⚏ 100/110
⌘ ⊙ P ☂ ♨ ⎕ WC TV

ROSDORF Niedersachsen   13

Rasthaus Göttingen Ost (MT)
Ostseite
☏ 05509-345
✉ 25548

1 ♪
13 ⚏
AE ⓞ E ⇌ ♦ P ⎔ ⎕ WC TV

Rasthaus Göttingen West (MT)
Westseite
☏ 05509-633
✉ 25548

33 ⚏
AE ⓞ E ⇌ ♦ P ☂ ♨ ⎔ ⎕ WC TV

ROSENHEIM Bayern   23

Goldener Hirsch (HR)   *AA ANWB*
Münchenerstr 40
☏ 08031-12029 fax 08031-32234
✉ 83022

The Hotel Goldener Hirsch is housed in an attractive, renovated building in the centre that dates back to 1875. The public areas are rustic looking and comfortably furnished: there are 2 restaurants, a luungo with an open fire and a Pilsbar Brasserie, Bonaparte. The bedrooms are modern, spacious and comfortable. In the summer, food is prepared on the charcoal grill in the beer garden.

* 15 ♪ 92/108
* 18 ⚏ 140/190
AE ⓞ E ⇌ ⊙ P ↕ ⎕ TV

ROTH AN DER OUR Rheinland-Pfalz   17

Schloß Roth (HA)   *AA ANWB*
Johanniterstr 17
☏ 06566-594 fax 06566-1312
✉ 54675

The apartment-hotel Schloss Roth has a lovely woodland setting near the German-Luxembourg border. A small 13th-century castle is the beautiful historic setting for the hotel. The classic furnishings in the lounges, dining rooms and the well equipped rooms are stylish and luxurious. There is a spacious, beautifully landscaped garden with seating. In the surrounding area, Vianden and Trier offer opportunities for day trips.

open 01.04 - 01.11
* - ♪ 70/-
* 10 ⚏ 90/155
AE ⌘ ♠ P ☂ ♨ ⎔ ⎕ WC TV ⓒ

ROTHENBURG OB DER TAUBER Bayern   19

Goldener Hirsch (HCR)   *AA ANWB*
Untere Schmiedgasse 16
☏ 09861-7080 fax 09861-708100
✉ 91534

The Hotel Goldener Hirsch has a wrought-iron façade and is situated in the medieval town of Rothenburg ob der Tauber. The lounges, guest rooms and restaurant all have good furnishings, and the restaurant overlooks the old fortress.

open 11.01 - 19.12
* 23 ♪ 140/210
* 57 ⚏ 180/320
AE ⓞ E ⇌ ♠ ⊙ P ☂ ♨ ↕ ⎔ ⎕ WC TV ⓒ

Reichs Küchenmeister (HCR)
Kirchpl 8
☏ 09861-2046 fax 09861-86765
✉ 91541

* 6 ♪ 95/150
* 46 ⚏ 120/220
AE ⓞ E ⇌ ♠ ⊙ P ☂ ♨ ⇌ ↕ ⎔ ⎕ WC TV ⊙ ⓒ

ROTHENBURG O.D.TAUBER/ SCHILLINGSFÜRST *Bayern* 19

Flair Hotel Die Post (HR)   AA ANWB
Rothenburgerstr 1
Schillingsfürst
☎ 09868-473 fax 09868-5876
✉ 91581

Hotel Die Post lies on the well known Romantische Strasse and was already a very popular inn during the horse-and-carriage era. The cosy rooms offer comfortable accommodation; the restaurant has a wide choice of regional specialities on the menu. There is a playground for younger guests. In the winter cross-country skiing facilities are available in the area.

* 1 ♂ 70/90
* 12 ♒ 96/150
E ι ▲ ⊕ P ᛏ ⚲ ⛁ ᛐ WC TV ⋈

ROTTACH-EGERN *Bayern* 23

Bachmair Am See (HCR)
Seestr 47
☎ 08022-6444
✉ 83700

76 ♂
92 ♒
⋋ ⚒ P ᛏ ⚲ ≼ ᛒ ⇅ ᛐ WC TV ⋈

Franzen (HR)
Karl Theodorstr 2 a
☎ 08022-6087 fax 08022-5619
✉ 83700

open 12.12 - 02.04 + 18.04 - 22.11
* 3 ♂ 115/155
* 11 ♒ 160/330
E ◈ ◆ P ᛏ ⚲ ᛒ ᛐ WC TV ⋈ ⊙

RÜDENHAUSEN *Bayern* 19

Bräurei Wolf (HCR)
Paul Gerhard Pl 7
☎ 09383-440
✉ 97355

3 ♂
6 ♒
ᛐ ⋈

RÜDESHEIM *Hessen* 18

Central Ringhotel (HCR)
Kirchstr 6
☎ 06722-3036 fax 06722-2807
✉ 65385

open 01.03 - 20.12
* 8 ♂ 99/113
* 45 ♒ 162/206
AE ⬢ E ⌨ ⋋ ⊙ P ᛏ ⇅ ᛐ ᛒ ᛐ WC TV ⋈ ⊙

Garni Dries (HR)
Kaiserstr 1
☎ 06722-2420 fax 06722-2663
✉ 65385

open 01.04 - 07.11
* 6 ♂ 80/-
* 38 ♒ -/120
P ᛏ ⚲ ≼ ᛐ WC ⋈ ⋈

Germania (HCR)
Rheinstr 10
☎ 06722-2584 fax 06722-3226
✉ 65385

4 ♂ 45/85
14 ♒ 78/140
AE ⬢ E ⌨ ⊙ ◆ P ᛒ ᛐ WC TV 🏠 ⊙

RÜDESHEIM/ASSMANNSHAUSEN *Hessen* 18

Krone Assmannshausen (HCR)
Rheinuferstr 10
Assmannshausen
☎ 06722-4030 fax 06722-3049
✉ 65385

open 01.03 - 31.12
* 15 ♂ 150/280 excl. breakfast
* 50 ♒ 250/850 excl. breakfast
AE ⬢ E ⌨ ⋋ ⚒ P ᛏ ⚲ ≼ ⇅ ᛐ ᛒ ᛐ WC TV

Café Post (HCR)
Rheinuferstr 2
Rüdesheim
☎ 06722-2326 fax 06722-48249
✉ 65382

open 16.03 - 15.11
* 4 ♂ 60/95
* 16 ♒ 80/175
AE ⬢ E ⌨ ⋋ ⚒ ⊙ P ᛏ ⚲ ᛒ ᛐ WC TV ⋈ ⊙

GERMANY 167

RUHPOLDING Bayern — 24

Diana (HR)
Kurhausstr 1
☎ 08663-9705 fax 08663-5859
✉ 83321

open 16.12 - 31.10
* 8 ♨ 57/70
* 18 ⌇ 110/140
⊙ P 🛉 🍴 📺 WC ⌂ 🕾

Steinbach (HR)
Am Westernberg
☎ 08663-1644 fax 08663-370
✉ 83321

21 ♨
51 ⌇
AE E ℄ ⊙ P 🛉 🍴 ⚡ 🛏 ⌂ WC TV 🕾

RUHSTORF Bayern — 24

Mathäser (HCR)
Hauptstr 19
☎ 08531-3074 fax 08531-3714
✉ 94099

* 6 ♨ 59/73
* 29 ⌇ 98/125
AE E ℄ ⊙ P 🛉 🍴 ⚡ ↕ 🛏 ⌂ WC TV 🕾 🚹 ☎

SAARBRÜCKEN Saarbrucken — 17

Mercure Kongress Saarbrücken (HCR)
Hafenstr 8
☎ 0681-38900 fax 0681-372266
res nr 0681-3890603
✉ 66111

* ♨ 140/190 excl breakfast
* 150 ⌇ 160/230 excl. breakfast
AE ① E ✕ ⊙ ◆ P 🛉 🍴 ⚡ 🛏 ⌂ WC TV 🕾

SACHRANG Bayern — 24

Sachrangerhof (HCR)
Dorfstr 3
☎ 08057-383
✉ 83229

2 ♨
8 ⌇
℄ ⊙ P 🛉 🍴 ⌂ WC TV 🕾

SAIG Baden-Württemberg — 21

Hochfirst (HCR)   AA ANWB
Dorfpl 5
☎ 07653-751 fax 07653-505
✉ 79853

The Hotel Hochfirst is situated in Saig, in the southern part of the Schwarzwald, and is a typical holiday hotel for summer and winter. Most of the rooms have a balcony and en suite toilet, shower/bath. The hotel has a pleasant restaurant, and guests can enjoy a drink in the *Gaststube* or on the terrace. Set at an altitude of over 1000m the region gets a lot of snow, making it the ideal venue for a winter-sports holiday. After skiing, guests can use the swimming pool and sauna.

open 20.12 - 02.11
* 5 ♨ 39/90
* 20 ⌇ 106/200
℄ ⊙ P 🛉 🍴 ⚡ 🛏 ⌂ WC 🕾

SALZBERGEN Niedersachsen — 6

Gutsschänke Holsterfeld (HCR)
Feldweg 30
☎ 05971-70650 fax 05971-81714
✉ 48499

open 20.01 - 24.12
6 ♨ 39/56
6 ⌇ 79/92
🚹 ⑤ ◆ P 🛉 🍴 WC TV 🕾

SAUERLACH Bayern — 23

Sauerlacher Post (HR)   AA ANWB
Tegernseer Landstr 2
☎ 08104-830 fax 08104-8383
✉ 82054

The Hotel Sauerlacher Post is built in Bavarian country-house style and situated 20km south of München. It features stylish rooms with en suite facilities, colour TV and telephone. The restaurant offers a wide choice of dishes with the emphasis on regional and international specialities. Guests can use the gym and sauna free of charge, and conference facilities for up to 110 persons are available.

→

GERMANY

* 11 ⌂ 130/195
* 40 ⌂ 150/235
[AE] ⓘ [E] ≡ ♨ ☉ ♦ P ⊺ ♨ ⇈ ☐ 🄴 [WC] [TV] ⦿

SAUERLACH/LOCHHOFEN Bayern   23

Zur Schmiede (HP)
Kirchstr 4
Lochhofen
☏ 08104-9421
✉ 8021

7 ⌂
12 ⌂
⚐ P ⊺ ⇈ ☐ 🄴 [WC] ⇞ ⦿

SCHANZE/SCHMALLENBERG
Nordrhein-Westfalen   12

Alfons Hanses (HCR)   [AA] [ANWB]
Schmallenberg
☏ 02975-473
✉ 57392

The Hotel Alfons Hanses is situated in the tiny village of Schanze (near Grafschaft), in the centre of the quiet Rothaargebirge nature park. This is the highest part of the Sauerland which is a good walking area in summer for walking, and in winter for skiing. The rooms are well furnished, there is a sauna and gym and the restaurant overlooks the surrounding area.

open 27.12 - 05.11
5 ⌂ -/48
11 ⌂ 88/92
⚐ ♨ ☉ P ⊺ ♨ [WC] ⦿ ⊙

SCHIEDER Nordrhein-Westfalen   7

Nessenberg (HCR)   [AA] [ANWB]
Nessenberg 1
☏ 05282-1008
✉ 32816

The Hotel Nessenberg is situated in the Weserbergland on Bundesstrasse 239 between Schieder and Bad Meinberg, 2km from the Emmerstausee. It is a comfortable hotel which could serve as an overnight stop and which has plenty of walks nearby for those staying longer. All rooms have a bathroom and TV. The restaurant offers trout and various game dishes, and there is a terrace at the front of the hotel.

* 4 ⌂ 40/60
* 12 ⌂ 80/120
[AE] ⓘ [E] ≡ ♨ ⌇ ♦ P ⊺ ♨ ☐ 🄴 [WC] [TV] ⦿ ⊙

SCHIEDER/SCHWALENBERG Nordrhein-Westfalen   7

Papiermühle (HP)
Niesetal 11
Schwalenberg
☏ 05282-458
✉ 4938

2 ⌂
4 ⌂
♨ ⌇ ☉ P ⊺ 🄴 [WC] ⇶

SCHIERKE Sachsen   14

Heinrich Heine (HCR)   [AA] [ANWB]
☏ 039455-345 fax 039455-357
✉ 38879

The Hotel Heinrich Heine is in a peaceful setting close to the highest mountain in the Harz. This partly renovated hotel is suitable as a stopover or as a base for walks in the wooded surroundings. The rooms, some of which have en suite toilet and shower facilities, are reached by a lift. There are plenty of recreational possibilities available nearby.

35 ⌂ 35/70
67 ⌂ 90/290
[AE] ⓘ [E] ≡ ⚐ ♨ ☉ P ⊺ ♨ ⇈ ☐ 🄴 [WC] [TV] ⦿ ⊙

GERMANY 169

Guest House-Café-Boarding House Alfons Hanses
D-57392 Schmallenberg-Schanze
Hoch Sauerland, 720 metres above sea level
Tel.: 02975-473

Located in the Rothaar hills scenic park, 720 metres above sea level with extensive stretches of deciduous and pine forest. The ideal spot for hiking with wonderful views in the country of a thousand mountains. Mild climate recommended in summer and winter.

The hotel is entirely geared to relaxation and peace and quiet. Wonderful rooms with shower and wc, balcony and attractive lounges with television, individual sauna and fitness room, ski lift and cross-country ski runs and midget golf.

We extend you a warm welcome.

A. HANSES

SCHILLINGEN Rheinland-Pfalz 17

Pension Wildgarten (HP) AA ANWB
Marscheiderweg 4
☎ 06589-7042
✉ 54429

Pension Wildgarten is a small peaceful hotel, situated on the edge of a forest, offering comfortable accommodation all year round. The rooms are well kept and a half-board option is also available. From the *Wintergarten* guests have splendid views of the animals in the hotel's private game reserve.

* - ♫ 28/32
* 4 ♫ 44/54
⚹ ♨ ☺ P ⚐ ⚑ ☂ WC ☺

SCHLEIDEN Nordrhein-Westfalen 11

Höddelbusch (HCR) AA ANWB
Gemündenerstr 39
☎ 02444-3222 fax 02444-1701
✉ 53937

The Hotel Höddelbusch is situated at the foot of a hill in the northern part of the Eifel, a mountainous region with woods and lakes. It can be reached via the B265, the road from Schleiden in the direction of Gmünd. This is a traditional holiday hotel; there are rooms with or without en suite facilities and TV, and a terrace at the front of the hotel.

* 7 ♫ 45/75
* 11 ♫ 70/110
♦ P ⚐ ⚑ ☂ WC TV ☺

SCHLEIDEN/GEMÜND Nordrhein-Westfalen 11

Friedrichs (HCR) AA ANWB
Alte Bahnhofstr 16
Schleiden
☎ 02444-600 fax 02444-3108
✉ 53937

The Hotel Friedrichs enjoys a good location at the convergence of the rivers Urft and Olef. The rooms in this family-run hotel have a shower, toilet, telephone and radio; TV is available on request. The hotel has a sun-bathing lawn, sauna and solarium, and a play lawn for younger guests.

* 6 ♫ 85/95
* 15 ♫ 120/150
AE ① E ⚑ ☺ P ⚐ ⚑ ☂ ▮ ▮ WC TV ☺

Zum Urfttal (HCR)
Alte Bahnhofstr 12
Schleiden
☎ 02444-3041 fax 02444-2688
✉ 53937

3 ♫
15 ♫
E ⚐ ☺ P ⚐ ⚑ ▮ ▮ WC TV ☺

SCHLESWIG Schleswig-Holstein 2

Strandhalle Ringhotel (HCR)
Strandweg 2
☎ 04621-9090 fax 04621-909100
✉ 24837

* 2 ♙ 105/140
* 23 ♙ 150/175
🆎 💳 🅴 ♒ ♿ ⓞ 🅿 🍽 🐕 🔔 🛏 🚻 📺 🍴

Waldhotel Am Schloß Gottorf (HCR)
Stampfmuhle 1
☎ 04621-23288 fax 04621-23289
✉ 24837

open 15.03 - 15.10
* 1 ♙ 75/80
* 8 ♙ 120/135
🆎 🅴 ♒ ♿ ⓞ 🅿 🍽 🐕 🚻 ☺

SCHLIERSEE Bayern 24

Schlierseer Hof (HCR)   *AA ANWB*
Seestr 21
☎ 08026-4071 fax 08026-4953
✉ 83727

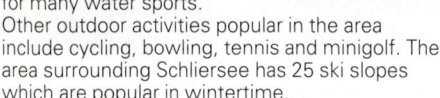

The Best Western Hotel Schlierseerhof is only a short distance from Munich, situated in a valley beside a lake which provides facilities for many water sports. Other outdoor activities popular in the area include cycling, bowling, tennis and minigolf. The area surrounding Schliersee has 25 ski slopes which are popular in wintertime.

* 2 ♙ 130/180
* 44 ♙ 180/280
🅴 ♒ ♿ ⊜ ⓞ ◆ 🅿 🍽 ⛷ ↑↓ 🛏 🚻 📺 🍴

SCHLITZ Hessen 13

Vorderburg (HCR)
An Der Vorderburg 1
☎ 06642-5041 fax 06642-7535
✉ 36110

open 25.01 - 20.12
* 13 ♙ -/65
* 15 ♙ -/108
♿ ⓞ 🅿 🍽 ↑↓ 🚻 📺 🍴

SCHLÜSSELFELD Bayern 19

Panorama (HR)
Attelsdorf 1
☎ 09552-1500 fax 09552-6224
✉ 96130

4 ♙
30 ♙
♿ 🅿 🍽 🐕 🛏 🚻 📺 🍴 🐾

Zum Storch (HR)
Marktpl 20
☎ 09552-1016 fax 09552-1006
✉ 96130

open 13.11 - 31.10
* 7 ♙ 40/57
* 31 ♙ 72/97
🆎 💳 🅴 ♒ ♿ ⓞ 🅿 🍽 🐕 ↑↓ 🛏 🚻 📺 🍴

SCHMALLENBERG Nordrhein-Westfalen 12

Zum Grubental (HR)   *AA ANWB*
Latrop 5
☎ 02972-6327
✉ 57392

The Hotel zum Grubental is situated in Latrop, a village near Schmallenberg in the Hochsauerland. It is an inviting holiday hotel, built in a typical regional style. The rooms have en suite facilities and some also have a TV. There is a pleasant restaurant and an attractively landscaped garden with a terrace. The surrounding area offers plenty of winter-sports opportunities, including many kilometres of cross-country skiing trails.

* 6 ♙ 62/68
* 10 ♙ 110/146
♿ ⚘ 🅿 🍽 🚻 📺 🍴 ☺

Waldhaus (HCR)
Ohlenbach 10
☎ 02975-840 fax 02975-8448
✉ 57392

open 01.12 - 10.11
10 ♙
50 ♙
🆎 💳 🅴 ♒ ♿ ⚘ 🅿 🍽 🐕 🔔 🛏 🚻 📺 🍴 🐾

GERMANY 171

SCHMALLENBERG/FREDEBURG 12
Nordrhein-Westfalen

Klein (HCR) AA ANWB
Kleins Wiese
Schmallenberg
☎ 02974-7029 fax 02974-5115
✉ 57392

The Klein is situated in the mountainous area of the Sauerland. It offers a range of modern comforts; all the rooms are equipped with a shower, toilet, TV and telephone. In addition, the hotel features various leisure facilities, including fitness room, sauna and solarium, and a minigolf course outside. The ski lift is 300m from the hotel.

open 26.12 - 26.11
* 6 ♨ 75/115
* 12 ⚏ 150/240
🛁 ♨ P ☎ ⚏ 🍴 WC TV 🍽 ☼

SCHMALLENBERG/GRAFSCHAFT 12
Nordrhein-Westfalen

Maritim Grafschaft (HR) AA ANWB
An De Almert 11
Schmallenberg
☎ 02972-3030 fax 02972-303168
res nr 0221-219672
✉ 57392

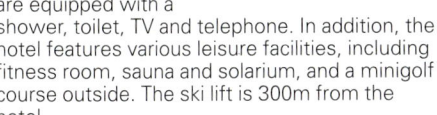

The Hotel Maritim is situated in the woods near Grafschaft, a village in the Hochsauerland. The hotel has spacious rooms with modern facilities, a good restaurant and a bar. There is a gym, a large swimming pool with sauna, tennis courts, golf and a riding school. In winter this is a good base for downhill and cross-country skiing.

* 24 ♨ 157/267
* 78 ⚏ 248/338
AE ◉ E ⚏ ♨ ✎ P ☎ ⚏ 🍴 ⚕ 🍽 WC TV ☼

SCHMALLENBERG/OBERKIRCHEN 12
Nordrhein-Westfalen

Landhotel Gasthof Schütte (HCR) AA ANWB
Eggeweg 2
Oberkirchen
☎ 02975-820 fax 02975-82522
res nr 02975-82501
✉ 57392

Built in 1774 this timbered house has become a hospitable hotel. There are communal lounges, a swimming pool, a sauna, sun beds, a large garden and a sunbathing lawn, all combining to create a relaxed atmosphere. The rooms at the Gasthof Schutte are comfortable, with toilet, colour TV, telephone and minibar.

open 27.12 - 20.11
* 15 ♨ 95/150
* 45 ⚏ 170/340
AE ◉ E ⚏ ♨ ✎ P ☎ ⚏ 🍴 ⚕ 🍽 WC TV ☼

Seidenweber (HP)
In Der Riemeske 15
Schmallenberg
☎ 02975-588
✉ 57392

2 ♨
6 ⚏
🛁 P ⚏ 🍴 🍽 WC ☼

SCHNEVERDINGEN Niedersachsen 7

Landhaus Höpen (HCR)
Höpener Weg 13
☎ 05193-820 fax 05193-8213
✉ 29640

10 ♨
34 ⚏
E 🛁 ♨ P ☎ ⚏ ✎ ⚕ 🍴 🍽 WC TV ☼

SCHÖMBERG Baden-Württemberg 18

Krone (HCR)
Liebenzellerstr 15
☎ 07084-7077 fax 07084-6641
✉ 75328

15 ♨ 60/85
20 ⚏ 100/130
◉ ♦ P ☎ ⚏ 🍴 🍽 ⚕ WC TV ☼

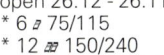

GERMANY

SCHÖMBERG/LANGENBRAND Baden-Württemberg 18

Sommer (HP) AA ANWB
Kiefernstr 2-4
Schömberg
☏ 07084-7062
✉ 75328

The Hotel Sommer is quietly situated outside the centre of Schomberg in the northern part of the Schwarzwald. It is a well maintained hotel-pension, with rooms equipped with en suite facilities and TV, and more than half with a balcony. A number of rooms have been turned into apartments with a private kitchen. There are reclining chairs in the garden, and the hotel has a sauna and solarium.

* 4 ♪ 30/37
* 17 ♯ 64/78
♣ ♠ ♦ P ♣ ♪ ■ ♪ WC TV ☺

SCHONACH Baden-Württemberg 21

Rebstock (HR) AA ANWB
Sommerbergstr 10
☏ 07722-5327
✉ 97993

The Hotel Rebstock can be found in the centre of the holiday and winter-sports town of Schonach, in one of the highest parts of the Schwarzwald. All the rooms have a toilet and shower, and some have TV. The restaurant offers a choice of typical Schwarzwald specialities, and the hotel also has a large swimming pool.

* 6 ♪ 66/-
* 23 ♯ 132/-
AE ① E ♣ ♠ ● P ♣ ♪ ■ ♪ ↑↓ ■ WC ☺

SCHONGAU Bayern 23

Alte Post (HCR)
Marienpl 19
☏ 08861-8058 fax 08861-7037
✉ 86956

open 11.01 - 24.12
* 4 ♪ 60/100
* 36 ♯ 100/180
E ● ♪ ♪ ■ ♪ WC TV ◎

Holl (HR)
Altenstädterstr 39
☏ 08861-4051 fax 08861-8943
✉ 86956

* 1 ♪ 75/90
* 21 ♯ 130/150
AE ① E ≡ ♣ ● P ♣ ■ ♪ WC TV ☺

SCHÖNHAGEN Schleswig-Holstein 2

Dorinthotel Schönhagen (HA)
Schloßstr 1
☏ 04644-1701 fax 04644-1370
res nr 0130-6605
✉ 37170

open 19.03 - 31.10
AE ① E ≡ ♣ ♠ ♣ ≡ ↑↓ ♪ WC TV ☺

SCHÖNMÜNZACH/BAIERSBRONN Baden-Württemberg 21

Holzschuh's Schwarzwaldhotel AA ANWB
(HCR)
Murgtalstr 655
Schönmünzach
☏ 07447-1088 fax 0744/-1004
✉ 72270

The Holzschuh's Schwarzwaldhotel is beautifully situated; most rooms have en suite facilities. There is an inviting bar and a restaurant serving good food, while dishes from the barbecue are served on the terrace. The hotel has an indoor swimming pool and on-site parking.

open 15.12 - 15.11
* 7 ♪ 57/99
* 17 ♯ 136/180
♣ P ♣ ♣ ≡ ↑↓ ♪ ■ ♪ WC TV ◎ ☺

SCHÖPPINGEN Nordrhein-Westfalen 6

Kongresshotel zum Rathaus (HR)
Hauptstr 52
☏ 02555-8290
✉ 48624

20 ♨

SCHRIESHEIM Baden-Württemberg 18

Neues Ludwigstal (HR)   AA ANWB
Strahlenbergerstr 2
☏ 06203-61028 fax 06203-61208
✉ 69198

The Hotel Neues Ludwigstal is situated in a green valley on the Bergstrasse just outside Schriesheim. It is a comfortable holiday hotel where the rooms have an en suite bathroom, and some also have a TV and balcony. There is a stylish, well furnished restaurant and a pleasant *Bierstube*. The hotel is a good base for day trips to the Odenwald, romantic Neckardal, and beautiful Heidelberg.

* 12 ♨ 55/72
* 22 ♨ 95/115

SCHRIESHEIM/ALTENBACH Baden-Württemberg 18

Waldhotel Bellevue (HCR)
Röschbachstr 1
Schriesheim
☏ 06203-1520 fax 06203-7213
✉ 69198

* 2 ♨ 55/65
* 8 ♨ 90/98

SCHWABACH Bayern 20

Löwenhof (HCR)
Rosenbergerstr 11
☏ 09122-2047 fax 09122-12625
✉ 91126

open 11.01 - 21.12
* 6 ♨ 90/95
* 20 ♨ -/150

SCHWÄBISCH GMÜND Baden-Württemberg 19

Das Pelikan (HR)
Türlensteg 9
☏ 07171-3590 fax 07171-359359
✉ 73525

19 ♨ 150/185
45 ♨ -/275

SCHWÄBISCH HALL Baden-Württemberg 19

Der Adelshof (HR)
Am Markt 12-13
☏ 0791-75890 fax 0791-6036
✉ 74523

26 ♨ 145/210
21 ♨ -/230

Hohenlohe (HCR)
Weilertor 14
☏ 0791-75870 fax 0791-758784
✉ 74523

* 40 ♨ 147/197
* 60 ♨ 218/288

SCHWANGAU Bayern 23

Hanselewirt (HCR)
Mitteldorf 13
☏ 08362-8237
✉ 87645

open 31.12 - 28.02 + 01.04 - 31.10
* 1 ♨ 38/48
* 11 ♨ 82/86

Post (HR)
Münchenerstr 5
☏ 08362-8235
✉ 87645

5 ♨
30 ♨

SCHWANGAU/HORN Bayern 23

Rübezahl (HCR) AA ANWB
Am Ehberg 31
Schwangau
☎ 08362-8327 fax 08362-81701
✉ 87645

The pleasant Hotel Rübezahl is situated in a beautiful area and offers views over the mountains, meadows and the castle of Neuschwanstein. The comfortable timbered rooms are equipped with en suite facilities. The restaurant serves delicious meals, prepared with fresh local produce; and after a walk, the guests can relax in the sauna, solarium or whirlpool.

open 15.12 - 15.11
* 5 ♪ 60/87
* 27 ♫ 108/154

SCHWEICH Rheinland-Pfalz 17

Leinenhof (HCR)
An Der L 141
☎ 06502-2657
✉ 54338

4 ♪
23 ♫

Zur Moselbrücke (HCR) AA ANWB
Brückenstr 1
☎ 06502-1068 fax 06502-7680
✉ 54338

Hotel Zur Moselbrücke stands near the river Mosel and has a welcoming atmosphere. The rooms - some with balcony - are well kept, and feature en suite facilities, colour TV and telephone. Guests can relax on the terrace or in the garden. The immediate surroundings offer a variety of recreational facilities.

open 01.02 - 31.12
* 4 ♪ 55/60
* 20 ♫ 110/120

SCHWEINFURT Bayern 19

Panorama Hotel (HG) AA ANWB
Am Oberen Marienbach 1
☎ 09721-2040 fax 09721-186391
✉ 97621

The Panorama Hotel lies at the heart of Schweinfurt, which is one of the oldest towns in Germany. The hotel is part of a building complex which also houses a supermarket, library, restaurant and shops. It has a pleasant breakfast room and all the bedrooms - some recently renovated - feature en suite facilities, TV and minibar.

open 04.01 - 24.12
* 8 ♪ 119/133
* 74 ♫ 158/200

SEEBRUCK/LAMBACH Bayern 23

Malerwinkel (HCR)
Lambach 23
Seebruck
☎ 08667-488 fax 08667-1408
✉ 83358

open 25.12 - 23.12
* 1 ♪ 90/130
* 19 ♫ 160/200

SEESEN Niedersachsen 8

Goldener Löwe Ringhotel (HCR)
Jacobsonstr 20
☎ 05381-1201 fax 05381-3840
✉ 38723

15 ♪
22 ♫

Wilhelmsbad (HCR)
Frankfurterstr 10
☎ 05381-1035 fax 05381-47590
✉ 38723

6 ♪ 70/95
12 ♫ 90/140

GERMANY 175

SENHALS Rheinland-Pfalz 17

Weinhaus Halfenstube (HCR)   AA ANWB
Moselweinstr 30
☎ 02673-4579 fax
02673-4133
✉ 56820

Not far from famous Cochem on the left bank of the Mosel lies Senhals; the Hotel Weinhaus Halfenstube is located by the river in this wine-producing town. The timbered rooms all have a toilet and shower, and there is a restaurant with a terrace. The garden on the other side of the street offers a view of the ships on the river and the vineyards on the hills.

2 ♊ -/60
11 ♋ -/120
🍴 🚗 🛏 P ♨ 🛗 ❄ WC 🍽 ☎

SIEDLINGHAUSEN Nordrhein-Westfalen 12

Schniederjost (HCR)
Brilonerstr 2
☎ 02983-562
✉ 59955

10 ♊
20 ♋
🚗 P 🅿 ♨ ⇅ 🛏 ❄ 🛗 TV 🍽

SIEGBURG Nordrhein-Westfalen 12

Raststätte Zur Alten Poststraße   AA ANWB
(HCR)
Autobahn A3
☎ 02241-66068 fax
02241-55863
✉ 53721

The Zur Alten Poststrasse/Siegburg West is one of the oldest establishments of its kind in Germany, and stands in wooded grounds on the Köln-Frankfurt motorway. The rooms are bright and tidy and have en suite toilet and washing facilities. There is a restaurant with a separate part for non-smokers. There is a pleasant terrace, and swimming and tennis facilities are available nearby.

* 8 ♊ 81/110 excl. breakfast
* 8 ♋ 114/175 excl. breakfast
♿ ☎ ◆ P ♨ 🛏 ❄ 🛗 WC TV 🍽

Siegblick (HCR)
Nachtigallenweg 1
☎ 02241-60077 fax 02241-60079
✉ 53721

open 11.08 - 31.12 + 19.01 - 14.07
* 3 ♊ 80/130
* 16 ♋ 115/165
E ⚙ ♿ ♣ ☎ 🌐 ♦ P ♨ ♨ ❄ 🛗 ❄ WC TV 🍽 ☎

SIEGEN Nordrhein-Westfalen 12

Kochs Ecke (HR)   AA ANWB
Koblenzerstr 53
☎ 0271-23036 fax
0271-21070
✉ 57072

The Hotel Kochs Ecke is particularly suitable for business people. It is situated in the centre of Siegburg, within walking distance of the station. The rooms have good sound insulation, and they have a good range of facilities, including a TV and minibar. The restaurant offers a wide choice of food from simple lunches to exquisite dinners. Parking facilities are available.

* 13 ♊ 62/102
* 28 ♋ 95/168
AE ◐ E ⚙ ◆ P ♨ ⇅ ❄ 🛗 ❄ WC TV 🍽 ☎

SIEGSDORF Bayern 24

Edelweiss (HR)   AA ANWB
Hauptstr 21
☎ 08662-9296 fax
08662-12722
✉ 83313

Siegsdorf is close to the München - Salzburg motorway, with the Bayern Alps serving as an impressive backdrop. The rooms, equipped with shower and toilet, are well kept. There is a restaurant and shady terrace.

open 01.12 - 31.10
* 3 ♊ 33/45
* 11 ♋ 58/85
AE E ◆ P ♨ ❄ 🛗 ❄ WC ⇧ ☎

Gasthof Neue Post (HR)
Kirchpl
☎ 08662-9278 fax 08662-9174
✉ 83313

open 15.12 - 02.11
2 ₰ 28/-
18 ₰ 50/84
[icons]

SIMMERATH/EICHERSCHEID Nordrhein-Westfalen 11

Haus Gertrud (HR)   AA ANWB
Bachstr 4
Eicherscheid
☎ 02473-1310
✉ 52152

The Haus Gertrud is a well kept family-run hotel, comfortably furnished, and with a relaxed atmosphere. The rooms are well furnished and have shower, toilet and balcony. The hotel features a sunbathing lawn, children's playground and private parking facilities. It is situated in the centre of Eicherscheid and is easily accessible. This is a popular walking area.

* - ₰ 31/42
* 6 ₰ 52/70
[icons]

SIMONSKALL/HÜRTGENWALD Nordrhein-Westfalen 11

Talschenke (HCR)   AA ANWB
Simonskall
☎ 02429-7153
✉ 5165

The Hotel Talschenke is peacefully situated in a valley in the small tourist town of Simonskall which is surrounded by woods. A pleasant looking house forms the setting for this friendly hotel, which has spacious rooms with en suite bathroom and minibar - some also have TV. The cosy restaurant offers a wide choice of excellent dishes, and the surrounding area provides plenty of scope for walking.

* - ₰ 65/70
* 12 ₰ 100/110
[icons]

SINDELFINGEN Baden-Württemberg 18

Appartement Hotel Central (HR)
Vaihinger Str 15
☎ 07031-869810 fax 07031-869870
✉ 71063

* 13 ₰ 60/135 excl. breakfast
* 15 ₰ 75/165 excl. breakfast
[icons]

Holiday Inn (HR)
Schwertstr 65
☎ 07031-61960 fax 07031-84990
res nr 0130-815131
✉ 71065

* 55 ₰ 170/290
* 130 ₰ 220/350
[icons]

Queens Hotel Bristol (HR)
Wilhelm Haspelstr 101
☎ 07031-6150 fax 07031-874981
res nr 0130-4433
✉ 71065

open 01.03 - 30.11
43 ₰ 128/268 excl. breakfast
100 ₰ 176/366 excl. breakfast
[icons]

SINDRINGEN Baden-Württemberg 19

Krone (HP)
Untere Str 2
☎ 07948-401 fax 07948-2492
✉ 74670

open 01.02 - 01.12
* 9 ₰ 55/65
* 14 ₰ 90/100
[icons]

SINGEN Baden-Württemberg 21

Jägerhaus (HR)   AA ANWB
Ekkehardstr 84
☎ 07731-65097 fax 07731-63338
✉ 75196

The Hotel Jägerhaus can be found in the centre of Singen, a town at the foot of a magnificent rock which features the ruin of Hohentwiel at the top. Because of its convenient position on the A81 motorway to Zürich, the hotel makes a good overnight stop. The rooms offer comfortable accommodation, and the stylish restaurant specialises in game and fish.

10 ♫ 85/95
18 ♫ 120/160
AE ⓘ E ✖ ⊙ ◆ P 🅿 ⇅ 🔲 📞 WC TV

SOEST Nordrhein-Westfalen 12

Andernach Zur Börse (HR)
Thomasstr 31
☎ 02921-4019
✉ 59494

6 ♫
8 ♫
AE ⓘ E ✖ ⊙ P 🅿 📞 WC TV ☺

Pilgrim Haus (HR)
Jakobistr 75
☎ 02921-1828 fax 02921-12131
✉ D-59494

open 02.01 - 23.12
* 2 ♫ -/110
* 4 ♫ -/165
AE E ✖ ⊙ P 🅿 ⇅ 🔲 📞 WC TV ⍩ ☺

SOMMERHAUSEN Bayern 19

Ritter Jörg (HR)
Maingrasse 14
☎ 09333-1221 fax 09333-1883
✉ 97286

8 ♫
14 ♫
✖ ⊙ P 🅿 ⇱ 🔲 📞 WC

Weinhaus Unkel (HR)
Maingasse 6
☎ 09333-227
✉ 97286

open 10.03 - 20.02
* 3 ♫ 44/55
* 9 ♫ 76/90
E ✖ ⊙ P 🅿 🔲 📞 WC

SPEYER Rheinland-Pfalz 18

Goldener Engel (HR)   AA ANWB
Mühlturmstr 1 a
☎ 06232-13260 fax 06232-132695
✉ 67321

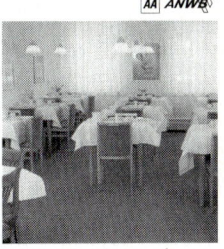

The Hotel Goldener Engel is peacefully situated on the edge of the town centre, near the Altpörtel. It is within walking distance of the famous Speyer cathedral via the grand Maximillianstrasse. This holiday and business hotel has spacious, comfortable rooms with en suite bathroom and TV, and a rustic restaurant. To find the hotel take the Speyer Dudeshofen exit from the B9 road, then follow de Dudenhofer and Schützenstrasse, and turn left at the railway.

open 02.01 - 23.12
12 ♫ 93/120
30 ♫ 140/190
AE ⓘ E ✖ ✖ ⊙ P 🅿 ⇅ 🔲 📞 WC TV ☺

Trutzpfaff (HR)
Webergasse 5
☎ 06232-78399
✉ 67346

8 ♫ -/95
AE ⓘ E ✖ ⊙ P 🅿 ⇱ 📞 WC TV ⍩ ✈

Am Wartturm (HG)
Landwehrstr 30
☎ 06232-36066
✉ 67346

6 ♫
8 ♫
⊙ P 🅿 📞 WC ✈

STARNBERG Bayern 23

Seehof (HR)
Bahnhofpl 06
☎ 08151-6001 fax 08151-28136
✉ 82319

7 ♫
24 ♫
AE ⓘ E ✖ ⊙ P 🅿 ⇅ 🔲 📞 WC TV ☺

ST BLASIEN Baden-Württemberg 21

Dom (HCR)
Hauptstr 4
☎ 07672-371 fax 07672-4655
✉ 79829

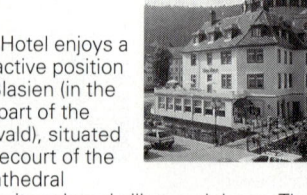

The Dom Hotel enjoys a most attractive position in Sankt Blasien (in the southern part of the Schwarzwald), situated on the forecourt of the Dom, a cathedral famous for its colossal pillars and dome. The hotel has a river flowing either side of it. Most of the rooms have private toilet and shower. The conservatory-restaurant and terrace over the water provide a panoramic view of the church and surrounding area.

* 3 ♿ 45/80
* 9 ⌂ 70/160
🅴 ⚘ ⊙ 🅿 🍽 ⌛ 🛏 🅿 🚽 🆆🅲 📺 🍴 ⚘

STEINFURT/BORGHORST Nordrhein-Westfalen 6

Posthotel Riehemann (HR)   AA ANWB
Münsterstr 8
Borghorst
☎ 02552-4050 fax 02552-62484
✉ 48565

The Posthotel Riehemann was first established in 1827 and has recently been renovated. All the rooms have good facilities, and there is a good restaurant. The area is good for cycling. Parking facilities are available.

open 09.01 - 26.12
6 ♿ 60/80
13 ⌂ 110/130
🆎 ⓪ 🅴 ⚘ ⊙ 🅿 🍽 ⌛ 🛏 🅿 🆆🅲 📺 🍴 ⚘

STEINGADEN Bayern 23

Moser (HP)
Wies 1
☎ 08862-503
✉ 86989

1 ♿
4 ⌂
⚘ ⊙ 🅿 🍽 ⌛ 🛏 🅿 🆆🅲 🍴

STEMWEDE Nordrhein-Westfalen 6

Berggasthof Wilhelmshöhe (HR)
Zur Wilhelmshöhe 14
☎ 05474-1010 fax 05474-1371
✉ 32351

open 18.02 - 23.01
* 6 ♿ 65/85
* 8 ⌂ 120/140
🆎 ⓪ 🅴 ⚘ ⚘ 🅿 🍽 ⌛ 🛏 🅿 🆆🅲 📺 🍴 ✈

ST ENGLMAR Bayern 24

Sporthotel (HCR)
Am Predigtstuhl 12
☎ 09965-1810 fax 09965-1314
✉ 94379

* 9 ♿ 53/74
* 45 ⌂ 132/188
🆎 ⓪ 🅴 ⚘ ⚘ 🅿 🍽 ⌛ 🎾 🛏 🅿 🆆🅲 📺 🍴

ST GEORGEN Baden-Württemberg 21

Hirsch (HR)
Bahnhofstr 70
☎ 07724-7125
✉ 88048

7 ♿
15 ⌂
⊙ 🅿 🍽 🛏 🅿 🆆🅲 📺

ST GOAR Rheinland-Pfalz 17

Zum Goldenen Löwen (HCR)
Heerstr 82
☎ 06741-1674
✉ 56329

6 ♿
9 ⌂
⚘ 🅿 ⌛ 🛏 🅿 🆆🅲 🍴

Hauser (HCR) AA ANWB
Heerstr 77
☏ 06741-333 fax 06741-1464
✉ 56329

The Hotel Hauser is situated in the centre of Sankt Goar, a tourist spot in the Rhine valley. It is famous for the Lorelei and the many ruins. The hotel overlooks the busy traffic on the river. Most of the rooms have washing facilities. The restaurant serves Rhineland specialities, and there is a terrace for sunny days.

open 01.03 - 01.11
* 3 ♦ 55/95
* 13 ♦ 98/130
AE ① E ☰ ⚡ ▲ ⊙ ♦ ♛ ▬ ☐ WC ⑩

Am Markt (HP)
Markt 1
☏ 06741-1689 fax 06741-1721
✉ 56329

open 01.03 - 15.11
* 3 ♦ 60/80 excl. breakfast
* 14 ♦ 100/120 excl. breakfast
AE ① E ☰ ⊙ ☂ ♛ ▬ ☐ WC ⑩ ✈

ST GOARSHAUSEN Rheinland-Pfalz 17

Pohls Rheinhotel Adler (HR)
Bahnhofstr 6
☏ 06771-2613 fax 06771-1447
✉ 56346

open 16.02 - 01.01
* 8 ♦ 50/62
* 59 ♦ 100/110
⊙ P ♛ ≋ ▬ ☐ WC ⑩

ST MÄRGEN Baden-Württemberg 21

Kranz (HR)
Südhang
☏ 07669-311
✉ 7811

4 ♦
8 ♦
▲ P ☂ ♛ ╫ ▬ ☐ WC ⑩

STOCKACH Baden-Württemberg 21

Goldener Ochsen (HR)
Zozneggerstr 2
☏ 07771-2031 fax 07771-2034
✉ 78333

* 19 ♦ 85/115
* 20 ♦ 130/170
AE ① E ☰ ⊙ ♦ P ☂ ♛ ╫ ▬ ☐ WC TV ⑩

GERMANY 179

STOCKSTADT AM MAIN Bayern 18

Haus Maria (HG)
Schulstr 44 a
☏ 06027-1307
✉ 63811

10 ♦
10 ♦
AE E ▲ ⊙ P ♛ ☐ WC ⑩

ST PETER Baden-Württemberg 21

Berghotel Kandel (HCR)
Panoramastr
☏ 07660-7091 fax 07660-7093
✉ 79271

open 18.12 - 07.11
* 1 ♦ 70/90
* 39 ♦ 104/148
AE E ☰ ▲ ♠ ⊙ P ☂ ╘ ▬ ☐ WC TV ⑩

Jägerhaus (HP) AA ANWB
Mühlgraben
☏ 07660-343 fax 07660-821
✉ 79271

The Hotel Jägerhaus is remotely situated in a valley, amid meadows, woods and mountains in the southern part of the Schwarzwald. It is a peaceful holiday and winter-sports hotel with rooms furnished in country style and equipped with good modern amenities. The restaurant offers a choice of regional specialities complemented with local wine. There is a garden with an attractive terrace and minigolf.

open 11.12 - 09.11
* 1 ♦ 67/-
* 5 ♦ 96/106
E ♠ P ☂ ♛ WC TV ⑩

ST PETER-ORDING Schleswig-Holstein 2

Ambassador International (Best Western) (HCR)
Im Bad 26
☏ 04863-7090 fax 04863-2666
res nr 0130-4455
✉ 25826

* 8 ♦ 170/250
* 82 ♦ 240/320
AE ① E ☰ ▲ ⊙ P ☂ ≋ ╫ ╘ ▬ ☐ WC TV ⑩

STRAUBING Bayern 24

Römerhof (HR)
Ittlingerstr 136
☎ 09421-61245 fax 09421-60697
✉ 94315

* 4 ♦ 65/85
* 16 ⚐ 105/125
AE ⓘ E ⚡ ⚒ ⦿ P ⚑ ⚓ ⬜ ⬛ WC TV

Seethaler (HR)   AA ANWB
Theresienpl 25
☎ 09421-12022 fax 09421-23390
✉ 94315

The historic Hotel Seethaler, with its decorated façade, is situated in the town centre of Straubing by the Danube. The hotel is particularly proud of its adorned ceilings and furnishings. All the rooms have a bathroom and TV; half of them have a minibar.

open 04.01 - 17.12
* 10 ♦ 95/105
* 10 ⚐ 150/160
AE E ⚡ ⦿ P ⚑ ⬜ ⬛ WC TV

Theresientor (HR)
Theresienpl 41
☎ 09421-8490 fax 09421-849100
✉ 94315

* 3 ♦ 105/170 excl. breakfast
* 30 ⚐ 145/240 excl. breakfast
AE ⓘ E ⚡ ⦿ P ⚑ ⚓ ⚒ ⬜ ⬛ WC TV ⍟

Villa (HCR)
Bahnhofpl 2
☎ 09421-23094 fax 09421-82482
✉ 94315

5 ♦
10 ⚐
AE ⓘ E ⚡ ⦿ P ⚑ ⚓ ⬜ ⬛ WC TV ⍟ ⊚

Gasthof Metzgerei Wenisch (HCR)
Innere Passauerstr 59-61
☎ 09421-22066 fax 09421-23768
✉ 94315

* 12 ♦ 50/85
* 22 ⚐ 90/130
AE ⓘ E ⚡ ⦿ P ⚑ ⬜ ⬛ WC TV ⊚

STROMBERG Rheinland-Pfalz 18

Burghotel Stromburg (HCR)
Schloßberg
☎ 06724-1026 fax 06724-3307
✉ 55442

* 4 ♦ 95/-
* 17 ⚐ 150/170
AE ⓘ E ⚡ ⚒ ♨ P ⚑ ⚓ ⬜ ⬛ WC TV ⍟ ⊚

Goldenfels (HR)   AA ANWB
August Gerlachstr 2 a
☎ 06724-3605 fax 06724-7260
✉ 55442

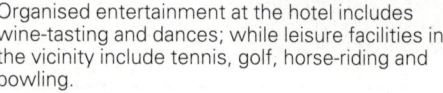

The family-run hotel Goldenfels lies 2km away from motorway 61. The rooms are pleasantly furnished and equipped with private en suite facilities. Organised entertainment at the hotel includes wine-tasting and dances; while leisure facilities in the vicinity include tennis, golf, horse-riding and bowling.

* 4 ♦ 40/55
* 14 ⚐ 85/100
E ⚡ ⦿ P ⬛ WC

STÜHLINGEN Baden-Württemberg 21

Krone (HR)
☎ 07744-321
✉ 79780

10 ♦
12 ⚐
⦿ P ⬛ WC TV ⍟

STUTTGART Baden-Württemberg 18

Mövenpick Stuttgart Airport (HR)   AA ANWB
Randstr 7
☎ 0711-79070 fax 0711-793585
res nr 06-0220717
✉ 70629

The Mövenpick Stuttgart Airport Hotel lies 200m from the terminals and 20 minutes by bus from the city centre. The rooms are modern and comfortably furnished. Drinks are served on the terrace or in the lounge bar, and excellent meals are served in the

Mövenpick restaurant, which has an attractive winter-garden. The hotel has facilities for disabled visitors and offers meeting rooms. There is a courtesy bus service to the terminals from the hotel.

* 87 ☐ 249/390 excl. breakfast
* 142 ☐ 289/430 excl. breakfast
🜚 🜚 E 🜚 🜚 P 🜚 ↕ 🜚 🜚 WC TV

Wartburg (HR)
Langestr 49
☎ 0711-20450 fax 0711-2045450
✉ 70174

open 04.01 - 24.12
* 18 ☐ 145/185
* 63 ☐ 240/265
🜚 🜚 E 🜚 🜚 P 🜚 ↕ 🜚 🜚 WC TV 🜚 🜚

STUTTGART/KIRCHHEIM UNTER TECK
Baden-Württemberg

Park Hotel (HR)   AA ANWB
Eichendorffstr 99
☎ 07021-80080 fax 07021-800888
✉ 73230

The Park Hotel is quietly situated at the foot of the Swäbische Alp. The bedrooms are convenient, and all have en-suite bathrooms and cable TV. There is a good atmosphere in the hotel restaurant, and food served here includes local specialities. The hotel is fairly central and there are conference facilities for business people. Facilities here include a sauna and beauty salon.

* 32 ☐ 138/178
* 33 ☐ 165/210
🜚 🜚 E 🜚 🜚 ♦ P 🜚 🜚 🜚 🜚 WC KTV 🜚

STUTTGART/SINDELFINGEN *Baden-Württemberg*   18

Senator Hotel (Best Western) (HR)   AA ANWB
Riedmühlestr 18-20
Sindelfingen
☎ 07031-6980 fax 07031-698600
res nr 0130-4455
✉ 71063

The Senator Hotel enjoys a central location 3 minutes from the the centre and the bus station. The rooms are large, comfortable and fully furnished. The pleasant bar-bistro serves meals from 20.00 until 24.00. Bicycles are available free for guests' use, and there is a sauna and solarium. The hotel is situated on the A81/A8 *Autobahn*. Courtesy transport service to the airport is available on request.

* 60 ☐ 99/149
* 43 ☐ 129/179
🜚 🜚 E 🜚 P 🜚 ↕ 🜚 WC TV

SULZBACH *Hessen*   18

Holiday Inn Main Taunus (HR)
Am Main Taunus Zentrum 1
☎ 06196-7630 fax 06196-72996
res nr 0130-815131
✉ 65843

* 106 ☐ 265/450 excl. breakfast
* 183 ☐ 305/470 excl. breakfast
🜚 🜚 E 🜚 P 🜚 🜚 🜚 TV

TAUBERBISCHOFSHEIM *Baden-Württemberg*   19

Adlerhof (HR)
Bahnhofstr 18
☎ 09341-2336 fax 09341-2143
✉ 97941

open 20.01 - 20.12
* 7 ☐ 69/89
* 11 ☐ 110/139
E 🜚 ♦ P 🜚 🜚 🜚 WC TV 🜚

Am Brenner (HR)   AA ANWB
Goethestr 10
☎ 09341-3091 fax 09341-5874
✉ 97941

Hotel Am Brenner is a modern and comfortable hotel, peacefully situated in the Taubertal. The rooms are spacious and equipped with modern

→

182 GERMANY

amenities. The excellent cuisine and personal attention are the hallmarks of this establishment. The terrace offers beautiful views over the town and hills, and the surrounding area provides plenty of opportunity for walking and bicycle rides.

* 10 ♫ 70/90
* 20 ⚏ 95/135
🆎 ⓘ 🇪 ⚒ ⚶ ⓢ 🅿 🍴 🏊 ⬇ ▬ 🅿 wc 📺 🍽

TECKLENBURG Nordrhein-Westfalen   6

Parkhotel Burggraf (HCR)   AA ANWB
Meesenhof 5-7
☏ 05482-425 fax 05482-6125
✉ 49545

The modern, 6-storey Parkhotel Burggraf is part of the Ringhotels group. It is surrounded by woods and stands at the edge of this historic town, where the houses are built in the traditional, regional style. A relaxed atmosphere prevails in this holiday and business hotel, and the rooms are equipped with good amenities. Both bedrooms and restaurant provide fine views of the green hills in the Teutoburgerwald. The hotel has a large swimming pool with sauna, and conference facilities are available.

* 4 ♫ 120/215
* 39 ⚏ 160/240
🆎 ⓘ 🇪 ⚒ ◆ ♨ ⓢ 🅿 🍴 🏊 ⬇ ▬ 🅿 wc 📺 🍽

Tecklenburger Land West (MT)
Grafenstr 17
☏ 05482-566 fax 05482-568
✉ 49545

* 6 ♫ 90/100
* 18 ⚏ 145/155
🆎 ⓘ 🇪 ⚒ ◆ 🅿 🍴 🏊 ⬇ ▬ 🅿 wc 📺 🍽

TEGERNSEE Bayern   23

Silencehotel Bayern (HCR)
Neureuthstr 23
☏ 08022-1820 fax 08022-3775
✉ 83684

30 ♫ 126/212
60 ⚏ 210/300
🆎 ⓘ 🇪 ⚒ ♨ ⓢ 🅿 🍴 🏊 ⬇ ▬ 🅿 wc 📺 🍽

TETTNANG Baden-Württemberg   22

Bären (HR)
Bärenpl 1
☏ 07542-6945
✉ 88069

18 ♫
21 ⚏
⊙ 🅿 🍴 ▬ 🅿 wc 🍽

Ritter (HR)
Karlstr 2
☏ 07542-52051 fax 07542-5797
✉ 88069

open 19.01 - 20.10 + 09.11 - 31.12
1 ♫ 72/80
23 ⚏ 110/145
🆎 ⓘ 🇪 ⚒ ⊙ ◆ 🅿 🍴 🏊 ⬇ ▬ 🅿 wc 📺 🍽 ⚲

THALFANG Rheinland-Pfalz   17

Berghof (HR)
Berghof 1
☏ 06504-8754
✉ 544245

2 ♫ 39/-
10 ⚏ 70/88
ⓢ 🅿 🏊 🅿 wc

Haus Vogelsang (HR)
Vogelsangstr 7
☏ 06504-1088 fax 06504-2332
✉ 54424

* 1 ♫ 43/51
* 11 ⚏ 78/96
🇪 ♨ ⓢ 🅿 🏊 🍴 🅿 wc 📺 🍽 🐾

TIMMENDORFER STRAND Schleswig-Holstein   3

Maritim Golf und Sporthotel (HCR)
An Der Waldkapelle 26
☏ 04503-6070 fax 04503-2996
res nr 0221-219672
✉ 23669

12 ♫ 167/283
194 ⚏ 238/392
♨ ⚒ ⓢ 🍴 🏊 🅿 ⚓ ⬇ ▬ 🅿 wc 📺 🍽 ⚲

Maritim Seehotel (HCR)
Strandallee 73 b
☏ 04503-6050 fax 04503-2932
res nr 0221-219672
✉ 23669

18 🛏
223 🛌
AE ⓘ E ⇌ 🚌 ⊙ P 🍴 🏊 🚤 ♨ 🛗 ▪ 📺 🐕

TITISEE-NEUSTADT Baden-Württemberg   21

Maritimhotel Titisee (HCR)   AA ANWB
Seestr 16
☏ 07651-8080 fax
07651-808603
res nr 0221-219672
✉ 79822

The Maritimhotel Titisee
is a modern,
comfortable holiday and
winter-sports hotel
situated on the wooded
shore of the Titisee.
Most of the spacious rooms have a balcony, and
full facilities. There is a restaurant, bar, swimming
pools, sauna with solarium and gym. The Titisee
offers plenty of opportunities for windsurfing and
sailing.

28 🛏 179/273
102 🛌 254/334
AE ⓘ D E ⇌ 🚌 ⊙ P 🍴 🏊 🚤 ♨ 🛗 ▪ 📺 🐕
🏨 ☎

Rauchfang (HP)   AA ANWB
Bärenhofweg 2
☏ 07651-8255 fax
07651-88186
✉ 79822

The Hotel Rauchfang is
situated on the shore of
the Titisee. The rooms
are well furnished and
have a toilet, shower or
bath and a TV. The
tables in the restaurant
are arranged around an open fire. The hotel
combines health and leisure, offering a
swimming pool with sauna and a garden. There is
plenty of walking and cross-country skiing in the
area.

open 26.11 - 14.12
* 2 🛏 -/90
* 15 🛌 -/176
ⓘ E ⇌ P 🍴 🏊 🚤 ▪ 📺 ☎

TODTMOOS Baden-Württemberg   21

Schwarzwaldstube (HR)
Grüntalstr 6
☏ 07674-400
✉ 79682

1 🛏
9 🛌
⊙ P 🍴 🏊 ♨ 📺 🐕

TODTNAU Baden-Württemberg   21

Sonne (HCR)
Meinrad Thomastr 1
☏ 07671-385 fax 07671-8956
✉ 79674

* 2 🛏 29/49
* 9 🛌 58/88
AE E ⇌ ⊙ P 🍴 📺 🐕

TODTNAUBERG Baden-Württemberg   21

Pension Elisabeth (HG)
Max Leipheimer Weg 6
☏ 07671-463
✉ 79674

1 🛏
7 🛌
🏊 P 🚤 📺

TRABEN-TRARBACH Rheinland-Pfalz   17

Rema Hotel Bellevue (HCR)
Am Moselufer
☏ 06541-7030 fax 06541-703400
✉ 56841

* / 🛏 95/155
* 43 🛌 190/280
AE ⓘ D E ⇌ ⊙ 🚤 ♨ ▪ 📺 🐕

TRAUNSTEIN Bayern   24

Parkhotel Traunsteinerhof (HR)
Bahnhofstr 11
☏ 0861-69041
✉ 83278

27 🛏
33 🛌
⊙ P 🍴 ♨ ▪ 📺 🐕

Rosenheimerhof (HCR)
Rosenheimerstr 58
☏ 0861-4900
✉ 83278

2 🛏
15 🛏
⊙ ◆ P 🅿 WC ⅏

TRAVEMÜNDE Schleswig-Holstein 3

Grüner Jäger (HR)
Ivendorfer Landstr 40/42
☏ 04502-2667 fax 04502-2065
✉ 23570

* - 🛏 75/85
* 28 🛏 100/150
AE ① E 🗷 ◑ P 🅿 WC TV ⅏

Kurhaus (KH)
Aussenallee 10
☏ 04502-810 fax 04502-74437
✉ 23524

* 40 🛏 189/277
* 64 🛏 274/350
AE ① E 🗷 ⸙ ◑ P 🛎 ≋ ↾ ⊟ 🅿 WC TV ⅏

Maritim Strandhotel (HR)
Trelleborgallee 2
☏ 04502-890 fax 04502-74439
res nr 0221-219672
✉ 23570

* 10 🛏 189/309
* 230 🛏 248/428
AE ① E 🗷 ⸙ ≋ ⊟ 🅿 WC

TRECHTINGHAUSEN Rheinland-Pfalz 18

Rheinblick (HCR)   AA ANWB
Mainzerstr 14
☏ 06721-6100 fax 06721-6722
✉ 55413

The Hotel Rheinblick is only separated from the river by a railway track. The restaurant offers a panoramic view of one of the most characteristic landscapes of Germany - the Rhine with its wine-producing slopes and the ruins of Rheinsteiun und Reichenstein. Most rooms have a private toilet, some also have a shower or bath. There is a terrace on the sunny side of the hotel.

4 🛏 30/45
13 🛏 60/80
⊙ P 🛎 ≋ ⊟ 🅿 WC TV

TRENDELBURG Hessen 13

Pension Habedank (HP)
Am Schaarbusch 49
☏ 05675-1418
✉ 34388

open 01.03 - 30.11
* 2 🛏 22/23
* 9 🛏 56/74
⸙ ⅏ P 🛎 ≋ ⸳ ↾ ⊟ 🅿 WC ⊛

TRIBERG Baden-Württemberg 21

Parkhotel Wehrle (HR)   AA ANWB
Gartenstr 24
☏ 07722-86020 fax 07722-860290
res nr 07722-860249
✉ 78094

The Parkhotel Wehrle is a luxury hotel situated in the centre of Triberg, one of the holiday and winter-sports resorts in the Schwarzwald. The rooms, some of them in the Gästehaus, have a full range of facilities. The restaurant and lounges are well furnished. There is a sauna and swimming pool inside, as well as an outdoor pool in the garden.

* 8 🛏 82/150 excl. breakfast
* 44 🛏 145/260 excl. breakfast
AE ① E 🗷 ⸙ ◑ P 🅿 🛎 ≋ ↾ ⸳ ⊟ 🅿 WC TV ⅏ ⊛

TRIER Rheinland-Pfalz 17

Eurener Hof (HR)
Eurenerstr 171
☏ 0651-88077 fax 0651-800900
✉ 54294

open 27.12 - 23.12
* 18 🛏 115/125
* 39 🛏 180/190
⸙ P 🛎 ≋ ↾ ⊟ 🅿 WC TV ⅏ ⊛

Fassbenders Central Hotel (HR)
Sichelstr 32
☏ 0651-978780 fax 0651-9787878
✉ 54290

open 08.01 - 20.12
* 2 🛏 75/80
* 30 🛏 130/160
AE E 🗷 ⸙ ◑ P 🛎 ⸳ ⊟ 🅿 WC TV ⅏

GERMANY

Zur Post (HR)   AA ANWB
Ruwererstr 18
☏ 0651-5100 fax 0651-57773
✉ 54292

The rooms in Hotel zur Post vary in size, but all have en suite bath/shower and toilet, and some also have a balcony. Fine beers are served in the *Bierstube*. It is pleasant to relax in the garden and on the terrace after activities on the skittle alley.

* 1 ♦ 68/88
* 20 ♦ 98/130
🅰🅴 ⓘ 🅴 ≡ 🔑 🅿 ☂ ♨ 🛏 🅿 WC TV 🍴

Weinhaus Haag (HG)   AA ANWB
Stockpl 1
☏ 0651-72366
✉ 54290

The Hotel Weinhaus Haag is situated on a quiet square in the town centre. This is a well maintained and good-value bed and breakfast hotel where most of the rooms have a private toilet and shower. The attractions of Trier, a pleasant town with a many historic sights and pavement terraces, are within walking distance.

* 7 ♦ 45/85
* 9 ♦ 80/145
🅰🅴 ⓘ 🅴 ≡ ♨ ⊙ 🅿 WC TV 🍴

TRIPPSTADT *Rheinland-Pfalz*   **18**

Gunst (HG)
Hauptstr 99 a
☏ 06306-1785
✉ 67705

2 ♦
9 ♦
♨ ⊙ 🅿 ☂ 🅿 WC

Schloßstube (HR)
Hauptstr 24
☏ 06306-442
✉ 67705

5 ♦
♨ ⊙ 🅿 ☂ 🅿 WC 🍴

TRITTENHEIM *Rheinland-Pfalz*   **17**

Moselperle (HCR)
Moselweinstr 42
☏ 06507-2221 fax 06507-6737
✉ 54349

open 15.01 - 30.11
* 2 ♦ 60/80
* 12 ♦ 90/120
🅰🅴 ⓘ 🅴 ≡ ⊙ ♦ 🅿 ☂ ♨ 🛏 🅿 WC TV

TÜBINGEN *Baden-Württemberg*   **21**

Am Bad (HCR)   AA ANWB
Europastr 2
☏ 07071-73071 fax 07071-75336
✉ 72072

The Hotel am Bad is a comfortable residential hotel situated in beautiful, park-like countryside on the Neckar, not far from the *Altstadt*. It is a well kept hotel where the rooms have en suite bathrooms. There is a pleasant restaurant and the terrace overlooks the large, outdoor swimming pool with its sunbathing lawns, which is adjacent to the hotel's garden. For younger guests there is a paddling pool and a playground. The hotel's recreational facilities include golf and tennis.

open 11.01 - 19.11
* - ♦ 75/106
* 15 ♦ 135/163
🅰🅴 🅴 ≡ ♨ ✎ 🅿 ☂ ♨ 🛏 🅿 WC TV 🐕

Domizil (HCR)   AA ANWB
Wohrdstr 5-9
☏ 07071-1390 fax 07071-139250
✉ 72072

The Hotel Domizil can be found in the heart of the historic town of Tübingen, and is situated on the river Neckar. This tastefully furnished hotel has pleasantly appointed rooms offering comfortable accommodation. A relaxed atmosphere prevails in the restaurant, from where there are splendid views over the river Neckar. Boats can be hired from the hotel.

* 41 ♦ 110/160
* 38 ♦ 160/195
🅰🅴 ⓘ 🅴 ≡ ♨ ✎ ⊙ 🅿 ☂ ♨ ↕ 🛏 🅿 WC TV 🍴

ÜBERLINGEN/BODENSEE Baden-Württemberg 22

Bad Hotel Kurgarten Und See (HR) AA ANWB
Christophstr 2
Überlingen
☎ 07551-61055 fax 07551-67079
✉ 88662

The Bad Hotel Kurgarten und See is on the banks of the Überlinger See, the northern tributary of the Bodensee. It is a traditional, chic residential and spa hotel in a beautiful building. The rooms are comfortable and overlook the lake, there is a pleasant atmosphere in the restaurant, and there is an attractive garden with a sunny terrace which stretches from the hotel to the lake.

* 20 ♦ 120/150
* 30 ♦ 170/230

Parkhotel St Leonhard (HR)
Obere St Leonhardstr 71
Überlingen
☎ 07551-808100 fax 07551-808531
✉ 88662

* 28 ♦ 130/177
* 117 ♦ 214/254

UFFENHEIM Bayern 19

Grüner Baum (HR) AA ANWB
Marktpl 14
☎ 09842-310 fax 09842-2115
✉ 97215

The Gasthof-Hotel Grüner Baum has an attractive façade, and is situated on a square in the town centre of Uffenheim, 5km from the A7 motorway. The hotel has rooms with private toilet and shower, and is very suitable for a comfortable overnight stop. Game and typical Bavarian dishes such as carp are the speciality of the restaurant.

7 ♦ 32/48
40 ♦ 64/96

ULM Baden-Württemberg 22

Neuthor (HR)
Neuer Graben 23
☎ 0731-15160 fax 0731-1516513
✉ 35753

36 ♦ 140/150
56 ♦ 170/205

ULM/GÖGGLINGEN Baden-Württemberg 22

Zum Ritter (HR) AA ANWB
Bertholdstr 8
Ulm
☎ 07305-7365 fax 07305-22935
✉ 35753

The Gasthof zum Ritter is situated in the centre of Gögglingen, south of Ulm, on the right bank of the Donau on the road from Neu-Ulm to Biberrach. The Gasthof is in a historic building and is suitable for an overnight stop or a longer stay. The restaurant has outstanding ceilings and wainscots and when the weather permits, guests can eat outside on the terrace.

2 ♦ 38/52
16 ♦ 65/95

UNKEL Rheinland-Pfalz 12

Rheinhotel Schulz (HCR)
Rheinpromenade
☎ 02224-2302 fax 02224-72111
✉ 53572

7 ♦ 95/115
18 ♦ 160/180

UNTERGRUPPENBACH Baden-Württemberg 19

Landgasthof Fromm (HR)
Happenbacherstr 54
☎ 07131-702040
✉ 74199

4 ♦
9 ♦

GERMANY 187

UNTEROESTHEIM/BEI ROTHENBURG O.T.
Bayern 19

Schwarzer Adler (HR)
Würzburgerstr 8
Unteroestheim
☎ 09868-382
✉ 95583

3 ♨
12 ⚐
🄴 ⚲ 🅿 ⛽ 🛌 🛏 🚻 📺 🍽 ☺

UNTERREICHENBACH *Baden-Württemberg* 21

Untere Kapfenhardter Mühle (HCR)
☎ 07235-223 fax 07235-7180
✉ 63633

4 ♨
29 ⚐
🄰🄴 ⓘ 🄴 🟰 ⛽ 🚻 📺

ÜRZIG *Rheinland-Pfalz* 17

Zum Weissen Rössel (HCR) 🄰🄰 ANWB
Rathauspl 11
☎ 06532-4087
✉ 54539

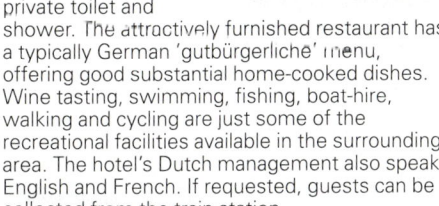

Hotel Zum Weissen Rössel lies in the centre of the small and romantic town of Ürzig on the river Mosel. The rooms are well maintained and have private toilet and shower. The attractively furnished restaurant has a typically German 'gutbürgerliche' menu, offering good substantial home-cooked dishes. Wine tasting, swimming, fishing, boat-hire, walking and cycling are just some of the recreational facilities available in the surrounding area. The hotel's Dutch management also speak English and French. If requested, guests can be collected from the train station.

open 01.02 - 31.10
* - ♨ 35/40
* 9 ⚐ 70/80
⚲ 🐎 ⚡ ⓘ 🚻 🍽 🐴

Ürziger Würzgarten (HCR) 🄰🄰 ANWB
Moselufer 44
☎ 06532-2083 fax 06532-2086
✉ 54539

The Hotel Ürziger Würzgarten is situated in the sunny valley of the Mosel at the edge of the village by the foot of a wine-producing mountain. It is a relaxed hotel with well furnished rooms; all have their own toilet and shower, and most overlook the Mosel on the other side of the street. The cellar houses famous local wines, and the hotel also has a swimming pool and sauna.

4 ♨ 50/70
29 ⚐ 50/80
⚲ 🅿 ⛽ 🛌 🏊 🚻 🛏 🗝 🚽 📺 🍽

USLAR *Niedersachsen* 13

Romantikhotel Menzhausen (HR) 🄰🄰 ANWB
Langestr 12
☎ 05571-2051 fax 05571-5820
✉ 37170

The picturesque town of Uslar is situated in the Weserbergland on the Deutsche Märchen Strasse. The Hotel Menzhausen is in the town centre and built in the distinctive regional timbered style. The bedrooms have luxurious furnishings, and the lounges and cosy restaurant are furnished in a characteristic rustic style. In the underground vaults a stock of selected wines quietly matures, and these can be enjoyed on the terrace in the courtyard.

* 15 ♨ 110/195
* 25 ⚐ 165/310
🄰🄴 ⓘ 🄴 🟰 ⓘ 🅿 ⛽ 🛌 🚻 🛏 🗝 🚽 📺 🍽 ☺

ÜTTINGEN *Bayern* 19

Fränkischer Landgasthof (HCR) AA ANWB
Marktheidenfelder Str 3
Uettingen
☎ 09369-8289 fax 09369-8094
✉ 97292

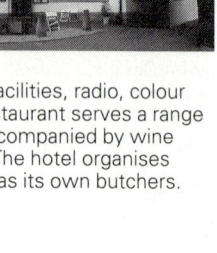

Fränkischer Landgasthof is a very well maintained hotel and very suitable for an overnight stay. The rooms are bright and tidy and feature en suite facilities, radio, colour TV and telephone. The restaurant serves a range of regional specialities, accompanied by wine from the local vineyards. The hotel organises wine-tasting events and has its own butchers.

open 26.11 - 07.11
* 3 ♪ 58/68
* 6 ∞ 94/-
🏠⊙◆ P 🅿 🕐 WC TV ✈

VALLENDAR *Rheinland-Pfalz* 12

Wolf (HCR) AA ANWB
Hellenstr 60-62
☎ 0261-60027 fax 0261-64838
✉ 56179

The Hotel Wolf can be found in Vallendar, a suburb of Koblenz, on the right bank of the Rhine. All the rooms have a balcony, and some are equipped with en suite toilet and shower. The restaurant enjoys a good reputation in the area. The Hotel Wolf can serve as a quiet base for visiting Koblenz and the famous Rhine valley. Parking is available.

open 01.08 - 01.06
* - ♪ 45/55
* 11 ∞ 90/110
Æ ⓓ E ⚏ 🏠 ⌇ ⊙ P 🅿 🕐 WC TV 🍴 ✈

VELBURG *Bayern* 20

Flair Hotel Winkler Braustüberl (HCR) AA ANWB
St Martinstr 6
☎ 09182-170 fax 09182-1710
✉ 92355

The history of this private brewery goes back to 1428, although the present building was constructed in 1903. The combination of brewery and hotel is not unusual in Germany and the Winkler beer is brewed by the owner of this hotel. The rooms of the Flairhotel Winkler Braustüberl are well equipped, and guests are made welcome.

open 26.12 - 02.01, 17.01 - 13.02 + 15.02 - 23.12
* 8 ♪ 81/98
* 47 ∞ 112/129
ⓓ E ⚏ 🏠 P 🅿 🐕 ⇅ 🛏 🚿 🕐 WC TV 🍴 ⊙

Zur Post (HCR) AA ANWB
Parsbergerstr 2
☎ 09182-1635 fax 09182-2415
✉ 92335

The blue and white façade of the Hotel zur Post is an eye-catching feature of Velburg marketplace. This is a large, typical Bayern family hotel with spacious rooms, all with en suite bathroom. There are 2 restaurants, one with rustic the other with classical furnishings. The brew-hall in the vaults and the *Bierstube* both serve traditional Bayern beer. The hotel can be reached from the Nürnberg to Regensburg motorway, Velburg exit.

* 15 ♪ 45/50
* 87 ∞ 72/76
🏠 ⊙ P 🅿 🕐 ⇅ 🛏 🚿 🕐 WC 🍴

Zur Traube (HP) AA ANWB
Untere Gasse 13
☎ 09182-1642 fax 09182-2239
✉ 93255

The Hotel zur Traube is situated in a narrow street in the centre of the town of Velburg close to the A3 Nürnberg - Regensburg motorway. It is a welcoming and well kept hotel in which all the rooms have a bathroom. There is a large garden at the back of the hotel, a luxurious sauna and the

Gaststube, which serves a good glass of beer.
* 2 ♦ 38/-
* 28 ♦ 68/-

VILSHOFEN *Bayern* 24

Bayerischer Hof (HR)
Vilsvorstadt 29
☎ 08541-5065 fax 08541-6972
✉ 94474

open 13.01 - 23.12
* 8 ♦ 65/78
* 19 ♦ 100/160

WACHENHEIM/WEINSTRASSE *Rheinland-Pfalz* 18

Goldbächel (HR)
Waldstr 99
Wachenheim
☎ 06322-94050 fax 06322-5068
✉ 67157

open 01.02 - 31.12
* 3 ♦ 63/108
* 13 ♦ 115/135

Gasthof Sonne (HR)
Weinstr 8
Wachenheim
☎ 06322-1827
✉ 67157

3 ♦
5 ♦

WALCHENSEE *Bayern* 23

Schwaigerhof (HCR)
Seestr 42
☎ 08858-232
✉ 82432

4 ♦
24 ♦

WALDECK *Hessen* 13

Seehof (HR)
Seeweg 2
☎ 05623-5488 fax 05623-6297
✉ 35413

* 3 ♦ 33/42
* 11 ♦ 54/84

WALDECK AM EDERSEE *Hessen* 13

Roggenland Ringhotel Waldeck (HCR)
Schloßstr 11
Waldeck
☎ 05623-5021 fax 05623-6008
✉ 34513

open 27.12 - 18.12
* 8 ♦ 110/130
* 43 ♦ 160/190

WALDENBURG *Baden-Württemberg* 19

Bergfried (HR)
Hauptstr 30
☎ 07942-544
✉ 74638

open 15.01 - 26.12
2 ♦ 40/65
8 ♦ 60/105

Panorama (HCR)
Hauptstr 84
☎ 07942-2001 fax 07942-8884
✉ 74638

29 ♦ 105/115
38 ♦ 140/150

WALTENHOFEN *Bayern* 22

Haus Kristall (HG)
Kreuzweg 24
☎ 08362-8594
✉ 87448

1 ♦
10 ♦

190　GERMANY

WANGEN Baden-Württemberg　22

Alpina (HG)
Am Waltersbühl 6
☎ 07522-4038
✉ 89186

6 🛏
17 🛌
P 🅿 † ⊟ 🄿 WC

WARENDORF Nordrhein-Westfalen　12

Landhaus Wieseнhof (HCR)
Lange Wieske 52
☎ 02581-78061 fax 02581-7552
✉ 48231

4 🛏 75/100
12 🛌 -/155
AE ① E ⊞ P ⚲ ⊟ 🄿 WC TV 🐕

WASSERBURG Bayern　22

Haus des Gastes (HCR)
Hauptstr 12
☎ 08382-24848
✉ 83512

3 🛏
6 🛌
⚲ P ⚲ 🄿 WC

WASSERBURG AM INN Bayern　23

Fletzinger (HR)
Fletzingergasse 1
☎ 08071-8010 fax
08071-40810
✉ 83512

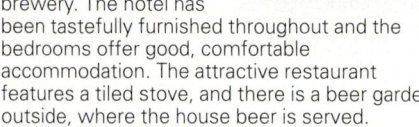

The Hotel Fletzinger is situated in the beautiful *Altstadt* of Wasserburg am Inn, and is set in what was the main building of a historic brewery. The hotel has been tastefully furnished throughout and the bedrooms offer good, comfortable accommodation. The attractive restaurant features a tiled stove, and there is a beer garden outside, where the house beer is served.

open 20.01 - 04.12
* 7 🛏 86/199
* 33 🛌 124/158
AE ① E ⚲ ① P 🅿 † ⊟ 🄿 WC TV 🍴 ☺

WEIBERSBRUNN Bayern　19

Brunnenhof (HCR)　　AA ANWB
Hauptstr 231
☎ 06094-364 fax
06094-1064
✉ 63879

The Hotel Brunnenhof lies 400m from the A3 Frankfurt to Nürnberg motorway, via the Wiebersbrunn exit. It stands amid peaceful meadows, offering guests an undisturbed night's sleep. Most of the rooms have en suite facilities and a balcony, and some have a TV. The restaurant offers a view over the surrounding hills. In fine weather, drinks are served on the sunny terrace.

* 7 🛏 60/98
* 45 🛌 98/136
E ⚲ ♥ P 🅿 ⚲ ⚲ † ⊟ 🄿 WC TV 🍴 ☺

Pension Diana (HG)　　
Hauptstr 15
☎ 06094-564 fax
06094-1064
✉ 63879

Pension Diana lies in the Spessart, and is a good base for walking in the area. The rooms - some with balcony - have en suite facilities. It has a restaurant, and covered parking space is available.

* 2 🛏 60/70
* 7 🛌 75/105
⚲ 🏠 ♥ P 🅿 ⚲ ⊟ 🄿 WC TV

Pension Gerlinde Amrhein (HG)
Hessenthalerweg 4
☎ 06094-315
✉ 8651

* - 🛏 35/40
* 6 🛌 55/60
E ● P 🅿 ⚲ ↕ 🄿 WC TV ☺

WEIDEN IN DER OBERPFALZ Bayern   20

Europa (HCR)
Frauenrichter Str 173
☎ 0961-25051 fax 0961-61562
res nr 0961-25051
✉ 92637

* 12 ♦ 65/95
* 14 ♦ 115/180
AE ① E ✳ ⊕ ◆ P 🅿 🍽 ⇅ 🛏 ⬜ WC TV 🍴

Stadtkrug (HR)
Wolframstr 5
☎ 0961-38890 fax 0961-36268
✉ 92637

open 06.01 - 24.12
* 20 ♦ 69/85
* 32 ♦ 120/160
AE ① E ✳ ⊙ P 🅿 🍽 🛏 ⬜ WC TV

WEIDENTHAL Rheinland-Pfalz   18

Berghof (HP)
Mainzertal 6
☎ 06329-324
✉ 67475

2 ♦
10 ♦
⛷ 🐾 P 🅿 🍽 ♨ ⛱ ⛰ ⬜ WC 🍴 ☺

WEIL AM RHEIN Baden-Württemberg   21

Victoria (HG)   AA ANWB
Elsasserstr 21
☎ 07621-70038
✉ 79576

The Hotel Victoria is a simple bed and breakfast hotel with functional furnishings throughout - none of the bedrooms have en suite facilities. The lounge has a TV for guests to use and there is a children's playground. Some on-site parking spaces are available.

open 08.01 - 23.12
* 4 ♦ 50/80
* 11 ♦ 90/130
⛷ ☕ P 🛏 🐾

WEINGARTEN/RAVENSBURG Baden-Württemberg   18

Mövenpick (HCR)   AA ANWB
Abt-Hyller-Str 37-39
Weingarten
☎ 0751-5040 fax 0751-504400
✉ 88250

The Mövenpick Hotel is situated in the Oberschwaben cultural and conference centre. The rooms and suites are comfortably and fully furnished. After a drink in the the bar guests can enjoy an excellent dinner in the Mövenpick restaurant. Recreational facilities in the surrounding area include a swimming pool, sauna and solarium. The hotel has bicycles for hire and has facilities for guests in wheelchairs. Meeting rooms are available. Travellers can reach Weingarten via the B30 Ulm/Friedrichshafen, or from the B32 Tübingen/Wangen.

* 22 ♦ 160/180 excl. breakfast
* 50 ♦ 190/210 excl. breakfast
AE ① E ✳ P 🍽 ⇅ ⬜ WC TV 🍴

WEINHEIM Baden-Württemberg   18

Fuchs'sche Mühle (HR)
Birkenauertalstr 10
☎ 06201-61031 fax 06201-12914
✉ 55232

* - ♦ 110/130
* 20 ♦ 150/170
AE ① E ✳ ◆ P 🅿 🍽 ⛱ ⇅ 🛏 ⬜ WC TV ☺

WENDELSTEIN Bayern   20

Gerner (HP)
Sudring 13
☎ 09129-6008
✉ 90530

open 13.01 - 14.08 + 31.08 - 24.12
* 7 ♦ 55/60
* 9 ♦ 100/110
⛷ P 🍽 ♨ ⬜ WC ☺

Gasthof Hotel Zum Wenden (HR)
Hauptstr 30-32
☎ 09129-90130 fax 09129-901316
✉ 90530

* 1 ♦ 98/128
* 5 ♦ 138/168
⊙ ⬜ WC 🍴

WENDEN/BRÜN Nordrhein-Westfalen 12

Sporthotel Wacker (HCR) AA ANWB
Mindenerstr 1
Brün
☎ 02762-8088 fax 02762-6200
✉ 57482

Brün is in gently undulating landscape characteristic of the wooded southern part of the Sauerland. The Sporthotel Wacker has a swimming pool, a sauna and solarium, and offers massage facilities and therapeutic exercises. There is a golf course nearby. The layout of the hotel is suitable for people in wheelchairs.

* 6 ♋ 85/145
* 40 ♌ 140/190

WENHOLTHAUSEN Nordrhein-Westfalen 12

Zur Post (HR) AA ANWB
Südstr 4
☎ 02973-570
✉ 59889

The Gasthof zur Post is situated next to the *Kurpark* of Wenholthausen in an area with hills, woods, lakes and fast-flowing streams. This well kept *Gasthof* has bedrooms with toilet and shower, some have TV. The rustic restaurant serves dishes, the meat comes from their own butcher. In summer this is an excellent base for walking or cycling holidays, and in winter for cross-country skiing.

* 4 ♋ 38/46
* 9 ♌ 72/96

WERNECK Bayern 19

Gasthof Krone Post (HR)
Balthasar Neumanstr 1-3
☎ 09722-5090 fax 09722-509199
✉ 97440

* 8 ♋ 80/120
* 50 ♌ 100/168

WERTHEIM Baden-Württemberg 19

Ross (HR)
Aalbachstr 45
☎ 09342-236
✉ 97877

2 ♋ -/40
3 ♌ -/70

Zum Schwan (HCR) AA ANWB
Mainpl 8
☎ 09342-1278 fax 09342-21182
✉ 97877

The Hotel zum Schwan enjoys a peaceful location in the town centre. It has been recently renovated and almost all of the rooms have en suite facilities, a large proportion also have TV. Special diet meals are available in the restaurant on request. The surrounding area offers plenty of opportunities for horse riding. The hotel has a pleasant terrace and private parking facilities are available.

* 5 ♋ 85/120
* 26 ♌ 120/160

WESTERNBÖDEFELD Nordrhein-Westfalen 12

Zur Schmitte (HCR) AA ANWB
Am Roh 2
☎ 02977-268
✉ 57392

The country hotel Gasthof zur Schmitte is quietly situated in the hills and woods in the highest part of the Sauerland area. Much loved by winter-sports fans, this is a traditional *Gasthof* with modern rooms - all have washing facilities, some have TV and a balcony. There is a restaurant with an open fire, as well as tennis courts, swimming pool and sauna.

open 15.12 - 15.11
* 2 ♋ 40/55
* 11 ♌ 75/95

GERMANY 193

WEYARN Bayern · 23

Weiglmühle (HCR)
Mühltal
☎ 0802-208

3 🛏
24 🛌
🛠 P 🅿 ⛽ 🅿 WC 🍽

WIEDEN Baden-Württemberg · 21

Heidi Wiesler (HP) *AA ANWB*
Steinbuhl 11
☎ 07673-7013 fax
07673-7014
✉ 83629

Hotel Heidi Wiesler has good facilities and occupies a beautiful position, close to a downhill and cross-country skiing area, and with plenty of opportunity for walking nearby. The rooms are comfortably furnished, with a rustic look; some have a balcony. There is a sauna, solarium, whirlpool and fitness room, and guests are free to use the parking facilities in front of the hotel.

open 15.12 - 10.11
2 🛏 -/45
9 🛌 76/90
P 🅿 🛁 🛏 P WC ☼

WIEDERSTEIN Nordrhein-Westfalen · 12

Blecher (HR) *AA ANWB*
Frankfurterstr 174
☎ 02735 2260
✉ 57290

The Hotel Blecher is a simple hotel, on a rather busy road. The bedrooms are on 2 floors, and some of them have washing facilities. The hotel has a garden and restaurant. Parking facilities are available.

* - 🛏 -/42
* 14 🛌 -/84
◆ P 🅿 P WC ☼

WIEHL Nordrhein-Westfalen · 12

Zur Post (HR) *AA ANWB*
Hauptstr 6-10
☎ 02262-9091 fax
02262-92595
✉ 51674

The Hotel zur Post is situated in the centre of Wiehl in the nature park of 'Bergische Land'. All rooms in this holiday hotel and conference centre have their own bathroom, TV and minibar, some have a balcony. The hotel offers a restaurant, a bar, a skittle alley, a swimming pool, a sauna with solarium and tennis courts.

* 3 🛏 90/145
* 50 🛌 136/190
AE ◉ E ⌿ ⊙ ◆ P 🅿 ≋ ⇅ ⌂ ⛁ P WC TV 🍽 🐕

WIESBADEN Hessen · 18

Holiday Inn Crowne Plaza (HR)
Bahnhofstr 10-12
☎ 0611-1620 fax 0611-304599
res nr 0130-815131
✉ 65185

111 🛏 275/330 excl. breakfast
122 🛌 315/370 excl. breakfast
AE ◉ E ⌿ ⊙ 🅿 ≋ ⇅ ⌂ ⛁ P WC TV 🍽 🛗 ☼

Am Kochbrunnen (HR)
Taunusstr 15
☎ 0611-522001 fax 0611-373044
✉ 65183

6 🛏 90/130
18 🛌 130/170
AE ⌿ ⊙ P 🅿 ≋ ⇅ ⛁ P WC TV ☼

Ramada Hotel Wiesbaden (HR)
Abraham Lincoln Str 17
☎ 0611-7970 fax 0611-761372
res nr 06-0227337
✉ 65189

* - 🛏 195/290 excl. breakfast
* 207 🛌 240/345 excl. breakfast
AE ◉ E ⌿ ◉ P 🅿 ≋ ⇅ ⌂ ⛁ P WC TV 🍽

GERMANY

WIESENT Bayern 23

Gästehaus Rösch (HG)
Regensburgerstr 10
☎ 09482-3706
✉ 93109

open 07.01 - 23.12
* 4 ⌂ 36/38
* 6 ⌂ 56/60

WILDEMANN Niedersachsen 13

Bremer Schlüssel (HR)
Im Spiegeltal 49
☎ 05323-6262
✉ 38709

10 ⌂
17 ⌂

Rathaus (HCR) AA ANWB
Bohlweg 37
☎ 05323-6261 fax 05323-6713
✉ 38709

The Hotel Rathaus is beautifully situated at the foot of a hill in the holiday and winter-sports centre of Wildemann, in the Harz region. The hotel is built of traditional stone and wood, and in front there is a terrace and a 1000- year-old lime tree. Most rooms have a shower and toilet, some also have a TV. The restaurant offers a choice of regional and international dishes.

open 20.12 - 15.11
* 3 ⌂ 40/45
* 8 ⌂ 74/96

Waldgarten (HCR)
Schützenstr 31
☎ 05323-6229
✉ 38709

8 ⌂ 43/60
25 ⌂ 85/120

WILHELMSHAUSEN Hessen 13

Zum Reinhardswald (HR)
Muenderstr 15
☎ 05541-8467
✉ 34233

2 ⌂
4 ⌂

WILHELMSHAVEN Niedersachsen 6

Zur Krone (HCR)
Ebertstr 104
☎ 04421-43048 fax 04421-42402
✉ 26382

* 3 ⌂ 78/115
* 45 ⌂ 110/185

WILLINGEN Hessen 12

Zum Hohen Eimberg (HCR) AA ANWB
Zum Hohen Eimberg 3 A
☎ 05632-4090 fax 05632-409333
✉ 34503

The splendidly situated, family-run Hotel zum Hohen Eimberg is a suitable venue for both summer and winter holidays, offering a good standard of comfortable accommodation. The rooms feature en suite toilet and shower/bath. As well as a swimming pool, sauna, solarium and billiards; the hotel is well known for its gourmet cuisine, dance evenings, après ski, guided walks and many other activities. The local ski lifts, ski schools and cross-country skiing are only 500m away.

* 2 ⌂ 99/230
* 68 ⌂ 178/385

GERMANY 195

Der Sauerland Stern (HCR) AA ANWB
Kneippweg 1
☎ 05632-4040 fax 05632-6119
✉ 34508

This large, modern holiday and sports complex in the centre of Willingen is especially suited to young, active people. All rooms have modern furnishings (with private bathroom facilities, telephone and colour TV), and there are extensive facilities for sports and relaxation. The Hotel der Sauerland Stern has a swimming pool, sauna, fitness room and table tennis. There is also a tennis and squash park, beach lake and covered ice rink.

* - ♪ 126/155
* 510 ♫ 146/230
🅰🅴 ⓞ 🅴 ⚒ ♣ ⊙ 🅿 ♒ 🚗 ↕ ⊡ ▣ 🅿 🆆🅲 📺 🍽 ☺

Waldhotel Willingen (HCR) AA ANWB
Köhlerhagen 3
☎ 05632-6016 fax 05632-69039
✉ 34508

The Waldhotel Willingen is quietly situated just outside Willingen, in the woods next to the ski slopes. The tastefully furnished rooms all have a toilet and shower, and some have a balcony and TV. The hotel also offers a restaurant and bar, swimming pool, sauna with whirlpool and tennis courts.

* 14 ♪ 82/135
* 28 ♫ 156/320
ⓞ 🅴 ⚒ ♣ ⊙ 🅿 ♒ 🚗 ↕ ⊡ ▣ 🅿 🆆🅲 📺 🍽 ☺

WILNSDORF Nordrhein-Westfalen 12

Danne (HR)
Frankfurterstr 9
☎ 02739-2214
✉ 57234

4 ♪
6 ♫
🅰🅴 🅴 ♣ ♠ ⊙ 🅿 🅿 🆆🅲 📺 🍽 ☺

Kölsch (HR) AA ANWB
Frankfurter Str 7
☎ 02739-2253
✉ 57234

The Hotel Kölsch is situated in the centre of Wilnsdorf, a small town in the Siegerland area, just off the Sauerland motorway. It is an ideal stopover for tourists who are travelling through. This is a quiet hotel set in a historic building with well furnished rooms, some of which have a shower. The woods in the surrounding area are good for a leisurely stroll.

open 11.01 - 23.12
* 4 ♪ 35/45
* 4 ♫ 78/88
🅰🅴 🅴 ♣ ♠ ⊙ 🅿 🚗 🅿 🍽 ☺

WINDECK/HALSCHEID Nordrhein-Westfalen 12

Pension Tannenhof (HP)
Oppersauerstr 48
Windeck
☎ 02292-5179
✉ 5227

2 ♪
10 ♫
🅿 🚗 🍽 ☺

WINTERBERG Nordrhein-Westfalen 12

Appart Hotel Zur Boppard (HCR) AA ANWB
Kapperundweg 4
☎ 02981-8060 fax 02981-806149
✉ 59955

A beautiful position is one of the major attractions at the Hotel zur Boppard. This family-run hotel, where children are made very welcome, has both bedrooms and apartments. Besides an attractive restaurant, bar and public lounge, it offers adults and children a large play room with table football, darts and billiards.

- ♪ 83/100
13 ♫ 130/150
🅰🅴 ⓞ 🅴 ⚒ ♣ ⊙ 🅿 ♒ 🚗 ↕ ⊡ ▣ 🆆🅲 📺 🍽

GERMANY

Der Brabander (HCR)
Am Waltenberg 65
☎ 02981-7024 fax 02981-3269
✉ 59955

The Hotel der Brabander is a family hotel situated just outside the centre of Winterberg. The surroundings are wooded, the ski slopes start in front of the hotel, and the garden has a terrace and minigolf. All the rooms have a toilet and shower and the hotel has a sauna.

2 ♬ 40/60
40 ⚏ 80/150
☼◆ P ⚐ 🛏 🚻 WC ⓘ ⊙

Haus Herrloh (HCR)
Herrlohweg 3
☎ 02981-470
✉ 59955

The Hotel Haus Herrloh is a good winter-sports hotel, situated at the edge of Winterberg close to the ski slopes and overlooking the ski-jump slope. A garden, terrace and minigolf make it a good place to stay in the summer too; it is a good base for a walking holiday. The rooms are well furnished and have washing facilities and TV. The hotel has a restaurant specialising in game dishes.

open 03.05 - 30.10 + 01.12 - 19.03
5 ♬
14 ⚏
E ⚑ ⚐ P ⚐ 🛏 🚻 WC TV ⓘ ⊙

Hessenhof (HCR)
Am Waltenberg 1
☎ 02981-2217 fax 02981-6995
✉ 59941

The stylish and well furnished Hotel Hessenhof is in the centre of Winterberg. The wooded surroundings and comfortable accommodation are attractive features; bedrooms are spacious, and some have balconies. The hotel has a large garden with a terrace; there is also a sauna, swimming pool and cosy and informal public rooms.

open 17.12 - 10.04 + 19.04 - 20.11
* 6 ♬ 68/76
* 41 ⚏ 120/150
⊙ E ≡ ⚑ ⊙ P ⚐ 🛏 🚻 WC ⓘ ⊙

Meurs (HCR)
Am Waltenberg 67
☎ 02981-7356 fax 02981-7356
✉ 59955

The Hotel Meurs is an attractive, family-run establishment which is situated amid splendid walking and skiing country just 300m from Winterberg. All the rooms in this cosy and informal hotel have en suite toilet and bath/shower facilities, and some also have balconies. The hotel is under Dutch management and features an attractive pancake restaurant.

1 ♬ 32/63
15 ⚏ 65/126
⚑ ⚐ P ⚐ 🛏 🚻 WC ⓘ ⊀

Schulte Werneke (HCR)
Alterhagen 1
☎ 02981-8266 fax 02981-1221
✉ 59955

The Hotel Schulte Werneke is situated in a wooded area at the foot of a hill in Siedlinghausen, a village between Winterberg and Meschede. The rooms are well maintained; all have a bathroom, and some also have a TV, minibar and balcony. The restaurant has a good atmosphere and there is also a bar, a terrace with a lovely view and a garden with a large pond. The hotel is well placed for walking trips, and for skiing in winter.

* 8 ♬ 58/70
* 16 ⚏ 62/85
⚑ P ⚐ 🛏 🚻 WC TV ⓘ ⬆ ⊙

GERMANY

A holiday with a touch of romance
Hotel-Café-Restaurant

Landhotel Grimmeblick

Our family-run hotel which welcomes children is beautifully situated at the edge of Winterberg. Here you can enjoy your holiday in one of our comfortable rooms. Our hotel has: room with fireplace, bar, Weinstube, sauna, solarium, fitness room, skittle alley and diving pool for sports divers, with filling station. Trips by covered wagon, torchlight walks around Burgberg with a knight's tournament. The outdoor swimming-pool is lovely in summer; the large playing field and our rooftop terrace have full restaurant facilities.

Children up to age 11 can stay free of charge.
Bed & breakfast DM 64,--, half board DM 89,--.

Our midweek offer: 3 nights including 3-course meal DM 199,-- per person (valid only outside school holidays), or 5 nights with half board DM 350,--.

Leenaert and Pool families. To apply for leaflets: 02981 - 7070 or 7079, Fax: 02981 - 3552.
Am Langen Acker 5, D-59955 Winterberg-Elkeringhausen.

WINTERBERG/ELKERINGHAUSEN *Nordrhein-Westfalen*   **12**

Landhotel Grimmeblick (HCR)   AA ANWB
Am langen Acker 5
Elkeringhausen
☏ 02981-7070 fax 02981-3552
✉ 59955

The Landhotel Grimmeblick is beautifully situated in the holiday resort of Elkeringhausen near Winterberg. The bedrooms, some with balconies, are large and well equipped. The hotel features a cosy and informal restaurant, and it has its own diving facilities.

* 2 ☏ 73/73
* 12 ✱ 138/138
AE ⓓ E ≡ ♃ ⓑ P ♉ ⬛ P WC TV ⊙ ☺

WINTERBERG/HILDFELD *Nordrhein-Westfalen*   **12**

Heidehotel Hildfeld (HCR)   
Am Ufer 13
Hildfeld
☏ 02985-8030 fax 02985-345
✉ 59955

The Heidehotel Hildfeld is a genuine country hotel and is situated on the edge of a forest. The rooms are well maintained and have many facilities. There is a relaxed atmosphere in the restaurant and leisure facilities include a sauna, solarium, swimming pool and fitness room. In addition, sailing facilities are available on the Hillesee.

4 ☏ 72/97
32 ✱ 140/224

WINTERBERG/NEUASTENBERG Nordrhein-Westfalen 12

Dorint Hotel und Ferienpark (HCR) *AA ANWB*
Postwiese
Neuastenberg
☎ 02981-8970 fax 02981-897700
res nr 0130-6605
✉ 59955

The well appointed Dorint holiday park comprises holiday bungalows and hotel rooms. The apartments and rooms are attractively furnished and comfortable. The restaurant has a relaxed atmosphere with a wide choice of appetising specialities. Paragliding, golf, tennis and horse-riding are among many recreational facilities available.

34 ♨ 145/165
53 ♨ 235/280
🅰🅴 ◐ 🄴 ⇌ ♠ ◉ ◆ 🅿 ☂ ♋ ⬚ ✦ ➡ ▣ WC TV ◉○ ⊙

WINTERBERG/SCHMALLENBERG Nordrhein-Westfalen 12

Störmann (HCR) *AA ANWB*
Weststr 58
Schmallenberg
☎ 02972-4055 fax 02972-2945
✉ 57392

The Hotel Stormann is situated on the sunny side of the Rothaar mountain range, which guarantees tradition, peace and comfort. All the rooms have a shower, toilet and telephone. There is a swimming pool, sauna, solarium, massage room, gym and stables for guests with horses. The hotel is also a good base for winter sports.

open 27.12 - 06.03 + 25.03 - 20.12
* 18 ♨ 75/120
* 21 ♨ 150/240
🅰🅴 ◐ 🄴 ⇌ ♠ ◉ ◆ 🅿 ☂ ♋ ⬚ ✦ ⥯ ➡ ▣ WC TV ◉○ ⊙

WINTERBERG/NIEDERSFELD Nordrhein-Westfalen 12

Cramer (HP) *AA ANWB*
Rührstr 50
Winterberg
☎ 02981-471 fax 02981-1528
✉ 59955

The Cramer is a good holiday hotel in Niederberg, almost 10km from Winterberg on the Brilon road. All the rooms have a toilet and shower. The restaurant offers specialities of game, trout and Westphalian ham. There is a *Bierstube*, a garden, an indoor pool, sauna and solarium.

* 10 ♨ 85/95
* 16 ♨ 150/190
🅰🅴 ◐ 🄴 ⇌ ◉ 🅿 ☂ ♋ ⬚ ➡ WC TV ⬆ ⊙

WINTERBERG/ZÜSCHEN Nordrhein-Westfalen 12

Hollands Hotel Züschenwald (HCR) *AA ANWB*
Nuhnetalstr 8
Züschen
☎ 02981-3477 fax 02981-3687
✉ 59955

In the surroundings of Winterberg stands the beautiful Hollands Hotel Züschenwald. The rooms are well maintained, and some feature private toilet and shower facilities. The restaurant boasts an extensive and varied menu, while the hotel also features a sauna, solarium, garden terrace and sunbathing lawn.

3 ♨ 44/49
29 ♨ 88/108
🅰🅴 ◐ 🄴 ⇌ ♠ ◉ ◆ 🅿 ☂ ➡ ▣ WC ◉○ ⊙

WUPPERTAL Nordrhein-Westfalen 11

Juliana Golfhotel (Best Western) (HCR)
Mollenkotten 195
☎ 0202-64750 fax 0202-6475777
res nr 0130-4455
✉ 42103

57 ♦ 195/285
81 ♦ 255/345
AE ⓘ E ≡ ⓢ P ♦ ♦ ↕ ■ ⓟ WC TV ⓞ

Kaiserhof (HCR)   AA ANWB
Döppersberg 50
☎ 0202-43060 fax 0202-456959
✉ 42103

* 72 ♦ 175/270 excl. breakfast
* 84 ♦ 290/350 excl. breakfast
AE ⓘ E ≡ ⓢ ♦ ♦ P ↕ ■ ⓟ WC TV ⓞ

WÜRZBURG Bayern 19

Amberger (HCR)
Ludwigstr 17-19
☎ 0931-50179 fax 0931-54136
✉ 97070

30 ♦ 145/155
40 ♦ 200/320
AE ⓘ E ≡ ⓢ ♦ P ↕ ■ ⓟ WC TV

Maritim (HCR)
Pleichertorstr 5
☎ 0931-30530 fax 0931-18682
res nr 0221-219672
✉ 97070

53 ♦ 217/337
240 ♦ 274/384
AE ⓘ E ≡ ⓢ ♦ ♦ P ♦ ♦ ↕ ⓛ ■ ⓟ WC TV

Rebstock (Best Western) (HCR)
Neubaustasse 7
☎ 0931-30930 fax 0931-3093100
res nr 0130-4455
✉ 97070

* 38 ♦ 176/248
* 43 ♦ 280/350
AE ⓘ E ≡ ⓢ P ↕ ■ ⓟ WC TV ⓞ ♦

Russ (HR)
Wolfhartsgasse 1
☎ 0931-50016 fax 0931-50969
✉ 97070

The Gasthof Russ is situated in the heart of Würzburg's historic town centre, near both the old town hall and the Residenz. A number of the well kept rooms have en suite facilities and TV. The gourmet restaurant serves meals, complemented with a glass of Franken wine from its own cellar. The hotel has a private parking garage.

12 ♦ 59/120
18 ♦ 100/160
♦ ⓞ P ♦ ■ ⓟ TV ⓞ

Schloß Steinburg (HCR)
Auf Dem Steinberg
☎ 0931-93061 fax 0931-97121
✉ 97070

10 ♦ 110/140
40 ♦ 170/200
AE ⓘ E ≡ ⓢ ♦ ⓢ P ♦ ♦ ↕ ⓛ ■ ⓟ WC TV

Walfisch (HR)   AA ANWB
Am Pleidenturm 5
☎ 0931-50055 fax 0931-51690
✉ 97070

The celebrated Hotel Walfisch is situated on the bank of the river Main and offers views over the ancient fortress of Mariënburg. The rooms are equipped with modern amenities. The cosy restaurant has an extensive choice of tasty dishes on the menu, including fish and vegetarian meals. The hotel has car parking, and conference facilities are available.

* 20 ♦ 160/180
* 20 ♦ 200/280
AE ⓘ E ≡ ♦ ⓞ ♦ ♦ P ↕ ⓛ ■ ⓟ WC TV ⓞ

WÜRZBURG/VERSBACH Bayern 19

Mühlenhof Daxbaude (HCR)
Frankenstr 205
Würzburg
☎ 0931-21001 fax 0931-29275
✉ 97078

* 4 ♫ 90/120
* 30 ♫ 160/185

ZELL Rheinland-Pfalz 17

Zur Post (HR)   AA ANWB
Schloßstr 21-25
☎ 06542-4217
✉ 56856

The Hotel zur Post is a pleasant and comfortable holiday hotel in the centre of the wine-producing town of Zell. The rooms are large and have washing facilities and a TV; most also have a balcony overlooking the Mosel and the surrounding mountains. The restaurant and the Mosel Terrace both offer panoramic views, and there is also a bar.

open 31.12 - 09.02 + 11.03 - 22.12
* 2 ♫ 60/65
* 14 ♫ 110/116

ZELL AM HARMERSBACH Baden-Württemberg 21

Sonne (HP)
Hauptstr 5
☎ 07835-1344 fax 07835-1278
✉ 77736

open 15.02 - 15.07 + 05.08 - 20.01
* 5 ♫ 65/70
* 14 ♫ 110/130

ZORGE Niedersachsen 14

Landhotel Kunzental (HCR)
Im Förstergarten 7
☎ 05586-1261 fax 05586-660
✉ 37449

open 21.12 - 19.11
* 2 ♫ 70/80
* 26 ♫ 110/120

ZUSMARSHAUSEN Bayern 22

Krone (HR)   AA ANWB
Augsburgerstr 9
☎ 08291-212 fax 08291-8232
✉ 86441

The Hotel Krone is a traditional *Gasthof* situated in the centre of Zumarshausen. It lies halfway between Ulm and Augsburg on the A8 motorway, making it an excellent overnight stop. Well furnished rooms have en suite toilet and shower, and the restaurant serves both German and international dishes.

* 6 ♫ 45/55
* 49 ♫ 80/100

ZWEIBRÜCKEN Rheinland-Pfalz 17

Europas Rosengarten (HCR)
Rosengartenstr 60
☎ 06332-49041
✉ 66482

47 ♫

Hitschler (HR)
Fruchtmarkt 8
☎ 06332-2574
✉ 66482

5 ♫
9 ♫

ZWIESEL Bayern 24

Bergfeld (HP)
Hochstr 45
☎ 09922-9553
✉ 94227

5 ♫ -/55
21 ♫ -/110

Deutscher Rhein (HCR)
Stadtpl 42
☎ 09922-1651 fax 09922-4477
✉ 94227

17 ♫

GERMANY 201

GERMANY

Kneipp Kurhotel Linde (HR)
Lindenweg 9
☎ 09922-1661 fax 09922-1650
✉ 94227

* 4 ♫ 70/88
* 35 ⚭ 130/166
🏔️🅿️🛎️🏊‍♂️🚡↕️🛗🍽️🛗🚾📺🍽️

Kurhotel Sonnenberg (HCR)
Augustinerstr 9
☎ 09922-2031
✉ 94227

5 ♫ -/50
16 ⚭ -/123
🐕🅿️🛎️🏊‍♂️🚡🛗🍽️🛗🚾📺☺

Zur Waldbahn (HR)
Bahnhofspl 2
☎ 09922-3001 fax 09922-3001
✉ 94221

open 29.11 - 27.10
* - ♫ 60/80
* 28 ⚭ 100/140
🐕👁️🅿️📞🛎️🍽️🛗🚾🐩

AUSTRIA

CAPITAL	Vienna
LANGUAGE	German
CURRENCY	Austrian schilling, divided into 100 groschen UK £1 = AS16.80 US $1 = AS11.35
EMERGENCY NUMBERS	Fire, telephone 122; police, telephone 133; ambulance, telephone 144
TOURIST INFORMATION	*In Britain:* Austrian National Tourist Organisation, 30 St George Street, London W1R 0AL, telephone 071-629 0461 *In USA:* Austrian National Tourist Office, 500 Fifth Avenue, New York, NY 10110, telephone 212 944 6880

MOTORING AND GENERAL INFORMATION ➢

For more information refer to the *Travellers' directory* on page IX.

Accidents If you are involved in an accident, you must stop and exchange particulars with the other party. If anyone is injured, you must seek medical assistance, and immediately report the incident to the police. Anyone who arrives at the scene of an accident is obliged to help unless it is obvious that everything necessary has already been done. See also *Warning triangle* below.

Breakdown If your car breaks down, try to move it so that it obstructs traffic as little as possible. The Austrian motoring club, Österreichischer Automobil-, Motorrad- und Touring Club (ÖAMTC) maintains a 24-hour roadside assistance *(Pannenhilfe)* and towing service *(Abschleppdienst)*; dial 120 from anywhere in Austria. A patrol service *(Strassenwacht)* operates around Vienna and on the south and west motorways when traffic is heavy. See also *Motorways* and *Warning triangle* below.

Children in cars Children under 12 are not permitted to travel as front-seat passengers unless using a suitable restraint system.

Driving licence A valid UK licence is also legally valid in Austria, though language difficulties may cause isolated misunderstandings. A free translation of your licence can be obtained from the head office of the Austrian motoring club (ÖAMTC) in Vienna. An International Driving Permit is recommended for holders of Republic of Ireland driving licences, and compulsory for holders of licences issued in Australia, Canada, New Zealand and the USA. The minimum age at which a visitor can use a temporarily imported motorcycle (exceeding 50cc) or car is 18 years.

First-aid kit In Austria, all vehicles (including motorcycles) must by law be equipped with a first-aid kit, and visitors are expected to comply. Motorists can be stopped at the scene of an accident and their first-aid kit demanded.

Fuel Credit cards are sometimes accepted at larger petrol stations. Up to 10 litres of petrol or diesel fuel in a can may be imported free of customs duty and tax. Leaded petrol is not available, but the 98 octane super unleaded has an additive which makes it suitable for use in cars normally requiring leaded petrol. Unleaded petrol *(bleifrei)* is available as *normal benzin* (91 octane), *Eurosuper* (95 octane) and *super unleaded* (98 octane) grades. Pumps dispensing unleaded petrol are marked with a green point or label indicating *Euro 95* or *Eurosuper* or *bleifrei*. In all but a few non-brand garages, octane ratings are clearly marked on the pumps. Only one grade of diesel *(diesel)* is sold for automotive use.

204 AUSTRIA

Hitch-hiking — Hitch-hiking is generally prohibited on motorways and highways. In Oberöstereich, Steiermark, Burgenland and Vorarlberg, hitch-hiking is prohibited if under 16.

Horn — Your horn must not be used where signs prohibit it. Generally it is prohibited at night in large towns and resort areas, and is forbidden at all times in Vienna.

Hotel classification — Hotels in Austria are awarded star ratings by the hoteliers' association, Fachgruppe der Beherbergungsbetriebe in der Bundeskammer der gewerblichen Wirtschaft. These range from a very luxurious hotel at five stars to a modest hotel, *pension* or *Gasthof* at one star.

Austria has a wide choice of hotels, especially in the modest and medium class categories. There are luxury international hotels in major cities and tourist centres. Both Austria and Germany have a special type of hotel called a *Kurhotel*, which is a health resort or spa. *Apartmenthotels* have a small kitchen, but guests can opt to use the hotel catering services. *Schlosshotels* are castles or country houses which have been converted to hotels, usually in the luxury categories. *Romantikhotels* are comfortable hotels, featuring a pleasant atmosphere and excellent restaurants. *Gasthöfe* are equivalent to small hotels; in the mountains they are sometimes called *Alpengasthof* or *Berggasthof*. Some *pensions* are classed as *Frühstückpensions*, and offer bed and breakfast only. *Fremdenheime* are addresses where you can rent a room, with or without breakfast.

Insurance — All temporarily imported trailers must be covered by a separate policy from that covering the towing vehicle.

Lights — Although it is prohibited to drive with undipped headlights in built-up areas, motorists may warn of approach by flashing their lights. It is prohibited to drive on unlit urban motorways and outside built-up areas with sidelights only. In poor visibility, fog lamps may be used with both sidelights and dipped headlights. Parking lights are not required if the vehicle can be seen from 50 metres (55yds).ABlueprint Lights on lamp posts ringed with red go off during the night; parking lights are required.

Motoring club — The Österreichischer Automobil-, Motorrad- und Touring Club (ÖAMTC) has its headquarters at 1010 Wien, Schubertring 1-3, telephone 0222 71199-0. It is represented in most towns either direct or through provincial motoring clubs, with other offices at frontiers. The offices are usually open 09.00 to 18.00 weekdays, 09.00 to 12.00 on Saturdays, closed Sundays and public holidays.

Motorways — A network of some 1000 miles of motorway *(Autobahn)* is now nearly complete. There are tolls on four motorways: the Brenner, the Karawanken Tunnel, the Tauern and the Pyhrn (Gleinalm and Bosruck Tunnels).

Triangles marked on motorway posts indicate the nearest emergency telephone, every 2km (1.25 miles). Lifting the speaking flap on the telephones automatically connects you to motorway control. Give your location (printed inside the speaking flap) before any message; if you subsequently find that you do not need help, you must contact motorway control again to let them know.

A flashing orange/yellow light at the top of telephone posts indicates danger ahead.

Parking — Where parking is allowed, cars must be parked in the direction of the traffic flow. Parking is forbidden on a main road or one carrying fast-moving traffic, and also where there are signs *Beschränkung für Halten oder Parken* (restriction for stopping or parking).

There is a total ban on stopping on roads which have priority (mostly federal roads) in the case of fog or poor visibility.

Between 15 December and 31 March, parking is prohibited at night on any roads with tram lines.

Blue zones are signed *Zone* or *Kurzparkzone*, and sometimes have blue road markings. The only signs are those marking the beginning of the zone; there are no further reminders. In the larger towns parking is allowed for up to three hours unless otherwise indicated. The whole city of Vienna (Wien, 1st district) is a *Kurzparkzone*, where parking is allowed for an hour and a half. You must buy a ticket in advance from the ÖAMTC, banks or tobacconists, and indicate the date and time of arrival on the ticket. In other towns you can park for up to 90 minutes in a blue zone if you display a parking disc, available free from any tobacconist.

Priority in traffic   Vehicles continuing straight ahead or making a right-hand turn at an intersection have priority over oncoming vehicles turning left, providing that there are no signs to the contrary; in this case even trams give way. To turn across the flow of traffic at a junction controlled by a policeman, pass in front of him unless otherwise indicated.

Public holidays 1994

January 1 New Year's Day	May 23 Whit Monday	December 8 Immaculate Conception
January 6 Epiphany	June 2 Corpus Christi	
April 4 Easter Monday	August 15 Assumption	December 25 Christmas Day
May 1 Labour Day	October 26 National Day	December 26 St Stephen's Day
May 12 Ascension Day	November 1 All Saints' Day	

Roads   Austria has a network of well engineered roads. The main traffic artery runs from Bregenz in the west to Vienna in the east, via the Arlberg tunnel, Innsbruck, Salzburg and Linz. Most of the major alpine roads are excellent. Service stations are fairly frequent, even on mountain roads.

In July and August, several roads across the frontier become congested, mainly on the Lindau – Bregenz road, at the Brenner Pass (a possible alternative is the Résia/Reschen Pass), at Kufstein, on the Munich – Salzburg *Autobahn* and on the Villach – Tarvisio road. Also, Klingenbach and Nickelsdorf on the Austria-Hungary border are very busy.

Speed limits   The beginning of a built-up area is indicated by the sign *Ortsanfang*, and at the end by the sign *Ortsende* and the name of the place. Here, the maximum speed is 50kph (31mph). Outside built-up areas, the speed limit for cars is 100kph (62mph), which increases to 130kph (80mph) on motorways, unless signs indicate otherwise. If you are towing a trailer there are lower limits – enquire at tourist office or motoring organisations.

Telephone   To make an international call from Austria, lift the receiver and then insert coins. Dial 00 followed by the country code (see under *General and touring information* in the *Travellers' directory*), the area code without the first 0, and then the number.

To call Austria from another country, the international code for Austria is 43; omit the first 0 from the area code.

Traffic lights   The green light flashes four times before the green phase ends; an orange light with the red light means that the green phase is about to begin.

Warning triangle   Compulsory in the event of an accident or breakdown, the warning triangle must be placed on the road an adequate distance behind the vehicle or obstacle, and must be clearly visible from 200 metres (220 yards).

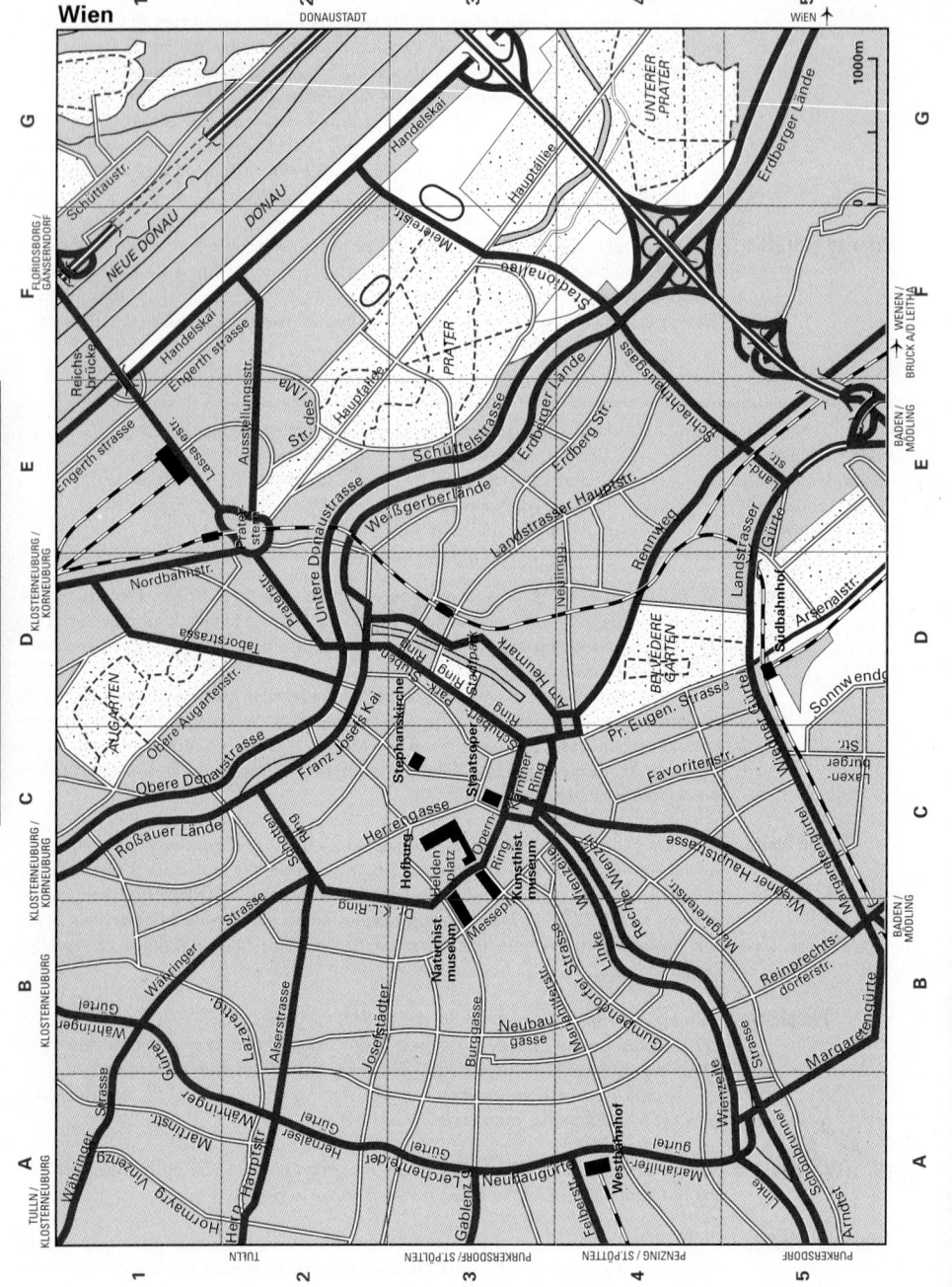

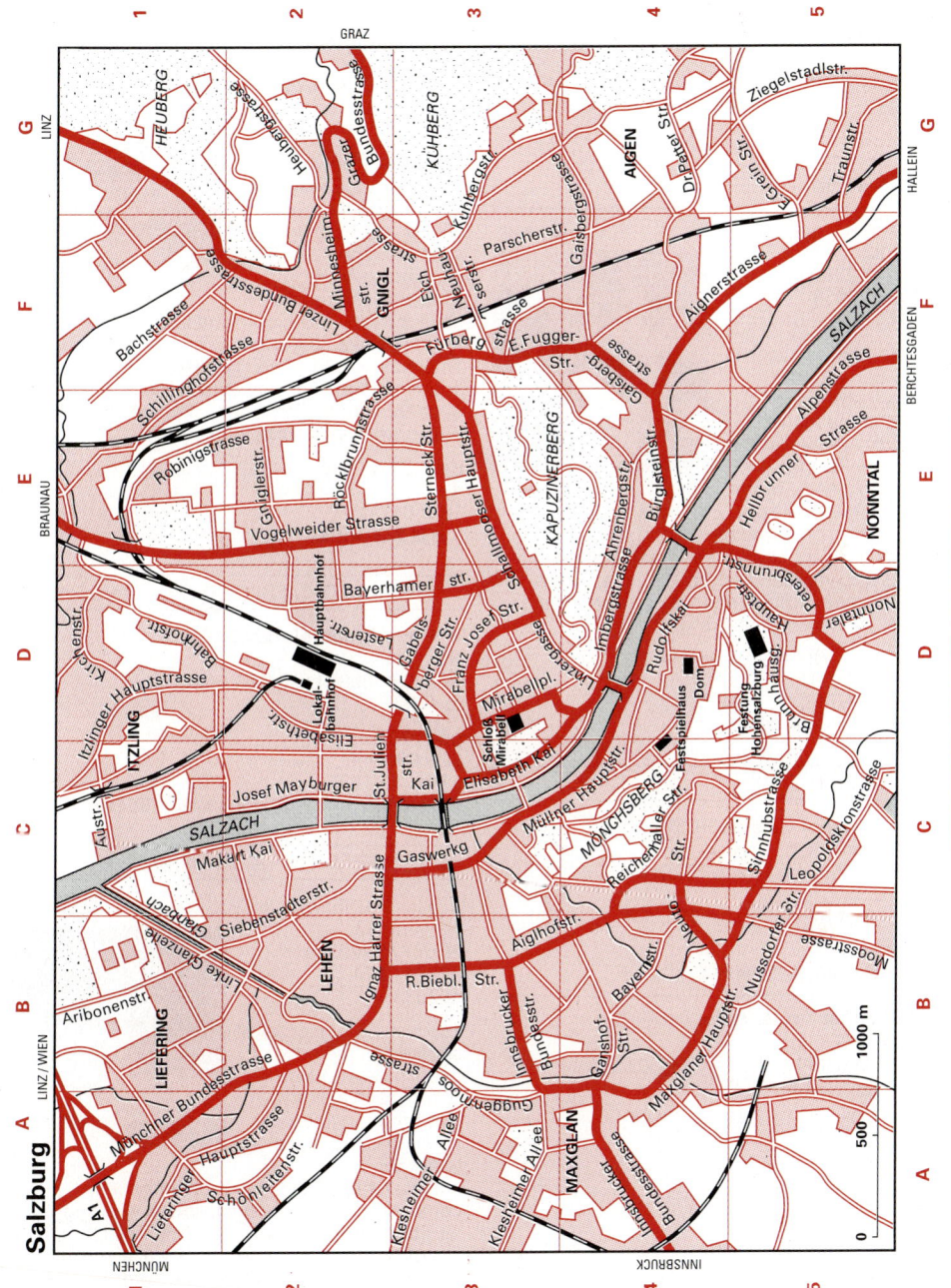

208 AUSTRIA

ABTENAU *Salzburg* 4

Panorama (HG)
Markt 183
☎ 06243-2386
✉ 5441

5 🛏
30 🛌
🚿 P 🛎 ↕ 🍴 ⌂ WC

★ ★ ★ **Roter Ochs** (HCR)
Markt 32
☎ 06243-2259 fax
06243-225959
✉ 5441

The Hotel Roter Ochs is a very comfortable holiday hotel in the centre of the tourist resort of Abtenau at the foot of the Tennen mountains. Most of the rooms in this well kept hotel have en suite bathrooms; some also have TV. The restaurant and the pleasant *Gaststube* ensure that the guests are well looked after. The hotel offers ample leisure facilities and the surrounding area is ideal for walking and skiing.

open 18.12 - 05.04 + 07.05 - 14.10
* 5 🛏 550/1100
* 40 🛌 550/1460
🎫 ● P 🛎 🍴 ⌂ WC TV 🍽 ⌂ ☺

ACHENKIRCH *Tirol* 3

★ ★ ★ **Gasthof Geisler** (HCR)
Achenkirch 130 b
☎ 05246-6533 fax 05246-6626
✉ 6215

2 🛏
28 🛌
🎫 🚿 ⊜ P 🛎 🍴 ⌂ WC TV 🍽 ☺

★ ★ **Gasthof Tiroler Adler** (HCR)
Hausnr. 371
☎ 05246-6206 fax 05246-6830
✉ 6215

open 15.05 - 31.10 + 19.12 - 10.04
* - 🛏 -/350
* 21 🛌 -/640
🚿 ● P 🛎 ⌂ WC 🍽 ☺

AFRITZ/VERDITZ *Kärnten* 4

★ ★ ★ **Lärchenhof** (HP) AA ANWB
Afritz
☎ 04247-2134 fax
04247-213411
✉ 9542

The Hotel Lärchenhof is situated in the village of Afritz and is surrounded by a large garden with a swimming pool and sunbathing lawn. Almost all the rooms have their own bathroom and balcony; the dining room has been decorated in country style. The hotel has its own sports facilities, with tennis courts on the other side of the road. The area is good for winter sports, and there are some lakes within walking distance of the hotel.

open 21.12 - 31.10
4 🛏
18 🛌 647/682
🚿 ♨ P 🛎 ⊜ 🍴 ⌂ WC

AIGEN AM BÖHMERWALD *Oberösterreich* 5

★ ★ ★ ★ **Waldhof Axberg** (HCR)
Berghansl 40
☎ 07281-8585 fax 07281-8584
✉ 4160

open 20.12 - 30.11
22 🛏 690/990
27 🛌 740/1880
🎫 ● 🎫 🚿 ♨ ⊜ P 🛎 ⊜ 🍴 ↕ ⌂ 🍴 ⌂ WC TV 🍽 ☺

ALTLENGBACH *Niederösterreich* 6

★ ★ ★ **Steinberger** (HCR) AA ANWB
Hauptstr 52
☎ 02774-2289 fax
02774-2874
✉ 3033

The Hotel Steinberger is situated on the edge of a wood, just outside Altlengbach which is close to the motorway to Vienna (A1). It is a well kept establishment, managed by a family; it has comfortable rooms, almost all with washing facilities and some with a balcony. The restaurant is large but has a good atmosphere, and drinks are served in the Stübel bar. The hotel also has an indoor pool, a luxurious sauna and solarium, and a large garden.

* 7 ∂ 400/480
* 51 ∂ 750/900
AE ① E ⊞ ⓑ ◆ P ⚡ ⚐ ⚡ ↕ ⚡ ■ ℗ WC TV ⊘ ⊙

AMSTETTEN Niederösterreich 5

★ ★ ★ Gasthof zum Mostviertler (HP)
Waidhofner Str 31
☎ 07472-63960 fax 07472-639607
✉ 3300

* 10 ∂ 300/320
* 21 ∂ 540/580
E ⊞ ⊙ ◆ P ⚡ ↕ ℗ WC ⊙

ANGATH Tirol 3

★ ★ ★ ★ Motor Hotel Rosenberger (MT)
Bosendorferstr 5
☎ 05332-7875 fax 05332-76478
✉ 6300

1 ∂ -/655
44 ∂ -/975
AE ① E ⊞ ▲ ◆ P ⚡ ↕ ⚡ ■ ℗ WC TV ⊙

ANNABERG IM ÖTSCHERLAND
Niederösterreich 5

★ ★ ★ Petermann (HCR)
☎ 02728-8243 fax 02728-8443
✉ 3222

* 3 ∂ 330/370
* 32 ∂ 660/740
⚐ ⊙ ⚡ ≡ ⚡ ■ ℗ WC ⚡ ⊙

AU Vorarlberg 2

★ ★ Gasthof Hubertus (HCR)
Bundesstr 397
☎ 05515-2342
✉ 6883

4 ∂
11 ∂
⚐ P ⚡ ℗ WC ⚡ ⚡

★ ★ ★ ★ Rössle (HP)
☎ 05515-2216 fax 05515-2484
✉ 6883

* - ∂ 490/520
* 32 ∂ 800/860
E ⊞ ⊙ ⚡ ↕ ⚡ ℗ WC TV ⊙

AU/BREGENZERWALD Vorarlberg 2

★ ★ ★ Adler (HCR)
Au
☎ 05515-2216 fax 05515-2484
✉ 6883

13 ∂
E ⊞ ◆ P ⚡ ⚡ ℗ WC ⚡ ⊙

★ ★ ★ Alpenrose (HCR)
Rehmen 91
Au
☎ 05515-2247 fax 05515-22477
✉ 6883

* 3 ∂ 470/540
* 22 ∂ 740/880
⊙ P ⚡ ⚐ ⚡ ■ ℗ WC TV ⊙ ⊙

AU/LÄNGENFELD Tirol 3

★ ★ ★ Bergwelt (HCR)
Längenfeld
☎ 05253-5301 fax 05253-5152
✉ 6444

5 ∂
27 ∂
⚐ ◆ ⚡ ↕ ⚡ ℗ WC TV ⚡ ⚡

AURACH BEI KITZBÜHEL Tirol 4

Gasthof Alpenhof (HR)
☎ 05356/4507 fax 05356/4507
✉ 6370

- ∂ 270/320
22 ∂ 270/320
AE ① E ⊞ ⚐ ⊙ ◆ ⚡ ▲ ⚡ ■ ℗ WC ⊙

★ ★ ★ Gasthof Hochenmoos (HCR)
☎ 05356-5288
✉ 6370

2 ∂ 320/420
24 ∂ 600/800
⚐ ◆ P ⚡ ■ ℗ WC ⊙

BADEN/WIEN Niederösterreich 6

★ ★ ★ ★ Herzoghof (HR)
Theresiengasse 5
Baden
☎ 02252-48395 fax 02252-42979
✉ 2500

34 ∂
52 ∂
⊙ P ⚡ ▲ ⚡ ↕ ⚡ ■ ℗ WC ⚡ ⊙

AUSTRIA

★ ★ ★ **Krainerhütte** (HCR)
Helenental
Baden
☎ 02252-44511 fax 02252-4451499
✉ 2500

22 🛏 900/1320
46 🛏 1320/1860
⓪ E ♨ ⓢ ◆ P 🅿 🏊 ↕ ⇅ 🍽 🛌 P WC TV ❙ ♿ ♻

★ ★ ★ **Parkhotel Baden** (HCR)   AA ANWB
Kaiser Franz Ring 5
Baden
☎ 02252-44386 fax 02252-80578
✉ 2500

The hotel has an attractive location in the *Kurpark* in the centre of Baden. The terrace of this well maintained hotel is one of the most frequented spots in this sophisticated spa town on the edge of the Wienerwald. The rooms are functional and have many wooden features. The Parkhotel has its own swimming pool, sauna and solarium.

* - 🛏 880/1170
* 90 🛏 1300/1800
AE ⓪ E ⌘ ♨ ⓢ ◎ P 🅿 🏊 ↕ ⇅ 🍽 🛌 P WC TV ❙

★ ★ ★ **Seminar Hotel Baden** (HR)
Trostgasse 23
Baden
☎ 02252-886620 fax 02252-88662504
✉ 2500

* - 🛏 1100/-
* 75 🛏 1650/-
AE ⓪ E ⌘ ♨ ⓢ P 🏊 ↕ ⇅ 🍽 🛌 P WC TV ❙ ♻

BADGASTEIN *Salzburg*   4

★ ★ ★ **Weismayr** (HCR)
Kaiser Franz Josef Str 6
☎ 06434-2594 fax 06434-259414
✉ 5640

open 16.12 - 29.09
17 🛏 774/1014
59 🛏 1172/1652
AE ⓪ E ⌘ ⓢ ◎ 🏊 ↕ ⇅ 🍽 🛌 P WC TV ❙ ♻

★ ★ ★ **Wildbad** (HCR)
☎ 06434-3761 fax 06434-376170
✉ 5640

open 18.12 - 09.04 + 07.05 - 08.10
* 20 🛏 630/960
* 20 🛏 1100/1760
♨ ◎ P 🅿 🏊 ↕ ⇅ 🍽 🛌 P WC TV ❙ ♻

BAD HOFGASTEIN *Salzburg*   4

Pension Iris (HP)
Achenstr 18
☎ 06432-6120
✉ 5630

6 🛏
17 🛏
♨ P 🏊 🛌 P WC TV

BAD ISCHL *Oberösterreich*   2

★ ★ ★ **Kurhotel** (HCR)
Voglhuberstr 10
☎ 06132-4271 fax 06132-7682
✉ 4820

45 🛏
70 🛏
AE ⓪ E ⌘ ◎ P 🅿 🏊 ↕ 🍽 🛌 P WC TV ❙

BAD KLEINKIRCHHEIM *Kärnten*   4

★ ★ ★ **Kapeller** (HP)
St Oswald 72
☎ 04240-482 fax 04240-48340
✉ 9546

open 21.12 - 09.04 + 21.05 - 19.10
* 2 🛏 650/950
* 19 🛏 1240/1800
P 🏊 🏊 🍽 P WC TV ♻

★ ★ **Pension Haus Mall** (HG)
Untertschern
☎ 04240-496
✉ 9546

4 🛏
5 🛏
♨ P 🏊 🛌 P WC ❙

★ ★ ★ ★ **Pulverer** (HCR)
☎ 04240-744
✉ 9546

open 15.12 - 01.11
20 🛏 920/1330
90 🛏 1660/2020
♨ ◎ P 🅿 🏊 ⚔ ↕ ⇅ 🍽 🛌 P WC TV ❙

AUSTRIA

BAD MITTERNDORF Steiermark 4

★ ★ ★ ★ **Batal Hotel Heilbrunn** (KH)
Neuhofen 108
☎ 03623-2486 fax 03623-248633
✉ 8983

open 01.12 - 30.11
* 39 ♨ 615/1010
* 66 ⚭ 1390/1830

BÄRNBACH Steiermark 7

★ ★ ★ ★ **Sport Hotel Glockenhof** (HCR)
Hochtregisterstr 25
☎ 03142-62334 fax 03142-62334
✉ 8572

* 3 ♨ 420/450
12 ⚭

BERWANG Tirol 2

★ ★ ★ ★ **Berwanger Hof** (HCR)
☎ 05674-8288 fax 05674-828835
✉ 6622

4 ♨ 290/530
61 ⚭ 580/1060

★ ★ ★ ★ **Sporthotel Singer** (HCR)
☎ 05674-8268 fax 05674-8436
✉ 6622

14 ♨
47 ⚭

BEZAU Vorarlberg 2

★ ★ ★ ★ **Gasthof Gams** (HCR)
Platz 44
☎ 05514-2220 fax 05514-222024
✉ 6870

open 15.12 - 15.11
* 10 ♨ 590/960
* 30 ⚭ 880/1620

★ ★ ★ ★ **Post** (HCR)
☎ 05514-2207 fax 05514-220722
✉ 6870

10 ♨
32 ⚭

BIRNBAUM Kärnten 4

★ ★ ★ **Gasthof Post** (HCR)
Birnbaum 1
☎ 04719-224 fax 04719-225
✉ 9652

open 01.12 - 31.10
* 4 ♨ 340/360
* 13 ⚭ 650/690

BIZAU Vorarlberg 2

★ ★ ★ **Gasthof Schwanen** (HCR)
☎ 05514-2133 fax 05514-213329
✉ 6874

open 25.12 - 10.01 + 30.01 - 15.11
* 4 ♨ 370/410
* 16 ⚭ 700/800

BLEIBURG Kärnten 7

Gasthaus Kraut (HP)
☎ 04235-2592
✉ 9150

15 ⚭

BLONS Vorarlberg 2

Adler (HCR) AA ANWB
Nr 2
☎ 05553-223
✉ 6700

The tiny mountain village of Blons is situated on the slopes of the Grosswalsertal. The design of the Hotel Adler, with its sloping roof, window shutters and balconies with geraniums, fits perfectly into the surrounding mountain-village scene. It is a modest, but well kept establishment. All rooms have a shower and toilet. Parking facilities are available.

* 1 ♨ -/300
* 9 ⚭ -/500

BLUDENZ Vorarlberg 2

★★★ **Löwen** (HR)
Mutterstr 7
☎ 05552-62206
✉ 6700

1 🛏
5 🛏🛏
🐕 ⊙ P 🅿 🍽 📺 WC TV ⏰

★★★★ **Schloß** (HCR) AA ANWB
Schloßpl 5
☎ 05552-630160 fax 05552-630168
✉ 6700

The Hotel Schloss is built on a rock just above the old town and has a covered terrace which overlooks Bludenz and the Rhätikon mountains. It is quiet, but close to the centre of town. The hotel is well furnished, and all the rooms have a bath/shower/toilet, radio/TV and a balcony. Parking facilities are available.

15 🛏 680/820
26 🛏🛏 1060/1180
AE ◐ E ⇌ 🐕 ⊙ P 🅿 🍽 🛎 🍴 P WC TV ⏰

BODENSDORF Kärnten 7

Haus Bergland (HP)
Trattenweg 4
☎ 04243-550
✉ 9551

* 1 🛏 225/260
* 6 🛏🛏 450/550
E 🐕 ⊙ P 🅿 ⚓ 🍴 P WC TV 🦌

★★ **Pension Marianne** (HP)
Fischerweg 2
☎ 04243-396
✉ 9551

3 🛏
11 🛏🛏
E ⚓ 🐕 ⊙ P 🅿 P WC ⏰ ⊛

BODENTAL Kärnten 7

★★★ **Lausegger Berggasthof** (HCR) AA ANWB
Bodental 182
☎ 04227-6260 fax 04227-626060
✉ 9163

The Lausegger Berggasthof is situated on a mountain plateau; it has a terrace and a large garden with a magnificent view. The rooms are well furnished, and most have a shower and toilet. The hotel owner organises and offers advice on mountain walks, as well as on trips with the hotel mini-bus. To reach the hotel, take the road from Klagenfurt to the Loible pass, exit Bodental. After about 5km turn right leading through woods towards the hotel.

* 1 🛏 -/280
* 16 🛏🛏 -/560
🐕 🦌 P 🅿 🍽 P WC ⏰ ⊛

BRAND Vorarlberg 2

★★★ **Alpenhof Zimba** (HP)
☎ 05559-3510 fax 05559-35140
✉ 6708

3 🛏
19 🛏🛏
🐕 P 🅿 🍽 🛎 P WC ⏰ 🏠 ⊛

★★ **Gulma** (HG)
Hausnr. 96
☎ 05559-246
✉ 6708

3 🛏
12 🛏🛏
🐕 ⊙ P 🅿 🍽 P WC TV

★★★ **Gasthof Jägerheim** (HCR)
Hausnr. 70
☎ 05559-217
✉ 6708

2 🛏
11 🛏🛏
⊙ P P WC ⏰

★ ★ ★ **Orchidee** (HG)
Hausnr. 201
☎ 05559-327 fax 05559-3279
✉ 6708

The holiday pension Orchidee is quietly situated on an Alpine pasture. It is well maintained and has spacious apartments with balcony, bath/shower/toilet, minibar, telephone and a radio (TV can be hired). The apartments are suitable for 2 to 5 people. The pension has a sunbathing lawn, a sun terrace and a children's playground.

* 8 ₰ 520/640

★ ★ ★ ★ **Sporthotel Beck** (HCR)
☎ 05559-306 fax 05559-30670
✉ 6708

open 15.05 - 31.10 + 15.12 - 12.04
1 ₰
* 30 ₰ 785/1540

BRAND/LAABEN Niederösterreich 6

★ ★ ★ ★ **Zur Post** (HCR)
Laaben
☎ 02774-8363 fax 02774-8333
✉ 3053

open 08.02 - 06.01
9 ₰
43 ₰

BRAUNAU AM INN Oberösterreich 4

★ ★ ★ **Gasthof Gfrörer** (HCR)
Bahnhofstr 50
☎ 07722-3320 fax 07722-33204
✉ 5280

8 ₰ 270/295
12 ₰

BRAZ BEI BLUDENZ Vorarlberg 2

★ ★ ★ ★ **Traube** (HR)
Klostertalerstr 12
Braz
☎ 05552-8103 fax 05552-810340
✉ 6751

The Hotel Traube in the tiny village of Ausserbraz in the Klostertal can be an excellent base for making day trips to the Arlberg and Rhätikon mountains. Almost all of the rooms have a bath/toilet, telephone, radio and balcony. The restaurant offers regional and international dishes.

open 11.12 - 01.11
* 2 ₰ 660/760
* 23 ₰ 920/1120

BREGENZ Vorarlberg 2

★ ★ **Gasthof Adler** (HCR)
Vorklostergasse 66
☎ 05574-31788 fax 05574-61953
✉ 6900

* 2 ₰ 200/220
* 6 ₰ 440/520

★ ★ ★ **Deutschmann** (HG)
Rheinstr 83 a
☎ 05574-67740 fax 05574-677412
✉ 6900

* 12 ₰ 780/950
* 71 ₰ 1100/1600

★ ★ **Pension Weidach** (HCR)
Landstr 17
☎ 05574-34142
✉ 6900

3 ₰
6 ₰

★ ★ ★ ★ **Weisses Kreuz (Best Western)** (HCR)
Römerstr 5
☎ 05574-4988 fax 05574-498867
res nr 0660-194
✉ 6900

open 25.01 - 20.12
* 11 ♪ 650/1270
* 34 ♖ 990/1930
AE ⓘ E ⚏ ⊙ ◆ P ♂ ⇅ ▤ ▣ WC TV ☺

BREITENBRUNN Burgenland 6

★ ★ ★ **Pension Rosenhof** (HCR)
☎ 02683-5200 fax 02683-520020
✉ 7091

open 01.04 - 30.11
* - ♪ 300/400
* 9 ♖ 520/620
⛰ ⓢ P ♂ ▤ WC TV ☺

BRUCK A.D. GROSSGLOCKNERSTRASSE
Salzburg 4

★ ★ ★ **Gasthof Zur Post** (HCR)
Raiffeisenstr 27
Bruck a.d. Grossglocknerstrasse
☎ 06545-215 fax 06545-658888
✉ 5671

open 01.05 - 29.10 + 19.12 - 09.04
* 4 ♪ 350/400
* 24 ♖ 640/740
⊙ P ⌂ ♂ ⇅ ▣ WC ☺

Sportpension Oberhof (HR)
Oberhofstr 40
Bruck a.d. Grossglocknerstrasse
☎ 06545-354
✉ 5671

open 01.01 - 31.10
1 ♪ 265/330
13 ♖ 500/660
⚘ P ♂ ▣ WC TV ⚔

BRUCK AN DER LEITHA Niederösterreich 6

★ ★ ★ **Rumpler** (HG)
Altstadt 86
☎ 02162-2739 fax 02162-5520
✉ 2460

2 ♪ 250/350 excl. breakfast
33 ♖ -/500 excl. breakfast
◆ P ⌂ ♂ ⇅ ↹ ▣ WC ☺

BÜRSERBERG Vorarlberg 2

★ ★ **Dunza** (HCR)   AA ANWB
Tschengla 223
☎ 05552-65308
✉ 6700

Situated in the mountains on the Tschengla plateau, the Hotel Dunza is easily reached from Bludenz or Bürserberg-Boden. It is family run, and all the rooms have a bath/shower/toilet and a balcony. The hotel is well placed as a base for mountain walks and has beautiful views from its sun terrace.

* - ♪ -/380
* 15 ♖ -/660
⚘ ⛰ P ♂ ⚏ ▣ WC ☺

Gasthof Schäfle (HP)
☎ 05552-62711
✉ 6700

open 16.12 - 31.10
1 ♪
6 ♖
⊙ P ♂ ⏇ ☺

BÜRSERBERG/DORF Vorarlberg 2

Matin (HCR)
Bürserberg
☎ 05552-63588 fax 05552-675776
✉ 6700

open 01.05 - 20.10 + 19.12 - 10.04
* 3 ♪ 500/660
* 25 ♖ 800/1120
AE ⓘ E ⚏ ⊙ P ♂ ⇅ ▤ ▣ WC TV ⏇ ☺

DAMÜLS Vorarlberg 2

★ ★ ★ **Alpenblume** (HCR)
Uga 78
☎ 05510-265 fax 05510-2656
✉ 6884

open 15.12 - 09.04 + 21.05 - 31.10
3 ♪
18 ♖
⚘ P ⌂ ♂ ▤ ▣ WC TV ⏇ ☺

★ ★ ★ ★ **Berghotel Madlener** (HCR)
Haus 22
☎ 05510-2210 fax 055 0-22115
✉ 6884

open 16.12 - 14.10
2 ♨
23 ⚐

DELLACH/MARIA WÖRTH Kärnten   7

★ ★ ★ **Seepension Ria** (HG)
Dellach 44
Maria Wörth
☎ 04273-2536
✉ 9082

open 01.04 - 31.10
* 10 ⚐ 700/1200

DORFGASTEIN Salzburg   4

★ ★ ★ ★ **Römerhof** (HR)
Nr 22
☎ 06433-209 fax 06433-20912
✉ 5632

open 04.12 - 23.10
7 ♨
32 ⚐

★ ★ ★ **Pension Steindlwirt** (HP)
☎ 06433-219
✉ 5632

5'♨
24 ⚐

DORNBIRN Vorarlberg   2

★ ★ ★ ★ **Katharinenhof** (HG)   AA ANWB
F. Michael Felderstr 2
☎ 05572-22577 fax 05572-225778
✉ 6850

Katharinenhof is a small, comfortable hotel in the centre of Dornbirn, close to the station. All rooms have a bath/shower/toilet, and the hotel also has a sauna and solarium. The town of Dornbirn is located along the Rheintal motorway, just south of Bregenz. The Bodensee, Bregenzerwald and Liechtenstein are all only a short distance away.

open 10.01 - 22.12
* 8 ♨ 625/750
* 10 ⚐ 1110/1220

★ ★ ★ ★ **Krone** (HR)
Hatlerstr 2
☎ 05572-22720 fax 05572-28078
✉ 6850

* 10 ♨ 520/850
* 17 ⚐ 900/1800

DROBOLLACH AM FAAKERSEE Kärnten   7

Kratschacherhof (HP)
Kratsacherweg 54
☎ 04254-2213
✉ 9580

1 ♨
19 ⚐

DÜRNSTEIN Niederösterreich   5

★ ★ ★ ★ **Richard Löwenherz** (HR)
Nr 8
☎ 02711-222 fax 02711-22218
✉ 13601

5 ♨
35 ⚐

EBENSEE Oberösterreich   4

★ ★ ★ **Ahamer** (HG)
Rindbachstr 20
☎ 06133-5202
✉ 4802

4 ♨
19 ⚐

EHRWALD Tirol 2

★ ★ ★ Stern (HR)
Innsbrucker Str 8
☎ 05673-2287 fax 05673-2287222
✉ 6632

open 21.12 - 04.04 + 20.05 - 15.10
* 3 ♦ 520/535
* 27 ♦ 820/870

EICHGRABEN/GROSSRAM Niederösterreich 6

★ ★ ★ Rosenberger Motorhotel   AA ANWB
(HCR)
West Autobahn
Eichgraben
☎ 02773-6651 fax 02773-6656
✉ 3033

The modern Rosenberger Motorhotel is situated in wooded surroundings close to Vienna. The rooms have a balcony, en suite bathroom, radio, TV, telephone, and minibar, and offer very comfortable accommodation. Both restaurants have a relaxed atmosphere and serve a range of good meals, complemented with a choice of Austrian wines. For private parties there is a large separate room with air conditioning.

* - ♦ -/750
* 42 ♦ -/1100

EISENKAPPEL Kärnten 7

Berghaus Brunner (HP)
Lobnig 4
☎ 04238-301
✉ 0354

4 ♦
16 ♦

★ ★ ★ Gasthof Besser (HG)
☎ 04238-342
✉ 9135

* - ♦ 195/285
* 14 ♦ 320/480

ELLMAU Tirol 3

★ ★ ★ ★ Sporthotel Ellmau (HP)
Dorf 139
☎ 05358-2721 fax 05358-2512555
✉ 6352

144 ♦

★ ★ ★ ★ Kaiserblick (HCR)
Dorf 51
☎ 05358-2230 fax 05358-2230402
✉ 6352

2 ♦ 510/870
52 ♦ 820/1580

ENGELHARTSZELL Oberösterreich 5

★ ★ Ronthalerhof (HCR)   AA ANWB
Ronthal 2
☎ 07717-8083 fax 07717-81827
✉ 4090

The Ronthalerhof is in a good location in the Danube valley, less than half an hour from the Nibelungenstrasse from Passau to Vienna. This is a popular overnight stop for bus touring companies and independent holiday travellers, which can make the dining room a little noisy. The hotel has clean rooms with bath/shower/toilet.

5 ♦ 400/500
20 ♦ 700/720

ENNS Oberösterreich 5

★ ★ ★ Goldenes Schiff (HCR)   AA ANWB
Hauptpl 23
☎ 07223-2327 fax 07223-232715
✉ 4470

The terrace and the traditional façade of the medium-sized modern Hotel Goldenes Schiff fronts on to the central square of Enns. All the rooms have a bath, shower and toilet. Enns is the oldest town in Austria and has some interesting sights; it makes a suitable place for an overnight stop if you are

travelling along the motorway to Vienna.
* 6 ⌬ 550/700
⌬⌬⌬⌬⌬⌬⌬⌬

ETMISSL Steiermark 7

★ ★ ★ **Etmisslerhof** (HR)
Etmissl 43
☏ 03861-8110 fax 03861-835540
✉ 8622

* 6 ⌬ 330/570
* 24 ⌬ 660/1110
⌬⌬⌬⌬⌬⌬⌬⌬⌬

EUGENDORF Salzburg 4

★ ★ ★ **Landgasthof Holznerwirt** (HR)
☏ 06225-8205 fax 06225-8772619
✉ 5301

open 16.01 - 01.01
6 ⌬ 560/630
26 ⌬ 1020/1260
⌬⌬⌬⌬⌬⌬⌬⌬⌬

FAAK AM SEE Kärnten 7

★ ★ ★ **Pension Duregger** (HG)
Bachstr 2
☏ 04254-2293
✉ 9583

1 ⌬ 220/350
9 ⌬ 600/700
⌬⌬⌬⌬⌬

FEISTRITZ IM ROSENTAL Kärnten 7

Pension Marianne (GH)
Sultschach 163
☏ 04228-2029
✉ 9181

4 ⌬
⌬⌬⌬⌬⌬⌬⌬⌬

FILZMOOS Salzburg 4

★ ★ ★ ★ **Golf und Sporthotel Filzmooserhof** (HCR)
☏ 06453-232 fax 06453-23266
✉ 5532

open 10.04 - 12.05 + 24.10 - 20.12
* 10 ⌬ 670/1020
* 20 ⌬ 1120/2300
⌬⌬⌬⌬⌬⌬⌬⌬⌬⌬

★ ★ ★ **Hammerhof** (HP)
☏ 06453-245 fax 06453-4144
✉ 5532

open 20.12 - 25.04 + 25.05 - 20.10
* 1 ⌬ 350/490
* 10 ⌬ 580/860
⌬⌬⌬⌬⌬⌬⌬

★ ★ ★ ★ **Hanneshof** (HR)   AA ANWB
☏ 06453-275 fax 06453-57421
✉ 5532

The Hanneshof is a comfortable hotel where the Mayr family provides a personal service to guests. It is attractively situated in the centre of Filzmoos on a mountain plateau above the Enntal and at the foot of the Dachstein. All the rooms have a bath/shower/toilet, balcony, radio, telephone and minibar. The hotel has a swimming pool with sauna and solarium. The restaurant serves meat from its own butcher's shop.

open 05.12 - 31.10
8 ⌬ 450/890
38 ⌬ 800/1600
⌬⌬⌬⌬⌬⌬⌬⌬⌬⌬⌬⌬⌬⌬⌬

Pension Rottenau (HP)
Filzmoos 58
☏ 06453-256
✉ 5532

1 ⌬
12 ⌬
⌬⌬⌬⌬⌬⌬⌬⌬

FISS Tirol 2

★ ★ ★ ★ **Chesa Monte** (HCR)
☏ 05476-6406 fax 05476-64067
✉ 6533

⌬⌬⌬⌬⌬

FLATTACH IM MÖLLTAL Kärnten 7

★ ★ **Gasthof zur Raggaschlucht** (HCR)
☏ 04785-224
✉ 9831

open 01.05 - 31.10
1 ⌬
4 ⌬
⌬⌬⌬⌬⌬⌬⌬⌬⌬

FÜGEN Tirol 3

★ ★ ★ **Kohlerhof** (HCR)
☎ 05288-2962 fax 05288-4130
✉ 6263

6 🛏
60 🛌

★ ★ ★ **Waldfriede** (HCR)   AA ANWB
Hochfuegenerstr 32
☎ 05288-2253 fax 05288-4220
✉ 6263

The Hotel Waldfriede lies outside the village of Fügen, just above the valley station of the Spieljochbahn. All the rooms have a bath/shower/toilet and there are good views of Fügen and its surroundings. This hotel is ideal for those wishing to combine the peace of a country hotel with the atmosphere of a Tyrolean holiday village.

* 5 🛏 525/535
* 47 🛌 850/900

FULPMES Tirol 3

★ ★ ★ ★ **Donnerhof** (HCR)
Waldraster Str 8
☎ 05225-2743 fax 05225-284520
✉ 6166

6 🛏 630/1300
34 🛌 1060/3060

★ ★ ★ **Stubaier Hof** (HCR)
☎ 05225-22660 fax 05225-226655
✉ 6166

- 🛏 620/1120
59 🛌 1000/2000

★ ★ ★ **Gästehaus Zinner** (HA)
Sonnensteinweg 3
☎ 05225-3502 fax 05225-3502
✉ 6166

* - 🛏 360/-

FUSCH A.D. GROSSGLOCKNERSTRASSE
Salzburg 4

★ ★ ★ **Lampenhausl** (HCR)   AA ANWB
Großglocknerstr
Fusch a.d.
Grossglocknerstrasse
☎ 06546-215302 fax 06546-215302
✉ 5672

The Hotel Lampenhausl is centrally located in the village of Fusch, along the Grossglockner-Hochalpenstrasse road and near the Hohe Tauern national park. The rooms are clean and have a bath, shower and toilet - some also have a balcony. The restaurant, with its south-facing terrace, offers a wide choice of dishes; the emphasis in this establishment is more on the restaurant than the hotel.

open 21.12 - 19.10
* 4 🛏 250/350
* 36 🛌 400/560

★ ★ ★ **Römerhof** (HCR)
Großglocknerstr 77
Fusch a.d. Grossglocknerstrasse
☎ 06546-2180 fax 06546-21816
✉ 5672

open 15.12 - 15.04 + 08.05 - 15.10
* 7 🛏 350/380
* 45 🛌 580/640

GABLITZ Niederösterreich 6

★ ★ ★ **Austria** (HCR)
Hauptstr 27
☎ 02231-2113 fax 02231-211399
✉ 3003

1 🛏 400/520
34 🛌 540/720

AUSTRIA

★ ★ ★ **Rosner** (HP) AA ANWB
Linzerstr 95
☎ 02231-2726 fax 02231-33306
✉ 3003

The Hotel Rossner is a comfortable hotel; all the rooms have bath/shower and toilet, telephone and radio, and some have a balcony. It is an attractive hotel for those visitors to Vienna who do not want to spend the night in the city itself, but can appreciate a comfortable overnight stop in the surrounding area. There is a frequent public bus service to Vienna. The small town of Gablitz is suitable as a base for day trips to the Wienerwald.

* 1 ♒ 390/445
* 28 ⚐ 590/630
🛁 ⊙ P ⛁ 🏨 🍴 🔑 WC 🐎

★ ★ ★ **Stadlmaier** (HCR)
Linzerstr 80
☎ 02231-3457 fax 02231-345727
✉ 3003

* 1 ♒ 310/330
* 29 ⚐ 620/660
⊙ ◆ P ⛁ 🏨 🍴 🔑 WC 🍽 ⊛

GALTÜR Tirol   2

★ ★ **Gasthof Alpina** (HCR)
Haus Nr 24a
☎ 05443-264
✉ 6563

1 ♒
19 ⚐
🛁 P ⛁ 🔑 WC

★ ★ ★ **Toni** (HP)
Haus Nr 64a
☎ 05443-282
✉ 6563

4 ♒
14 ⚐
🛁 P 🍴 🔑 WC TV 🍽

GARGELLEN Vorarlberg   2

★ ★ ★ **Alpenrose** (HCR)
☎ 05557-6314 fax 05557-63146
✉ 6787

open 15.12 - 25.04 + 15.06 - 15.10
17 ⚐
🍷 🛁 ⊙ P ⛁ 🍴 🔑 WC TV 🍽 🛎 ⊛

GASCHURN Vorarlberg   2

★ ★ ★ **Monika** (HP)
☎ 05558-8291 fax 05558-8126
✉ 6793

open 10.12 - 11.04 + 15.05 - 01.11
* 3 ♒ 480/880
* 22 ⚐ 760/1760
🛁 ⊙ P ⛁ 🍴 🔑 WC 🍽 🛎 ⊛

★ ★ ★ ★ **Pfeifer** (HCR)
☎ 05558-8620 fax 05558-8808
✉ 6793

21 ⚐
💧 P ⛁ 🍴 🔑 WC TV 🍽 ⊛

★ ★ ★ **Posthotel Rössle** (HR)
☎ 05558-8331
✉ 6793

8 ♒
46 ⚐
🛁 ⊙ P ⛁ 🍴 🏊 ⛱ ↕ 🔑 WC TV 🍽

★ ★ ★ **Verwall** (HCR)
☎ 05558-82060 fax 05558-8149
✉ 6793

6 ♒ 535/570
35 ⚐ 930/1000
🛁 ⊙ ◆ P ⛁ ⛱ ↕ 🔑 WC TV 🍽 ⊛

GERLOS Tirol   3

★ ★ ★ ★ **Gaspingerhof** (HCR)
☎ 05284-5216 fax 05284-533549
✉ 6281

open 13.12 - 17.04 + 15.06 - 15.10
7 ♒ 670/900
93 ⚐ 1240/1700
🛁 ⊙ P ⛁ 🍴 ⛱ 🔑 WC 🍽

220 AUSTRIA

Gerloserhof (HR)
☎ 05284-5224
✉ 6281

4 🛏
23 🛌
⊙ P 🖵 🖸 WC 🍽

★ ★ ★ **Platzer Hotel** (HCR)   AA ANWB
☎ 05284-5204 fax 05284-520444
✉ 6281

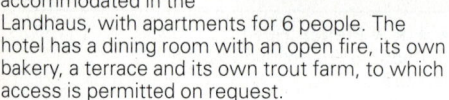

The Hotel Platzer is a family-run hotel in the centre of Gerlos. All the rooms have a bath/shower/toilet, telephone and balcony. Large families can be accommodated in the Landhaus, with apartments for 6 people. The hotel has a dining room with an open fire, its own bakery, a terrace and its own trout farm, to which access is permitted on request.

open 01.06 - 31.10 + 01.12 - 30.04
* 2 🛏 500/570
* 28 🛌 860/1540
AE ⓘ E ⚡ ⊙ P 🅿 ⚡ ↑↓ 🖵 🖸 WC TV 🐕

★ ★ ★ ★ **Sporthotel Alpina** (HCR)
☎ 05284-5305 fax 05284-5526
✉ 6281

6 🛏
37 🛌
⚡ ⊙ P ⚡ ↑↓ 🖵 🖸 WC TV 🍽 🏠 🐕

GMÜND IM LIESERTAL Kärnten   4

★ ★ ★ **Alte Mühle** (HP)   AA ANWB
Pongratzenvorstadt 2
☎ 04732-2257
✉ 9853

The Alte Mühle is on the outskirts of the town of Gmünd, not far from the Salzburg - Villach motorway. This is a small, relaxed hotel in which the owner does her utmost to look after the guests. The clean rooms have a bath, shower and toilet. The hotel has a large garden with seats and is suitable for families with children.

1 🛏 300/350
9 🛌 560/660
E ⚡ ⊙ P ⚡ 🖵 🖸 WC

★ ★ ★ **Gasthof Kohlmayr** (HCR)   AA ANWB
Hauptpl 7
☎ 04732-2149 fax 04732-2153
✉ 9853

Situated on the town square of Gmünd, the Gasthof Kohlmayr is decorated in rustic style. The restaurant serves both good plain fare and à la carte meals. The comfortable rooms have large, modern bathrooms, and the hotel has a small terrace on the square.

open 25.11 - 31.10
* 2 🛏 330/400
* 21 🛌 600/700
E ⊙ P 🅿 ⚡ ⚡ 📞 🖵 🖸 WC TV 🍽 🐕

★ ★ ★ **Pension Platzer** (HP)   AA ANWB
Vorstadt 26
☎ 04732-2745 fax 04732-3313
✉ 9853

The Platzer is a clean bed and breakfast establishment with modest rooms that have a shower, and most also have a toilet. There is a large garden along the River Malta with a sunbathing lawn and seats. All the rooms overlooking the river have a balcony. This is an attractive stopover close to the Tauern motorway, and is also a good base for making trips to the beautiful Malta valley.

open 16.05 - 14.10 + 25.12 - 14.04
* 3 🛏 450/470
* 15 🛌 740/780
🐕 🔑 ⊙ P ⚡ 🖸 WC TV 🍽 🏠 🐕

GNESAU Kärnten   7

Gasthof Biermann (HP)
☎ 04278-273 fax 04278-27314
✉ 9563

8 🛌 -/600
⊙ ◆ P 🖵 🖸 WC TV 🏠 🐕

AUSTRIA

GOLLING Salzburg 4

★ ★ ★ Goldener Stern (HR) [AA] [ANWB]
Am Marktpl 56
☎ 06244-2200 fax 06244-691242
✉ 5440

The Hotel Goldener Stern is situated in the centre of Golling, a town in the Salzach valley, south of Salzburg and only a few minutes' drive from the Tauern motorway. The hotel's exterior and interior have a country style, and the rooms have good facilities. There is a sauna and solarium in the hotel and a sun terrace at the adjacent nature park. The hotel has its own butcher's shop.

* 7 ♬ 350/550
* 30 ♭ 650/1000

★ ★ ★ Torrenerhof (HCR)
Torren 24
☎ 06244-380 fax 06244-7769
✉ 5440

open 01.12 - 31.10
5 ♬
60 ♭

GÖTZENS Tirol 3

★ ★ Pension Elizabeth (HP)
☎ 05234-32225
✉ 6091

2 ♬
14 ♭

GRAZ Steiermark 8

★ ★ ★ ★ Daniel (HCR)
Europapl 1
☎ 0316-911080 fax 0316-911085
✉ 8021

open 11.01 - 22.12
* 13 ♬ 1030/1525
* 87 ♭ 1550/2000

★ ★ ★ ★ Erzherzog Johann (HR)
Sackstr 3-5
☎ 0316-811616 fax 0316-811515
✉ 8010

* 34 ♬ 1150/1300
* 36 ♭ 1750/1950

★ ★ ★ ★ Top Hotel Europa Graz (HCR)
Bahnhofgürtel 89
☎ 0316-90760 fax 0316-9076606
✉ 8020

114 ♭

★ ★ ★ ★ Weitzer (HCR)
Grieskai 12-14
☎ 0316-913801 fax 0316-9138088
✉ 8011

* 33 ♬ 1215/1630
* 166 ♭ 1770/2210

GRAZ/STRASSGANG Steiermark 8

★ ★ ★ ★ Süd (HCR)
Stemmerweg 10
Graz
☎ 0316-281860 fax 0316-285862
✉ 8054

* 1 ♬ 610/650
* 21 ♭ 900/960

GRÖBMING Steiermark 4

★ ★ ★ Sonnhof (HR)
Hofmanning 203
☎ 03685-22101 fax 03685-2210137
✉ 8962

open 16.12 - 31.10

GROSSARL Salzburg 4

★ ★ ★ Alpina (HP)
Markt 206
☎ 06414-308
✉ 5611

open 01.06 - 18.09 + 27.12 - 02.04
* 11 ♭ 610/1110

★ ★ ★ Toferer (HP)
Markt 186
☏ 06414-312
✉ 5611

* 2 ⌀ 280/480
* 14 ⌀ 560/920

GSCHNITZ Tirol 3

★ ★ Gschnitzerhof (HCR)
Im Gschnitztal
☏ 05276-213 fax 05276-321
✉ 6150

open 02.06 - 14.10 + 19.12 - 14.03
* 5 ⌀ 270/320
* 25 ⌀ 540/640

HAINZENBERG Tirol 3

★ ★ ★ Dörflwirt (HCR)
Hainzenberg 35
☏ 05282-3162 fax 05282-4231
✉ 6280

open 01.11 - 15.12 + 15.04 - 15.05
* 6 ⌀ 485/495
* 24 ⌀ 840/860

HALDENSEE Tirol 2

Tyrol (HP) AA ANWB
Nr 6
☏ 05675-6231
✉ 6673

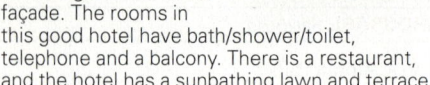

The Tyrol Hotel is situated on the Haldensee lake in the Tannheimer valley. It is especially pretty in the summer months when flowers grace the white façade. The rooms in this good hotel have bath/shower/toilet, telephone and a balcony. There is a restaurant, and the hotel has a sunbathing lawn and terrace.

* 6 ⌀ 560/740
* 39 ⌀ 1060/1380

HEILIGENBLUT Kärnten 4

Ederhof (HG)
Fleiss 1
☏ 04824-2411
✉ 9844

9 ⌀

★ ★ ★ ★ Kaiser Franz Joseph (Best Western) (HCR)
Großglockner Hochalpenstr
☏ 04824-2512 fax 04824-250313
res nr 0660-194
✉ 9844

1 ⌀
50 ⌀

★ ★ ★ ★ Post (HCR)
Hof 1
☏ 04824-2245 fax 04824-224581
✉ 9844

open 19.12 - 05.04 + 30.05 - 15.10
* 7 ⌀ 480/850
* 44 ⌀ 840/890

HENNDORF AM WALLERSEE Salzburg 4

★ ★ Pension Gollackner (HP)
Olling 4
☏ 06214-509
✉ 5302

open 15.01 - 01.11
2 ⌀
12 ⌀

HINTERBRÜHL Niederösterreich 6

★ ★ ★ ★ Höldrichsmühle (HCR)
Gaadnerstr 34
☏ 02236-262740 fax 02236-48729
✉ 2371

* 5 ⌀ 800/-
* 15 ⌀ 1200/1400

HINTERGLEMM *Salzburg* 4

Tirolerhof (HCR)
☎ 06541-497
✉ 5754

9 🛏
28 🛌

HIPPACH *Tirol* 3

★ ★ ★ **Alpenblick** (HCR)
Schwendau 91
☎ 05282-3627 fax 05282-3547
✉ 6283

open 15.12 - 25.10
5 🛏 420/700
16 🛌 760/1100

HIRSCHEGG/KLEINWALSERTAL *Vorarlberg* 2

★ ★ ★ **Gemma** (HP)   AA ANWB
Schwarzwassertalstr 21
Hirschegg
☎ 05517-5360 fax 05517-6861
✉ 6992

The Hotel Gemma is situated in a quiet spot in the village of Hirschegg in the Kleinwalser valley. This is a modern hotel with comfortable rooms, many with a south-facing balcony. The apartments on the top floor have a roof terrace. There is a swimming pool, sauna, solarium, table-tennis room, parking garage, sun terrace and winter garden. The Parsenn ski lift passes by the hotel.

open 10.12 - 03.11
* 3 🛏 98/148
* 21 🛌 160/366

HOCHNEUKIRCHEN *Niederösterreich* 8

★ ★ **Höhwirt** (HR)
Beim Hohwirt 1
☎ 02648-213
✉ 2852

* 1 🛏 180/230
* 4 🛌 320/460

HOCHSÖLDEN *Tirol* 3

Edelweiss (HCR)
☎ 05254-2298
✉ 6450

1 🛏
39 🛌

HOFKIRCHEN IM MÜHLKREIS *Oberösterreich* 5

★ ★ ★ **Falkner** (HCR)
Marsbach 2
☎ 07285-223 fax 07285-22320
✉ 4142

2 🛏
10 🛌

HOHENTAUERN *Steiermark* 7

★ ★ ★ **Moscher** (HR)
☎ 03618-204 fax 03618-204
✉ 8785

1 🛏
20 🛌 1180/1320

HOPFGARTEN IM BRIXENTAL *Tirol* 3

★ ★ ★ **Hopfgarten** (AH)
Brixentaler Str 39
☎ 05335-3920 fax 05335-3923
✉ 6361

32 🛌

★ ★ **Gasthof Mamooserhof** (HCR)
Penningberg 90
☎ 05335-2014
✉ 6361

10 🛌

IGLS *Tirol* 3

★ ★ ★ **Alpenhof** (HCR)
Iglerstr 47
☎ 0512-77491
✉ 6080

9 🛏
29 🛌

AUSTRIA

★ ★ ★ **Batzenhäusl** (HCR)
Lanserstr 12
☎ 0512-38618 fax 0512-386187
✉ 6080

open 16.12 - 14.10
* 1 ♭ 600/1100
* 35 ♭♭ 1000/1800
🅿 🗄 🖨 🍴

★ ★ ★ **Sonnenhof** (HCR)
Fernkreuzweg 16
☎ 0512-77379 fax 0512-773795
✉ 6080

* 1 ♭ 550/700
* 17 ♭♭ 800/1000
🐕 🅿 ♨ 🗄 🖨 📺 ☕

IMST *Tirol* 2

★ ★ ★ **Romantikhotel Post** (HCR)
☎ 05412-2554 fax 05412-251955
✉ 6460

open 01.02 - 31.10
* 3 ♭ 570/870
* 30 ♭♭ 900/1500
AE ⓘ E ⚡ ⊙ 🅿 🎾 ♨ ⛷ ↥ 🗄 🖨 WC 📺 🍴 ☕

INNSBRUCK *Tirol* 3

Capital of the Tirol and fourth largest city in Austria, Innsbruck stands at a strategic position, with the Scharnitz Pass to the north, the Brenner Pass to the south, the Arlberg Pass to the west, and the Inn valley to the east. The city is spectacularly set on a double bend of the river Inn, with the top peaks of the Karwendelgebirge towering over the city from the north. Twice the venue of the Winter Olympic Games, Innsbruck has grown rapidly over recent years, and is a flourishing winter-sports resort. One of the most photographed sights in the city is from Maria-Theresien-Strasse, with the Spitalkirch and the tower of Annasäule against a backdrop of the mountains. In Herzog- Frederich-Strasse there is another famous city landmark, the Goldenes Dachl - a lavishly decorated loggia protected by a roof covered with gold-plated tiles, built in 1500 by Maximilian I as a royal box from which he could view events below. The Hofburg contains state rooms displaying the glories of the Habsburg monarchy, and inside the Hofkirch is the splendid mausoleum of Maximilian I. The Tiroler Vokskunstmuseum, with its vast collection of folk art, is probably the best museum of its kind in Austria.

★ ★ ★ ★ **Austrotel Innsbruck** (HCR)
Bernhard Hofel Str 16
☎ 0512-443330 fax 0512-44428
✉ 6020

* 7 ♭ 1140/1420
* 120 ♭♭ 1780/2060
🐕 🅿 ♨ ↥ ⛔ 🗄 🖨 WC 📺 🍴 ☕

★ ★ ★ ★ **Central** (HCR)
Gilmstr 5
☎ 0512-5920 fax 0512-580310
✉ 6020

open 01.12 - 31.10
* - ♭ 1050/1300
* 65 ♭♭ 1400/1900
AE ⓘ E ⚡ ⊙ ♨ ⛷ ↥ 🗄 🖨 WC 📺 🍴 ☕

★ ★ ★ ★ **Grauer Bär** (HR)
Universitätsstr 5-7
☎ 0512-5924 fax 0512-574535
✉ 6020

* 16 ♭ 930/1100
* 65 ♭♭ 1460/1860
AE ⓘ E ⚡ ⊙ ◆ 🅿 ↥ 🗄 🖨 WC 📺 🍴

★ ★ ★ ★ **Maria Theresia (Best Western)** (HCR)
Maria-Theresienstr 31
☎ 0512-5933 fax 0512-575619
res nr 0660-194
✉ 6020

* 25 ♭ 1000/1400
* 80 ♭♭ 1500/2100
AE ⓘ E ⚡ ⊙ 🅿 🎾 ↥ 🗄 🖨 WC 📺 🍴

★ ★ ★ **Mozart** (HCR)
Müllerstr 15
☎ 0512-59538 fax 0512-595386
✉ 6010

* 9 ♭ 550/700
* 33 ♭♭ 900/1200
AE ⓘ E ⚡ 🅿 🎾 ↥ 🗄 🖨 📺 ☕

★ ★ ★ ★ **Sailer** (HR)
Adamgasse 6-10
☎ 0512-5363 fax 0512-53637
✉ 6020

* 14 ♭ 650/800
* 72 ♭♭ 900/1400
AE ⓘ E ⚡ ⊙ 🅿 🎾 ♨ ↥ 🗄 🖨 WC 📺 🍴 🐾

★ ★ ★ ★ **Tourotel Breinössl** (HR)
M Theresienstr 12
☎ 0512-584165 fax 0512-58416524
✉ 6020

* - ♨ -/950
* 41 ⛌ -/1440
🅰🅴 ⓞ 🅴 ☰ ⊙ ◆ 🅿 ↑↓ ⛌ 🅵 🆆🅲 🆃🆅 ☺

ISCHGL Tirol   2

★ ★ ★ ★ **Albona** (HP)
☎ 05444-5500 fax 05444-56727
✉ 6561

1 ♨
31 ⛌
♨ ⊙ 🅿 🅿 ↑↓ ⛌ 🅵 🆆🅲 🆃🆅 🍽 🛌 ☺

★ ★ ★ **Charly** (HP)
Haus Nr 5
☎ 05444-5434 fax 05444-543454
✉ 6561

open 04.12 - 02.05 + 20.06 - 30.09
2 ♨
* 16 ⛌ 700/1200
♨ ⊙ 🅿 ⛌ 🅵 🍽 🛌 ☺

★ ★ ★ **Garni Lasalt** (HG)
☎ 05444-5121 fax 05444-55266
✉ 6561

1 ♨
14 ⛌
♨ ⊙ 🅿 🅵 🆆🅲 🆃🆅 ☺

★ ★ ★ ★ **Salnerhof** (HCR)
☎ 05444-5272 fax 05444-518247
✉ 6561

8 ♨
32 ⛌
⊙ 🅿 🅿 ↑↓ ⚓ ⛌ 🅵 🆆🅲 🆃🆅 🍽 🛌 ☺

★ ★ ★ ★ **Seespitz** (HCR)
☎ 05444-5214 fax
05444-57084
✉ 6561

The Hotel Seespitz is situated in the heart of the winter-sports resort of Ischgl. This holiday hotel has a good atmosphere; the comfortably furnished rooms have en suite facilities, and most also have a balcony or terrace. The hotel's recreational facilities include a fitness room, sauna, mud-bath and solarium. There are extensive winter-sports facilities in the region.

open 04.12 - 02.05 + 04.07 - 02.10
* 3 ♨ 1070/1320
* 28 ⛌ 1800/2400
🅰🅴 ⓞ ♨ ⊙ 🅿 🅿 ↑↓ 🍽 🛌 ☺

★ ★ ★ ★ **Solaria** (HCR)
☎ 05444-5205
✉ 6561

40 ⛌
♨ ⊙ 🅿 🅿 ⚓ ↑↓ ⛌ 🅵 🆆🅲 🆃🆅 🍽 🛌

JENBACH Tirol   3

★ ★ ★ **Esterhammer** (HP)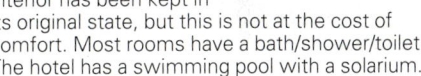
Rotholz Bei Jenbach
☎ 05244-2212 fax
05244-3200
✉ 6200

The Hotel Esterhammer is an old Tyrolean *Gasthof* in the Inn valley south of Jenbach and not far from the motorway. The hotel's interior has been kept in its original state, but this is not at the cost of comfort. Most rooms have a bath/shower/toilet. The hotel has a swimming pool with a solarium.

* 4 ♨ 260/406
* 16 ⛌ 506/692
♨ 🅿 🅿 ⚓ ⛌ 🅵 🆆🅲 🍽 ☺

★ ★ ★ **Toleranz** (HCR)
Bahnhofstr 18
☎ 05244-2366 fax 05244-267814
✉ 6200

8 ♨
15 ⛌
♨ 🅿 🅿 ⚓ ↑↓ ⛌ 🅵 🆃🆅 🍽

JERZENS Tirol   2

★ ★ ★ **Hirchenklause** (HCR)
☎ 05414-291
✉ 6460

1 ♨
10 ⛌
🅿 ⛌ 🅵 🍽

JUNGHOLZ Tirol — 2

Adler Sporthotel (HR)
☎ 08365-8102
✉ 8965

20 🛏
45 🛌
⌘ P ⌂ 🍴 ≋ ↟ ▬ 🔑 WC TV ❙◯❙

KALWANG Steiermark — 7

★ ★ ★ **Kalwangerhof** (HCR)
☎ 03846-214
✉ 8775

2 🛏
12 🛌
⌘ P ⌂ 🍴 🔑 ❙◯❙

KAPRUN Salzburg — 4

★ ★ ★ **Gasthof zur Künstleralm** (HCR)
Kesselfalkstr 166
☎ 06547-8560 fax 06547-856082
✉ 5710

open 26.10 - 24.09
* 2 🛏 400/550
* 23 🛌 800/1040
AE ⓞ P ⌂ 🍴 ↟ ▬ 🔑 WC TV ❙◯❙ ✕

★ ★ ★ **Toni** (HCR)
Nikolaus Gassnerstr 620
☎ 06547-7113 fax 06547-711355
✉ 5710

2 🛏
* 36 🛌 700/1200
AE ⓓ E ⚡ ⓞ P ⌂ 🍴 ≋ ↟ 🔑 WC TV ❙◯❙ ✕

★ ★ ★ ★ **Vier Jahreszeiten** (HCR)
☎ 06547-8316 fax 06547-831644
✉ 5710

- 🛏 550/920
- 🛌 940/1700
AE ⓓ E ⚡ ⌘ ❙◯❙

KEUTSCHACH Kärnten — 7

Pension Allesch (HR)
Plescherken 6
☎ 04273-2421
✉ 9074

1 🛏
50 🛌
⌘ 🚗 P ⌂ 🍴 ▬ 🔑 WC ❙◯❙

Pension Seeblick (HP)
Keutschach 24
☎ 04273-21143
✉ 9074

9 🛌
⌘ ⓞ P ⌂ WC ✕

KIRCHBERG IN TIROL Tirol — 3

★ ★ ★ ★ **Alpen Hotel Tiroler Adler** (HCR)
Kitzbühlerstr 10
☎ 05357-2327 fax 05357-2327205
✉ 6365

open 01.12 - 01.11
6 🛏 470/1000
34 🛌 900/2300
☾ ◆ P ⌂ ↟ ⌬ ▬ 🔑 WC TV ❙◯❙ ☺

★ ★ ★ **Bechlwirt** (HCR)
Dorfpl 5
☎ 05357-2959 fax 05357-3459
✉ 6365

4 🛏 270/380
49 🛌 560/600
AE ⓓ E ⚡ ⓞ ◆ P ⌂ ▬ 🔑 WC TV ❙◯❙ ✕

★ ★ ★ ★ **Sporthotel Happy Kirchberg** (HCR)
Aschauerstr 45
☎ 05357-2842 fax 05357-2842-406
✉ 6365

- 🛏 925/1370
42 🛌 1750/2440
☾ ◆ P ⌂ ≋ ↟ 🔑 WC TV ❙◯❙ ☺

★ ★ ★ **Gasthof Metzgerwirt** (HCR)
☎ 05357-2325 fax 05357-232549
✉ 6365

6 🛏 720/820
48 🛌 1040/1560
AE ⓓ E ⓞ P ⌂ ↟ ▬ 🔑 WC TV ❙◯❙

★ ★ ★ ★ **Sonne** (HR)
☎ 05357-2402 fax 05357-24088
✉ 6365

10 🛏 940/1720
106 🛌 2000/3240
AE ⓓ E ⚡ ⓞ P ⌂ ≋ ↟ ⌬ ▬ 🔑 WC TV ❙◯❙ ⇧ ☺

KIRSCHENTHEUER *Kärnten* 7

Tischler (HP)
Kirschentheuer 10
☎ 04227-2468 fax 04227-278350
✉ 9162

3 ♨ 300/330
13 ⚏ 540/700
🛇 ⊙ P ☏ ♨ ⇌ 🔳 ℙ WC ☼

KITZBÜHEL *Tirol* 4

★ ★ ★ **Resch** (HG)
Franz-Reisch-Str
☎ 05356-2294 fax 05356-5006
✉ 6370

2 ♨ 450/600
21 ⚏ 900/1200
AE ⊙ E ⇌ ⊙ ◆ P ☏ ↕ 🔳 ℙ WC TV ☼

★ ★ ★ **Schwarzer Adler** (HCR)
☎ 05356-2286 fax 05356-5001
✉ 6370

5 ♨ 650/850
87 ⚏ 1300/1700
AE ⊙ E ⇌ ⊙ P ☏ ♨ ↕ 🔳 WC 🍴 ☼

★ ★ ★ ★ **Zur Tenne** (HR)
Vorderstadt
☎ 05356-4444 fax 05356-480356
✉ 6370

* - ♨ 900/1300
* 51 ⚏ 1350/2100
AE ⊙ E ⇌ ⊙ ☏ ↕ 🔳 ℙ WC TV ☼

KITZBÜHEL/GUNDHABING *Tirol* 4

★ ★ ★ **Foidl** (HP) AA ANWB
Gundhabing 25
Kitzbühel
☎ 05356-2189
✉ 6370

The pension Foidl is situated in the tiny village of Gundhabing on the road from Kirchberg to Kitzbühel. The hotel is surrounded by woods and Alpine pastures. The rooms in this clean pension have a balcony, and the area is good for active holidays, both in summer and winter. Parking facilities are available.

open 19.12 - 09.04 + 14.05 - 15.10
* 2 ♨ 300/480
* 13 ⚏ 500/840
🛇 ⊙ P ☏ ⇌ 🔳 ℙ WC TV 🍴 ☼

KLAGENFURT *Kärnten* 7

★ ★ ★ **Kurhotel Carinthia** (HG)
Maistr 41
☎ 0463-511645 fax 0463-5116721
✉ 9020

11 ♨ 770/1000
17 ⚏ 1010/1540
AE ⊙ E ⇌ ⊙ P ☏ ↕ 🔳 ℙ WC TV ☼

★ ★ ★ **Romantikhotel Musil** (HCR)
10 Oktoberstr 14
☎ 0463-511660 fax 0463-5116604
✉ 9020

open 28.12 - 15.12
* 1 ♨ 1400/2000
* 11 ⚏ 1800/2600
AE ⊙ E ⇌ ⊙ ◆ P ☏ 🔳 ℙ WC TV 🍴 ☼

★ ★ ★ ★ **Sandwirt (Best Western)** (HCR)
Pernhartgasse 9
☎ 0463-56209 fax 0643-514322
✉ 9020

* 1 ♨ 980/1100
* 40 ⚏ 1420/1800
P 🔳 ℙ

★ ★ ★ ★ **Wörthersee** (HCR)
Villacherstr 338
☎ 0463-211580 fax 0463-211588
✉ 9020

3 ♨
22 ⚏
⊙ ⇌ 🛎 🛇 ◆ P ☏ ☂ ⚓ 🔳 ℙ WC TV 🍴 ☼

KLOSTERNEUBURG *Niederösterreich* 6

★ ★ ★ **Anker** (HCR) AA ANWB
Niedermarkt 5
☎ 02243-2134 fax 02243-213462
✉ 3400

The Hotel Anker is situated on the market square, but nearly all of the rooms are at the back and therefore there is little traffic noise. The rooms are spacious, and the hotel has a bar, café and restaurant in the vaults. There is a gym,

→

swimming pool, skittle alley and gymnastics hall only 300m away.

3 ♨ 420/550
34 ⚭ 640/940
[AE] [◐] [E] [≖] [⚲] [◉] [P] [⛱] [⚜] [♨] [☰] [☐] [WC] [◉] [☻]

KOLLERSCHLAG Oberösterreich 5

★ ★ **Gasthof zur Linde** (HCR)
☎ 07287-8118
✉ 4154

1 ♨
10 ⚭
[P] [☰] [☐] [◉]

KÖTSCHACH-MAUTHEN Kärnten 4

Pension Edelweiss (HP)
☎ 04715-284
✉ 9640

10 ♨
22 ⚭
[⚲] [◉] [P] [⛱] [⚜] [☐] [WC] [◉] [⚞]

★ ★ ★ ★ **Naturabenteuer Hotel Post** [AA] [ANWB]
(HCR)
Nr 66
☎ 04715-221 fax 04715-22253
✉ 9640

The Hotel Post is situated in the most southern and sunny valley of Austria, the Gailtal. The village of Kötschach is well known as a spa, but as a winter-sports resort it also offers many opportunities. The rooms in this first-class hotel are equipped with good amenities. The pleasant bar and garden are festively floodlit at night.

open 20.12 - 31.10
* 2 ♨ 590/780
* 10 ⚭ 1200/1400
[E] [≖] [⚲] [◉] [P] [⛱] [⚜] [⚞] [☰] [☐] [WC] [TV] [◉] [⇧] [☻]

KRAIG Kärnten 7

Kraigersee (HP)
☎ 04212-3565
✉ 9311

3 ♨
17 ⚭
[⚲] [⚞] [P] [⛱] [⚜] [☰] [☐] [WC] [◉] [⇧] [⚞]

KREMS Niederösterreich 5

★ ★ **Gästehaus Einzinger** (HG)
Steiner Landstr 82
☎ 02732-82316
✉ 3500

* 1 ♨ 300/320
* 7 ⚭ 500/650
[⚲] [P] [⚜] [☰] [☐] [WC] [TV] [☻]

KRIMML Salzburg 3

Falkenstein (HCR)
Falkensteinweg
☎ 06564-284
✉ 5743

1 ♨
5 ⚭
[⚲] [⚞] [P] [⛱] [⚜] [☐] [WC] [◉]

★ ★ ★ ★ **Krimmlerfaelle** (HCR)
Wasserfallstr 42
☎ 06564-203 fax 06564-473
✉ 5743

open 01.12 - 31.10
* 6 ♨ 550/970
* 51 ⚭ 980/1640
[AE] [⚲] [⚞] [P] [⛱] [⚞] [☰] [☐] [WC] [TV] [◉]

★ ★ ★ **Gasthof zur Post** (HCR)
☎ 06564-3580 fax 06564-55831
✉ 5743

open 01.05 - 30.10 + 05.12 - 20.04
* 2 ♨ 370/390
* 32 ⚭ -/800
[AE] [◐] [E] [≖] [⚲] [⚞] [P] [⛱] [⚜] [☰] [WC] [TV] [◉] [☻]

KRUMPENDORF Kärnten 7

Pension Seehof (HG)
Kochelstr 19
☎ 04229-2258
✉ 9201

3 ♨
17 ⚭
[⚲] [⚞] [P] [⛱] [⚜] [⚞] [☰] [☐] [WC]

KUFSTEIN Tirol   3

★ ★ ★ ★ **Zum Bären** (HCR)
Salurnerstr 36
☎ 0043-05372 fax 05372-6222941
✉ 6330

open 11.12 - 14.11
* 6 ♪ 550/-
* 27 ⚏ 1050/-
🌒🌓◆🅿🍴⇅🛏🚻🛁📺🍽🍸

★ ★ ★ **Kufsteinerhof** (HCR)
Franz Josefs Pl 1
☎ 05372-64884 fax 05372-61363
✉ 6330

* 3 ♪ -/580
* 39 ⚏ -/935
🆎🌒🅴🚌⊙◆🅿🍴⇅🛏🚻🛁📺🍽

★ ★ ★ **Stimmersee** (HR)
☎ 05372-62756 fax
05372-627567
✉ 6330

Set in a peaceful
location in the middle of
a wood, the Hotel
Stimmersee guarantees
its guests a relaxed
holiday. All the rooms in
this 2-storey hotel have
en suite facilities. There
is an inviting swimming pool and an attractive
terrace. The restaurant has a wide choice of good
dishes on the menu. Parking facilities are
available.

open 16.12 - 14.10
* 4 ♪ 285/315
* 28 ⚏ 560/640
🅴🚌♘🏨🚶🅿🛏🚻🛁📺🍽🍸

★ ★ ★ **Tiroler Hof** (HR)   AA ANWB
Am Rain 16
☎ 05372-62331 fax
05372-61909
✉ 6330

The Hotel Tiroler Hof is
situated in the border
town of Kufstein
surrounded by
mountains and lakes. In
the centre of the town
is an imposing fortress
containing the largest open-air organ in the world.
All the rooms have a shower, toilet, radio, TV and
balcony. The restaurant offers a good choice, and
drinks are served on the terrace.

1 ♪ 350/450
10 ⚏ 600/730
🅴🚌♘🅿🍴⇅🛏🚻🛁📺🍽🍸

LANDECK Tirol   2

★ ★ ★ **Pension Enzian** (HP)
Adamhofgasse 6
☎ 05442-62066 fax 05542-61260
✉ 6500

* 4 ♪ 300/380
* 16 ⚏ 650/750
🅴♘🅿🛁🛀🛏🚻

Kristille (HP)   AA ANWB
☎ 05442-62524 fax 05442-62524
✉ 6500

Landeck is at an altitude of 816m and is an ideal
base for trips to Switzerland and south Tirol. Most
of the rooms have a shower and toilet. The
Kristille Hotel organises barbecues on summer
evenings and mountain trips for experienced
walkers. There is also a sunbathing lawn.

open 01.01 - 10.04 + 02.06 - 25.09
* 12 ⚏ 520/580
♘🌓🅿🍴⇅🛀🛏🚻🐎

★ ★ ★ **Mozart** (HCR)
Adamhofgasse 7
☎ 05442-64222 fax 05442-6469211
res nr Orwt 210
✉ 6500

open 16.12 - 14.04 + 16.05 - 14.10
* 1 ♪ 430/490 excl. breakfast
* 22 ⚏ 760/880 excl. breakfast
🅿🛏🛁

★ ★ ★ **Post** (HCR)
☎ 05442-6911 fax 05442-62360
✉ 6500

1 ♪
88 ⚏
🆎🌒🅴🚌⚬⊙🅿🍴⇅🛏🚻🛁🍽

Sonne (HCR)
Herzog Friedrichstr 10
☎ 05442-62519 fax 05442-6251917
✉ 6500

6 ♪
30 ⚏
♘🅿🍴⇅🛏🛁🚻🍽

LÄNGENFELD *Tirol* 3

★ ★ ★ **Sulztalerhof** (HCR)   AA ANWB
☏ 05253-5113 fax 05253-511350
✉ 6444

The Hotel Sulztalerhof is situated in the Sulz valley, an offshoot of the Oetz valley. This is a well maintained hotel, where most of the rooms have a spacious balcony. The restaurant serves international food, and game dishes are the speciality. There is a gym, a whirlpool and a terrace on the sunny side of the hotel.

open 01.01 - 15.04 + 15.05 - 01.11
* - ♫ 250/300
* 32 ♬ 550/650
🅴 ⛳ 👤 🅿 ⛵ 🍴 🛏 🅱 🚻 📺 🍽

LECH AM ARLBERG *Vorarlberg* 2

★ ★ ★ ★ **Berghof** (HR)
Lech
☏ 05583-2636 fax 05583-26355
✉ 6764

46 ♬
⊙ 🅿 ⛵ 🍴 🛏 🅱 🚻 📺

★ ★ ★ ★ **Tannenbergerhof** (HCR)   AA ANWB
Dorf 111
Lech
☏ 05583-2202 fax 05583-3313
✉ 6764

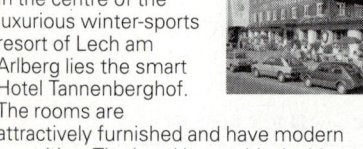

In the centre of the luxurious winter-sports resort of Lech am Arlberg lies the smart Hotel Tannenberghof. The rooms are attractively furnished and have modern amenities. The hotel has a chic, inviting restaurant and the disco-bar is open until the small hours. Leisure facilities include a swimming pool with bar, sauna with solarium and whirlpool, sun-terrace and sunbathing lawn.

open 05.12 - 26.04 + 05.07 - 14.09
* 9 ♫ 600/650
* 22 ♬ 1140/1240
🅿 ⊙ ⛵ 🍴 🛏 🅱 🚻 📺 🍽

LEOGANG *Salzburg* 4

★ ★ ★ ★ **Salzburger Hof** (HR)
☏ 06583-7310-20 fax 06583
✉ 5771

6 ♫ 470/850
39 ♬ 820/1620
🛏 ⛳ 🅿 ⛵ 🍴 🛏 🅱 🚻 📺 🍽

★ ★ ★ ★ **St Leonhard** (HP)
☏ 06583-5420 fax 06583-54285
✉ 5771

8 ♫ 560/1180
57 ♬ 920/2160
🛏 ⛳ 🅿 ⛵ 🍴 🛏 🅱 🚻 📺 🍽

LERMOOS *Tirol* 2

★ ★ ★ **Bergland** (HCR)
Reuttener Str 1
☏ 05673-2913 fax 05673-295835
✉ 6631

9 ♫ 580/770
34 ♬ 920/1300
⊙ ⛳ 🅿 ⛵ 🍴 🛏 🅱 🚻 📺 🍽

★ ★ ★ **Drei Mohren** (HCR)
☏ 05673-2362 fax 05673-3538
✉ 6631

open 21.12 - 19.03 + 01.05 - 19.10
* 5 ♫ 400/760
* 45 ♬ 600/1320
🆎 ⓞ 🅴 ⛳ 🛏 🅿 ⛵ 🍴 🛏 🅱 🚻 📺 🍽 ⬆ ⊙

★ ★ ★ **Lärchenhof** (HA)   AA ANWB
Gries 16
☏ 05673-2197 fax 05673-21975
✉ 6631

This apartment-hotel is situated just outside the tourist and winter-sports resort of Lermoos, at the foot of the Zugspitze. The rooms and apartments are well furnished, and some have a balcony. The hotel has a terrace, and there is a campsite next to the hotel.

open 18.12 - 15.04 + 20.05 - 13.10
* 4 ♫ 245/340
* 14 ♬ 410/580
🛏 🅿 ⛵ 🍴 🛏 🅱 🚻 ⊙

★ ★ ★ ★ **Post** (HCR)
Kirchpl 6
☏ 05673-22810 fax 05673-228141
✉ 6631

open 21.12 - 14.04 + 16.05 - 25.10
* 2 ♬ 530/830
* 26 ♭ 860/1400
🅴🔘🅿️⛽🏊🍴🛌📺🔲📶

LEUTASCH Tirol   3

★ ★ ★ ★ **Aparthotel Xander** (HCR)
Kirchplatzl 147
☏ 05214-6581 fax 05214-6943
✉ 6105

3 ♬
60 ♭
🐕🔘🅿️⛽🏊🔑🛌📺🔲📶

★ ★ ★ ★ **Quellenhof** (HR)
☏ 05214-6782 fax 05214-6369
✉ 6105

open 15.05 - 20.10 + 20.12 - 15.04
* - ♬ 675/1195
* 70 ♭ 990/2560
🅰🔘🅴🔳🐕🔘🅿️⛽🏊🍴🛌📺🔲📶

LIENZ Tirol   4

★ ★ ★ **Gasthof Falken** (HCR)
Eichholz 1
☏ 04852-64022 fax 04852-640326
✉ 9900

open 26.12 - 09.10
* 2 ♬ 380/420
* 6 ♭ 740/820
🚗🐕🔘⛽🏊🍴🛌🔲📶

★ ★ ★ ★ **Sonne (Best Western)** (HR)
Südtirolerpl
☏ 04852-63311 fax 04852-63314
res nr 0660-194
✉ 9900

* 19 ♬ 800/1150
* 37 ♭ 1200/1900
🅰🔘🅴🔳🔘🅿️⛽🏊🍴🛌📺🔲📶

★ ★ ★ ★ **Traube** (HCR)   AA ANWB
Hauptpl 14
☏ 04852-64444 fax 04852-64184
✉ 9900

The Romantikhotel Traube is in the town centre of Lienz and has a colourful façade. The rooms are luxurious and the bathrooms even have golden taps. The lounges, restaurant and *Bierstube*, under the old vaults, are all well furnished and the swimming pool, on the top floor, overlooks the Lienzer Dolomites.

* 16 ♬ 830/1100
* 35 ♭ 1660/2600
🅰🔘🅴🔳🔘🅿️⛽🏊🍴🛌📺🔲📶

LINGENAU Vorarlberg   2

★ ★ ★ **Gasthof Adler** (HCR)   AA ANWB
Hof 43
☏ 05513-6367 fax 05513-63675
✉ 6951

The Gasthof Adler is situated in the centre of Lingenau, a rural village in the Bregenzer Wald, not far from Bregenz. The hotel is surrounded by greenery and has a garden. The rooms are clean, and most have washing facilities and a balcony. There is a bar-discotheque and skittle alley.

open 05.12 - 02.11
* 3 ♬ 300/340
* 16 ♭ 520/540
🅴🚗🔘⛽🏊🛌🔲🐕✈

LINZ Oberösterreich   5

★ ★ ★ ★ **Spitz (Best Western)** (HR)
Fiedlerstr 6
☏ 0732-2364410 fax 0732-230841
res nr 0660-194
✉ 4041

* 4 ♬ 1190/1460
* 52 ♭ 1460/1800
🅰🔘🅴🔳🔘🅿️⛽🏊🍴🛌📺🔲📶

★ ★ ★ ★ **Trend Hotel Linz** (HCR)
Untere Donaulaende 9
☎ 0732-7626 fax 0732-76262
✉ 4020

* - ♿ -/1190
* 176 ♿ -/1490

LOFER Salzburg 4

★ ★ ★ **Lintner** (HCR)
Rauchenbergstr 59
☎ 06588-240
✉ 5090

4 ♿
22 ♿

★ ★ ★ **Post** (HCR)
Hauptpl
☎ 06588-3030 fax 06588-30359
✉ 5090

7 ♿
28 ♿

LOIBICHL/MONDSEE Oberösterreich 4

★ ★ ★ ★ **Restop Mondsee Panoramahotel** (HCR)
Innerschwand 150
Loibichl
☎ 06232-2876 fax 06232-28765
✉ 5311

* 1 ♿ -/900
* 40 ♿ -/1320

MAISHOFEN Salzburg 4

★ ★ ★ **Hettlerhof** (HG)
Oberreit 2
☎ 06542-8757
✉ 5751

7 ♿

MALLNITZ Kärnten 4

★ ★ ★ **Apart Hotel Garni Kärntnerhof** (HR)
Im
☎ 04784-413 fax 04784-676
✉ 9822

open 18.12 - 09.04 + 29.05 - 09.10
* - ♿ 350/450
* - ♿ 600/800

MARIA ALM Salzburg 4

Pension Langeck (HP)
Aberg 14
☎ 06584-338
✉ 5761

open 08.11 - 31.10
1 ♿
23 ♿

★ ★ ★ **Gasthof Niederreiter** (HCR)
Nr 110
☎ 06584-7754 fax 06584-775456
✉ 5761

5 ♿ 360/600
34 ♿ 660/1200

★ ★ ★ ★ **Salzburger Hof** (HR)
☎ 06584-7724 fax 06584-2026
✉ 5761

4 ♿
38 ♿

★ ★ ★ **Urslauerhof** (HR)
Hinterthal 66
☎ 06584-8164 fax 06584-820841
✉ 5761

4 ♿
18 ♿

MARIA WÖRTH Kärnten 7

★ ★ ★ ★ **Seehotel Wulfenia** (HP)
Süduferstr 84
☎ 04273-2213 fax 04273-221330
✉ 9082

open 01.04 - 31.10
* 3 ♿ 600/1000
* 20 ♿ 1100/1900

MARIAZELL Steiermark　　　　　　　5

★ ★ ★ Goldene Krone (HR)
Grazerstr 1
☏ 03882-2583 fax 03882-258333
✉ 8630

open 20.12 - 10.11
* 4 ♦ 360/420
* 18 ♦ 640/760

★ ★ ★ Landgasthof Sulzberg (HCR)
Fadental 3
☏ 03882-2130 fax 03882-306938
✉ 8630

* 2 ♦ 320/340
* 13 ♦ 640/680

MAURACH Tirol　　　　　　　　　3

Alpenblick (HP)
☏ 05243-5315
✉ 6212

7 ♦
28 ♦

★ ★ ★ Huber Hochland (HP)　　AA ANWB
☏ 05243-5311 fax 05243-6210
✉ 6212

Maurach, on the Achensee, is an ideal holiday resort both in summer and winter. In summer it is a good base for water sports and mountain trips, in winter there is plenty of skiing. The rooms in the Hotel Huber Hochland all have a shower and toilet, and there is also a sauna and a gym. Parking facilities are available.

open 20.12 - 20.10
* 5 ♦ 540/645
* 43 ♦ 920/1240

★ ★ ★ Mauracher Hof (HCR)
☏ 05243-5338 fax 05243-5338606
✉ 6212

10 ♦
62 ♦

MAYRHOFEN Tirol　　　　　　　　3

★ ★ Gästehaus Kröll (HCR)
Talstr 126
☏ 05285-2580 fax 05285-2580
✉ 6290

5 ♦ 145/-
11 ♦ 200/270

★ ★ ★ Neue Post (HCR)
☏ 05285-2131 fax 05285-36666
✉ 6290

20 ♦ 570/810
73 ♦ 1040/1480

★ ★ ★ ★ Neuhaus (HCR)
☏ 05285-2203 fax 05285-3808
✉ 6290

35 ♦ 450/750
105 ♦ 900/1500

★ ★ ★ ★ Gasthof Rose (HCR)
Brandbergstr 353
☏ 05285-2229 fax 05285-3321
✉ 6290

2 ♦ 480/540
53 ♦ 800/960

Strolz (HP)　　AA ANWB
☏ 05285-2256 fax 05285-3909
✉ 6290

Most of the rooms in Hotel Strolz have en suite facilities. The surrounding area provides many opportunities for walking and horse-riding, and there is a pleasant view from the hotel garden. There is a restaurant, parking garage and conference facilities.

open 23.05 - 15.10 + 20.12 - 10.04
8 ♦ 690/-
40 ♦ 1310/1510

★ ★ **Zillertal** (HCR)
Burgstall 388
☎ 05285-2304 fax 05285-23046
✉ 6290

The Hotel Zillertal is situated in an area which is well known for its many walking and skiing trails. This family hotel is only a few hundred metres from the centre of the town. The rooms are comfortable, and most have a shower and toilet. There is a bar and minigolf. Parking facilities are available.

open 22.12 - 14.04 + 16.05 - 29.09
* 8 ♦ 250/300
* 29 ♦ 500/550
▱ ♦ ⌁ ⊙ P ♇ ♨ ▭ ⛉ P' WC |◉| ☺

MELK Niederösterreich 5

Central (HCR)
Hauptpl 10
☎ 02752-2278
✉ 3390

4 ♦
28 ♦
⊙ P ♇ ♨ ▭ P' WC |◉|

METNITZ Kärnten 7

★ ★ ★ **Metnitzerhof** (HR)
☎ 04267-600 fax 04267-6006
✉ 9363

* 1 ♦ 250/280
* 13 ♦ 500/560
♠ P ↑ ♇ P' WC |◉| ☺

MILLSTATT Kärnten 4

★ ★ ★ **Zur Glocke** (HCR)
Am Marktpl 6
☎ 04766-2040
✉ 9872

2 ♦
11 ♦
▱ ⊙ P ♇ ▭ P' WC |◉|

★ ★ ★ **Marchetti Strandhotel** (HCR)
Seemühlgasse 83
☎ 04766-2075 fax 04766-208465
✉ 9872

7 ♦
26 ♦
▱ ▭ P ♇ ⌁ ↑ ▭ P' WC |◉|

MITTELBERG/KLEINWALSERTAL Vorarlberg 2

Alpenhaus Walsertal (HR)
Von Klenze Weg 5
Mittelberg
☎ 05517-5551
✉ 6993

▱ P ♇ ⌁ ▭ P' WC

★ ★ ★ **Alte Krone** (HP)
Walserstr 87
Mittelberg
☎ 05517-5728 fax 05517-3157
✉ 6993

open 21.12 - 31.03 + 01.05 - 19.10
* 11 ♦ 74/104
* 22 ♦ 156/200
P ♇ ⌁ ⛉ ↑ ▭ P' WC

MITTERSILL Salzburg 4

★ ★ ★ **Ferienhotel Paß Thurn** (HCR)
Pass Thurn 11
☎ 06562-8377 fax 06562-837790
✉ 5730

open 02.12 - 15.04 + 01.05 - 31.10
6 ♦ 330/540
42 ♦ 560/1220
AE ◑ E ▭ ◆ P ↑ ♇ ↕ ▭ P' WC TV |◉|

★ ★ ★ **Sonnberghof** (HCR)
Lamerbühel
☎ 06562-8311
✉ 5730

open 10.05 - 30.10 + 01.12 - 15.04
1 ♦ 250/280
11 ♦ 500/540
▱ ♠ P ↑ ♇ ▭ P' WC TV |◉|

MÖDLING Niederösterreich 6

★ ★ ★ ★ Babenbergerhof (HCR) AA ANWB
Babenbergergasse 6
☏ 02236-22246 fax 02236-222466
✉ 2340

Mödling is an old town which, it is said, inspired Beethoven to write the 'Missa Solemnis'. It is also a good base for trips to the famous Wienerwald. The Hotel Babenbergerhof has recently been renovated, all its rooms have a bath, shower, toilet, radio, TV, telephone and minibar. The restaurant offers a good choice.

* 10 ♦ 800/850
* 40 ♦ 1200/1400

MÖLLBRÜCKE Kärnten 7

★ ★ ★ Kreinerhof (HCR)
Hauptstr 6
☏ 04769-2221 fax 04769-222133
✉ 9813

* 5 ♦ 240/380
* 50 ♦ 480/760

MUHLBACH AM HOCHKÖNIG Salzburg 4

★ ★ ★ Bergheimat (HCR) AA ANWB
Manndlwaldstr 159
☏ 06467-72260 fax 06467-722713
✉ 5505

The Hotel Bergheimat is situated in a mountainous area; in summer there are walks to the Hochkönig mountain and in winter there is plenty of skiing. The hotel has a Tyrolean atmosphere, it has a sauna, dining rooms and a large sun terrace. The hotel organises a weekly entertainment programme.

open 18.12 - 04.04 + 11.06 - 09.09
* 3 ♦ 360/880
* 35 ♦ 600/1180

NAUDERS Tirol 2

★ ★ ★ ★ Alpenhotel Naudererhof (HR)
☏ 05473-777 fax 05473-22146
✉ 6543

4 ♦
41 ♦

★ ★ ★ Astoria (HCR)
☏ 05473-310 fax 05473-310312
✉ 6543

open 15.12 - 02.04 + 22.05 - 01.10
* 1 ♦ 670/1140
* 24 ♦ 980/2300

★ ★ ★ Gasthof Lamm (HCR)
☏ 05473-257
✉ 6543

2 ♦
23 ♦

★ ★ ★ Post (HCR)
☏ 05473-202 fax 05473-202521
✉ 6543

open 01.06 - 14.10 + 16.12 - 14.04
4 ♦
40 ♦

★ ★ ★ Schwarzer Adler (HCR) AA ANWB
Dr Tschiggfreystr 33
☏ 05473-2540 fax 05473-624
✉ 6543

The Schwarzer Adler lives up to the ideal of a traditional Austrian family hotel. The decor throughout maintains a traditional theme of wooden beams, and exposed stone and plasterwork. The rooms are fully equipped and attractively furnished. Both in summer and winter the surrounding area offers many recreational facilities, including water and winter sports. The hotel's unique location makes it convenient for visiting Austria, Switzerland and Italy.

open 16.12 - 14.04 + 01.06 - 14.10
* - ♦ 670/1250
* 45 ♦ 1090/2500

NEUFELDEN *Oberösterreich* 5

★ ★ ★ ★ Sammer (HCR)
Neufelden 15
☎ 07282-223 fax 07282-2407
✉ 4120

4 🛏
14 🛏
🛉 ⊙ P 🅿 ⛱ 🔥 ▬ 🗎 🏳 WC TV 🍴 ☺

NEUKIRCHEN AM GROSSVENEDIGER
Salzburg 3

★ ★ ★ Gassner (HCR)
☎ 06565-6232 fax 06565-6232400
✉ 5741

- 🛏 380/450
50 🛏 720/760
🛉 P ⛱ 🔥 ▬ 🗎 TV

★ ★ ★ Jagdschloß Graf Recke (HCR)
Neukirchen am Grossvenediger
☎ 06565-6417
✉ 5741

7 🛏
21 🛏
🛉 P 🅿 ⛱ ◢ 🗎 🏳 WC TV 🍴

NEUSTIFT IM STUBAITAL *Tirol* 3

★ ★ ★ ★ Forster (HP)
☎ 05226-2600 fax 05226-2682
✉ 6167

6 🛏 470/680
12 🛏 740/1400
🛉 P ⛱ 🔥 ▬ 🗎 🏳 WC TV ☺

★ ★ ★ Hoferwirt (HCR)
Nr 108
☎ 05226-2560 fax 05226-220122
✉ 6167

11 🛏
19 🛏
AE ◐ E ⇌ ⊙ P ⛱ 🔥 🏳 WC TV 🍴 ☺

★ ★ ★ Tiroler Hof (HP)
Dorf 702
☎ 05226-3278 fax 05226-3278112
✉ 6167

- 🛏 520/700
26 🛏 840/1200
⊙ P ⛱ 🔥 ▬ 🗎 🏳 WC TV 🍴 ☺

OBERDRAUBURG *Kärnten* 4

★ ★ ★ Pontiller (HCR)   AA ANWB
Marktstr 17
☎ 04710-2244 fax 04710-224466
✉ 9781

This family hotel is situated on the River Drau in a village with many sports facilities - tennis, swimming, fishing, horse riding and golf. The Hotel Pontiller is well maintained and has spacious rooms with good facilities. There is a large garden and terrace behind the hotel. The hotel has its own fishing lake.

open 10.12 - 02.11
* 6 🛏 300/380
* 28 🛏 600/700
🛉 ⊙ P 🅿 ⛱ 🔥 ▬ 🗎 🏳 WC TV 🍴 🐕

OBERGURGL *Tirol* 3

★ ★ ★ ★ Alpina (HP)
☎ 05256-2950 fax 05256-234
✉ 6456

open 21.06 - 19.09 + 26.11 - 30.04
* 10 🛏 600/1600
* 66 🛏 600/1700
⊙ P ⛱ 🔥 ▬ 🗎 🏳 WC TV 🍴 🛗 🐕

★ ★ ★ ★ Crystal (HP)
☎ 05256-454 fax 05256-36995
✉ 6456

open 28.11 - 18.04 + 03.07 - 20.09
* 6 🛏 560/1400
* 31 🛏 600/2800
⇌ ◐ ◆ P 🅿 ⛱ 🔥 ▬ 🗎 🏳 WC TV 🍴 🛗 ☺

★ ★ ★ ★ Hochfirst (HP)
☎ 05256-231 fax 05256-303
✉ 6456

open 22.06 - 28.09 + 01.12 - 27.04
15 🛏
68 🛏
◐ E ⇌ 🛉 ◐ P 🅿 ⛱ 🔥 ▬ 🗎 🏳 WC TV 🍴 🛗

OBERMÜHL AN DER DONAU *Oberösterreich* 5

★ ★ Bruckwirt (HP)   *AA ANWB*
☎ 07286-321
✉ 4131

The Hotel Bruckwirt lies amid woods by the river Mühl, with the Donau only 3km away. Most of the rooms in this well equipped hotel have a private toilet and shower. There is a good restaurant with Mühlviertel Essen on the menu. The hotel has its own fishing lake, and guests who are staying for longer than one week can obtain a permit for trout-fishing.

* 6 🛏 280/-
* 7 🛏 500/-

OBERTAUERN *Salzburg* 4

★ ★ ★ Berghotel Pohl (HCR)
☎ 06456-209 fax 06456-39720
✉ 5562

open 28.11 - 17.04
* - 🛏 720/120
* 17 🛏 1120/1140

OBERVELLACH *Kärnten* 4

★ ★ ★ Pension Schloß Trabuschen (HP)
Obervellach 77
☎ 04782-2042
✉ 9821

open 01.04 - 31.10
4 🛏 300/560
11 🛏 420/560

OBSTEIG *Tirol* 3

Tyrol (HCR)   *AA ANWB*
Am Sonnenplateau
☎ 05264-8181 fax 05264-8183
✉ 6416

The Tyrol Hotel is situated at the foot of the Tyrolean Alps, a real outdoor and winter-sports hotel. There is a restaurant and *Stüberle*, and drinks are served by the open fire. Some of the spacious rooms have TV, and there is a gym, swimming pools, sauna, indoor tennis courts and plenty of skiing in winter.

18 🛏 495/1380
102 🛏 770/2500

OETZ *Tirol* 2

★ ★ Drei Mohren (HCR)
Hauptstr 54
☎ 05252-6301 fax 05252-6301
✉ 6433

open 15.12 - 30.09
* 7 🛏 323/389
* 21 🛏 646/758

★ ★ ★ Posthotel Kassl (HCR)
☎ 05252-6303 fax 05252-2176
✉ 6433

5 🛏
44 🛏

PATERNION *Kärnten* 4

★ ★ ★ Gasthof Tell (HCR)   *AA ANWB*
Marktpl 14
☎ 04245-2931 fax 04245-3026
✉ 9711

The Gasthof Tell is situated halfway between Spittal and Villach next to the Tauernautobahn in the Drau valley. The hotel has a 16th-century atmosphere - the dance hall and bar are furnished in the style of the age of chivalry, and the chairs and benches are upholstered in leather. The restaurant offers a wide choice of food, the rooms are comfortable, and the garden has a large terrace.

* 4 🛏 350/400 excl. breakfast
* 13 🛏 640/740 excl. breakfast

PERCHTOLDSDORF *Niederösterreich* 6

★ ★ ★ Central Garten Hotel (HR)
Marktpl 17
☎ 1-8653410 fax 1-865431056
✉ 2380

* 2 🛏 690/790
* 23 🛏 -/13320

PERTISAU Tirol   3

★ ★ ★ ★ **Pfandler** (HCR)
☎ 05243-52230 fax 05243-522362
✉ 6213

7 ♨ 750/900
53 ⚭ 1300/1800
⊙ P 🔺 ⚓ ↕ ▬ 🅿 WC TV 🍽 ☺

★ ★ ★ **Strandhotel Entner** (HCR)   AA ANWB
Seepromenade 72
☎ 05243-5559 fax 05243-5985113
✉ 6213

The Strandhotel overlooks the Achernsee; the rooms at the front have a balcony and a panoramic view. The hotel has a restaurant and disco. The lake is suitable for swimming and rowing, and in winter the hotel is a good base for cross-country and downhill skiing.

open 07.05 - 27.10 + 17.12 - 08.04
* 8 ♨ 830/1250
* 71 ⚭ 1220/2200
🐕 ☕ 🚡 ⊙ P 🔺 ⚓ 🚞 ↕ ▬ 🅿 WC TV 🍽 ☺

★ ★ ★ ★ **Wiesenhof** (HP)
Achensee 9
☎ 05243-5246 fax 05243-542648
✉ 6213

2 ♨
34 ⚭
⊙ P 🔺 ⚓ ↕ ▬ 🅿 WC 🍽 ☺

PFUNDS Tirol   2

★ ★ ★ **Kajetansbrücke** (HCR)
☎ 05474-5831 fax 05474-58318
✉ 6542

open 19.12 - 19.04 + 20.05 - 24.10
* 3 ♨ 440/620
* 31 ⚭ 720/1060
🄴 🐕 🚡 ⊙ P 🔺 ⚓ ↕ ▬ 🅿 WC TV 🍽 ☺

★ ★ ★ **Kreuz** (HCR)
Hausnr 143
☎ 05474-5218
✉ 6542

1 ♨
12 ⚭
🐕 P 🔺 ⚓ ▬ 🅿 WC TV 🍽

PFUNDS/LAFAIRS Tirol   2

★ ★ ★ ★ **Lafairserhof** (HCR)
Pfunds
☎ 05474-5251 fax 05474-575740
✉ 6542

open 16.05 - 19.10 + 19.12 - 14.04
* - ♨ 570/680
* 35 ⚭ 1120/1300
🄴 🐚 ◆ P 🔺 ⚓ 🚞 ↕ ▬ 🅿 WC TV 🍽 ✈

PICHL-MANDLING Steiermark   4

★ ★ ★ **Erlebnis Hotel Steirerhof** (HCR)
Vorberg am Dachstein
☎ 06454-372 fax 06454-7480
✉ 8973

open 01.06 - 31.10 + 16.12 - 14.04
* 1 ♨ 523/773
* 28 ⚭ 926/1426
P ▬ 🅿

PIESENDORF Salzburg   4

★ ★ ★ **Schett** (HCR)
Fürth 51
☎ 06549-7251 fax 06549-72516
✉ 5721

open 16.05 - 19.04
1 ♨
* 18 ⚭ 520/740 excl. breakfast
🐕 P 🔺 ⚓ ▬ 🅿 🍽 🛗

PILL/NIEDERBERG Tirol   3

★ ★ **Jägerhof** (HCR)
Pillbergstr
Pill
☎ 05242-5490
✉ 6130

1 ♨
13 ⚭
🐕 P 🔺 WC 🍽 🛗 ✈

PÖRTSCHACH AM WÖRTHERSEE Kärnten   7

★ ★ **Haus Florian** (HG)
St Oswalerstr 125
☎ 04272-3242
✉ 9210

10 ⚭
🐕 P ▬ 🅿 WC

PRÄGRATEN *Tirol* 4

★★★ **Hohe Tauern** (HG)
St. Andrea 73
☎ 04877-5213 fax 04877-547720
✉ 9974

open 15.05 - 30.10 + 20.12 - 15.03
* 2 ♦ 220/240
* 11 ♦ 280/340

PRESSBAUM *Niederösterreich* 6

★★★ **Pressbaumerhof** (HCR)
Hauptstr 55
☎ 02233-23190 fax 02233-231950
✉ 3021

open 03.04 - 29.11
* 3 ♦ 470/-
* 23 ♦ 740/-

PURKERSDORF *Niederösterreich* 6

★★★ **Gasthof Goldener Adler** (HCR)
Hauptpl 10
☎ 02231-2195 fax 02231-5336
✉ 3002

open 13.07 - 30.06
* 4 ♦ 480/520
* 23 ♦ 800/850

★★★ **Landgasthof Moder Sommer** AA ANWB
(HCR)
Deutschwaldstr 10
☎ 02231-3387 fax 02231-5378
✉ 3002

The Hotel Moder is in the middle of the Wienerwald only 12km from the centre of Vienna, making it an ideal base for day trips. The hotel has a main building and an annexe, and all the rooms have a shower and a toilet. There is a large garden, a terrace and minigolf, and parking facilities are available.

open 01.12 - 14.11
* 5 ♦ 380/580
* 24 ♦ 680/980

RAMSAU AM DACHSTEIN *Steiermark* 4

★★ **Gasthof Gsenger** (HCR)
Hirzegg 26
☎ 03687-81280
✉ 8972

1 ♦
19 ♦

RAMSAU/HAINFELD *Niederösterreich* 6

★★ **Gasthof zum Touristen** (HCR)
Ramsau 7
Hainfeld
☎ 02764-70050 fax 02764-7005200
✉ 3172

2 ♦ 200/300
20 ♦ 560/-

RAURIS *Salzburg* 4

★★★ **Grimming** (HR)
Markt 87
☎ 06544-6268
✉ 5661

3 ♦
20 ♦

REITH BEI SEEFELD *Tirol* 3

★★★★ **Steigenberger Hotel Alpenkönig** ()
Auland
☎ 05212-3320 fax 05212-3320700
✉ 6103

* 25 ♦ 1410/1930
* 125 ♦ 2020/5320

RENNWEG *Kärnten* 4

★★★ **Waldhauser** (HP)
Abwerzg 1
☎ 04734-298
✉ 9863

* 1 ♦ 250/260
* 8 ♦ 500/530

AUSTRIA

REUTTE Tirol 2

★ ★ ★ **Alpenhotel Ammerwald** (HR)
☎ 05672-8131 fax 05672-8132200
✉ 6600

14 🛏
87 🛌

AE ① E ⚡ ♨ 🍴 P 🅿 🏊 ⛷ ↕ 🛗 ⬛ ⬜ WC TV 🍽

★ ★ ★ **Urisee** (HR)
Urisee 6
☎ 05672-2301
✉ 6600

The Hotel Urisee is situated outside Reutte by the lake, which is ideal for fishing and swimming. Most rooms have a shower/bath and toilet, as well as a balcony overlooking the mountains. There is a dining room, several lounges, a terrace offering good views, and the hotel has its own beach.

* 3 🛏 -/430
* 14 🛌 -/800

⚡ 🌊 🍴 P 🅿 🏊 ⛷ ⬛ ⬜ WC 🙂

REUTTE/EHENBICHL Tirol 2

★ ★ ★ **Maximilian** (HCR)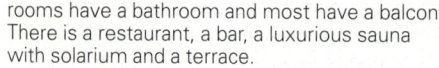
Reuttenerstr 1
Reutte
☎ 05672-2585 fax 05672-258554
✉ 6600

The Hotel Maximilian is situated on the outskirts of Reutte, a village on the Lech. It is a comfortable holiday and winter-sports hotel - all rooms have a bathroom and most have a balcony. There is a restaurant, a bar, a luxurious sauna with solarium and a terrace.

open 02.04 - 05.04, 01.05 - 16.10 + 19.12 - 20.03
4 🛏 450/520
32 🛌 800/1000

⚡ 🍴 P 🅿 🏊 ↕ ⬛ ⬜ WC TV

RIED IM OBERINNTAL Tirol 2

★ ★ ★ ★ **Mozart** (HCR) AA ANWB
☎ 05472-6919 fax 05472-693784
✉ 6531

The Hotel Mozart is surrounded by green woods; the area offers a range of recreational facilities including fishing, tennis, horse riding and skiing. The hotel has skis for hire.
The rooms are equipped with good amenities, there is a sauna and solarium, and there is a bar and a restaurant serving excellent meals.

open 18.12 - 09.04 + 21.05 - 15.10
* 5 🛏 490/870
* 66 🛌 910/1680

⚡ ♨ 🍴 P 🅿 🏊 ⛷ ↕ ⬛ ⬜ WC TV 🍽 🙂

★ ★ ★ ★ **Truyenhof** (HP)
☎ 05472-6513 fax 05472-601644
✉ 6531

open 15.12 - 31.10
* - 🛏 480/690
* 45 🛌 940/1440

E ⚡ ♨ P 🅿 🏊 ↕ ⬛ ⬜ WC 🍽 🙂

RIEGERSBURG Steiermark 6

★ ★ ★ **Fink** (HCR)
☎ 03153-216 fax 03153-7357
✉ 8333

4 🛏
29 🛌

♨ 🌊 ① P 🅿 🏊 ⬛ ⬜ WC TV 🍽 🙂

RIEZLERN/KLEINWALSERTAL Vorarlberg 2

★ ★ ★ ★ **Appartementshotel Wagner** (HA) AA ANWB
Walserstr 1
Riezlern
☎ 05517-5248 fax 05517-3266
✉ 6991

The winter-sports and holiday hotel Wagner is situated on the edge of the woods, only 8 minutes from the centre of Riezlern. All rooms and apartments have washing facilities and most have a TV and a balcony. The hotel has a restaurant, and the Bermuda-Halle contains the swimming pool and sauna with whirlpool. The Kleinwalzertal can be reached from the German Oberstdorf.

open 16.12 - 19.04 + 21.05 - 31.10
* 3 ♫ 72/80
* 17 ♫ 140/160
🅔 🌣 ⓞ 🅟 🍴 🛏 🚻 📺 🍽 ☺

ROHRBACH Oberösterreich 5

★ ★ ★ **Dörfner** (HCR)
Marktpl 25
☎ 07289-332
✉ 4150

1 ♫
12 ♫
🌣 ⓞ 🅟 🍴 🚻 🛏

ROHR IM GEBIRGE Niederösterreich 6

★ ★ ★ **Kaiser Franz Josef** (HCR)
☎ 02667-8200 fax 02667-820094
✉ 2663

8 ♫
19 ♫
🅔 ⓞ 🅟 🍴 🚻 📺 🍽 🛏 ☺

RUSSBACH Salzburg 4

★ ★ ★ **Alpenhotel** (HCR)
☎ 06242-226 fax 06242-2269
✉ 5442

The Alpenhotel is situated in the centre of Russbach, close to the swimming pool and other sports facilities. This town is surrounded by woods and mountains and is good as a base for winter sports. All rooms have a bath, shower, toilet and balcony.

open 18.12 - 15.10
* 5 ♫ 319/467
* 20 ♫ 512/808
🌣 ⓞ 🅟 🛏 🚻 🛏

SAALBACH Salzburg 4

★ ★ ★ ★ **Bergers Sporthotel** (HCR)
Dorfstr 33
☎ 06541-577 fax 06541-57760
✉ 5753

The Sporthotel Bergers is situated in the centre of the winter-sports resort of Saalbach. This luxury holiday hotel has spacious, comfortable rooms with en suite bathroom and TV - some also have a balcony. The Stüberl and the cosy restaurant both provide good food, and the disco is open well into the small hours. The vast skiing area of Saalbach-Hinterglemm offers many winter-sports facilities.

open 15.12 - 31.03 + 20.05 - 30.09
* 10 ♫ 600/1650
* 45 ♫ 1000/2800
🅐🅔 ⓞ 🅔 🌣 ⓞ 🅟 🍴 🛏 🍽 🛏 📺 🍽 🛏 ✻

Gasthof Iglsbergerhof (HCR)
Schönleitenweg 340
☎ 06541-491
✉ 5753

1 ♫
7 ♫
◆ 🅟 🍴 🛏 🛏 🚻 🍽

★ ★ ★ **Neuhaus** (HCR)
Dorfstr 38
☎ 06541-71510 fax 06541-715174
✉ 5753

open 16.12 - 09.04 + 21.05 - 14.10
* 14 ♫ 500/1400
* 56 ♫ 800/2700
🅔 ⓞ 🅟 🍴 🛏 🍽 🛏 🚻 ☺

SAALBACH/HINTERGLEMM Salzburg 4

★ ★ ★ **Pinzgauerhof** (HCR)
Reiterkogelweg 223
Hinterglemm
☎ 06541-417 fax 06541-4177
✉ 5754

open 21.05 - 19.10 + 21.12 - 29.04
* 4 ♫ 390/910
* 26 ♫ 620/1620
🌣 ⓞ 🅟 🍴 🍽 🛏 🚻 📺 🍽 🛏

SALZBURG *Salzburg*   4

This city is one of the glories of Europe. The new town, on the northeastern banks of the river Salzach, is overlooked by the Kapuziner Kloster, and the old town on the opposite bank is set under the sheer face of the Mönchsburg and the great mass of the Hohensalzburg fortress. Salzburg is a place of spacious squares and narrow alleyways, elegant shops and cafés, interesting churches, palaces and museums, but most of all it is a city of the arts - especially music - of the highest international standard. This is the city where Mozart was born and lived, and the prestigious annual music festival is held in his honour each year at several venues, including the modern Festspielhaus, with its 2,300-seat auditorium and a 130-metre-high stage cut into the Mönchsburg rock. The Hohensalzburg, once a stronghold of the prince-archbishops of the city, has an interesting museum and offers a panoramic view over the city. Sights in the old city include the Romanesque basilica of Stiftskirche St Peter with its cemetery; the Rezidenz, main residence of the prince-archbishops; and, of course, Mozart's birthplace, now a museum. The narrow streets of Getreidegasse and Judengasse are attractive and lively shopping areas, with decorative wrought-iron signs adorning the tall buildings.

See city plan on page 207.

★ ★ ★ **Airporthotel Salzburg** (HCR)
Loigstr 20 A
☎ 0662-850020 fax 0662-85002044
res nr 020-6102551
✉ 5020

* 15 ♫ 1100/1400
* 22 ♬ 1560/1960
[AE] [◐] [E] [⌸] [◉] [◆] [P] [🅿] [⚓] [⛴] [▬] [▭] [WC] [TV] [🍴] [☺]

★ ★ ★ **Auersperg** (HCR)
Auerspergstr 61
☎ 0662-88944 fax 0662-8894455
✉ 5027
City Plan D3

* 13 ♫ 920/1400
* 41 ♬ 1100/2180
[AE] [◐] [E] [⌸] [P] [▬] [▭] [WC] [TV]

★ ★ ★ ★ **Bristol** (HCR)
Makartpl 4
☎ 0662-873557 fax 0662-8735576
✉ 5020
City Plan D3

open 15.03 - 03.01
* 15 ♫ 1950/2810
* 51 ♬ 2300/5200
[AE] [E] [⌸] [P] [▬] [▭]

★ ★ ★ ★ ★ **Fondachhof** (HR)
Gaisbergstr 46
☎ 0662-641331 fax 0662-641576
✉ 5020
City Plan F4

open 24.03 - 31.10
12 ♫ 1300/2100
16 ♬ 2500/4000
[AE] [◐] [E] [⌸] [◉] [P] [🅿] [⚓] [⛴] [⇅] [▬] [▭] [WC] [TV] [☺]

★ ★ ★ **Gablerbräu** (HR)
Linzergasse 9
☎ 0662-88965 fax 0662-8896555
✉ 5020
City Plan D4

* 14 ♫ 750/995
* 38 ♬ 1300/1600
[AE] [◐] [E] [⌸] [◉] [⇅] [▬] [▭] [WC] [TV] [🍴] [☺]

★ ★ ★ **Zum Hischen** (HR)
St Julienstr 21-23
☎ 0662-889030 fax 0662-8890358
✉ 5020
City Plan C2

open 01.12 - 31.10
* 15 ♫ 550/1100
* 55 ♬ 900/1800
[AE] [◐] [E] [⌸] [◉] [P] [⇅] [▬] [▭] [WC] [TV] [☺]

★ ★ ★ ★ **Holiday Inn Crowne Plaza** (HR)
Rainerstr 6-8
☎ 0662-889783 fax 0662-878893
✉ 5020
City Plan D3

- ♫ 1700/4200
- ♬ 2600/4800
[AE] [◐] [E] [⌸] [◉] [◆] [P] [🅿] [⇅] [▬] [TV] [🍴]

★ ★ ★ **Kaserehof (Best Western)** (HCR)
Alpenstr 6
☎ 0662-21265 fax 0662-2126550
res nr 0660-194
✉ 5020
City Plan E5

open 01.03 - 31.01
* 1 ♫ 1360/2260
* 44 ♬ 2010/3560
[AE] [◐] [E] [⌸] [◉] [P] [⇅] [▬] [▭] [WC] [TV]

AUSTRIA 243

★ ★ ★ ★ **Kobenzl (Best Western)** (HCR)
Am Gaisberg
☎ 0662-641510 fax 0662-642238
res nr 0660-194
✉ 5020

open 15.03 - 15.11
3 ⬦ 1650/2900
17 ⬦ 2050/5400

★ ★ ★ ★ **Lasserhof** (HG)
Lasserstr 47
☎ 0662-873388 fax 0662-8733886
✉ 5020
City Plan D3

* 6 ⬦ 810/1450
* 16 ⬦ 1290/2310

★ ★ ★ **Parkpension Kasern** (HG)
Wickenburgallee 1
☎ 0662-50062 fax 0662-51188
✉ 5028

open 01.01 - 31.10
* - ⬦ -/600
* 15 ⬦ 700/1100

★ ★ ★ ★ **Rosenberger Salzburg (Best Western)** (HCR)
Bosendorferstr 5
☎ 0662-435546 fax 0662-43951095
res nr 0660-194
✉ 5020
City Plan B1

- ⬦ 1060/1250
120 ⬦ 1460/1800

★ ★ ★ ★ **Schaffenrath** (HR)
Alpenstr 115
☎ 0662-6231530 fax 0662-629314
✉ 5020

* - ⬦ 1050/1600
* 47 ⬦ 1380/1880

★ ★ ★ **Scherer** (HP)
Plainstr 37
☎ 0662-871706 fax 0662-876568
✉ 5020
City Plan C2

The Hotel Scherer is close to the station, the Festspiele and the Festung in this town of Mozart. It is modern and all the rooms have a shower, toilet, telephone and TV. The hotel has a restaurant, bar and lounge. Parking facilities are available.

* 8 ⬦ 790/1480
* 42 ⬦ 980/1980

★ ★ ★ ★ **Stieglbräu (Best Western)** (HR)
Bosendorferstr 5
☎ 0662-77682 fax 0662-7769271
res nr 0660-194
✉ 5020
City Plan D3

10 ⬦
40 ⬦

★ ★ ★ ★ **Wolf Dietrich** (HR)
Wolf Dietrichstr 7
☎ 0662-871275 fax 0662-882320
✉ 5020
City Plan D3

open 16.03 - 01.02
* 12 ⬦ 850/1020
* 18 ⬦ 1320/1920

SCHLEIDEN/GEMÜND *Niederösterreich* 5

★ ★ ★ ★ **Krone und Kaiserhof** (HCR)
Maria Taferl
☎ 07413-6355 fax 07413-635583
✉ 53937

The Hotels Krone and Kaiserhof lie close together in Maria Taferl, both overlooking the Donau valley. The 2 hotels, which are part of one enterprise, complement each other, with good leisure facilities available. The rooms have en suite bathroom and TV, and there are stylish, well

→

furnished restaurants. The Hotel Krone has an indoor swimming pool with luxury sauna, whirlpool and roof terrace; while the Hotel Kaiserhof has a large sunbathing lawn and an outdoor swimming pool.

open 01.03 - 31.12
* 3 ♫ 620/670
* 57 ⚭ 1040/1200
🛏⊙🅿🍴♨≋↕🚻📞WC🍽

SCHÖNBERG IM STUBAITAL Tirol 3

★★★ **Gasthaus Handl** (HR)
☏ 05225-2574 fax 05225-25748
✉ 6141

open 15.12 - 15.10
* 2 ♫ 360/430
* 18 ⚭ 540/640
🅴⚡⊙🅿🍴↕🚻📞WC📺☺

SCHRUNS/MONTAFON Vorarlberg 2

★★★ **Krone** (HR)
Ausserlitzstr 2
Schruns
☏ 05556-72255 fax 05556-74879
✉ 6780

open 05.04 - 21.05 + 16.10 - 24.12
* 1 ♫ 380/500
* 8 ⚭ 700/1120
🛏⚡⊙🅿🍴🚻📞WC🍽☺

SCHWAZ Tirol 3

★★★ **Gasthof Goldener Löwe** (HR)   AA ANWB
Husslstr 4
☏ 05242-62373
✉ 6130

The Gasthof-Pension Goldener Löwe is quietly situated on the outskirts of Schwaz, a small town in the Inntal. It is a traditional, family-run establishment with a welcoming atmosphere, where the rooms are very well kept and have a private shower and toilet. The restaurant serves a range of hearty Austrian dishes. As the hotel is not far from the motorway in the direction of Innsbruck and the Brenner, it makes a good overnight stop.

* 5 ♫ 315/355
* 25 ⚭ 570/650
🅴🛏⊙🅿🍴♨↕🚻📞WC📺🍽☺

SEEBODEN Kärnten 4

★★★ **Club Fliegenpilz** (HCR)   AA ANWB
Süduferweg 123 -125
☏ 04762-81708 fax 04762-81708
✉ 9871

The Hotel Club Fliegenpilz is situated on the Millstättersee, and is ideal for guests who like sports - various water sports, tennis, table-tennis, fishing are available. A number of the rooms have en suite facilities and a balcony; some have views of the lake. Accommodation is on half-board basis; in the morning there is a comprehensive breakfast buffet, and in the evening there is a menu and a salad bar. The hotel offers an extensive activity programme, and there is a beach, sunbathing lawn and sun-terrace.

open 15.05 - 10.10
2 ♫ 420/550
19 ⚭ 420/690
🏠⛱🚤🅿🍴≋↕🚻📞WC📺🏠☺

SEEFELD Tirol 3

★★★ **Alpenhof** (HCR)
Münchenerstr 76
☏ 05212-2249 fax 05212-4311
✉ 6100

open 19.12 - 08.04 + 22.05 - 09.10
* 6 ♫ -/700
* 25 ⚭ 800/1400
🅰🅴⊙🅴⚡⊙🅿≋↕🚻📞WC🍽☺

★★★★ **Alpina** (HCR)
Geigenbuhel
☏ 05212-2601 fax 05212-260166
✉ 6100

10 ♫
35 ⚭
🅰🅴⊙🅴⚡⊙🅿🍴♨≋↕🚻📞WC📺🍽☺

★ ★ ★ ★ **Astoria** (HCR)   AA ANWB
☎ 05212-22720 fax 05212-2272100
✉ 6100

The Hotel Astoria lies above Seefeld at an altitude of 1200m, and is popular both as a summer and winter hotel. The rooms are well furnished, there is a restaurant, a bar, and a swimming pool in the garden with views of the surrounding mountains.

* 5 ♦ 840/1390
* 39 ⚏ 1680/2880
⚝ ⊙ P ☂ ♨ ⇥ ⏏ ■ ✝ WC TV ☺

★ ★ ★ ★ **Prachenskyhof** (HP)
Panoramaweg 560
☎ 05212-2722
✉ 6100

10 ⚏
⚝ ☂ ♨ ⇥ ⏏ ■ WC TV ⚑

★ ★ ★ ★ **Stefanie** (HG)
Reitherspitzstr 384
☎ 05212-2466 fax 05212-235843
✉ 6100

open 20.12 - 10.04 + 25.05 - 10.10
* 4 ♦ 700/880
* 38 ⚏ 1300/1600
AE ⊙ E ⇌ ☯ P ☂ ♨ ⇥ ⏏ ■ ✝ WC TV ⚑ ☺

★ ★ ★ ★ **Tyrol** (HCR)
Münchenerstr 114
☎ 05212-2221 fax 05212-4311
✉ 6100

open 19.12 - 08.04 + 22.05 - 10.10
* 6 ♦ 700/1350
* 41 ⚏ 1200/2600
AE ⊙ E ⇌ P ☂ ♨ ⇥ ⏏ ■ ✝ WC TV ◎ ☺

SEMMERING Niederösterreich   6

★ ★ ★ ★ **Alpenheim Gartenhotel** (HCR)
Villenstr 55
☎ 02664-322
✉ 2680

9 ♦
15 ⚏
⚝ ♨ P ☂ ⇥ WC TV ◎ ✝

SERFAUS Tirol   2

★ ★ **Alpenrose** (HP)
Muhlbachweg 6
☎ 05476-6272
✉ 6534

2 ♦
10 ⚏
⚝ ⊙ ☂ ■ ✝ WC ✝

★ ★ ★ ★ **Alte Schmiede** (HCR)
☎ 05476-6492 fax 05476-62707
✉ 6535

open 01.12 - 01.05 + 01.06 - 01.10
7 ♦ 570/1150
39 ⚏ 590/1400
⚝ ⊙ P ☂ ♨ ⇥ ⏏ ■ ✝ WC TV ◎ ☺

★ ★ ★ ★ ★ **Cervosa** (HCR)   AA ANWB
Herrenanger 11
☎ 05476-6211 fax 05476-6211141
✉ 6535

Just outside the pleasant winter-sports resort of Serfaus, the Hotel Cervosa stands against a sunny south-facing slope. This holiday and winter-sports hotel is situated at an altitude of 1400m and has rooms with en suite bathroom, TV, minibar and a balcony with a fine view. The grill-restaurant serves a range of good dishes. Leisure facilities include a large swimming pool with sauna, gym, tennis and squash.

open 01.06 - 14.10 + 16.12 - 19.04
* 10 ♦ 1360/1640
* 58 ⚏ 2000/4820
AE ⊙ ⇌ ⚝ ☯ P ☂ ♨ ⇥ ⏏ ■ ✝ WC TV ◎ ⚑ ☺

★ ★ ★ **Pension Edelweiss** (HP)
Archleweg 5
☎ 05476-6223 fax 05476-6843
✉ 6534

open 18.04 - 14.06 + 26.09 - 14.12
* 3 ♦ 280/930
* 15 ⚏ 520/1960
⚝ ☯ P ☂ ■ ✝ WC TV ◎ ☺

Rex (HCR)
☎ 05476-6264
✉ 6535

4 ♦
21 ⚏
⊙ P ☂ ⇥ ⏏ ✝ WC ◎ ⚑

★ ★ ★ ★ **St Zeno** (HCR)
☎ 05476-6328 fax 05476-632865
✉ 6535

18 ♉
42 ⛁
🆎 💳 🅴 ⚖ ♌ 🅿 🅿 ♒ ♒ ♉ 🍴 ▭ 🆆🅲 📺 🔔 🏠 ☺

SILZ Tirol 2

Oberland (HCR)
Tirolerstr 8
☎ 05263-6405
✉ 6424

The Hotel Oberland is situated in the fairly quiet high street of Silz. It is a small hospitable, residential, hotel not far from the popular winter-sports areas of Oetztal and Seefeld. The hotel has a relaxed and friendly atmosphere; the rooms - some with en suite facilities - are simply furnished but well maintained. There is an attractive dining room and a bowling alley.

open 26.11 - 31.10
* 2 ♉ 270/310
* 12 ⛁ 440/520
🌀 🅿 🅿 ♒ ▭ 📧 🆆🅲

SÖLDEN Tirol 3

★ ★ ★ ★ **Bergland** (HCR)
☎ 05254-2234 fax 05254-2656510
✉ 6450

14 ♉ 530/620
72 ⛁ 1160/1400
🆎 🅴 ⚖ ● ◆ 🅿 🅿 ♒ ♒ ♉ 🍴 ▭ 📧 🆆🅲 📺 🔔 🏠 🦌

★ ★ ★ ★ ★ **Central** (HCR)
☎ 05254-22600 fax 05254-2260511
✉ 6450

open 10.07 - 09.04
* 20 ♉ 1040/2110
* 52 ⛁ 1920/3620
🏊 ● 🅿 🅿 ♒ ♉ 🍴 ▭ 📧 🆆🅲 📺 🔔 ☺

Hubertus (HCR)
☎ 05254-2608 fax 05254-2731
✉ 6450

3 ♉ 680/1000
22 ⛁ 1260/1880
● ◆ 🅿 🅿 ♒ ▭ 📧 🆆🅲 📺 🔔 🏠 🦌

SPITAL AM PYHRN Oberösterreich 7

★ ★ ★ **Berghotel Hengl** (HCR)
Wurzeralm 211
☎ 07563-281
✉ 4582

15 ♉
17 ⛁
🏊 ♌ ♒ ⚓ 📧 🅿 🆆🅲 🔔

SPITZ Niederösterreich 5

★ ★ ★ **Haus Burkhardt** (HG)
Kremserstr 19
☎ 02713-2356
✉ 3620

open 01.04 - 31.10
* 1 ♉ 280/290
* 6 ⛁ 550/630
🏊 ● 🅿 🅿 ♒ 📧 🅿 🆆🅲

★ ★ ★ **Garni zum Ruine Hinterhaus** (HR)
Hinterhaus 8
☎ 02713-2254 fax 02713-2875
✉ 3620

2 ♉
10 ⛁
🆎 🅴 ♌ 🅿 🅿 ♒ 🍴 ▭ 🅿 🆆🅲 🔔 ☺

STADL AN DER MUR Steiermark 7

★ ★ **Ortner Seerainer** (HP)
☎ 03534-2284 fax 03534-2284
✉ 8862

The Gasthof Ortner Seerainer is situated in Steiermark, which has only recently been discovered by tourists. All rooms have washing facilities and some have a large balcony; the restaurant serves Austrian specialities. This is a good base for walking and cross-country skiing.

7 ♉ 300/320
25 ⛁ 520/560
💳 🏊 ● 🅿 ♒ 🅿 🆆🅲 🔔

ST ANTON AM ARLBERG Tirol 2

Alpenhof (HCR)
☎ 05446-2700 fax 05446-270033
✉ 6580

2 ♨
33 🛏

★ ★ ★ **Alte Post** (HR)
Hauptstr 58 A
☎ 05446-25530 fax 05446-255441
✉ 6580

open 01.06 - 10.10 + 04.12 - 01.05
* 9 ♨ 840/2120
* 32 🛏 1680/4240

★ ★ ★ **Garni Mössmer** (HG)
Haus Nr 35
☎ 05446-2727 fax 05446-272750
✉ 6580

open 01.12 - 31.10
5 ♨ 300/750
23 🛏 600/1500

★ ★ ★ ★ **Sporthotel (Best Western)** (HCR)
St Anton 52
☎ 05446-3111 fax 05546-311170
res nr 0660-194
✉ 6580

open 01.06 - 01.10 + 01.12 - 30.04
* 1 ♨ 620/1880
* 56 🛏 1150/3600

ST CORONA AM WECHSEL Niederösterreich 6

★ ★ ★ **Ödenhof** (HR)
St Corona 15
☎ 02641-2279 fax 02641-22793
✉ 2880

open 21.12 - 30.10
* 7 ♨ -/450
* 29 🛏 -/800

STEINACH AM BRENNER Tirol 3

★ ★ **Post** (HCR)   AA ANWB
Brennerstr 45-47
☎ 05272-6239
✉ 6150

Most of the rooms in the Hotel Post have en suite facilities. The location of this beautiful and peaceful hotel makes it an excellent base for trips in the area. The hotel has a pleasant bar, and the restaurant has a friendly and welcoming atmosphere. There is a garden with a terrace, and on-site parking is available.

* - ♨ 780/880
* 34 🛏 1400/1600

★ ★ ★ **Gasthof zur Rose** (HP)   AA ANWB
Brennerstr 30
☎ 05272-6221 fax 05272-2224
✉ 6150

The Gasthof zur Rose is in the centre of Steinach am Brenner. Almost all the rooms have washing facilities and there is a public lounge with a TV. Parking facilities are available.

open 20.12 - 05.04 + 01.06 - 14.10
* 5 ♨ 480/640
* 32 🛏 800/1120

★ ★ ★ **Sporthotel Wilder Mann** (HCR)   AA ANWB
Brennerstr 38-40
☎ 05272-6210 fax 05272-621054
✉ 6150

The Sporthotel Wilder Mann has a classic façade and is situated in the centre of rural Steinach. This hotel is a good base for summer and winter-sports holidays. All rooms have a bathroom. There is a restaurant, lounge with open fire, and an indoor swimming pool with sauna and gym overlooking the garden and sunbathing lawn.

open 01.05 - 20.10 + 19.12 - 05.04
* 12 ♨ 560/1020
* 37 🛏 920/2240

AUSTRIA 247

★ ★ ★ ★ **Weisses Rössl** (HR)
Brennerstr 23
☎ 05272-6206 fax 05272-620622
✉ 6150

9 🛏
34 🛌

STEINDORF AM OSSIACHERSEE *Kärnten* 7

★ ★ ★ **Gasthof Pension Laggner** (HP)
Seestr 5
Steindorf
☎ 04243-318 fax 04243-8659
✉ 9552

open 01.06 - 30.09
* 5 🛏 380/430
* 20 🛌 720/900

ST JOHANN IM PONGAU *Salzburg* 4

★ ★ ★ **Alpenblick** (HP)
Plakenau 4
☎ 06412-6234
✉ 5600

2 🛏
8 🛌

★ ★ ★ **Hirschenwirt** (HCR)
Bundesstr 1
☎ 06412-6012 fax 06412-805275
✉ 5600

open 01.06 - 31.10 + 01.12 - 08.05
* 2 🛏 330/390
* 25 🛌 540/660

★ ★ ★ **Talblick** (HR)
Talblickstr 6
☎ 06412-7293
✉ 5600

open 01.01 - 10.04 + 10.05 - 31.10
* 6 🛌 440/770

ST JOHANN IN TIROL *Tirol* 4

Schöne Aussicht (HCR)
Berglehen 23
☎ 05352-2270 fax 05352-4626
✉ 6380

The name of Hotel Schöne Aussicht indicates its prime attraction. It is situated on a mountain slope and offers a splendid view of Sankt Johann and the surrounding mountain peaks. The rooms in this holiday and winter-sports hotel all have en suite bathroom and a balcony. The hotel has a cosy restaurant, a sunny garden and a panoramic terrace; it lies in the middle of an area which provides a complete range of winter-sports facilities. One of the ski-lifts is next to the hotel.

open 18.12 - 30.03 + 09.05 - 30.09
* 3 🛏 370/410
* 45 🛌 640/720

ST KOLOMANN *Salzburg* 4

★ ★ ★ **Motel Kneipbad Sommerau** (HP)
☎ 06241-212
✉ 5423

4 🛏
18 🛌

ST LEONHARD AM WALDE *Niederösterreich* 5

★ ★ **Harreither** (HCR)
Am Platz 1
☎ 07442-7212
✉ 3340

3 🛏
27 🛌

ST MICHAEL IM LUNGAU *Salzburg* 4

★ ★ ★ **Aparthotel Staigerwirt** (HA)
Marktstr 66
☎ 06477-206 fax 06477-20620
✉ 5582

10 🛌

ST PÖLTEN *Niederösterreich* 6

★★ Gasthof Graf (HP)
Bahnhofpl 7
☎ 02742-52757
✉ 3100

3 ♪ 420/520
19 ♫ 540/740
⊙ ◆ P ♛ ⌂ ▬ ⓟ WC ↑ ☺

STRASS IM ATTERGAU *Oberösterreich* 4

Strobl Waldfrieden (HP)
Powang 32
☎ 07667-7095
✉ 4881

1 ♪
16 ♫
↳ P ♛ ⌐ ⓟ WC

STUMM *Tirol* 3

Zum Pinzger (HCR)
☎ 05283-2265
✉ 6272

8 ♪
48 ♫
↳ ⊙ P ♛ ↕ ⌂ ▬ ⓟ WC ⓘ

ST VEIT AN DER GLAN/MURAUNBERG *Kärnten* 7

★★★ Pension Muraunerhof (HP)
Muraunberg 1
St Veit an der Glan
☎ 04212-3183 fax 04212-71451
✉ 9300

* 8 ♪ 350/-
* 30 ♫ 580/-
↳ P ♛ ♕ ⌐ ⌂ ⓟ WC ⓘ

ST WOLFGANG *Oberösterreich* 4

Belvédère (HG)
☎ 06138-2302
✉ 5360

5 ♪
13 ♫
⌐ ⊙ ◆ P ♛ ⌂ ▬ ⓟ WC

★★★★ Post (HR)
Markt 87
☎ 06138-2346 fax 06138-23467
✉ 5360

* - ♪ 1250/1650
* 30 ♫ 1900/2400
AE ⓘ E ⊠ ⊛ ⊙ P ♛ ♕ ⌐ ⌂ ↕ ▬ ⓟ WC TV ☺

★★★ Schloß Eibenstein (HG)
Markt 107
☎ 06138-2342 fax 06138-23467
✉ 5360

open 16.03 - 31.10
* 10 ♪ 570/980
* 61 ♫ 920/1660
AE ⓘ E ⊠ ⊛ ⌐ ⊙ P ♛ ♕ ⌐ ⌂ ↕ ▬ ⓟ WC TV ☺

★★★★ Villa Gastberger (HG)
Markt 17
☎ 06138-2346 fax 06138-23467
✉ 5360

open 01.05 - 31.12
* 6 ♪ 900/1650
* 34 ♫ 1800/2400
AE ⓘ E ⊠ ⊛ ⌐ ⊙ P ♛ ♕ ⌐ ⌂ ↕ ▬ ⓟ WC TV ☺

SULZ IM WIENERWALD *Niederösterreich* 6

★★★ Lindenhof (HP) **AA ANWB**
Kirchenpl 6
☎ 02238-8111
✉ 2392

The 200-year-old Lindenhof is rich in tradition, and enjoys a splendid and quiet location in the centre of Sulz, in the heart of the Wienerwald with its beautiful country scenery. The hotel has well kept rooms, and is the ideal venue for a relaxed stay in these beautiful surroundings; it is also a good base for trips to the centre of Vienna, 25km away.

open 01.02 - 31.10
* 2 ♪ 220/400
* 5 ♫ 550/600
↳ ⊙ P ♛ ⌂ ▬ ⓟ WC ☺

AUSTRIA

TEICHALPE/TEICHALM Steiermark 8

★ ★ ★ ★ **Teichwirt** (HCR)
Teichalpe
☎ 3179-7169 fax 3179-716988
✉ 8163

30

THOMATAL Salzburg 4

★ ★ ★ **Gasthof Gell** (HCR)
☎ 06476-253
✉ 5591

1
26

TRINS Tirol 2

★ ★ ★ **Gasthof Hohe Burg** (HCR) AA ANWB
Haus Nr 107
☎ 05275-5204 fax 05275-5204
✉ 6152

The Gasthof Hohe Burg is on the outskirts of Trins, a holiday and winter- sports resort in the Schnitztal. The hotel is at an altitude of 1200m and wood is a major feature of both the interior and exterior. The rooms are comfortable, and there is a restaurant and a terrace with a view of the surrounding mountains.

open 19.12 - 24.10
* 25 310/360
* - 500/640

TSCHAGGUNS Vorarlberg 2

★ ★ ★ **Gasthof Löwen** (HCR)
Zelfenstr 3
☎ 05556-2247
✉ 6774

4

★ ★ ★ ★ **Montafoner Hof** (HR)
Hausnr 3
☎ 05556-44000 fax 05556-44006
✉ 6774

8
40

TÜRNITZ Niederösterreich 5

Gravogl (HP) AA ANWB
Pichlrotte 16
☎ 02769-201
✉ 3184

Situated on the B20 from St Pölten to the south, the Hotel Gravogl is pleasant and quiet, set in the greenery of Niederösterreich. The rooms are comfortable and have washing facilities, and the hotel is a good base for walking and cycling.

open 15.11 - 20.10
1 -/200
5 320/380

VELDEN AM WÖRTHERSEE Kärnten 7

★ ★ **Pension Bergfrieden** (HP)
Oberjeserz West 47
☎ 04274-3760
✉ 9220

open 01.12 - 31-10
* 1 200/320
* 6 320/680

★ ★ ★ **Gästehaus Rosanna** (HP)
Schanzenweg 17
☎ 04274-3763
✉ 9220

open 03.04 - 31.10
* 2 230/300
* 14 460/600

VENT *Tirol* 2

★ ★ ★ Alpenrose (HCR)
Haus Nr 30
☎ 05254-8178 fax 05254-819633
✉ 6458

3 ♨ 350/600
23 ☰ 600/1100

VILLACH *Kärnten* 7

Ebner (HR)
☎ 04242-23910
✉ 9580

50 ☰

★ ★ ★ ★ Europa (Best Western) (HG)
Bosendorferstr 5
☎ 04242-26766 fax 04242-2676650
res nr 0660-194
✉ 9580

The Hotel Europa is situated in the centre of Villach, opposite the station. It is a comfortable, well kept town hotel with spacious rooms equipped with en suite bathroom, TV and minibar. The cosy Wiener Kaffeehaus serves coffee and breakfast. The hotel has its own parking garage and lies just one km from the Salzburg to Klagenfurt motorway.

* 7 ♨ 690/950
* 37 ☰ 1090/1700

★ ★ ★ Mosser (HG)
Bahnhofstr 9
☎ 04242-24115 fax 04242-24115222
✉ 9580

* 6 ♨ 600/800
* 25 ☰ 900/1400

★ ★ ★ Romantikhotel Post (HCR)
Hauptpl 26
☎ 04242-261010 fax 04242-26101420
✉ 9580

* 19 ♨ 570/1500
* 57 ☰ 1030/1700

VILLACH/MARIA GAIL *Kärnten* 7

★ ★ ★ Gasthof Moser (HCR)
18 November Pl 8
Maria Gail
☎ 04242-34933 fax 04242-35426
✉ 9580

* 5 ♨ 250/400
* 26 ☰ 400/700

VILLACH/WARMBAD *Kärnten* 7

★ ★ ★ ★ Der Karawankenhof (HG)
Kadischenallee 25-27
Villach
☎ 04242-30020 fax 04242-300261
✉ 9504

* 18 ♨ 950/1400
* 62 ☰ 1450/3800

WALDHAUSEN IM STRUDENGAU
Oberösterreich 5

★ ★ ★ Ettlinger (HR)
Schlossberg 27
☎ 07418-206 fax 07418-397
✉ 4391

open 01.01 - 31.10
4 ♨ 300/360
14 ☰ 540/620

WALD IM PINZGAU *Salzburg* 3

★ ★ ★ Jagdschloß Graf Recke (HCR)
☎ 06565-6417 fax 06565-6920
✉ 5742

open 01.01 - 21.03 + 22.05 - 05.10
7 ♨ 620/800
20 ☰ 1100/1400

WEISSBRIACH *Kärnten* 7

★ ★ Zur Post (HCR)
Weissbriach 13
☎ 04286-238
✉ 9622

11 ☰

WELS Oberösterreich 4

★ ★ ★ ★ Rosenberger Wels (HCR) AA ANWB
Adlerstr 1
☎ 07242-62236 fax 07242-6223660
✉ 4600

The Hotel Rosenberger is situated in the centre of Wels which hosts annual fairs and conferences. This modern hotel with its spacious comfortable rooms is especially appealing to business people; because of its location on the Passau-Vienna road it is also suitable for a relaxed overnight stop. The hotel has a pleasant restaurant and a luxurious sauna and whirlpool.

* - ♬ 995/-
* 106 🛏 1295/-
AE ⓘ E ⌘ ⊙ ◆ P 🅿 ⌇ ♨ ▤ 🅒 WC TV 🍴

WERFENWENG Salzburg 4

★ ★ ★ Sporthotel (HCR)
☎ 06466-450 fax 06466-4507
✉ 5453

14 ♬
47 🛏
AE ⓘ E ⌘ ♦ P 🅿 ⌇ ⛵ ☎ ▤ 🅒 WC 🍴

WESTENDORF Tirol 3

★ ★ ★ Briem (HCR) AA ANWB
Bahnhofstr 34
☎ 05334-6310 fax 05334-6023
✉ 6363

The Hotel Briem enjoys a fine, quiet position near the station of Westendorf. Most of the rooms have en suite facilities. There is an attractive terrace and a children's playground. After an apéritif in the bar, guests can enjoy a good meal in the restaurant.

open 22.01 - 25.03 + 15.05 - 27.09
* 6 ♬ 240/510
* 44 🛏 480/960
AE ⓘ E ⌘ ♦ P 🅿 ⌇ ♨ ☎ ▤ 🅒 WC 🍴 ⓣ

★ ★ ★ Glockenstuhl (HCR)
☎ 05334-6175 fax 05334-2472
✉ 6363

2 ♬ 690/745
18 🛏 1240/1390
ⓘ ⓘ ◆ P 🅿 ▤ 🅒 WC TV 🍴 ⛲ ⓣ

★ ★ ★ Schermer (HCR)
☎ 05334-6268 fax 05334-2384
✉ 6363

5 ♬
27 🛏
ⓘ E ⌘ ⊙ ♦ P 🅿 ⌇ ⛵ ♨ ▤ 🅒 WC 🍴 ⓣ

WEYREGG AM ATTERSEE Oberösterreich 4

★ ★ ★ Landgasthof Zur Post (HR)
Haus Nr 47
Weyregg
☎ 07664-202 fax 07664-65355
✉ 4852

9 ♬
24 🛏
E ⌘ 🌐 ⊙ P 🅿 ▤ 🅒 WC 🍴 ⓣ

WIEN Wien 6

For centuries Vienna was at the heart of the vast Habsburg empire, a stronghold of Christianity against the Turks, and cultural focus of central Europe. Today the city is still one of the world's major tourist centres, confident and cosmopolitan, but still with its own charm and native flair. The façades of the grand baroque buildings - the churches, palaces and elegant residences - still bear witness to the epithet 'Vienna gloriosa' here. The arts flourish here now as they always have; many of the world's great composers have lived and worked in Vienna, and the Staatsoper (State Opera) plays an important part in the social, cultural and political life of the city.

The city radiates southwestwards from the Donau Kanal; the old city lies between it and the grand Stephansdom, its 137-metre spire piercing the sky. The old city with its long narrow streets of houses and hotels are full of character, and the pedestrianised areas around the cathedral, Kärtner Strasse, the Hofburg and the Staatsoper are busy and elegant shopping streets with boutiques and jewellers, and porcelain, glass and china shops.

The complex of the Hofburg, once the favourite residence of the Habsburgs, now contains the old imperial apartments, as well as the Burgkapelle, Schatzkammer (treasury), the principal collection of the Österreichische Nationalbibliothek (national library), porcelain and silver collections, a display of arms and amour, and the Spanish Riding School.

There is a full programme of cultural entertainment in the city, but for informal moments Viennese cafés are a famous institution: meeting places for the locals and a delight for visitors, with tables outside in summer,

and of course the traditional strong, aromatic Viennese coffee.
See city plan on page 206.

★ ★ ★ ★ **Albatros** (HR)
Liechtensteinstr 89
☏ 1-343508 fax 1-34350885
res nr 1-343508
✉ 1090
City Plan B1

* 7 ♨ 1030/1280
* 46 ⚭ 1420/1880

★ ★ ★ **Altwienerhof** (HR)
Herklotzgasse 6
☏ 1-8926000 fax 1-89260008
✉ 1150
City Plan A4

* 9 ♨ 460/650
* 15 ⚭ 960/2000

★ ★ ★ ★ **Pension Arenberg (Best Western)** (HCR)
Stubenring 2
☏ 1-5125291 fax 1-5139356
res nr 0660-194
✉ 1010
City Plan D3

* 1 ♨ 720/950
* 23 ⚭ 1280/1650

★ ★ ★ **Austria** (HG)
Fleischmarkt 20
☏ 1-51523 fax 1-51523506
✉ 1011
City Plan C2

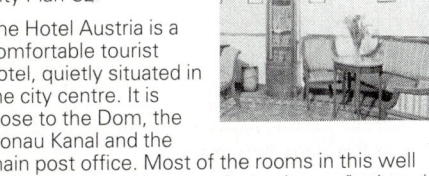

The Hotel Austria is a comfortable tourist hotel, quietly situated in the city centre. It is close to the Dom, the Donau Kanal and the main post office. Most of the rooms in this well maintained hotel have a private shower/bath and toilet; a large proportion also have TV. The linen-covered breakfast tables give guests a stylish start to the day. Terms are bed and breakfast only.

* 8 ♨ 580/1080
* 46 ⚭ 850/1590

★ ★ ★ ★ **Pension Aviano** (HP)
Marco D'aviano Gasse 1
☏ 1-5128330 fax 1-512816565
✉ 1010
City Plan C3

* 2 ♨ 740/-
* 15 ⚭ 1040/-

★ ★ ★ **Pension Bardnesse** (HP)
Lange Gasse 61
☏ 1-4051061 fax 1-405106161
✉ 1080
City Plan A2

6 ♨ 560/680
33 ⚭ 880/1120

★ ★ ★ ★ **Beethoven (Best Western)** (HG)
Milloeckergasse 6
☏ 1-5874482 fax 1-5874442
res nr 0660-194
✉ 1060
City Plan C3

* 2 ♨ 900/-
34 ⚭

★ ★ ★ ★ **Bellevue** (HCR)
Althanstr 5
☏ 1-313480 fax 1-31348801
✉ 1091
City Plan C1

* 17 ♨ 1115/1295
* 113 ⚭ 1670/2200

★ ★ ★ ★ **Am Brillantengrund** (HG)
Bandgasse 4
☏ 1-932219 fax 1-5261330
✉ 1070
City Plan A/B

* 9 ♨ 860/1300
* 27 ⚭ 1150/1760

★ ★ ★ **Pension Christina** (HP)
Hafnersteig 7
☏ 1-5332961 fax 1-533296111
✉ 1010
City Plan D2

6 ♨ 560/680
27 ⚭ 1040/1200

★ ★ ★ ★ **Erzherzog Rainer (Best Western)** (HCR)
Bosendorferstr 5
☎ 1-501110 fax 1-50111350
res nr 0660-194
✉ 1150
City Plan C4

1 🛏
84 🛏

🆎 ⓓ 🅴 ≡ ⦿ 🅿 ↕ 🔲 🅿 🆆🅲 🆃🆅

★ ★ ★ ★ **Jäger** (HG)
Hernalser Hauptstr 187
☎ 1-48666200 fax 1-48666208
✉ 1170

* 3 🛏 900/1000
* 15 🛏 1300/1600

🅴 ≡ ⚡ ↕ 🔲 🅿 🆆🅲 🆃🆅 ☺

★ ★ ★ ★ **K + K Palais** (HCR)
Rudolfspl. 11
☎ 222-5331353 fax 222-33135370
res nr 222-5331353
✉ 1010
City Plan C2

* 6 🛏 1200/1590
* 60 🛏 1550/2070

🆎 ⓓ 🅴 ≡ ⦿ 🅿 ↕ 🔲 🅿 🆆🅲 🆃🆅

★ ★ ★ ★ **Kaiserhof (Best Western)** (HCR)
Frankenberg
☎ 1-5051701 fax 1-505887588
res nr 0660-194
✉ 1040
City Plan C4

13 🛏 1000/1300
73 🛏 1200/3000

🆎 ⓓ 🅴 ≡ ⦿ 🅿 ↕ 🔲 🅿 🆆🅲 🆃🆅 ☺

★ ★ ★ ★ **Kaiserin Elisabeth** (HG)
Weihburggasse 3
☎ 1-51526 fax 1-515267
✉ 1010
City Plan C3

This stately hotel has a rich tradition. It is situated opposite the famous cathedral and close to the main shopping street of Vienna. The classic rooms are well furnished and there is a smoking room with an imposing glass dome. The Hotel Kaiserin Elisabeth has beautiful Persian carpets and lovely chandeliers.

* 16 🛏 950/1350
* 47 🛏 1800/2100

🆎 ⓓ 🅴 ≡ ⚡ ⦿ 🅿 ↕ 🔲 🅿 🆆🅲 🆃🆅 ☺

★ ★ ★ **Kärtnerhof** (HG)
Grashofgasse 4
☎ 1-5121923 fax 1-513222833
✉ 1011
City Plan C2

The Hotel Kärntnerhof is situated on the Grashofgasse close to Stephansdom. The Staatsoper and Hofburg are only a few minutes' walk away. Practically all rooms have a toilet and a shower or bath. There is a sunny roof terrace at the back with a view of the roofs and towers of this part of Vienna.

* 10 🛏 980/1040
* 33 🛏 1000/1660

🆎 ⓓ 🅴 ≡ ⚡ ⦿ 🅿 ↕ 🔲 🅿 🆆🅲 ☺

★ ★ ★ ★ **Mate** (HCR)
Ottakringerstr 34
☎ 1-40455 fax 1-40455888
✉ 1170

* 10 🛏 980/1460
* 115 🛏 1580/2060

🆎 ⓓ 🅴 ≡ ⦿ 🅿 🍴 ≋ ↕ 🆃🆅 🍽 ☺

★ ★ ★ **Mate Dependance** (HCR)
Bergsteiggasse 22
☎ 1-40466 fax 1-40455888
✉ 1170
City Plan A2

* 7 🛏 760/990
* 40 🛏 1020/1680

ⓓ 🅱 🅿 ≋ ↕ 🔲 🅿 🆆🅲 🍽 ☺

★ ★ ★ ★ **Mercure Wien Zentrum** (HCR)
Fleischmarkt 1 A
☎ 1-534600 fax 1-53460232
✉ 1010
City Plan C2

* 7 🛏 1230/1600
* 148 🛏 1590/2110

🆎 ⓓ 🅴 ≡ ⦿ ↕ 🔲 🅿 🆆🅲 🆃🆅 🍽 ☺

★ ★ ★ **Nikolaus Berger** (HCR)
Bruennerstr 126
☎ 1-391665
✉ 1010

8 🛏
30 🛏

★ ★ ★ Opernring (HCR)
Opernrring 11
☎ 1-5875518 fax 1-587551829
✉ 1010
City Plan C3

* 1 ♦ 990/1680
* 35 ⚭ 1190/2280
AE ◉ E ⚏ ⊙ P ▯ ☎ TV

★ ★ ★ Pertschy (HP)
AA ANWB
Habsburgergasse 5
☎ 1-534490 fax 1-5344949
✉ 1010
City Plan C3

The Hotel Pertschy is in the small Cavriani palace. It is situated in a side street off the Graben, in the heart of Vienna. This hotel-pension has well furnished rooms and apartments; it does not have a restaurant, but does serve snacks. Drinks are served in the lounge.

* 5 ♦ 640/740
* 38 ⚭ 1140/1280
E ⚏ ⚐ ⊙ ↕ ▯ WC TV ☺

★ ★ ★ ★ President Wien (HCR)
Wallgasse 23
☎ 1-59990 fax 1-5967646
✉ 1060
City Plan B4

* - ♦ 790/1350
* 77 ⚭ 1104/1950
AE ◉ E ⚏ ⚐ ☏ ↕ ▯ WC TV ⎍ ☺

★ ★ ★ ★ Pullman Sofitel (HCR)
Neumarkt 35-37
☎ 1-716160 fax 1-71616844
res nr 06608194
✉ 1030
City Plan D3

18 ♦ 1240/1580
166 ⚭ 1730/2000
P ↕ ▯ WC TV

★ ★ ★ ★ Reither (Best Western) (HCR)
Bosendorferstr 5
☎ 1-856165 fax 1-855244
res nr 0660-194
✉ 1150
City Plan A4

1 ♦
50 ⚭
AE ◉ E ⚏ ⊙ P ☎ ▯ ☏ TV ⎍

★ ★ ★ ★ Römischer Kaiser (Best Western) (HCR)
Annagasse 16
☎ 1-5127751 fax 1-512775113
res nr 0660-194
✉ 1010
City Plan C3

* - ♦ 1600/1900
* 23 ⚭ 1800/2800
AE ◉ E ⚏ ⊙ ↕ ▯ WC ⎍ ⇌

★ ★ ★ Savoy (Best Western) (HCR)
AA ANWB
Lindengasse 12
☎ 1-934646 fax 1-934640
res nr 0660-194
✉ 1070
City Plan B3

The bed and breakfast hotel Savoy is situated in one of the most important shopping areas of Vienna, within walking distance of the Ringstrasse. The rooms have modern furnishings and offer comfortable accommodation. The hotel has a private parking garage, and tram and bus stops are nearby.

* 2 ♦ 640/1080
* 41 ⚭ 990/1630
AE ◉ E ⚏ P ↕ ▯ WC TV ☺

★ ★ ★ Schild (HG)
Neustift Am Walde 97-99
☎ 1-4421910 fax 1-44219153
✉ 1190

* 13 ♦ 390/920
* 20 ⚭ 1100/1420
⊙ P ☏ ⚲ ↕ ▯ WC TV ☺

AUSTRIA

★★★ Schloß Wilhelminenberg (HCR) AA ANWB
Savoyenstr 2
☎ 1-458503 fax 1-454876
✉ 1160

The imposing Schloss Wilhelminenberg is an exceptional hotel. The hotel itself is a large majestic country house, beautifully situated in a wooded and peaceful area. All the rooms have a shower, toilet and telephone. The hotel has a large garden, bowling alley and minigolf as well as a swimming pool.

* - ♪ 790/950
* 90 ⚭ 1170/1400
AE ⓓ E ≖ ♪ ♨ ⓢ P ⚐ ⇌ ↕ ⇤ ▬ ⌂ WC TV ⓘ

★★★★ Am Schubertring (HG)
Schubertring 11
☎ 1-717020 fax 1-7139966
✉ 1010
City Plan C/D

* 6 ♪ 1050/1650
* 34 ⚭ 1350/2500
AE E ≖ ⓢ ↕ ▬ ⌂ WC TV ⓘ

★★★★ Stefanie (Best Western) (HCR) AA ANWB
Taborstr 12
☎ 1-211500 fax 1-21150160
res nr 0660-194
✉ 1020
City Plan D2

The Hotel Stefanie is quietly situated only a 5-minute walk from the town centre, on the far side of the Donau Kanal. This is a luxury hotel with beautifully furnished rooms, fitted with en suite bathroom, TV and minibar. Most of the rooms are at the back of the hotel and overlook the courtyard garden where lunch and dinner are served in style. The hotel has its own underground car park.

* 30 ♪ 1340/1620
* 100 ⚭ 1620/2140
AE ⓓ E ≖ ♪ ⓢ P ⓟ ↕ ⇤ ▬ ⌂ WC TV ⓘ

★★★★ Am Stephansplatz (Best Western) (HCR) AA ANWB
Stephanspl 9
☎ 1-534050 fax 1-53405711
res nr 0660-194
✉ 1010
City Plan C3

The Hotel am Stephansplatz enjoys a privileged location in the heart of Vienna, directly opposite the grand Stephansdom. Many of the luxurious, comfortable rooms overlook the square with its tourists and *fiakers* - typical Viennese horse-drawn carriages. The chic gourmet restaurant on the first floor offers a wide choice of excellent dishes. There are several parking garages near the hotel.

* 20 ♪ 1190/1420
* 42 ⚭ 1630/2160
AE ⓓ E ≖ ♪ ⓢ ↕ ▬ ⌂ WC TV ⓘ

★★★ Tabor (HG)
Taborstr 25
☎ 1-21117000 fax 1-211171522
✉ 1020
City Plan D2

* 6 ♪ 690/890
* 88 ⚭ 1060/1360
AE ⓓ E ≖ ⓢ ↕ ▬ WC TV ⓘ

★★★ Terminus (HG)
Fillgradergasse 4
☎ 222-58773860 fax 15-87738676
✉ 1060
City Plan B3

13 ♪ 450/670
31 ⚭ 760/1120
AE ⓓ E ≖ ⓢ ↕ ⇤ ▬ ⌂ WC ⓘ

★★★★ Tigra (Best Western) (HCR)
Tiefer Graben 18
☎ 1-5339641 fax 1-5339645
res nr 1-5339641
✉ 1010
City Plan C2

* 1 ♪ 650/1280
* 40 ⚭ 980/1650
AE ⓓ E ≖ P ▬ ⌂

Trend Hotel Oberlaa (HCR)
Kurbadstr 8
☎ 1-681631 fax 1-681641235
✉ 1100

* 252 ♦ 1290/-
* 256 ⚭ 1580/-
🅿 ⚡ ↕ 🛏 🅿 WC TV 🍴

WIEN/VÖSENDORF Niederösterreich 6

City Club Vienna (HCR)
Parkallee 2
Vösendorf
☎ 1-693535 fax 1-693317
✉ 2334

* - ♦ -/2080
* 471 ⚭ 2570/7000
AE ⓞ E ⚡ ♦ 🅿 ⚡ ↕ 🛏 🅿 WC TV 🍴

WIESING Tirol 3

Gästehaus Waldrand (HP)
Rofansiedlung 455
☎ 05244-2624
✉ 6200

* 2 ♦ 210/230
* 13 ⚭ 380/400
♦ 🅿 ⚡ ♦ 🅿 WC

★★★ **Gasthof Waldruh** (HCR)
in 402
☎ 05244-2367
✉ 60200

29 ⚭
♦ 🅿 ⚡ 🅿 WC

WÖRGL Tirol 3

★★★★ **Motorhotel Angath** (MT)   AA ANWB
Inntal Autobahn
☎ 05332-7875 fax
05332-76468
✉ 6300

The Best Western Motorhotel Angath is close to the Inntall motorway and can be reached via the Kufstein-Süd exit. There is a *Stüberle* and a restaurant. All the rooms have a bathroom and TV, and most have a minibar.

* 1 ♦ -/695
* 44 ⚭ -/1045
AE ⓞ E ⚡ ♦ 🅿 ⚡ ↕ 🛏 🅿 WC TV 🍴

ZAMS Tirol 2

★★★ **Zammerhof** (HP)   AA ANWB
☎ 05442-63620
✉ 6511

The Hotel Zammerhof is a well maintained hotel, and has a recently added swimming pool and sunbathing lawn. All the rooms have a bath/shower and TV; some have a toilet. Guests may relax in the sauna or on the terrace in the garden. There is a restaurant and a playground for younger guests. The hotel is closed from the end of April to mid May and between mid October and the end of December.

open 25.12 - 20.04 + 20.05 - 15.10
* 1 ♦ 400/430
* 13 ⚭ 680/740
⊙ 🅿 ⚡ ⚡ 🛏 🅿 WC TV 🍴

ZELL AM MOOS Oberösterreich 4

★★★ **Seepension Steininger** (HP)
Hof 53
☎ 06234-280
✉ 4893

3 ♦
16 ⚭
♦ 🅿 ⚡ 🛏 🅿 WC ♦

ZELL AM SEE Salzburg 4

★★★★ **Porschehof** (HR)
☎ 06542-7248 fax 06542-6878
✉ 5700

open 16.12 - 14.11
* 7 ♦ 600/880
* 36 ⚭ 1100/1640
AE E ⚡ ♦ 🅿 ⚡ ↕ 🛏 🅿 WC TV 🍴 ♦

ZELL AM ZILLER Tirol 3

★★★ **Sporthotel Theresa** (HR)   AA ANWB
Bahnhofstr 15
☎ 05282-2286 fax 05282-4235
✉ 6280

The Zillertal is a popular region both in summer and winter. In the heart of this area lies the luxurious Sporthotel Teresa with its own swimming pool and sauna. There are well kept rooms with good amenities. The restaurant offers Tyrolean and

international dishes, and drinks are served in the cosy bar or the Toni-keller.

* 2 ♊ 1150/-
* 63 ♊ 850/1400
⟨symbols⟩

★ ★ ★ **Tiroler Hof** (HCR)
☎ 05282-2227 fax 05282-2227351
✉ 6280

4 ♊ 400/460
36 ♊ 680/800
⟨symbols⟩

★ ★ ★ **Gasthof Untermetzger** (HCR)
Unterdorf 5
☎ 05282-2386 fax 05282-238623
✉ 6280

open 20.12 - 30.03 + 20.05 - 10.10
* 4 ♊ 360/380
* 21 ♊ 640/680
⟨symbols⟩

ZIRL *Tirol* 3

★ ★ ★ ★ **Goldener Löwe (Best Western)** (HR)
Bosendorferstr 5
☎ 05238-2330 fax 05238-263138
res nr 0660-194
✉ 6170

11 ♊
17 ♊
⟨symbols⟩

ZÖBERN *Niederösterreich* 8

★ ★ ★ **Czerwenka** (HCR)
☎ 02642-8480 fax 02642-848088
✉ 2871

20 ♊
24 ♊
⟨symbols⟩

Index

A

Aachen 41
Aalen 41
Abtenau 208
Achenkirch 208
Achern 41
Afritz/Verditz 208
Ahorn 42
Ahrweiler 42
Aigen Am Böhmerwald 208
Aiterhofen/Straubing 42
Alf 42
Alfeld/Marienhagen 42
Allenbach 42
Allensbach 43
Allershausen 43
Allmershausen 43
Alpirsbach 43
Alsfeld 43
Alsfeld/Romrod 43
Altenahr 43
Altenkirchen 44
Altensteig 44
Altensteig/Berneck 44
Altlengbach 208
Alzenau 44
Alzey 44
Amberg 45
Amecke 46
Amorbach 46
Amstetten 209
Andernach 46
Angath 209
Anholt 46
Annaberg Im Ötscherland 209
Annweiler 46
Ansbach 46
Appenweier 47
Arnbruck 47
Arnsberg 47
Arolsen 47
Aschaffenburg 47
Assmannshausen 48
Attendorn 48
Au 209
Au/Bregenzerwald 209
Auderath 48
Augsburg 48
Au/Längenfeld 209
Aurach Bei Kitzbühel 209

B

Bacharach 48
Bad Aibling 48
Bad Bellingen 49
Bad Bergzabern 49
Bad Berleburg 49
Bad Bertrich 49
Bad Bramstedt 49
Bad Breisig 49
Bad Brückenau 50
Bad Camberg 50
Bad Dürkheim 50
Bad Ems 50
Bad Friedrichshall 51
Bad Gandersheim 51
Bad Griesbach Im Rottal 52
Bad Grund 52
Bad Harzburg 52
Bad Herrenalb 53
Bad Hofgastein 210
Bad Homburg Vor Der Höhe 53
Bad Iburg 53
Bad Ischl 210
Bad Kissingen 54
Bad Kleinkirchheim 210
Bad Königshofen 54
Bad Kreuznach 54
Bad Krozingen 54
Bad Laasphe 54
Bad Laasphe/Feudingen 55
Bad Lauterberg 55
Bad Lippspringe 55
Bad Mergentheim 55
Bad Mitterndorf 211
Bad Münder Am Deister 56
Bad Münstereifel 56
Bad Nauheim 56
Bad Nenndorf 56
Bad Neuenahr 56
Bad Neuenahr/Ahrweiler 56
Bad Oeynhausen 56
Bad Oldesloe 57
Bad Orb 57
Bad Peterstal 57
Bad Pyrmont 57
Bad Reichenhall 58
Bad Rippoldsau 58
Bad Rothenfelde 59
Bad Sachsa 59
Bad Salzuflen 59
Bad Sassendorf 59
Bad Schönborn 59
Bad Segeberg 59
Bad Soden 59
Bad Soden-Salmünster 60
Bad Tölz 60
Bad Waldsee 60
Bad Wiessee 60
Bad Wildungen 60
Bad Wimpfen 60
Baden-Baden 50
Baden/Wien 209
Badgastein 210
Baiersbronn 61
Bamberg 61
Battenberg/Eder-Dodenau 61
Baunatal 61
Bayerisch Eisenstein 61
Bayrischzell 62
Beilngries 62
Beilstein 62
Bensberg 62
Bensheim 62
Beratzhausen 62
Berchtesgaden 63
Berg Kreis Starnberg 63
Berghaupten/Schwarzwald 63
Berghausen 63
Berlebeck 63
Berlin 63
Bernau Am Chiemsee 65
Bernkastel-Kues 65
Bernkastel/Wehlen 65
Bernried 65
Berwang 211
Besigheim 65
Bestwig/Valme 65
Beverungen 66
Bexbach 66
Bezau 211
Biebelried 66
Bielefeld 66
Biersdorf 67
Bingen 67
Binzen 67
Birkenau 67
Birnbaum 211
Bischofsgrün 67
Bischofswiesen 67
Bizau 211
Blankenheim 67
Bleiburg 211
Bliesen 68
Blons 211
Bludenz 212
Bochum 68
Bodenmais 68
Bodensdorf 212
Bodental 212
Bollendorf 68
Bonn 69
Bonn-Bad Godesberg 70
Bonndorf 70
Boppard 70
Bosen 71
Boxberg 71
Brand 212
Brand/Laaben 213
Braunau Am Inn 213
Braunlage 71
Braunschweig 72
Braunschweig/Wenden 72
Braz Bei Bludenz 213
Bregenz 213
Breisach/Hochstetten 73
Breitenbrunn 214
Bremen 73
Bremerhaven 73
Bretten 73
Brilon 74
Bärnbach 211
Bruchsal 74
Bruck An Der Leitha 214
Bruck A.D. Grossglocknerstrasse 214
Brühl 74
Brunnen/Schwangau 74
Bühlertal 75
Bullay 75
Burbach 75
Burgbrohl 75
Bürserberg 214
Bürserberg/Dorf 214

INDEX

C

Celle 75
Cham 76
Cobbenrode 76
Coburg 76
Cochem 76
Creglingen 78
Cuxhaven 78

D

Dahn 78
Damüls 214
Darmstadt 78
Darscheid 79
Dauchingen 79
Daun 79
Deidisheim 80
Delecke 80
Dellach/Maria Wörth 215
Denkendorf 80
Dernau 80
Dernbach 80
Detmold/Hiddesen 81
Dierdorf 81
Diessen Am Ammersee 81
Dillenburg 81
Dinkelsbühl 81
Donaueschingen 82
Donauwörth/Parkstadt 82
Dorfgastein 215
Dorfgütingen/Feuchtwangen 82
Dornbirn 215
Dörndorf 82
Dornstetten 82
Dörrenbach 83
Dorsten 83
Dortmund 83
Dortmund/Hohensyburg 84
Dreieich 84
Drobollach Am Faakersee 215
Drolshagen 84
Drolshagen/Öringshausen 84
Drolshagen/Schreibershof 84
Dudeldorf 84
Duderstadt 85
Duisburg 85
Dülmen 85
Dürnstein 215
Düsseldorf 85
Düsseldorf/Ratingen 86

E

Ebensee 215
Echternacherbrück 87
Edenkoben 87
Ediger-Eller 87
Egestorf 87
Ehr 87
Ehrwald 216
Eichgraben/Grossram 216
Eichstatt 87
Eisenkappel 216
Eisenschmitt 88

Eitorf 88
Ellmau 216
Emmelshausen 88
Engelhartszell 216
Engen 88
Enns 216
Eppstein/Vockenhausen 88
Erlangen 89
Eslohe 89
Eslohe/Wenholthausen 89
Essen 89
Essen/Kettwig 89
Etmissl 217
Ettal 89
Ettenheim 90
Ettlingen 90
Eugendorf 217
Eutin 90

F

Faak Am See 217
Fallingbostel 90
Farchant 90
Feistritz Im Rosental 217
Felsberg 90
Feucht 90
Feuchtwangen 90
Filzmoos 217
Finnentrop/Fretter 91
Finsterweiling 91
Fischen Im Allgäu 91
Fiss 217
Flattach Im Mölltal 217
Flensburg 91
Forbach 91
Frankenthal In Der Pfalz 91
Frankfurt Am Main 92
Frankfurt An Der Oder/Lichtenberg 94
Frankfurt/Bad Weilbach 94
Frankfurt/Karben 95
Frankfurt/Langen 95
Fredeburg 95
Freiburg 95
Freilassing 96
Freinsheim 96
Freising 96
Freudenberg 96
Freudenstadt 97
Freyung 97
Friedrichshafen 97
Frittlingen 97
Fügen 218
Fulda 97
Fulpmes 218
Fusch A.D. Grossglocknerstrasse 218
Füssen 98
Füssen/Hopfen Am See 98

G

Gablitz 218
Gaggenau/Selbach 98
Galtür 219

Gammertingen 98
Garbsen 99
Gargellen 219
Garmisch-Partenkirchen 99
Gaschurn 219
Gau-Bickelheim 99
Geilenkirchen 100
Geiselwind 100
Geisenhausen 100
Gelsenkirchen 100
Gerlos 219
Gernsbach 100
Gerolstein 100
Gersfeld/Rhön 101
Gillenfeld 101
Glottertal 101
Gmund Am Teg 101
Gmünd Im Liesertal 220
Gnesau 220
Golling 221
Gondorf 101
Goslar 102
Goslar/Hahnenklee 102
Götzens 221
Graben-Neudorf 103
Grainau 103
Grassau 103
Graz 221
Graz/Strassgang 221
Gröbming 221
Grönenbach 103
Gross Gerau 103
Gross Reken 103
Grossarl 221
Grünstadt/Asselheim 103
Gschnitz 222
Guldental 104
Gummersbach/Lieberhausen 104
Gundelfingen 104
Gütenbach/Furtwangen 104

H

Haan 105
Hagen 105
Hagnau 105
Hainzenberg 222
Haldensee 222
Haldenwang 105
Hallenberg/Hesborn 105
Haltern 105
Hamburg 106
Hameln 107
Hanau/Steinheim 108
Hannover 108
Hannoversch-Münden 109
Hasborn 109
Hassloch 110
Hausach 110
Heede 110
Heidelberg 110
Heidelberg/Walldorf 111
Heidenheim An Der Brenz 111
Heilbronn/Flein 111
Heiligenblut 222
Heiligenroth 111
Heimbach/Hergarten 112

Helmstedt 112
Hengersberg 112
Henndorf Am Wallersee 222
Heppenheim 112
Herbitzheim 112
Herborn/Bürg 113
Herbrechtingen 113
Herdorf 113
Herford 113
Herscheid 113
Herzberg 113
Herzberg/Sieber 113
Herzogenaurach 114
Hessdorf 114
Hilchenbach 114
Hilchenbach/Lützel 114
Hilpoltstein 114
Hindelang 114
Hinterbrühl 222
Hinterglemm 223
Hinterzarten 115
Hippach 223
Hirschegg/Kleinwalsertal 223
Hochneukirchen 223
Hochsölden 223
Höchstadt/Wachenroth 115
Hockenheim 115
Hofkirchen 115
Hofkirchen Im Mühlkreis 223
Hohegeiss 115
Hohenau 115
Hohentauern 223
Höhr-Grenzhausen 115
Homberg 116
Hopfgarten Im Brixental 223
Horb/Dettingen 116
Hösbach 116
Höxter 116
Hügelsheim 116
Hürtgenwald/Vossenack 116

I

Ibbenbüren 116
Idar-Oberstein 117
Idotoin 117
Iggensbach 117
Igls 223
Illertissen 117
Ilshofen 117
Immenstaad 117
Immenstadt 118
Imst 224
Ingelheim Am Rhein 118
Ingolstadt 118
Innsbruck 224
Inzell 118
Irschenberg 118
Ischgl 225
Isenburg 118
Isny 119

J

Jagsthausen 119
Jena 119

Jenbach 225
Jerzens 225
Jungholz 226

K

Kaiserslautern 119
Kaiserslautern/Hohenecken 119
Kallstadt 119
Kalwang 226
Kandel 120
Kaprun 226
Karlsruhe 120
Kassel 120
Kassel/Lohfelden 121
Kassel/Niederzwehren 121
Kassel/Wilhelmshöhe 121
Kaub 121
Kelheim 121
Kell 121
Kerpen/Sindorf 121
Keutschach 226
Kiel 121
Kinding/Enkering 122
Kipfenberg/Pfahldorf 122
Kirchberg In Tirol 226
Kirchen/Katzenbach 122
Kirchheim 122
Kirchheimbolanden 123
Kirchheim/Hessen 123
Kirchhundem 123
Kirn 123
Kirschentheuer 227
Kitzbühel 227
Kitzbühel/Gundhabing 227
Kitzingen 123
Klagenfurt 227
Kleinich 123
Klosterneuburg 227
Koblenz 124
Kochel Am See 124
Kochel Am See/Ried 124
Kollerschlag 228
Köln 124
Köln-Mühlheim 126
Köln-Porz 126
Königstein Im Taunus 126
Königswinter 127
Köningsbronn 127
Konstanz 127
Kordel 128
Kothen 128
Kothen-Rhön 128
Kötschach-Mauthen 228
Kraig 228
Krefeld 128
Krekel 128
Krems 228
Kressbronn 128
Kreuzwertheim 129
Krimml 228
Krumpendorf 228
Krün 129
Kufstein 229
Kulmbach 129
Künzelsau 130
Kyllburg 130

L

Lackenhäuser/Neureichenau 130
Lage/Hörste 130
Laichingen/Feldstetten 130
Lamspringe 131
Landau In Der Pfalz 131
Landeck 229
Landshut 131
Langenargen 131
Langenburg 131
Langscheid 131
Lautenbach 132
Lauterbach 132
Lauterecken 132
Lech Am Arlberg 230
Leiwen 132
Leiwen/Mosel 132
Lenggries 132
Lennestadt 132
Lensahn 132
Leogang 230
Leonberg 133
Lermoos 230
Leutasch 231
Lich 133
Lienz 231
Liesenich 133
Limbach 133
Limburg An Der Lahn 133
Lindau 133
Lindenfels 134
Lindenholzhausen 134
Lindlar 134
Lingenau 231
Linz 134
Linz 231
Längenfeld 230
Lofer 232
Lohmar/Wahlscheid 134
Loibichl/Mondsee 232
Lorsch 134
Lübeck 134
Lübeck/Travemünde 135
Lüdenscheid 135
Ludwigsburg 135
Ludwigshafen 135

M

Mainz 135
Mainz/Nierstein 135
Maishofen 232
Mallnitz 232
Malsfeld/Beiseförth 136
Manching 136
Manderscheid 136
Mannheim 136
Marburg 137
Maria Alm 232
Maria Wörth 232
Mariazell 233
Markdorf 137
Marktheidenfeld 137
Marktleugast 138
Marktoberdorf 138
Marquartstein 138

262 INDEX

Marsberg 138
Maurach 233
Mayen 138
Mayrhofen 233
Mayschoss 139
Meersburg 139
Melk 234
Melle 139
Memmelsdorf 140
Memmingen 140
Menden 140
Mendig/Maria Laach 140
Merklingen 140
Meschede 140
Meschede/Freienohl 141
Metnitz 234
Mettendorf 141
Mettlach/Orscholz 141
Miesbach 141
Millstatt 234
Minden 141
Mindersdorf 141
Mittelberg/Kleinwalsertal 234
Mittenwald 142
Mitterfirmiansreuth 142
Mittersill 234
Möckmühl 142
Mödling 235
Mohrweiler 142
Möllbrücke 235
Mölln 142
Mönchengladbach 142
Monschau 143
Monschau/Höfen 143
Mosbach 144
Moselkern 144
Motten 144
Müggenbrunn 144
Muhlbach Am Hochkönig 235
Mühlhausen Im Täle 144
Müllheim 144
Müllheim/Niederweiler 145
München 145
München Airport/Hallbergmoos 147
München/Neubiberg 147
Münster 147
Mürlenbach 148
Murnau Am Staffelsee 148
Mutterstadt 148

N

Nauders 235
Neckargemünd 148
Neckarsulm 148
Neckarwestheim 149
Nesselwang 149
Netphen/Sohlbach 149
Neuenbürg 149
Neuerburg 149
Neufahrn Bei Freising 150
Neufelden 236
Neukirchen Am Grossvenediger 236
Neukirchen/Knüllgebirge 150
Neumarkt 150

Neustadt An Der Aisch 150
Neustadt An Der Weinstrasse 150
Neustift Im Stubaital 236
Neu-Ulm 150
Nickenich 151
Nideggen 151
Niederdürenbach 151
Niederkall 151
Niederzissen 151
Niefern 151
Niefern/Öschelbronn 151
Nittel An Der Mosel 152
Nördlingen 152
Nürnberg 152
Nürtingen 153

O

Oberammergau 153
Oberau 153
Oberaudorf 153
Oberderdingen 153
Oberdrauburg 236
Obergurgl 236
Oberhausen 154
Oberjoch 154
Oberkirch 154
Oberleichtersbach/Breitenbach 154
Obermühl An Der Donau 237
Oberstdorf 154
Obertauern 237
Oberteischbach 155
Obervellach 237
Oberweis 155
Oberwesel 155
Oberwolfach 155
Obsteig 237
Ochsenfurt 155
Ochtrup 156
Oetz 237
Offenburg 156
Offenburg/Fessenbach 156
Ohlsbach 157
Ohmenheim 157
Ohrenbach/Oberscheckenbach 157
Olpe/Drolshagen 157
Olsberg 157
Olsberg/Wiemeringhausen 158
Oppenau/Löcherberg 158
Ortenberg 158
Osnabrück 158
Osnabrück/Harderberg 159
Osterode/Lerbach 159

P

Paderborn 159
Parsberg 159
Passau 160
Paternion 237
Perchtoldsdorf 237
Pertisau 238
Pfettrach 160
Pforzheim 160

Pfunds 238
Pfunds/Lafairs 238
Pfungstadt 160
Pichl-Mandling 238
Piesendorf 238
Pill/Niederberg 238
Pirmasens 160
Plaidt 161
Pölich 161
Pörtschach Am Wörthersee 238
Pressbaum 239
Prägraten 239
Prüm 161
Prüm/Baselt 161
Prümzurlay 161
Purkersdorf 239

R

Radolfzell 162
Raesfeld 162
Rahden 162
Ramsau 162
Ramsau Am Dachstein 239
Ramsau/Hainfeld 239
Rathsmannsdorf 162
Rauris 239
Ravensburg 162
Regen 163
Regensburg 163
Reith Bei Seefeld 239
Rellingen/Krupunder 163
Remagen/Kripp 163
Remscheid 163
Rendsburg 164
Rennweg 239
Reutte 240
Reutte/Ehenbichl 240
Rheda-Wiedenbrück 164
Rheinböllen 164
Ried Im Oberinntal 240
Riegel 164
Riegersburg 240
Rieneck 164
Riezlern/Kleinwalsertal 240
Rimsting 164
Rinteln 164
Rockenhausen 164
Rohr Im Gebirge 241
Rohrbach 241
Rosdorf 165
Rosenheim 165
Roth An Der Our 165
Rothenburg Ob Der Tauber 165
Rothenburg O.D.Tauber/Schillingsfürst 166
Rottach-Egern 166
Rüdenhausen 166
Rüdesheim 166
Rüdesheim/Assmannshausen 166
Ruhpolding 167
Ruhstorf 167
Russbach 241

S

Saalbach 241
Saalbach/Hinterglemm 241
Saarbrücken 167
Sachrang 167
Saig 167
Salzbergen 167
Salzburg 242
Sauerlach 167
Sauerlach/Lochhofen 168
Schanze/Schmallenberg 168
Schieder 168
Schieder/Schwalenberg 168
Schierke 168
Schillingen 169
Schleiden 169
Schleiden/Gemünd 169
Schleiden/Gemünd 243
Schleswig 170
Schliersee 170
Schlitz 170
Schlüsselfeld 170
Schmallenberg 170
Schmallenberg/Fredeburg 171
Schmallenberg/Grafschaft 171
Schmallenberg/Oberkirchen 171
Schneverdingen 171
Schömberg 171
Schömberg/Langenbrand 172
Schonach 172
Schönberg Im Stubaital 244
Schongau 172
Schönhagen 172
Schönmünzach/Baiersbronn 172
Schöppingen 173
Schriesheim 173
Schriesheim/Altenbach 173
Schruns/Montafon 244
Schwabach 173
Schwangau 173
Schwangau/Horn 174
Schwaz 244
Schwäbisch Gmünd 173
Schwäbisch Hall 173
Schweich 174
Schweinfurt 174
Seeboden 244
Seebruck/Lambach 174
Seefeld 244
Seesen 174
Semmering 245
Senhals 175
Serfaus 245
Siedlinghausen 175
Siegburg 175
Siegen 175
Siegsdorf 175
Silz 246
Simmerath/Eicherscheid 176
Simonskall/Hürtgenwald 176
Sindelfingen 176
Sindringen 176
Singen 177
Soest 177
Sölden 246
Sommerhausen 177
Speyer 177

Spital Am Pyhrn 246
Spitz 246
St Anton Am Arlberg 247
St Blasien 178
St Corona Am Wechsel 247
St Englmar 178
St Georgen 178
St Goar 178
St Goarshausen 179
St Johann Im Pongau 248
St Johann In Tirol 248
St Kolomann 248
St Leonhard Am Walde 248
St Michael Im Lungau 248
St Märgen 179
St Peter 179
St Peter-Ording 179
St Pölten 249
St Veit An Der Glan/Murauenberg 249
St Wolfgang 249
Stadl An Der Mur 246
Starnberg 177
Steinach Am Brenner 247
Steindorf Am Ossiachersee 248
Steinfurt/Borghorst 178
Steingaden 178
Stemwede 178
Stockach 179
Stockstadt Am Main 179
Strass Im Attergau 249
Straubing 180
Stromberg 180
Stühlingen 180
Stumm 249
Stuttgart 180
Stuttgart/Kirchheim Unter Teck 181
Stuttgart/Sindelfingen 181
Sulz Im Wienerwald 249
Sulzbach 181

T

Tauberbischofsheim 181
Tecklenburg 182
Tegernsee 182
Teichalpe/Teichalm 250
Tettnang 182
Thalfang 182
Thomatal 250
Timmendorfer Strand 182
Titisee-Neustadt 183
Todtmoos 183
Todtnau 183
Todtnauberg 183
Traben-Trarbach 183
Traunstein 183
Travemünde 184
Trechtingshausen 184
Trendelburg 184
Triberg 184
Trier 184
Trins 250
Trippstadt 185
Trittenheim 185
Tschagguns 250

Tübingen 185
Türnitz 250

U

Überlingen/Bodensee 186
Uffenheim 186
Ulm 186
Ulm/Gögglingen 186
Unkel 186
Untergruppenbach 186
Unteroestheim/Bei Rothenburg O.T. 187
Unterreichenbach 187
Ürzig 187
Uslar 187
Üttingen 188

V

Vallendar 188
Velburg 188
Velden Am Wörthersee 250
Vent 251
Villach 251
Villach/Maria Gail 251
Villach/Warmbad 251
Vilshofen 189

W

Wachenheim/Weinstrasse 189
Walchensee 189
Wald I'm Pinzgau 251
Waldeck 189
Waldeck Am Edersee 189
Waldenburg 189
Waldhausen Im Strudengau 251
Waltenhofen 189
Wangen 190
Warendorf 190
Wasserburg 190
Wasserburg Am Inn 190
Weibersbrunn 190
Weiden In Der Oberpfalz 191
Weidenthal 191
Weil Am Rhein 191
Weingarten/Ravensburg 191
Weinheim 191
Weissbriach 251
Wels 252
Wendelstein 191
Wenden/Brün 192
Wenholthausen 192
Werfenweng 252
Werneck 192
Wertheim 192
Westendorf 252
Westernbödefeld 192
Weyarn 193
Weyregg Am Attersee 252
Wieden 193
Wiederstein 193
Wiehl 193
Wien 252

Wien/Vösendorf 257
Wiesbaden 193
Wiesent 194
Wiesing 257
Wildemann 194
Wilhelmshausen 194
Wilhelmshaven 194
Willingen 194
Wilnsdorf 195
Windeck/Halscheid 195
Winterberg 195
Winterberg/Elkeringhausen 197
Winterberg/Hildfeld 197
Winterberg/Neuastenberg 198
Winterberg/Niedersfeld 198
Winterberg/Schmallenberg 198
Winterberg/Züschen 198
Wittlich 199
Woffelsbach 199
Wolfsburg 199
Wolfstein 199
Wörgl 257
Worms 199
Wörth An Der Donau 199
Wuppertal 200
Würzburg 200
Würzburg/Versbach 201

Z

Zams 257
Zell 201
Zell Am Harmersbach 201
Zell Am Moos 257
Zell Am See 257
Zell Am Ziller 257
Zirl 258
Zöbern 258
Zorge 201
Zusmarshausen 201
Zweibrücken 201
Zwiesel 201